MW00416241

INSIGHTS:
A TALMUDIC
TREASURY

Selected Maxims, Moralisms and "Mamorim"
Analyzed, Annotated and Arranged
in Alphabetical Sequence

by
RABBI SAUL WEISS

volume two

FELDHEIM PUBLISHERS
Jerusalem ◆ New York

First published 1996
ISBN 0-87306-754-1

FELDHEIM PUBLISHERS
200 Airport Executive Park   POB 35002
Nanuet, NY 10954   Jerusalem, Israel

Printed in Israel

Dedicated in reverent memory of

הגאון הגדול מאור הגולה
רבן של ישראל
הרב יוסף דוב הלוי סולוביצ׳יק זצ״ל
Rabbi Joseph Ber Soloveitchik
Rebbe and guide, Gaon and teacher

whose historic accomplishments on behalf
of Torah, scholarship, and the Jewish community
have been an inspiration to his disciples
and a legacy for generations to come.

Congregation Kneseth Israel

EMPIRE AVENUE & SAGE STREET
FAR ROCKAWAY, NEW YORK 11691
327-7545

בס"ד

Ralph Pelcovitz
Rabbi

David Weinberger
Assistant Rabbi

Herbert Lazar
President

Rev. Yechiel Hecht
Ritual Director

Joel Kaplan
Cantor

The book "Insights: A Talmudic Treasury" by Rabbi
Saul Weiss is indeed a treasure! Sprinkled throughout the
Talmud and Midrash are countless 'pitgamim' - maxims and
moralistic gems - covering a variety of subjects. All of
them are priceless and timeless. Rabbi Weiss has used
excellent taste in choosing these Talmudic sayings, and
has skillfully illuminated them by drawing from numerous
Rabbinic luminaries, ranging from the Rishonim through the
Acharonim. These annotations, culled from Halachic and
Aggadic sources, elucidate the deeper meaning of these
classic Talmudic maxims, enriching the teachings of our
Sages.

This work, arranged alphabetically, makes it most
convenient for reference and will prove to be of great
benefit to many, be they well versed in the Talmud or the
average reader who is eager to discover the wisdom of
Torah reflected in these pithy sayings. Rabbi Weiss has made
a great contribution to modern traditional Jewish literature.

Rabbi Ralph Pelcovitz
Far Rockaway, N.Y.

PREFACE

"Insights: A Talmudic Treasury" contains five hundred selected dicta and maxims culled from our vast Torah reservoir of the Babylonian and Jerusalem Talmuds and midrashic writings. A varied collection of alphabetically arranged "mamorim" are interpreted and analyzed in a novel format.

Numerous rabbinic commentaries ranging from Rabbeinu Saadiah Gaon to Rav Yosef Dov Soloveitchik, from R. Moshe ben Maimon to R. Moshe Feinstein, are gathered to illuminate and illustrate obscure and misunderstood talmudic expressions.

In many of the annotations presented we are able to glimpse into the noble lives of such Torah giants as the Baal Shem Tov, the Vilna Gaon, R. Chaim of Volozhin, R. Nachman of Breslov, R. Chaim of Brisk, the Chasam Sofer, R. Levi Yitzchak of Berditchov, R. Yisroel Salanter, R. Menachem Mendel of Kotzk, R. Shimshon Raphael Hirsch, R. Avraham Yitzchak Kook, the Chazon Ish, the Chafetz Chaim, R. Chaim Shmulevitz and R. Yaakov Kamenetsky among many others.

I have tried to be eclectic in an objective fashion, without showing any preference for either chassidic or mithnagdic authorities. The commentary selection was largely determined by what I considered to be the most incisive and morally instructive interpretation of a particular dictum that I could find, and by first hand knowledge of the thoughts of some of our great men." I have attempted to follow the principle outlined in this work [# 385], in my homiletical analysis of the following talmudic dictum.

"From what time may one recite the "Shema" in the morning? . . . [Others say] From the time that one sees his friend who is a distance of four cubits (away) and he recognizes him" [Berakoth 9b].

When are you spiritually qualified to recite the "Shema" and accept upon yourself the yoke of the Heavenly Kingdom — to enter into an intimate relationship with the Almighty? It is only when you are willing to recognize the religious philosophy of one who is not in your "daled ammoth" — the "four cubits" of your particular religious life-style, i.e., he has within halachah, a slightly different approach, and yet you accept the reality that "no two minds are alike" [Bamidbar Rabbah 21:2], and you do not try to fit him into your mold, then you are spiritually mature to recite the "Shema" and to begin your day in the good graces of the Almighty.

ABOUT THE AUTHOR

Rabbi Saul Weiss received his rabbinical ordination [*semichah*] from Rabbi Yaakov Kamenetsky at Mesivta Torah Vodaath, in Brooklyn, New York. He is a graduate of Brooklyn College, where he majored in philosophy, and a graduate of Brooklyn Law School, where he was an editor of the Law Review.

He is the founder of the South Shore Hebrew Academy in Brockton (where he served as Rabbi), Chaplain of the New England Sinai Hospital in Stoughton, and Associate Justice of the Rabbinical Court of Massachusets.

Rabbi Weiss is the author of *Torah Values: A Midrashic Approach* and *Insights: A Talmudic Treasury* (volume one). He has also written extensively in *The Jewish Press* on some of the ideas expressed by Rabbi Joseph Ber Soloveitchik זצ"ל.

Rabbi Weiss is married to Peggy Gopin, former New England Regional Director of the Orthodox Union and National Conference of Synagogue Youth. They are the parents of Ariela and Mendel Balk, Adina and Bruce Broder, Bracha and Pinny Marcus, and Menachem Mendel Weiss.

CONTENTS

א

¶ 501 ¶

אַבָּב חֲנוּאָתָא נְפִישִׁי אָחִי וּמְרַחֲמִי,
אַבָּב בְּזִיּוֹנִי לָא אָחִי וְלָא מְרַחֲמִי

"At the gate of the shop there are many brothers and friends;
at the gate of loss, there are neither brothers nor friends"
(*Shabbath* 32a).

Prosperity attracts relatives and friends whereas "adversity has no friends." "The greatest *university* is *adversity*" (Shraga Silverstein, *A Candle by Day*, p. 16).

See, however, *Prov.* 17:17, "A friend loves at all times, and a brother is born for adversity." The Malbim comments: "The definition of a *true* friend is that he loves a person constantly, even more in times of trouble."

Cf. *Baba Mezia* 59a, "When the barley is gone from the pitcher, strife comes knocking at the door." Discord abounds when there is a shortage of food.

Rabbi Moshe Avigdor Amiel comments: "In years of plenty, people are close to and friendly with each other, whereas in years of famine people become indifferent to the needs of others."

See *Beraishith Rabbah* 89:4. "On the verse, 'And they fed in the *achu*' [reed-grass], the midrash comments: In years of prosperity men become brothers. This is a play on words: the word *achu* suggests *achva* [brotherliness]" (*Hegyonoth El-Ami*, vol. 2, p. 238).

"*False* friends are like migratory birds; they fly away in cold weather" (Lazerov, *Enciklopedie fun Idishe Vitzen*, #478).

See *Insights*, vol. 1, #50, "Strife is prevalent in a house only on account of food" (*Baba Mezia* 59a).

◊ 502 ◊

אַבּוּב לְחָרֵי זֶמֶר,
לְגַרְדָּאֵי לָא מְקַבְּלוּה מִינֵיה
"A flute is musical to nobles,
but give it to weavers — they will not accept it"
(*Yoma* 20b).

"The flute is an important musical instrument with a most pleasant sound, dating back to the days of Moshe Rabbeinu. Weavers, however, who are accustomed to inferior musical instruments cannot appreciate the 'refined' music of the flute" (*Maharsha*).

Cf. *Arakhin* 10b, "There was a flute in the Sanctuary which was smooth and thin, made of reed, and from the days of Moshe [and its sound was pleasant]. The king commanded to overlay it with gold, whereupon its sound was no longer pleasant. Then the overlay was removed and its sound was pleasant again as before."

Rabbi Abraham Besdin comments: "The flute from the days of Moshe, metaphorically, stands for *Torath Moshe* [revealed at Sinai]. Since 'all Israel are royal children' [*Shabbath* 67a], only they could appreciate the Torah for 'the words of Torah are compared to nobility' [ibid. 88b]. Consequently, when it was offered to the weavers [the nations of the world], they rejected it (*Abodah Zarah* 2b).

Regarding the tampering with the flute by overlaying it with gold, Rabbi Besdin admonishes: "The Torah is G-d's masterpiece. Don't modify it in order to add glitter and attractiveness. Real connoisseurs know that the original was better."

Cf. *Rosh Hashanah* 27a, "If it [the Shofar] was overlaid with gold at the place where the mouth is applied, it is invalid."

See *Insights*, vol. 1, #462.

◊ 503 ◊   אָבֵל אֵין לוֹ פֶּה

"A mourner has no mouth" (*Baba Bathra* 16b).

"Just as the lentil has no mouth (no cleft) so the mourner has no mouth [for speech]" (ibid. This is one of the reasons for serving lentils as the first meal given to mourners.)

Cf. *Beraishith Rabbah* 63:14, "As a lentil has no mouth, so a mourner is prohibited to speak" [on ordinary topics].

See *Yoreh De'ah* 378:9 regarding the custom of mourners to eat eggs or lentils. See *Shach* 378:9 (8).

In the course of the funeral for the *Sfath Emeth* [Rabbi Yehudah Aryeh Alter], one of his sons, R. Menachem Mendel of Kalisch, asked his brother R. Avraham Mordechai if he recalled how their father had interpreted the statement of our sages, 'A mourner has no mouth.' R. Avraham Mordechai's first reaction was to object, '*But a mourner has no mouth!*' But then he relented, and answered his brother's question. 'Father said, even if a mourner complains against the decree of Heaven he is not punished, for a man is not judged in the moment of his anguish'" (Rabbi A.Y. Bromberg, *Rebbes of Ger*, p. 144).

In a homiletical sense we may apply the above maxim, "A mourner has no mouth" to Rabbi Joseph Ber Soloveitchik's analysis of *aninuth* (the first phase of mourning, beginning with death and ending with burial). "In this period the mourner is exempt from the performance of *mitzvoth*." Rav Soloveitchik explains: "How can man pray and address himself to G-d if he doubts his very humanity, if speech is stripped by his doubts of its human characteristics and turned into mere physical sound? How can the mourner pronounce a benediction or say "*omein*" if he is speechless?" (Adapted from the eulogy delivered at the *sheloshim* observance for Rabbi M. Z. Twersky — 1972).

∬ 504 ∬

אָדָם צָרִיךְ לְהַחֲזִיק טוֹבָה לְמָקוֹם שֶׁיֵּשׁ לוֹ
הַנָאָה מִמֶּנּוּ

"A man must be grateful [and do something beneficial]
to a place where he derives some benefit"
(*Beraishith Rabbah* 79:6).

When Jacob dwelled in the city of *Shchem* he instituted something for the welfare of the city. "Rav said: 'He instituted coinage for them' [in place of barter]. Shmuel said: 'He instituted markets for them.' R. Yochanan said: 'He instituted baths for them' " (*Shabbath* 33b).

"This principle also applies to someone who comes to a yeshiva. Although a student may not be able to assist in the physical betterment of the yeshiva, he is able to assist in the spiritual betterment. How? By serving as a good example for others. He should come to *davening* and *seder* [study sessions] on time so that others will do likewise." (Rabbi Chaim Shmulevitz, cited by Rabbi Zelig Pliskin, *Love Your Neighbor*, p. 108).

Reb Chaim Shmulevitz's life exemplified the above dictum. He would be eternally grateful for the slightest favor. At the last "study session" of the semester he would thank his students for giving him the opportunity to say *shiurim* [Torah lectures].

Cf. *Baba Kamma* 92b, "Cast no mud into the well from which you have drunk." See *Insights*, vol. 1, #101.

∬ 505 ∬

אֱהֹב אֶת הַמְּלָאכָה וּשְׂנָא אֶת הָרַבָּנוּת

"Love work and hate lordship" (*Aboth* 1:10).

"Pursuit of an office and of political power causes trials and adversities . . . Thus [our sages] have said: Once a person becomes a leader of a community below, he is regarded as a transgressor above" (Rambam, *Commentary on Aboth*). See #522.

"Chassidic wisdom has it that 'Love work and hate lordship' implies that if a man accepts a call to a rabbinic post, he must consider as the reason for his acceptance not the love for lordship and authority, but love of endeavor on behalf of the community's spiritual betterment" (Rabbi Reuven P. Bulka, "Characteristics of Rabbinic Leadership — A Psychological View," *Tradition and Transition*, p. 90).

Similarly, Irving M. Bunim writes: "Love the creative achievement possible in the rabbinate, but despise the horrific trappings that accompany the position" (*Ethics from Sinai*, vol. 1, p. 75).

"It is especially important for those in the public eye to eradicate feelings of lordship. *Shulchan Aruch* (*Orach Chaim* 53:1) gives this admonition to the cantor who leads the congregation in prayer:

'He should stand before G-d in a solemn and reverent spirit, filled with trepidation and fear. If his purpose is to show his beautiful voice, and his heart rejoices in his cantorial skills — this is repulsive'" (Rabbi Avrohom Chaim Feuer, *A Letter for the Ages*, p. 66).

Cf. *Aboth D'Rabbi Nathan* 11:2, "And hate lordship" — What does it mean? It teaches that no man should put a crown on his head, but others should put it on him."

Cf. *Yoma* 86b, "Authority [power] buries those who possess it." See #659.

[506]

אַהֲבָה מְקַלְקֶלֶת אֶת הַשּׁוּרָה
וְשִׂנְאָה מְקַלְקֶלֶת אֶת הַשּׁוּרָה

"Love upsets the natural order
and hate upsets the natural order"
(*Beraishith Rabbah* 55:8).

Through love or hate a man acts as he would not otherwise, disregarding his own dignity.

Rabbi Yehudah Loew b. Bezalel [Maharal miPrague] declares that he who loves someone does not care in the slightest if the other is sitting while he is standing, even in cases where this would be contrary to social etiquette. This sweeping aside of conventional norms and barriers is a sign of love — of that inner closeness and devotion that makes nothing of all the externals of life: 'Love upsets the natural order.'

It was this perfection of ultimate love that G-d promised Abraham — so

dear would Israel be to Him that all the normal demands of respect and
deference will be neglected, the judges of Israel would sit while He [so to
speak] would stand in the counsel of judges (*Gur Aryeh*, Gen. 18:1).

Cf. *Sanhedrin* 105b, "Love nullifies the rule of dignified conduct. . . Hate
nullifies the rule of dignified conduct."

In Abraham's great love for G-d and in his eagerness to carry out His
commands, he rose up early and saddled his donkey himself [in preparation
of the Divine command to sacrifice Isaac]. Similarly, regarding hatred,
"Balaam rose up in the morning and saddled his donkey." His hatred
towards Israel was so intense that he did not ask his servants to saddle the
donkey which would take him to Midian to curse Israel.

Rabbi Avraham Pam, in discussing the concept of *Mishkal HaChasidus*
[weighing of one's deeds in relation to *saintliness*] in *Mesilas Yesharim*,
suggests the following homiletical and poignant interpretation of our maxim:

"*Ahava*" — an inordinate "love" of a particular *mitzvah* — may "*mekalkeles
es hashura*" — upsetting the *shuras hadin* [the requirement of the law]. Rav
Pam cited many examples from the life of Rabbi Yisrael Salanter, who was
the personification of *Mishkal HaChasidus*.

Once Reb Yisrael was told by his host, "Rabbi, this time you can perform
netilas yadayim with as much water as you like, for I have a Jewish maid who
draws the water for us." Reb Yisrael answered, "I have no intention of doing
a *hidur mitzvah* [a commandment performed in the most exemplary fashion]
at the expense of a poor maid" (*Erev Shabbos Shiurim*).

⦚ 507 ⦚ אוֹ חַבְרוּתָא אוֹ מִיתוּתָא
"Either friendship or death" (*Ta'anith* 23a).

In commenting on the dictum in *Aboth* 1:6, "Acquire a friend for yourself," Rambam cites the above maxim, "Either friendship or death" and
writes: "If he does not find one [a friend] he should persevere with all his
heart . . .How excellent was Aristotle's statement, 'The friend is one [with
yourself]' " (See *Nicomachean Ethics* 9:4).

Rambam then lists three types of friends: "*The friend of usefulness, the friend
of comfort and the friend of virtue.*

"Concerning the friend of usefulness [his friendship is] as the friendship of partners . . . The friend of comfort is of two types: the friend of satisfaction and the friend of trust. *Satisfaction* — as the friendship of males and females, and the like. *Trust* obtains where a man would have a friend in whom his soul would trust. He would not be guardful of him either in deed or in speech, and he would make known all his interests to him — the good as well as the unseemly . . .

"The friend of virtue obtains where the desire of both, and their purpose, will be related to a single matter, namely, the good, wherein each will wish to assist his friend in attaining that good for both jointly. This is the friendship we are instructed to acquire. It is illustrated by the devotion of a teacher to his student and of the student to his teacher" (*Commentary on Aboth* 1:6).

〖 508 〗

אוֹהֵב לִפְרוֹק וְשׂוֹנֵא לִטְעוֹן,
מִצְוָה בְּשׂוֹנֵא כְּדֵי לָכוֹף אֶת יִצְרוֹ

"If a friend requires unloading [a donkey] and an enemy requires loading, one's obligation is towards his enemy [first] in order to subdue his evil inclinations" (*Baba Mezia* 32b).

See Ex. 23:5 and Deut. 22:4 for the mitzvah of "unloading" and "loading" another's animal.

"If one encounters two animals, one crouching under its burden and the other unburdened because the owner cannot find anyone to help him load, he is obliged to unload first to relieve the animal's suffering and then to load the other. This applies only if the owners of the animals are both friends or both enemies [of the person who comes upon them]. But if one is an enemy and the other a friend, he is obligated to load for the enemy first, in order to subdue his evil impulse" (*Mishneh Torah, Hil. Rotzeach* 13:13).

Cf. *Pesahim* 113b, An enemy [in the above context] is a Jew who had committed a transgression in your presence.

See *Tosaf.* s.v. *Sherahah:* "Why is it necessary to subdue one's inclination towards such an 'enemy' since it is a *mitzvah* to 'hate' him?" *Tosafoth* answers that this [legitimate] hatred may degenerate into [illegitimate] animosity.

Similarly, Rabbi Moshe Avigdor Amiel suggests that the "enemy" in the

above dictum refers to one who is indeed hated by another not "for the sake
of Heaven" [because he committed a transgression], but out of "personal
animosity." Hence, one must first assist this "enemy" in order to subdue his
evil inclination (*Hegyonoth El-Ami*, vol. 2, p. 221).

The Yehudi HaKadosh of Pshischa commented: "Though the *halacha*
permits us to hate a sinner, that is only when he is actually committing the
sin. Immediately afterwards, one must love him again" (Shmuel Himelstein,
Words of Wisdom, Words of Wit, p. 109).

◊ 509 ◊

אוֹי לָנוּ מִיּוֹם הַדִּין
אוֹי לָנוּ מִיּוֹם הַתּוֹכֵחָה

"Woe unto us because of the day of judgment;
woe unto us because of the day of rebuke"
(*Beraishith Rabbah* 93:10).

"Joseph was the youngest of the tribes, yet [his brothers] could not
answer him [when he said: 'I am Joseph — is my father still alive'?] because
they were confounded by him. When the Holy One, blessed be He, comes
and rebukes each individual for what he is . . . how much more will he be
confounded" (ibid.).

The Brisker Rav, R. Yosef Dov Ber Soloveitchik, comments: "This is what
the Midrash means by each individual being rebuked 'for what he is.' The
Almighty will show how one's very actions nullify any excuses he might
make for himself. For instance, one who does not give enough *tzedakah*
excuses himself by saying that his income is meager while his expenses are
great . . . But on the day of judgment this poor man will be shown how
much money he squandered for lust, for honor, etc. . . . . Then he will be
punished twofold '*for what he is.*'

"Hence the distinction between 'the day of judgment' and the 'day of
rebuke': the day of judgment refers to the judgment of the sin itself, and the
day of rebuke to its attempted mitigation" (*Beis HaLevi, VaYigash*, trans. by
Yisrael Isser Zvi Herczeg, pp. 167-169).

Rabbi Chaim Shmulevitz remarks that "often a person will perform an act
with the knowledge that something is wrong, but he nevertheless feels the

act is justified for it is but a means leading to a worthy end. When that end, or goal, however, is proven false or meaningless then not only is the act without any redeeming value, but it stands out in its fullest measure of evil" (*Reb Chaim's Discourses, VaYigash* p. 99).

〖 510 〗

אוֹתוֹ הַיּוֹם שֶׁמֵּת רַבִּי בָּטְלָה קְדוּשָׁה. . .

"On the day on which Rebbi [R. Yehudah HaNassi] died holiness was suspended" (*Kethuboth* 103b).

In other words, even priests were able to participate in his burial, for his death was through the *Divine Kiss* and not through the "Angel of Death." Priests could therefore be engaged in his burial without becoming defiled, because only the Angel of Death "can cause a corpse to convey impurity" (Rabbeinu Bachya, *Kad Hakemach, Ahavah*).

See *Shabbath* 118b for the reasons why Rebbi was called Rabbeinu HaKadosh [our Holy Rabbi].

Cf. *Sotah* 49a, "When Rebbi died, humility and fear of sins ceased."

See *Tosaf., Kethuboth* 103b, s.v. *Osso HaYom* — "Rabbi Chaim HaKohen said: 'Had I been present when Rabbeinu Tam [R. Yaakov ben R. Meir of Ramerupt] died, I would have defiled myself for him [although he was a *Kohen* and would normally be forbidden to do so] for [the phrase] *"batlah kedushah"* [holiness was suspended] mentioned here refers to the holiness of the priesthood' [i.e. the sanctity of priests was suspended on the day Rebbi died due to Rebbi's great holiness — the same holds true for Rabbeinu Tam].'"

When Rabbeinu Avraham b. Dovid of Posquières [*Ravad*] died, his disciples proclaimed: "*Batlah Kedushah* — the sanctity of priests is suspended" and priests are permitted to participate in his burial (R. Avraham Zacuto, *Sefer Yuchsin HaShalem,* v. p. 220b).

511

אַטּוּ יִרְאַת שָׁמַיִם מִילְתָא זוּטַרְתָּא הִיא? . . .
לְגַבֵּי מֹשֶׁה מִילְתָא זוּטַרְתָּא הִיא

"Is the fear of Heaven such a small thing . . .
For Moshe it was a small thing" (Berakoth 33b).

In citing the verse, "And now Israel, what does the L-rd your G-d require of you, but (only) to fear . . ." [Deut. 10:12], the Talmud asks, "Is the fear of Heaven such a small thing . . ."

"*L'gabe Moshe*" — in the presence of Moshe, in his generation it was easy to be G-d fearing [through Moshe's influence] (R. Yaakov Yosef of Polonoye, *Toldoth Yaakov Yosef*, 96C).

Rabbi Moshe Feinstein offers a novel interpretation: "If fear of Heaven is a small thing for Moshe then it is surely a small thing for us, for it is easier for 'greater' people to be mislead. Educated individuals may wander off [deviate from the proper path], whereas ordinary people will obey blindly" (Rabbi Abraham Fishelis, *Bastion of Faith*, p. 186).

Rabbi Joseph B. Soloveitchik suggests that we divide the [above] dictum into two parts. "Is the fear of Heaven such a small thing . . . "Yes, with respect to Moshe." At this point we should pause and explain — "Yes" — if they treat Moshe Rabbeinu with fear, honor and respect — then "It is a small thing" (it is not difficult to acquire fear of Heaven).

This dictum alludes to the necessity of having a *Rebbe*. *Yiras Sha'mayim* (fear of Heaven) does not exist in a vacuum. He who lacks a *Rebbe* will not reach the heights of *Yiras Sha'mayim*, (*Hamevaser*, vol. 29 no. 2, p. 6). It is significant to note that the Baal Shem Tov suggests a similar interpretation. See *L'kutei Bosar L'kutei*, *Devarim*, p. 88.

Rabbi Shneur Zalman of Liadi writes: "Present in the soul of every Jew is an aspect, a spark of Moshe Rabbeinu, hence the demand to the Jews of all generations is justified. By virtue of that part of Moshe, every Jew has the power to fear G-d" (*Tanya*, ch. 42).

Cf. *Berakoth*, 36b, "Everything is in the hands of Heaven except the fear of Heaven." See *Insights*, vol. 1, #172.

Cf. *Hullin* 139b, "Where is Moshe alluded to in the Torah?" . . .
See #883.

▯ 512 ▯

אִי סַיָּיפָא לָא סַפְרָא,
וְאִי סַפְרָא לָא סַיָּיפָא

"If one is a robber he is not a scholar,
and if one is a scholar he is not a robber"
(*Avodah Zarah* 17b).

Literally, "If a sword, then not a book; and if a book, then not a sword."
Rabbi Menachem Mendel of Kotzk made the following observation: "If
there is a *sword* dividing the mind and the heart, i.e. if the mind and the
heart do not function on the same track, then one cannot be a scholar"
(Rabbi Ephraim Oratz, *And Nothing But The Truth*, p.74).

Cf. *"The sword and the book descended intertwined from Heaven."* Israel was
told, if you observe the Torah written in this (the Book), you will be delivered from this (the Sword), and if not . . . (*Sifri, Ekeb* 11:12). See *Insights*,
vol. 1, #183.

▯ 513 ▯

אֵיזֶהוּ עָשִׁיר? הַשָּׂמֵחַ בְּחֶלְקוֹ

"Who is wealthy?
He who rejoices in his portion"
(*Aboth 4:1*).

"One who is happy with his portion is one who delights in the toil of his
own hands and has enough for his daily needs. He does not seek the
luxuries of life. He will merit both this world and the World to Come for he
will have ample time to engage in the study of the Torah" (R. Menachem B.
Shlomo HaMeiri).

The Vilna Gaon writes: "It is good to associate with poor and humble
people. This way, one will acquire the trait of contentment and will be
happy with his lot" (*Even Sheleimah*, ch. 3:8).

"The lust for money can never be satisfied. A man's craving for more and
more wealth may well grow to such excess that the lack of what he does not
now possess may actually mar his joy in whatever he does have at present"

(Rabbi Samson Raphael Hirsch, *Commentary on Avoth*, p. 60).

Rabbi Avraham Pam often quotes this simple but profound saying: "People search desperately all over the world to find the 'city of happiness' — not realizing that it can only be found in the 'state of mind'!" (*Erev Shabbos Shiurim*).

Rabbi Joseph Breuer withdrew from public speaking and writing at the age of 85. "He would tell confidants that as long as his mind could function, he could make peace with the infirmities of age. Self-deprecatingly, he would say, 'Who is the wealthy man, one who rejoices *be'chelko* ["in a portion of himself"] — even if one retains only a portion of his powers, he should still rejoice'" (*The Torah World*, p. 228).

Cf. *Koheleth Rabbah* 1:13, "He who possesses one hundred desires two hundred." See *Insights*, vol. 1, #397.

〔 514 〕

אֵיזֶהוּ שׁוֹטֶה
הַיּוֹצֵא יְחִידִי בַּלַּיְלָה
וְהַלָּן בְּבֵית הַקְּבָרוֹת
וְהַמְקָרֵעַ אֶת כְּסוּתוֹ

"Who is a *shoteh*?
One who goes out alone at night;
one who spends the night in the cemetery;
and one who tears his garments" (*Hagigah* 3b).

"R. Huna said: 'They must all be [done] together.' R. Yochanan said: 'Even if [he does only] one of them'" (ibid.).

"The *shoteh* is disqualified by biblical law from serving as a witness because he is not subject to the commandments . . . Anyone who is mentally deranged with the result that his mind is constantly confused with regard to some matter, even though he converses and asks questions to the point with respect to other matters, is disqualified . . ." (*Mishneh Torah, Hilchos Eduth* 9:9-10).

Rambam maintains that the talmudic criteria for the definition of a *shoteh* are illustrative only, for any type of manifestly irrational behavior may

constitute mental incompetence (*Beth Yosef, Even HaEzer* 121).
According to Rambam a *shoteh* with regard to *one matter* is exempt from all *mitzvoth*. Rabbi Moshe Feinstein offers an explanation. "The Torah does not establish partial obligations with regard to *mitzvoth*. A person cannot be obligated with regard to some commandments and exempt from others. A *shoteh* is clearly exempt from the *mitzvoth* for which he lacks mental competence, hence he must be exempt from all *mitzvoth*" (*Iggeroth Moshe, Even HaEzer* I, no. 120).

◊ 515 ◊

אֵיזֶהוּ תַּלְמִיד חָכָם?
זֶה הָרוֹאֶה טְרֵפָה לְעַצְמוֹ

"Who is a Torah scholar?
He who would declare his own animal *trefah* [unfit]"
(*Hullin* 44b).

The word of a scholar can be trusted for he declares his own animal *trefah* when there has arisen some doubt concerning it. Hence, his lost articles are returned to him by "*teviath ayin*" [sight identification] i.e. without supplying a *siman* [identification mark]. See Tosaf. s.v. *Ezaihu*. See *Baba Mezia* 23b.

Rabbi Yitzchak Mordechai Podavah derives a moral lesson from the above dictum. "*Ha'roeh trefah*" — a Torah scholar who happens to see his neighbor committing a *trefah* [an improper act], then "*l'atzmo*" — let him look to himself. Perhaps he is guilty of the very same transgression. Since no man sees his own blemishes, it may have been providential for him to witness this impropriety in his neighbor, thereby enabling him to detect it in himself.

Similarly, the Baal Shem Tov declares: "When we detect a mean quality in man, we do so because we possess it ourselves. Heaven wants us to become aware of it, thereby hinting at the need for our repentance."

Cf. *Kiddushin* 70a, "Whoever disqualifies, disqualifies with his own blemish." See *Insights*, vol. 1, #296.

〚 516 〛

אִילְמָלֵא נִתְּנָה תּוֹרָה,
הָיִינוּ לְמֵדִין עֲרָיוֹת מִיּוֹנָה

"Had the Torah not been given,
we would have learnt.. [what is] forbidden intercourse
from the dove (*Eruvin* 100b).

The dove was a paragon of chastity among birds. The Talmud [*Sanhedrin* 108a] explains the verse, "For all flesh had corrupted its way upon the earth . . ." [Gen. 6:12] as follows: "Beasts and animals copulated indiscriminately with one another as they did with man." The sin which brought about the "Flood" was unbridled promiscuity.

It is significant to note that the olive leaf which the dove brought back to Noach in the Ark was the sign to him that the flood waters had substantially subsided. In plant life, the Talmud points out that hybrid plants can be produced from the grafting of all trees except the olive (*Yerushalmi, Kilaim* 1:7).

Rabbi Joseph Sherashevsky of Slonim suggests that the combination of the dove — a paragon of chastity among birds, and the olive — the unique example of lack of promiscuity among trees brought to Noach the heartening message that not only had the flood subsided, but also the perversion of nature which brought it about (Rabbi Louis I. Rabinowitz, *Torah and Flora*, p. 4).

〚 517 〛

אִילְמָלֵא לֹא נִשְׁתַּבְּרוּ לוּחוֹת הָרִאשׁוֹנוֹת
לֹא נִשְׁתַּכְּחָה תּוֹרָה מִיִּשְׂרָאֵל

"If the first tablets had not been broken
the Torah would never have been forgotten in Israel
(*Eruvin* 54a).

This is derived from the phrase, "Graven upon the tablets" [Ex. 32:16]. Had the tablets not been broken by Moshe [upon witnessing the collective sin of the Golden Calf], it would have remained "graven" forever.

Rabbi Eleazar Shlomo Shick [a Breslover leader] interprets the above dictum in a most unusual "positive" fashion. He writes: "The first tablets were broken before their miraculous appearance could make an impression on the Jewish people. Had Israel seen the tablets while they were still in a state of degradation [collective idolatry] they would have suffered from unbearable shame and unworthiness. Such a degenerate feeling would have been impossible to forget. Now, however, with the breaking of the tablets [before being received], Israel could repent and forget their grave sin, and begin anew. Hence, by breaking the tablets, Moshe revealed the tremendous power of 'forgetting' and starting anew after repentance" (A Voice Calls Out to G-d, p. 25).

⇡ 518 ⇣

אִילְמָלֵא מְשַׁמְּרִין יִשְׂרָאֵל
שְׁתֵּי שַׁבָּתוֹת כְּהִלְכָתָן מִיָּד נִגְאָלִים
"If Israel were to keep two Sabbaths
according to the laws thereof,
they would be redeemed immediately"
(Shabbath 118b).

Rabbi Zvi Elimelech of Dinov in a novel interpretation of this dictum suggests that "two Sabbaths" is an allusion to Yom Kippur [called Shabbos Shabboson] which coincides with the regular Sabbath. This, in effect is the observance of two Sabbaths at one and the same time. Israel will be redeemed when they learn how to observe these "two Sabbaths" (B'nai Yissachar).

Rabbi Aharon Soloveitchik comments: "On the surface, this [the above] statement appears difficult: Why only if the Jews observe two Shabbos days will they be redeemed — is not one Shabbos enough to show their devotion to the day? The answer is that the Talmud makes reference not to two Shabbos days, but rather to one Shabbos day and the extension of its spirit to the remainder of the week [called a Shabbos], so that every day becomes enlightened with the sanctity and restfulness of Shabbos. Only when they accomplish this will B'nei Yisrael be worthy of redemption" (The Warmth and *the Light*, p. 52).

Cf. *Niddah* 13b, "R. Jose stated: The son of David will not come until all the souls in *Guf* will have been disposed of." See Tosef. s.v. *Ahd.*

⎩ 519 ⎭ אִילְמָלֵא עָלַיָּא לָא מִתְקַיְּימִין אִיתְכָּלַיָּא

"Were it not for the leaves
the clusters [of grapes] could not exist" (*Hullin* 92a).

"Word was sent from Israel, 'let the clusters [the Torah scholars] pray for the leaves [the untutored], for were it not for the leaves the clusters could not exist.' "

"Just as the leaves of the vine withstand the wind and protect the clusters of grapes from the burning heat and the sun, so the 'untutored' common people plough, sow, and reap [provide food] so that the Torah scholars can eat" (Rashi).

When Israel worshipped the Golden Calf, the Almighty said to Moshe, "Descend from your greatness. I have only given you greatness for the sake of Israel — and now that Israel has sinned, why do I want you?" (*Berakoth* 32a). Rabbi Moshe Feinstein comments: "Were it not for the leaves [the children of Israel], the clusters [Moshe Rabbeinu and all the leaders of Israel] could not exist" (*Dorash Moshe*, p. 354).

Rabbi Ovadiah Sforno cites the above dictum in his commentary on "The seven lamps shall give light" [Num. 8:2]. Rabbi Raphael Pelcovitz explains: "The central shaft of the menorah represents the Divine light. The three wicks on the right represent the Torah scholars while the three on the left represent the supporters of Torah. Both are necessary, and together they exalt G-d's Name" (*Notes on Sforno* [trans.] vol. 2, p. 603).

Cf. *Yerushalmi, Sotah* 7:4. See #931.

⎩ 520 ⎭ אֵין אָדָם דָּר עִם נָחָשׁ בִּכְפִיפָה אַחַת

"No person can live with a serpent in one cage"
(*Yebamoth* 112b).

"Metaphorically, a husband and wife cannot live together when one must be constantly on guard against the harm of quarrelling or resentment of the other.

"This principle acts as a reason for declaring a marriage null *ab initio* (retrospective annulment), and for terminating a marriage through divorce" (ibid).

One of the many moral maxims ascribed to Rabbi Yisrael Salanter is a profound commentary on the above dictum. "A man cannot be expected to live in the same cage as a serpent. Yet anyone who cannot live with a serpent is 'a serpent' himself" (Rabbi Dov Katz, *Tenuath HaMussar*, trans. by Rabbi Leonard Oschry, *The Mussar Movement*, vol. 1, part 2, p. 124).

⎰ 521 ⎱   אֵין אָדָם כּוֹפֵר בַּעֲמִיתוֹ, עַד שֶׁכּוֹפֵר בָּעִיקָר

"No man deals falsely with his neighbor unless he first rebels against G-d" (*Tosefta, Shevuoth* 3:5).

This is based on the scriptural verse: "If anyone sins and rebels against the L-rd and deals falsely with his neighbor . . ." (Lev. 5:21).

Rabbi Moshe Meiselman comments: "Since belief in G-d is the basis of all morality, the rejection of morality is ultimately based on the rejection of G-d. The talmud sees a similar idea in the order of the Ten Commandments (*Kiddushin* 31a). The first commandment is: 'I am the L-rd your G-d . . .' [Ex. 20:12]. This provides a basis for the subsequent universal commands of human morality. Man himself cannot be the source of morality" (*Jewish Woman in Jewish Law*, p. 6).

In commenting on the above *Tosefta*, Rabbi Joseph Ber Soloveitchik remarked that "history certainly confirms this declaration and Soviet Russia is our contemporary example. It is true that the West is guilty of many serious moral aberrations and is often hypocritical! But it is still sensitive to moral issues and it feels the need to justify itself in moral terms . . . Russia, however, is morally bankrupt; there is no debate, reproach, argument; facts and history are distorted. Here we see, '*If one rebels against G-d* (atheism), *he will deal falsely with his neighbor*'" (Adapted from a lecture delivered at the

18 INSIGHTS: A TALMUDIC TREASURY

RCA Convention - 1970).

◊ 522 ◊

אֵין אָדָם עוֹלֶה לִגְדוּלָּה
אֶלָּא אִם כֵּן מוֹחֲלִין לוֹ עַל כָּל עֲוֹנוֹתָיו

"One does not attain greatness unless all his sins are forgiven"
(Sanhedrin 14a).

Cf. Aboth 1:10, "Hate lordship." Rambam writes: "Pursuit of an office and lordship causes trials and adversities. A man's faith will suffer if people become envious and are opposed to him. Thus they have said: 'Once a person becomes a leader of a community below, he is regarded as a transgressor above" (Comm. on Aboth).

How do we reconcile the above dictum with the one cited by Rambam? The Ein Eliyahu explains that "the relationship of a leader to his community is analogous to that of a husband to his wife. 'If one is worthy, she is a help to him, if he is unworthy, she is against him' (Yebamoth 63a). Similarly, if the leader 'is worthy' and leads his community in a righteous manner so that they accept his leadership then 'all his sins are forgiven.' However, 'if he is unworthy' and the people reject his leadership then he 'is regarded as a transgressor above'" (Rabbi Shmuel Alter, L'kutei Bosar L'kutei, [Agadoth], vol. 5, p. 17).

◊ 523 ◊

אֵין אֲרִי נוֹהֵם מִתּוֹךְ קוּפָּה שֶׁל תֶּבֶן,
אֶלָּא מִתּוֹךְ קוּפָּה שֶׁל בָּשָׂר

"A lion does not roar over a basket of straw, but over a basket of flesh" (Berakoth 32a).

Moshe attempted to mitigate the grave sin of the Golden Calf by arguing in defense of Israel that it occurred as a result of the "silver and gold" which the Almighty showered upon them; i.e. the "basket of flesh" caused them to "roar." "He whose stomach is full increases deeds of evil" (ibid).

Rabbi Aharon Yitzchok HaLevi Epstein [the *Aruch Hashulchan's* father] cited the above dictum in explaining the reason for his own observance of so many voluntary fasts. "In my mind," he said, "the whole practice of fasting is only a means to an end. Its whole purpose is to humble a person and break his haughty spirit. When a person fills his stomach with food and drink, his spirits rise, and he feels very pleased with himself. In this state it is only natural for him to become arrogant and unfeeling, veering off the path that is pleasing to G-d and man. Our sages mean this when they say, 'A lion only roars over a basket of flesh.' The true purpose of fasting is to humble a man's heart and to cause him to ponder the real purpose of his life — to refrain from bad character traits and cling to good ones, to be pleasant to people and righteous before G-d" (R. Baruch HaLevi Epstein, *Makor Baruch*, cited in *Recollections* [trans.] p. 22).

〚 524 〛 אֵין בֶּן דָּוִד בָּא עַד שֶׁיִּתְיָיאֲשׁוּ מִן הַגְּאוּלָה

"The son of David will not come . . . until the redemption is despaired of . . ." (*Sanhedrin* 97a).

Rabbi Yaakov Kamenetsky observed that this statement seems to contradict all the scriptural as well as rabbinic sources which assert categorically that we are never to lose hope in the advent of *Moshiach*. Says Reb Yaakov, the above dictum should be interpreted in the following manner: Jews are misguided when they turn to the gentile nations for political and military aid or for financial handouts to assist in the redemption of the Holy Land. *Moshiach* will come only when we put our full faith in the Almighty and trust in Him to send the true Redeemer, because we have given up all hope that the gentile nations will be our savior (Rabbi Avrohom Chaim Feuer, *Shemoneh Esrei*, p. 222).

See #518.

〚 525 〛

אֵין בָּשָׂר הַמֵּת שֶׁבְּחַי מַרְגִּישׁ בְּאִיזְמֵל

"The dead flesh in a living person does not feel the scalpel"
(*Shabbath* 13b).

Just as a piece of dead flesh which is cut off from the body of a living man feels nothing [no accompanying pain], so too, we are "dead" [numbed] to many troubles that have befallen us.

"We are like corpses who do not feel anything, and it is no exaggeration to say that we are dead . . . . Every man must bestir himself to become a living, feeling person, recognizing the true nature of reality, that 'there is none besides Him'" (Rabbi Yechezkel Levenstein, Ponevesh Yeshiva discourse).

Cf. *Berakoth* 18a, "The righteous in their death are called living." See *Insights*, vol. 1, #460.

〚 526 〛

אֵין הָעוֹלָם מִתְקַיֵּים אֶלָּא בִּשְׁבִיל
הֶבֶל תִּינוֹקוֹת שֶׁל בֵּית רַבָּן

"The world endures only for the sake of the breath of school children" (*Shabbath* 119b).

According to the renowned Kabbalist, Rabbi Chaim ben Attar, the structure of Jewish society may be divided into four classes of people corresponding to four categories of specific days in the Jewish calendar — *Shabbath*; *Yom Tov*; *Chol Ha'moed* and weekdays. "On the highest level of purity and innocence are the youngsters who study Torah. These children are completely consecrated to G-d and totally immersed in nothing but the diligent study of His Word. 'The entire universe endures only for the sake of the breath of school children.' These youngsters may be compared to the Sabbath.

Adults [who are not so pure] are comparable to the Festivals for they rejoice in the study of Torah and in the performance of *mitzvoth* [resembling a joyous festival].

On the third level are those who cannot study themselves but who support those who do . . . . Thus they resemble the Intermediate Festival days which are a mixture of the sacred and the mundane.

On the fourth level are the unlearned who shun the Torah and Torah scholars. They waste their time in the pursuit of all sorts of pleasure. They are like the weekdays — devoid of sanctity" (*Ohr HaChaim*, trans. by Rabbi Chaim Feuer, *Light of Life*, p. 36).

Cf. *Shabbath* 119b, "'Touch not my anointed' (*Divrei HaYomim* 16:22) — this refers to young school children." See #547.

527

אֵין הקב"ה מַשְׁרֶה מַשְׁכִינָתוֹ אֶלָּא עַל
גִּבּוֹר וְעָשִׁיר, וְחָכָם וְעָנָיו.

"The Holy One, blessed be He, does not place His Presence except on a person who is strong, wealthy, wise and humble" (*Nedarim* 38a).

Rabbi Chaim of Volozhin raises the following question: "Why doesn't the Almighty cause his *Shechinah* to descend on a person who even before birth was destined to be poor or infirm, as stated in *Niddah* 16b, 'What shall be the fate of this seed? Shall it produce a strong man or a weak man, a wise man or a fool, a rich man or a poor man?' If one lives a decent life and performs good deeds why doesn't G-d allow His spirit to rest on him?"

Says Reb Chaim, "The overriding quality required for a man to be worthy of the Divine Presence is the trait of humility. See *Abodah Zarah* 20b . . . . Now, a man who has no [outstanding] qualities at all cannot be considered a humble person, even if he humbles himself — for he has nothing to be proud of. On the other hand, a person endowed with many admirable attributes, who nevertheless is not aware of his merits but is meek and unpretentious — that person can be characterized as humble. A man in whom all the world's good qualities converge, who still maintains perfect humility, is the most humble of all. The three values mentioned in the dictum [above] power, wealth and wisdom, represent the sum total of mankind's aspirations. If a man, having attained all of these, still remains truly modest, he is indeed humble and worthy of receiving the *Shechinah*."

(Ruach Chaim on *Aboth* 4:1).

Moshe Rabbeinu's physical handicap (his speech defect) was an exception to the requirement of physical superiority. Had Moshe been a brilliant orator, then the Jews' acceptance of the Torah could have been ascribed to his eloquence and oratorical skill (Rabbeinu Nissim Gerondi, *Droshoth HaRan*, 65).

Cf. *Shabbath* 92a, "The Divine Presence rests only on a person who is wise, strong, wealthy and of stature." See #530.

〖 528 〗
אֵין הקב״ה נִפְרַע מִן הָאָדָם
עַד שֶׁתִּתְמַלֵּא סָאָתוֹ

"The Holy One, blessed be He, does not exact punishment of a man until his measure [of guilt] is filled" (*Sotah* 9a).

Rabbi Moshe Chaim Luzzatto writes: "It is necessary to realize that there is a limit placed on the amount of evil that a person can do. Once this limit is reached, G-d no longer gives the individual a chance, but obliterates him from the face of the earth. This is what our sages mean by the expression 'the measure is filled.'

"For this reason, it is also possible that the wicked should be successful in order that the door remain open for their destruction. With regard to this, our sages taught us, 'When one comes to defile himself, the door is opened for him' [*Yoma* 38b]. When this limit is reached, however, destruction is imminent. G-d's anger is aroused, and a catastrophe comes, totally annihilating such an individual" (*Derech HaShem*, II, chap. 3).

⦗ 529 ⦘

אֵין הַקּוֹמֶץ מַשְׂבִּיעַ אֶת הָאֲרִי
וְאֵין הַבּוֹר מִתְמַלֵּא מֵחוּלְיָתוֹ

"A handful cannot satisfy a lion, nor can a pit be filled with its own soil" (*Berakoth* 3b).

When the wise men of Israel said to David, "Our lord, the King, Israel your people require sustenance," he answered them, "Go let each sustain himself from the other." They said to him, "A handful cannot satisfy a lion . . ." [ibid.].

The poor cannot remain satisfied with a meager handout anymore than a handful will satisfy a hungry lion. Moreover, a nation needs external sources of supply. It cannot live on itself just as the soil taken out of a pit will not completely fill the cavity (Rashi). See Tosaf. s.v. *Ain HaBor*.

Rabbeinu Tam [Rabbi Yaakov ben Meir] explains "a pit cannot be filled up with its own soil" to mean "a well is never filled up with the water that flows into it" [water does not fill the well — the rich cannot satisfy the poor]. *Ri* [Rabbi Yitzchak of Dampière] offers the following explanation: "You will never fill a pit by digging in its bottom, moving soil from one place to another. The soil you add here is taken from there. Similarly, the money you take from the rich will be missing from the rich."

The *Baal Hafla'ah*, Rabbi Pinchas Horowitz, explains the question posed by the wise men of Israel in this fashion: "We have no concern with those who are engaged in commerce for they can support themselves, but what are the sages to do — how are they to live." To which, David replied that the merchants will support the scholars. Thereupon, they said to him, "*Ain hakometz* — the '*kamtzan*' [close-fisted] will not satisfy the '*Ari*' [the lion-hearted sage] because '*ain bor*' [the boorish person] is never '*filled*' [satisfied] with what he possesses [how do you expect him to satisfy the needs of others]" (*Ksav Sofer, Bamidbar* 4:4).

530

אֵין הַשְׁכִינָה שׁוֹרָה אֶלָּא עַל
חָכָם גִבּוֹר וְעָשִׁיר וּבַעַל קוֹמָה

"The Divine Presence rests only on a person who is wise, strong, wealthy and of stature" (*Shabbath* 92a).

The story is told concerning the Rebbe, R. Nachum of Tchernobil, who was accustomed to befriend poverty-stricken chassidim but was abrupt with wealthy ones. "A rich chassid asked him: 'Rebbe, does not the Talmud teach us that the *Shechinah* rests upon him who is wise, strong and wealthy? Doesn't this prove that the Almighty loves the rich?'"

The Rebbe smiled and said: "Do you really believe that G-d is concerned for that which is external to man? The wise, strong and wealthy man on which the *Shechinah* rests, is the one described in *Pirkei Aboth* 4:1. 'Who is wise? He who learns from all men. Who is mighty? He who conquers his own passions. Who is wealthy? He who rejoices in his own portion'" (D.L. Meklar, *Fun. Rebin's Hauf*, p. 39).

Cf. *Nedarim* 38a, "The Holy One, blessed be He, does not place His Presence except on a person who is strong, wealthy, wise and humble."
See #527.

531

אֵין זוֹרְקִין אֶת הָאוֹכְלִין

"Eatables should not be thrown" (*Berakoth* 50b).

The renowned kabbalist, Rabbi Moshe Cordovero writes: "Divine wisdom is extended to all created things — minerals, plants, animals and humans. This is the reason for the Rabbis warning us against despising food [one may not throw articles of food] . . . . One should despise no created thing, for they were all created in wisdom. One should not uproot anything which grows, nor kill any living thing unless it is necessary . . . to elevate them higher and higher, from plant to animal and from animal to human" (*Tomer Devorah*, Ch. 3).

Rabbi Shraga Feivel Mendelowitz once scolded a young boy at Camp

Mesivta for ripping a leaf from a tree: "That leaf was saying *Shira* [singing] to *Hashem*; why did you have to destroy it?" When another student absent-mindedly tore up a blade of grass, Reb Shraga Feivel chided him: "The Gemara relates that every blade of grass has a *maloch* [angel] in Heaven that says 'grow' and you say 'no!'" (Rabbi Yitzchak Chinn, "Ohr Shraga — The Light of Shraga Feivel," *The Jewish Observer* 17, no. 2 [Sept. 1983]:10).

Cf. *Beraishith Rabbah* 10:7, "There is no blade of grass without a guiding star in Heaven, which strikes it and commands, 'Grow.'"

Cf. *Eruvin* 64b, "We do not walk over food."

◊ 532 ◊ אֵין חָבוּשׁ מַתִּיר עַצְמוֹ מִבֵּית הָאֲסוּרִים

"A prisoner cannot release himself from the house of detention" (*Berakoth* 5b).

Similarly, a patient who may know how to prescribe for others cannot cure himself.

"Sometimes one can pray for others and be answered, while prayers for himself are not . . . . The reason for this may be because 'a prisoner cannot release himself from the house of detention'" (Rabbi Yehudah HaChasid, *Sefer Chassidim* 753).

An opposing view was suggested by Rabbi Yehudah Leow, the Maharal of Prague, who writes: "In the case of prayer, we do not say 'a prisoner cannot release himself,' since it is G-d who releases him" (*Gur Aryeh*).

See *Beraishith Rabbah* 53:14, "A sick person's prayers on his own behalf are more efficacious than those of anyone else." See #706.

"The only time one [who prays] cannot release himself is when he cannot concentrate on his prayers. If he can, however, his own prayers are best" (Rabbi Eliahu Mizrachi).

In a metaphysical vein, Rabbi Meir Leibush b. Yechiel writes: "Man is a composite of body and soul. The soul is locked and imprisoned within the body and cannot release itself from the body until the day of death" (Malbim, *HaTorah VeHaMitzvah*, Ex. 2:3).

After citing the above dictum, the *Chasam Sofer* writes: "It would be advisable for a community under siege to send away its Rabbi . . . . When the Rabbi is in a safe place, his prayers on behalf of the community are much more likely to be accepted . . . [for] when his life is also threatened, his prayers are tinged by a selfish nature . . ." (*Sefer Zikaron*, trans. *Pressburg Under Siege*, p. 64).

〚 533 〛

אֵין יִשְׂרָאֵל נִגְאָלִין
עַד שֶׁיִּהְיוּ כּוּלָן אֲגוּדָה אַחַת

"Israel will not be redeemed until they become one band" (*Midrash Tanchuma, Nitzavim*).

"You stand this day all of you . . ." [Deut. 29:9]. Only when they stand together — when Israel is united, only then will they merit Redemption.

The Torah records: "When you cross the Jordan and settle in the land that the L-rd your G-d causes you to inherit, and He grants you safety from all your enemies around you, and you will live in security" [Deut. 12:10]. "The phrase 'You will live in security' is a *condition precedent* to the fulfillment of the Divine promise, 'he will grant you safety from all your enemies around you.' For 'living in security' implies inner peace and domestic tranquility amongst the divergent elements of the nation. Hence, when Israel is not divided into sects who are at war with each other, then they need not concern themselves with the threat of foreign invasion" (Rabbi David Moskowitz, *Gelilai Zahav*, cited in *Parpera'ot La'Torah*, vol. 5, p. 92).

Rabbeinu Saadiah Gaon observes that the Torah unifies the Jewish people. Whatever internal struggles or differences of temperament and opinion that may exist, the Torah remains the basis for uniting the people (*Emunoth VeDeioth*, ch. 6).

Rabbi Naftali of Ropschitz sadly comments: "The only moment of true unity our people ever knew was at Sinai. After that, every experience was characterized by divisiveness (Rashi, Ex. 19:12). Apparently, even then, everybody claimed that his version of the Torah was the only correct one" (Rabbi Abraham J. Twersky, *Smiling Each Day*, p. 131).

Rabbi Moshe Sherer pointed out that *Tehillim* ends with *Kol haneshama t'hallel Koh* ["All the soul will praise G-d"], using the singular for the word "soul." The message is, "If all of us are united as one soul, with one heart, one goal, one dream — then we will eventually bring all of *K'lal Yisrael* [all Jews] to say *'Hallelu Koh'"* (*Agudath Israel of America, 73rd Anniversary Dinner,* May 21, 1995).

Cf. *Yebamoth* 13b, "'You shall not cut yourselves' (Deut. 14:1), you shall not form separate sects." See *Insights*, vol. 1, #359.

〚 534 〛 אֵין כָּל הַגָּלֻיּוֹת הַלָּלוּ מִתְכַּנְּסוֹת
אֶלָּא בִּזְכוּת מִשְׁנָיוֹת

"All the exiles will be gathered in, only through the merit of [the study of] the *Mishnah*" (*Va'yikra Rabbah* 7:3).

The *Sheloh HaKadosh* [Rabbi Isaiah Horowitz] writes: "The *Mishnah*, being the crown of the Oral Law, can cause a great *Tikkun* [spiritual improvement] for all Israel . . . . Through an intensive study of it, all salvations of Israel are aroused above, causing their power to shine and come down below.

Apart from the beneficial effect for all Israel, the study of the *Mishnah* is of immense benefit for the individual soul. Man should study the *Mishnah* continually . . . . Happy is he who is privileged to know the Six Orders of the Mishnah by heart, because thereby man makes a ladder for his soul on which he advances to the highest degree, the sign being that the letters of *Mishnah* (*mem, shin, nun, hey*) correspond to the letters of *Neshamah* (*nun, shin, mem, hey*) — soul" (*Sheney Luchoth HaBrith*, 1, p. 181 b).

It is interesting to note, that after the expulsion from Spain [1492], the Jews longed for redemption. Consequently, the kabbalists [more than others] engaged in an intensive study of the *Mishnah* (Rabbi E. Newman, *Life and Teachings of Isaiah Horowitz*, p. 99).

〚 535 〛 אֵין לְמֵידִין מְקוֹדֶם מַתַּן תּוֹרָה

"Laws may not be deduced from events which occurred before the Torah was given [on Sinai]" (*Yerushalmi, Moed Katan* 3:5).

"We regulate our actions only by G-d's commandments through Moshe our teacher and not by His commands to pre-Mosaic prophets. E.g., we may not eat a limb cut from the living, not because the Almighty forbade this to Noah; we practice circumcision not because the Almighty ordered Abraham to do so; we do not eat the *"gid hanoshe"* (the thigh muscle) because it was prohibited to Jacob — all these are binding on us because they are part of the 613 *mitzvoth* given to Moshe on Sinai" *(Rambam, Comm. on the Mishnah, Hullin,* ch. 7 end).

Rabbi Moshe Feinstein pointed out that "before the Torah was given, people were taught to observe certain *mitzvoth* and to abstain from certain activities because of social, psychological or other logical reasons . . . . After the Torah was given, however, the Jews were taught to observe the *mitzvoth* simply because this is the will of *Hashem* and we are obligated to carry out His commands" (Rabbi Abraham Fishelis, *Bastion of Faith,* p. 136).

The Lubavitcher Rebbe [Rabbi Menachem Mendel Schneerson] comments: "The principle of 'We do not learn from events which occurred before the Torah was given,' relates expressly to *halachoth* [legal rulings], because when the Torah was given, *halachah* was renewed [*Baba Bathra* 110b]. Elements relating to human character traits, however, can be learned even from events prior to Sinai because in this context there is no difference between periods before and after the Torah was given" *(L'kutei Sichoth,* vol. 1: *Beraishith).*

See *Encyclopedia Talmudith* vol. 1 for exceptions to this principle of not deducing laws from pre-revelation sources. Some authorities reject the principle entirely, and hold that we do indeed infer laws that were given prior to Sinai.

⇕ 536 ⇕   אֵין מְקַבְּלִין גֵּרִים לִימוֹת הַמָּשִׁיחַ

"Proselytes will not be accepted in the days of the Messiah"
(Yebamoth 24b)

Israel will then be prosperous and prospective converts will be attracted by worldly and not spiritual considerations.

Rabbi Chaim ben Attar comments: "When the Jews sinned with the Golden Calf, G-d declared to Moshe: 'Go down, for your nation which you brought out of Egypt has become corrupt' [Ex. 32:7]. Our sages explain that G-d criticized Moshe because he accepted many Egyptians who wanted to convert to Judaism when they saw the miracles which the Almighty had wrought for the Jews. These converts were opportunists who did not believe in G-d and who had not abandoned their pagan beliefs . . . . It was they who influenced the Jews to fashion the Golden Calf . . . .

In the future, during our final redemption, Moshe will right this wrong — for Moshe Rabbeinu will rule during the Messianic Era . . . . He will reject the insincere converts and will thus make amends for those he accepted during the Exodus from Egypt" (*Ohr HaChaim*, Ex. 32:10).

Cf. *Yebamoth* 47b, "Proselytes are as bad for Israel as a sore on the skin." See *Insights*, vol.1, #470.

Cf. *Abodah Zarah* 3b, "Dragged-in proselytes." See #605.

〚 537 〛

אֵין פּוּרְעָנוּת בָּאָה לְעוֹלָם
אֶלָּא בִּשְׁבִיל יִשְׂרָאֵל

"Punishment comes into the world only on Israel's account" (*Yebamoth* 63a).

"As it is said, 'I have cut off nations, their corners are desolate'" . . . . "I said: 'Just fear Me, O Israel; learn a lesson . . . .'" [Zephaniah 3:6-7].

Rabbeinu Nissim ben Reuben Gerondi writes: "Sometimes events erupt at great distances and in far away continents in order that Israel should be aroused to repentance and should experience awe and fear, lest these disasters strike them. This is the meaning of the prophecy, 'I have cut off nations . . . .' And when the Jewish people do not learn a lesson from the troubles of others, the disasters begin moving closer and closer . . . . Therefore, there is no doubt that at such times, it is proper to search painstakingly for a remedy for the soul" (*Ran, Derashoth* #6).

〚 538 〛

אֵין קָטֵיגוֹר נַעֲשֶׂה סַנֵּיגוֹר

"The accuser cannot become the defender" (*Rosh Hashanah* 26a).

An object used for a transgression may not be used for performing a *mitzvah*. Thus Aaron, who "sinned" with gold [for his complicity in the Golden Calf incident], was forbidden to enter the "Holy of Holies" on *Yom Kippur* while wearing his priestly garments of gold.

Rabbi Chaim ben Attar writes: "On the day of the dedication of the Tabernacle, Aaron was instructed to bring a calf for his sin-offering since he was not directly responsible for the construction of the Golden Calf. The Israelites, however, were instructed to bring a goat, and not a calf, for their collective sin-offering, for they were directly responsible for the Golden Calf, and bringing a calf for a sin-offering would violate the principle that 'The accuser cannot become the defender'" (*Ohr HaChaim*, Lev. 9:2).

Cf. *Berakoth* 32b, "A priest who has committed manslaughter should not lift up his hands [to say the priestly benediction] since it says, 'Your hands are full of blood'" [Isaiah 1:15]. "As he killed with his hands, the accuser [his hands] may not become the defender [by invoking a blessing]" (*Tosaf. Yebamoth* 7a, s.v. *Sh'ne'emar*).

See *Yerushalmi, Sukkah*, ch. 3, A stolen *lulav* is invalid for performing the *mitzvah*, since the accuser [the theft] cannot become his defender. This is similar to the *Talmud Bavli's* reason for invalidating a stolen *lulav* because it is "a mitzvah that is fulfilled through a transgression."

Cf. *Sukkah* 30a. See *Insights*, vol. 1, #416.

⟦ 539 ⟧   אֵין שָׁלִיחַ לִדְבַר עֲבֵירָה

"There can be no agent for a wrongdoing" (*Kiddushin* 42b).

The ruling that "a man's agent is as himself" (ibid. 41b), does not apply to an offense. Any wrongful act committed through an agent on the instructions of the principal is not accounted as an act of the principal, but of the agent himself (Rashi).

The reason for the above ruling is explicitly stated in the Talmud: "[When] the words of the master and the words of the student [are in conflict], whose are obeyed?" Obviously the master's. Hence, if the principal Reuven [the student] instructs the agent Shimon to do an act [which constitutes a transgression] against G-d [the Master], then Shimon acts on his own accord, for were he merely carrying out instructions, he would obey his Master's instructions.

See *Shach, Chosen Mishpat* 348:6.

Cf. *Kiddushin* 41b, "A man's agent is as himself." See *Insights*, vol. 1, #485.

▯ 540 ▯

אֵין תּוֹרָה כְּתוֹרַת אֶרֶץ יִשְׂרָאֵל
וְאֵין חָכְמָה כְּחָכְמַת אֶרֶץ יִשְׂרָאֵל

"There is no Torah like the Torah of the Land of Israel and no wisdom like the wisdom of the Land of Israel"
(*Va'yikra Rabbah* 13:5).

Rabbi Avraham Yitzchak Kook writes: "The difference between Torah in the Land of Israel and other lands is mighty and powerful. In the Land of Israel the flow of the Holy Spirit bursts forth, ready to invade the minds of the scholars who seek to study Torah for its own sake . . . the kind of sweetness and light of holiness that it offers in Israel to scholars who seek G-d is not found at all in other lands. I can testify to this fact out of my own experience" (*Great Jewish Thinkers of the Twentieth Century*, p. 82).

"The *Chazon Ish* (Rabbi Avraham Yeshaya Karlitz) once said that from the day he had arrived in *Eretz Yisrael* he had felt that his study of the Torah had improved, because of the *kedusha* (holiness) and spirituality in the Land" (Raphael Halpern, *20 Years Beside the Chazon Ish*, p. 23).

Rabbi Eliyahu E. Dessler writes: "There is something about *Eretz Yisrael* that makes the mind work better and the spirit grow stronger than else-where" (*Michtav Me-Eliyahu*, vol. 2, p. 55).

Cf. *Baba Bathra* 158b, "The climate of the Land of Israel makes one wise." See *Insights*, vol. 1, #11.

Cf. *Kiddushin* 49b, "Ten *kabs* [a measurement] of wisdom descended to the world, nine were taken by the Land of Israel and one by the rest of the world."

Cf. *Va'yikra Rabbah* 34:7, "Even the ordinary conversations of the people of the Land of Israel is Torah [requires study as if it were Torah]."

Cf. *Mechilta*, Bo 12:1, "Prophecy is attainable only in *Eretz Yisrael*."

〚 541 〛

אֵינָשֵׁי בָּדוּחֵי אֲנַן, מִבַדְּחִינַן עֲצִיבֵי

"We are jesters, we make people laugh when they are depressed"
(*Ta'anith* 22a).

Rabbi Beruka asked the prophet Eliyahu in the marketplace, "Can you show me someone who is assured of a place in the World to Come?" When Eliyahu pointed to two ordinary looking people, Rabbi Beruka asked them their occupation.

"We are jesters who make people laugh when they are depressed," they replied.

Rashi comments on the word *b'duchei* (jesters): "We are joyful and we cause others to rejoice."

It is significant to note, that at the conclusion of the *Tochocha* [a series of curses suffered by the Jewish people] the Torah admonishes us: "Because you did not serve the L-rd your G-d with joyfulness and with gladness of heart . . . ." [Deut. 28:47]. Rabbi Yitzchak Luria comments: "*Simchah* [joy] is fundamental to the service of G-d. Even if our service was lacking in other aspects, if we were happy while serving G-d, we never would have been exiled."

"Rejoicing in the fulfillment of the commandment and in the love of G-d who has prescribed the commandment is a supreme act of divine worship" (*Mishneh Torah, Hil. Lulav* 8:15).

Cf. *Ma'aser Sheni* 5:12, "'I have done entirely as you commanded me' — I have rejoiced and I have given joy to others therewith." See #929.

〚 542 〛

אִיתְּתָךְ גּוּצָא גְּחֵין וְתִלְחוֹשׁ לָהּ

"If your wife is short, bend down and hear her whisper" (*Baba Mezia* 59a).

One should listen to his wife's counsel in matters pertaining to the household [ibid.].

"The [above] talmudic advice points to a true one-to-one relationship [between husband and wife]. One can listen to someone shorter without bending down; the bending down is a symbolic concept of perceiving the relationship as that between two respecting equals" (Rabbi Reuven P. Bulka, *Jewish Marriage*, p. 202).

One Friday evening at twilight when the Alter of Slobodka's *mussar* discourse lasted longer than usual, his *Rebbetzin* opened the door a crack and whispered, "They have wives."

The Alter instantly stopped his speech and began the *Ma'ariv* prayers for Shabbos (Rabbi Chaim Ephraim Zaitchik, *HaMeoroth HaGedolim*).

Cf. *Yebamoth* 62b, "A man who loves his wife as himself and honors her more than himself, . . . Scripture says, 'And you shall know that your tent is in peace'" [Job 5:24]. See #614.

See Rambam, *Mishneh Torah, Hil. Ishuth* 15:19.

〚 543 〛 אָכַל וְלֹא הָלַךְ ד' אַמּוֹת אֲכִילָתוֹ מַרְקֶבֶת

"One who eats without walking four cubits, his food rots" (*Shabbath* 41a).

Rashi comments: "Without walking four cubits before he goes to sleep — for then his food will not be properly digested."

"At a Rabbinical Convention in Kovna, the Chafetz Chaim was forced to eat supper while sitting in bed, due to his weakened condition. After the meal the Chafetz Chaim strengthened himself and walked about four cubits away from his bed and said: 'I believe that I have already walked *dalet ammoth* [four cubits] and I have fulfilled my obligation, more than that I am not obligated'" (*Chafetz Chaim Al HaTorah*, p. 226).

As a matter of principle, the Chafetz Chaim was extremely concerned about the *mitzvah* of guarding one's health. In his yeshiva, he would enter the *Beth Midrash* after midnight and put out the lamps, pleading with the youngsters to go to sleep and take care of their health (Rabbi Moses M. Yoshor, *The Chofetz Chaim*, vol. 1, p. 93).

The Sanzer Rav, Rabbi Chaim Halberstam, was once ill on *Pesach* and his doctor told him that it was forbidden for him to eat *maror* because it would be dangerous to his health. At the *Pesach seder*, Rav Chaim took a large piece of *maror* and made a blessing, "Blessed are You who sanctified us with His commandments and commanded us to guard our health," and immediately returned the *maror* to the table (Rabbi Mordechai Cohen, *Al HaTorah*).

〚 544 〛   אֲכָלִית, אַשְׁקִית, לַוֵּית

"When you have given your guest food and drink, escort him" (*Beraishith Rabbah* 48:20).

So runs the proverb. In fact, "whoever escorts a guest on his way receives a reward comparable to the other services provided him," such as feeding, clothing and lodging.

Rabbi Shneur Kotler in discussing the *mitzvah* of "hospitality to guests" questions the "greater" importance attributed to escorting guests over feeding or providing lodging for them.

Says Rabbi Kotler: "Many times a guest overstays his welcome. At other times, the host is gracious to a guest but prays for the moment when the guest departs so that tranquility and privacy may once again prevail in his home. Accordingly, when this guest leaves, the host is privately overjoyed at his departure.

Hence, to escort a guest out of one's home is a positive sign that his departure is not one of joy but of sadness. [He stays with his guest until the very last minute when he must take leave of him.] This is indicative that his previous hospitality — the feeding, the clothing and lodging were sincere acts of wisdom and joy" (Rabbi J. Simchah Cohen, "Halachic Questions," *The Jewish Press*, 6/29/90).

Although one is halachically required to accompany his friend no more than four *amoth* (approximately eight feet), even that type of "escorting" suffices to show the one being accompanied that he is not alone but is connected to others. This spiritual connection gives the one accompanied the merit of the *tzibbur* (public), which is a potent protection against harm (*Maharal*, cited by Rabbi Zev Leff, *Outlooks and Insights*, p. 70).

Cf. *Sotah* 46b, "A person may be compelled to escort [a visitor] because the reward for escorting is limitless."

⟦ 545 ⟧

אַל יִפָּטֵר אָדָם מֵחֲבֵירוֹ אֶלָּא מִתּוֹךְ דְּבַר
הֲלָכָה שֶׁמִּתּוֹךְ כָּךְ זוֹכְרֵהוּ

"In taking leave of his fellow a man should always finish with a
matter of *halachah*, so that he should remember him thereby"
(Berakoth 31a).

Rabbi S. Joshua Zanibrowsky suggests that the meaning [of the above
dictum] is not that which is commonly understood, i.e. that through the
words of Torah the person departing from his friend will be remembered,
but rather "the words of the Torah" will thereby be remembered.

"When two friends take leave of each other their hearts are tender and
extremely receptive to words of Torah and *mussar* [moral instruction]. One
should therefore not be lax in speaking such 'memorable' words to his friend
on the day he takes leave of him. This is an opportune time for his words
to enter his friend's heart" *(Chemdas Yehoshua,* p. 31).

"Words that come from the heart enter the heart" (R. Moshe Ibn Ezra,
Shiras Yisroel, 156) See *Insights,* vol. 1, #138.

⟦ 546 ⟧

אַל תְּבַקֵּשׁ גְּדֻלָּה לְעַצְמֶךְ

"Do not seek greatness for yourself" *(Aboth* 6:5).

"A person becomes jealous when he sees that his neighbor has status and
advantages such as property and wealth, since he wishes to be greater than
his neighbor. If, however, a person does not seek greatness for himself, it
is certain that he will not be jealous of his neighbor" *(MeAm Lo'ez).*

Rabbi Moshe Avigdor Amiel analyzes the source of man's continued
striving and dissatisfaction until he dies without repose or contentment.
"After Adam and Eve ate from the 'Tree of Knowledge,' the Torah declares,
'And their eyes were opened and they knew that they were naked' [Gen.
3:7]. Until now they had been tranquil and content with their lot, envying
no creature, undisturbed in spirit and mind, until they ate of the fruit of the
forbidden tree. Then the poison entered their minds; their eager restless eyes

were opened, seeking after vanity, to be distinctive, to 'go one better' than the rest. They made themselves girdles of fig-leaves, sufficient to satisfy their pride and their assertion of superiority . . . .

"Man has multiplied in the world, his interests have become more varied, but the same principles animate him: the desire to 'go one better' than his neighbor, to have just that fig-leaf which his neighbor does not possess" (*Derashos El-Ami*, vol. 1, p. 3).

▯ 547 ▯

"אַל תִּגְּעוּ בִּמְשִׁיחָי",
אֵלּוּ תִּינוֹקוֹת שֶׁל בֵּית רַבָּן

"'Touch not my anointed' [*Divrei HaYomim* I 16:22] — this refers to young school children" (*Shabbath* 119b).

School children are designated as "anointed," for it was customary to rub children with oil (Rashi).

Rabbi Eliezer Zusman Sofer writes: "If you want to succeed in raising children imbued with Torah ideals, you must make them feel spiritually "anointed." They should feel that Torah study leads to royalty and that *middoth* (noble traits) are a form of majesty" (*Melayah Katoreth*).

Rabbi Yehudah Loew b. Bezalel [Maharal miPrague] explains the "child-*moshiach*" appellation in the following fashion: "A child is like a vessel which can be sanctified. Before he has been "tainted" [by becoming an adult], he is like the holy vessels in the Temple ready to receive sanctity" [*Nesivoth Olam, Nesiv HaTorah*, chap. 10). See Rabbi Yitzchak Hutner's *Pachad Yitzchak, Kuntrus V'zos Chanukah, Maamer* 11:9,10 on the Maharal's explanation.

Cf. *Shabbath* 119b, "We do not disrupt the learning of school children even for the building of the Temple."

In commenting on our dictum which, in effect, designates the young school children as the "messiahs of mankind," Rabbi Jacob Schacter writes: "The child is the perennial regenerative force in humanity, because through each child G-d continually gives mankind new chances to make good its mistakes" (*Ingathering*, p. 93).

Cf. *Shabbath* 119b, "The world endures only for the sake of the breath of school children." See #526.

⎰ 548 ⎱

אֵלוּ וָאֵלוּ דִּבְרֵי אֱלֹקִים חַיִּים

"These [statements] and these [statements] are the words of the living G-d" (*Erubin* 13b).

For three years Beth Shammai and Beth Hillel were disputing, the former asserting, "'The *halacha* is in accord with our views' while the latter contended, 'The *halacha* is in accord with our views.' A *Bath Kol* [Heavenly voice] announced: 'These and these [views] are the words of the living G-d, but the *halacha* is in accord with Beth Hillel.' Now, since both 'are the words of the living G-d,' why was the *halacha* fixed in accord with Beth Hillel? Because they were kindly and modest. They studied their own ruling as well as those of Beth Shammai and were so modest as to mention Beth Shammai's decisions before their own" [ibid.].

Rabbi Yehudah Loew b. Bezalel [Maharal miPrague] commented: "Modesty should not be the decisive factor in any case of law. But arrogant self-assertion blinds a person to truth, whereas patient humility allows one to see the opponent's logic or force of argument. The former is motivated by ill-will, often hatred of the other side, while the latter honors no goal except attaining truth and justice. Truth resides in the mansion of the humble searcher after its meaning" (*Be'er Hagolah*, vol. 5).

"Controversy in matters of Jewish Law is normal as long as there is an overarching authority to resolve the controversy by rendering an *halachic* decision and thus forestall a schism in Jewish life" (Rabbi Mendell Lewittes, "The Nature and History of Jewish Law," *Studies in Torah Judaism*, 9, p. 26).

Unfortunately, the above dictum is often cited by those who have rejected the words of the living G-d, i.e., the historical revelation of G-d on Mount Sinai. How ludicrous to proclaim that the words of both those who affirm *Torah miSinai* and those who reject this fundamental principle are "the words of the living G-d"!

⦅ 549 ⦆

אַלְיָה וְקוֹץ בָּהּ

"A fat tail with a thorn in it" (*Rosh Hashanah* 17a).

A certain breed of sheep in the East has very long tails which are esteemed a great delicacy, but as they trail on the ground they often pick up thorns. Hence the maxim, "A fat tail with a thorn in it" — a good thing containing a snag.

Rabbi Moshe Avigdor Amiel applies this maxim to the response given by the children of Heth to Abraham when he inquired about purchasing a burial site for his beloved wife Sarah.

The Hittites said: "Hear us, my lord, you are a prince of G-d in our midst . . ." [Gen. 23:6]. Says Rabbi Amiel, "This statement is 'A fat tail with a thorn in it,' and the thorn is greater than the tail. 'A fat tail' — Yes, it is true [they said] that you are a 'prince of G-d,' but 'with a thorn in it' — you are 'in our midst.' As long as you reside amongst us [the Hittites implied] you are as one of us. You can be a prince of G-d as long as you go along with us and give us your 'stamp of approval'" (*Hegyonoth El-Ami*, part 2, p. 102).

Cf. *Ketuboth* 105b, "If a scholar is loved by the townspeople, [their love] is not due to his superiority, but [to the fact] that he does not rebuke them for [neglecting] matters of Heaven." See #619.

If a Rabbi is very popular and is loved by his entire congregation [a fat tail], most probably he does not rebuke them concerning 'the *mitzvoth* between man and G-d' [there is a thorn in it].

English proverb: "A fly in the ointment."

⦅ 550 ⦆

אִם אֲנִי כָּאן הַכּל כָּאן

"If I am here, everyone is here" (*Sukkah* 53a).

During the rejoicing of the *Simchath Beis HaShoeivah* [Drawing of Water] on the festival of *Succoth*, Hillel the Elder would declare in the name of the Almighty [as if G-d Himself were declaring], "If *I* am here, everyone is here. As long as *I* favor this House [the Holy Temple] and My *Shechinah* dwells here, then all will come here. But if they [the Israelites] sin and I remove My *Shechinah*, who will come here?" [Rashi].

Tosafoth citing the *Yerushalmi* interprets Hillel's aphorism as referring to *Klal Yisroel* [the Israelites], i.e., "If I [Israel] am here, everyone is here . . . ."

The *Chasam Sofer* citing the *Sefer Hafla'ah* gives a literal interpretation to the above declaration. Hillel said: "If I [a man of little worth] am here," then "everyone is here" [all are qualified to be here]. If you will ask, "Indeed, what right do you have to be here?" i.e., "If I am not here," then "who is here?" — each person would disqualify himself and no one would visit the Holy Temple" (Rabbi Shmuel Alter, *L'kutei Bosar L'kutei* [*Aggadoth*, vol. 2, p. 179]).

In Mesivta Torah Vodaath, Reb Shraga Feivel Mendelowitz would often direct the singing and dancing on *Shabbos* and *Yom Tov*. On *Succoth*, one of his favorite songs was Hillel's aphorism. "*Im Ani Kahn, Hakol Kahn*" ["If I am here, everyone is here"]. He would say: "*Bachurim, tanzt Rashi's p'shat*" ["Boys, dance Rashi's version" (that 'I' refers to G-d)]. Then a while later, he would say: "*Bachurim, tanzt Tosafoth's p'shat*" ["Boys, dance Tosafoth's version" (that 'I' refers to Israel)] (Rabbi Yitzchak Chinn, "Ohr Shraga — The Light of Reb Shraga Feivel," *The Jewish Observer* 17, no. 2 [Sept. 1983]:8).

551

אִם בָּאָה עַל אָדָם צָרָה,
לֹא יִצְוַח לֹא לְמִיכָאֵל וְלֹא לְגַבְרִיאֵל,
אֶלָּא לִי יִצְוַח וַאֲנִי עוֹנֶה לוֹ

"If trouble should come upon an individual, he shall pray neither to [the angel] Michael, nor to [the angel] Gavriel, but he shall pray only to Me, and I will answer him at once"
(*Yerushalmi, Berakoth* 9:1).

This is the fifth principle of the 13 principles of faith formulated by Rambam. "It is He alone, blessed is He, whom it is fitting to worship . . . . Nor shall one do likewise in regard to any lower beings, be they angels, stars . . . . Nor is it proper to worship them, that they may serve as intermediaries [through which] to approach Him . . . . (*Comm. on the Mishnah*, Intro.

to *Perek Chelek*).

There are certain *piyyutim* [poetical liturgical prayers] which are addressed to *malachim* [angels], who are in turn requested to pray to G-d in our behalf, such as *machnisei rachamim* recited during *Selichoth*. The Maharal miPrague and Rabbi Chaim Volozhin and others felt that it would be proper to amend the text so that the prayers would be directed towards the Almighty (Rabbi Zechariah Fendel, *Torah Faith*: The *Thirteen Principles*, p. 101). See R. Yehudah Loew b. Bezalel, *Nesivoth Olam*, vol. 1, *Nesiv HaAvodah, Perek* 12.

Similarly, Rabbi Yaakov Emden and Rabbi Chaim Volozhin and others opposed the recitation of *Shalom Aleichem* on Friday night, for the stanza *Borchuni L'shalom* [Bless me for peace] is in violation of the above dictum. Angels have no independent power to confer blessing. Most authorities, however, maintain that this is not a "blessing" but merely good wishes for the future. See ArtScroll *Zemiroth*, p. 42.

◊ 552 ◊

אִם דּוֹמֶה הָרַב לְמַלְאַךְ ה' צְבָאוֹת, יְבַקְשׁוּ
תּוֹרָה מִפִּיו, וְאִם לָאו, אַל יְבַקְשׁוּ תּוֹרָה מִפִּיו

"If the Rav is like a messenger of the L-rd of Hosts, they should seek the law at his mouth. . ." (*Moed Katon* 17a).

Rabbi Aharon Soloveitchik points out that "at Sinai the children of Israel heard the 'Voice of G-d' and they also experienced these words '*mitoch ha'eish*' [amidst the fire]. Both Ramban and Rabbeinu Bachya tell us that in transmitting Torah to our children we must convey to them both of these components: the Voice and the Fire of Sinai.

What is the "Fire of Sinai"? Rabbi Soloveitchik cites the above dictum in explaining this concept. "For a teacher to be able to transmit the 'Fire of Sinai' to his students, he must bear a similarity to a '*Malach HaShem Tz'vokos*,' a messenger of the L-rd of Hosts. This demands at least three prerequisites on the part of the teacher or parent: (1) consistency; (2) a sense of Divine mission; (3) an abundance of love.

"It is not enough that we transmit the 'Voice of Sinai,' we must also *consistently* present to the child the full pattern of Torah living that is to accompany those words.

"Secondly, the teacher must consider himself an actual messenger of G-d . . . he must consider teaching not as a mere profession but as a *Divine mission*.

"The third prerequisite for Torah teachers . . . is the communication of an unlimited love of people as well as an *unlimited love of fellow Jews*" (*Building Jewish Ethical Character*, pp. 11-18).

⦗ 553 ⦘

אִם לֹא עַכְשָׁיו, אֵימָתָי?

"If not now, when?" (*Aboth* 1:14).

"If I will not acquire virtues now, in the period of youth, when shall I acquire them — in the period of old age? No, for it is difficult to turn aside from dispositions at that time because traits and attributes have become firm and permanent . . . ." (*Rambam, Commentary on the Mishnah*).

When Rabbi Hillel Lichtenstein became extremely ill, his doctors ordered him not to study Torah, but he ignored them. The *Chasam Sofer* sent a message to R' Hillel: "Why are you disobeying the doctors at a time when your life is in grave danger?"

"That is exactly the point," replied R' Hillel. "If I do not learn now, then when?" (Shmuel Himelstein, *A Touch of Wisdom, A Touch of Wit*).

[Nevertheless, the *Chasam Sofer's* "message" is the *halacha*!]

Irving M. Bunim cites the Chafetz Chaim's poignant illustration of the above popular maxim. The life of the average person may be compared to someone on vacation who writes to his friend on a picture postcard. At the top go the date, the salutation, the usual formal introduction — and before he has gotten around to writing what he really wanted to, he suddenly realizes with a sickening feeling that he has no more room! He has come to the end of the card! Desperate, the writer frantically begins to print in tiny letters, he turns the card over and attempts to write even in the margin.

Does not man cut the same pathetic figure as he manages his life? In our early years we "scribble" away so much of our time in trivia, in nonsense, in activities with no lasting meaning. Suddenly, with a shock we awake to the awful truth that life is a "picture postcard" with deceptively little time, and that we haven't even begun to do the job for which we were placed on earth (*Ethics From Sinai*, vol. 1, p. 94).

⟦ 554 ⟧

אִם נִתְיַשְׁנוּ דִּבְרֵי תוֹרָה בְּפִיךָ,
אַל תְּבַזֶּה עֲלֵיהֶן

"If the words of Torah have become old in your mouth, do not
despise them" (*Yerushalmi Berakoth*, 68a).

This is a talmudic interpretation of the verse, "And despise not your
mother when she is old" [Prov. 23:22].

Rabbi Yitzchak Elchanan applied the above talmudic passage to the
Maskilim of his day. He writes that on the surface, the phrase [in the dictum]
"in your mouth" seems superfluous. He explains that the "anti-traditional-
ists" fall into two categories. "To the first group belong those who do not see
fit to study Torah for the fear of being classed as 'old fashioned.' To the
second, belong those who not only do not study, but are even ashamed to
discuss ways and means of lightening the financial burden of those who
study Torah. They refuse to talk about it because it is too 'old fashioned' a
subject. Hence, the term [If the words of Torah have become old] '*in your
mouth*' is used in the talmud" (*Etz Pri*, p. 31, cited by Rabbi Ephraim
Shimoff, *Rabbi Isaac Elchanan Spektor, His Life and Works, p. 52*).

⟦ 555 ⟧

אִם שְׁגוּרָה תְּפִלָּתִי בְּפִי,
יוֹדֵעַ אֲנִי שֶׁהוּא מְקוּבָּל

"If my prayer is fluent in my mouth I know that it is accepted"
(*Berakoth* 34b).

Rabbi Chanina ben Dosa was able to predict the outcome of his prayers
for the sick by the fluency of his words before the Almighty.

Rabbi Elimelech of Lizhensk writes: "At first glance the expression *shegura*
[fluent] does not apply here. What Rabbi Chanina ben Dosa should have
said was, 'If I can say the prayer without hesitancy or error, I know that it
is accepted.'" [The word "fluent" indicates that the prayer had been prac-
ticed and reviewed earlier.]

"In order to explain this, we must understand why a righteous person can pray for the sick and cause him to be healed. This would seem to involve a change in G-d's mind . . . . The concept is this. At first, before the universe was brought into being, all worlds existed potentially in the Infinite Being. Then when He decided to create, He brought them from potential into actuality.

"Everything that would ever be, therefore, had potential existence in the blessed Infinite Being. Therefore, [when a person is healed as a result of prayer], there is no change. All this already existed potentially. The entire sequence existed there — namely, that an individual would be sick, that a righteous person would pray for him, and that prayer would have a beneficial effect . . .

"This explains what Rabbi Chanina ben Dosa meant when he said: 'If my prayer is fluent in my mouth, I know that it is accepted.' He was saying that the prayer was familiar, like something with which he was already acquainted. He knew that the prayer would be accepted for it already existed potentially in the Infinite Being, and nothing changes before Him" (*Noam Elimelech, Vayechi*, 27a, cited by Rabbi Aryeh Kaplan, *The Light Beyond*, p. 60).

⁅ 556 ⁆   אִם שָׁמוֹעַ בַּיָשָׁן, תִּשְׁמַע בֶּחָדָשׁ

"If you will hear the old, you will [be able to] hear the new"
(*Berakoth* 40a).

This is one interpretation of the verse, "If hearing you will hear" [Ex. 15:26].

"If you will hear the old" — "If you will review that which you have already learnt, then, you will hear the new. You will thereby gain the insight to comprehend the new from the old" (*Rashi, Sukkah* 46b).

In a letter to his son, Rabbi Avraham Yitzchak Kook makes the following observation on the above maxim: "The whole sickness of this generation is that they think that once a subject has been studied, it is no longer necessary to review it and to understand it properly, and they seek the new without possessing the old. Under no circumstances will they be able to achieve this, for the new cannot be properly established unless it is drawn from the roots of the old, which becomes new each day to one who studies it with an upright heart; and one who truly serves G-d is one who reviews his studies one hundred and one times (*Hagigah* 9b). This applies to all subjects of study" (*Iggrot* I, *Letter* 29).

Rabbi Zundel of Salant was a great believer in repeating [his studies] and in repeating them aloud. "His advice was: 'Study the new and review the old' . . . . On the other hand, he warned against excess." (Rabbi Dov Katz, *Tenuath HaMussar*, vol. 1).

The Vilna Gaon declared: "One who studies Torah without reviewing constantly what he has studied, will be left with nothing. Our sages (*Erubin* 54b) liken this to a fowler who hunts birds. If he fails to secure what he has caught, the birds will fly away and he will be left with nothing" (*Comm. to Mishle* 12:27).

Sefer Menuchah U'Kedushah writes, "I have heard that the Vilna Gaon would submit a prospective student to the following test: He would instruct him to review a given matter many times. If the more he reviewed, the more his love grew in his heart, [inspiring him] to continue to review it without interruption — with this he found favor in his [the Gaon's] eyes to be accepted as his disciple" (Rabbi Shimon Finkelman, *Inspiration and Insight*, vol. 2).

Cf. *Hagigah* 9b, "He that repeated his chapter a hundred times is not to be compared with him who repeated it a hundred and one times." See *Insights*, vol. 1, #55.

⌑ 557 ⌑ „אָנֹכִי" נוֹטָרִיקוֹן אֲנָא נַפְשִׁי כְּתִיבַת יְהָבִית

"*Anochi* is an acronym [for the words] *ana nafshi k'sivat y'havis* [I Myself have given the script] (*Sabbath* 105a).

This is the standard translation of this dictum. It is a confirmation that G-d Himself has written the script of the Decalogue.

Rabbi Baruch HaLevi Epstein suggests the following insightful interpretation: Psychologists have hypothesized that by analyzing a person's handwriting and language one can get a pretty good idea of his personality, temperament, and outlook on life. There is a French saying — "*le style c'est l'homme*" [the style is the man]. Similarly, I explain the meaning [of our dictum] as follows: [Literally translated] "I have given My soul in writing." G-d is saying in the word *"Anochi,"* that if you want to know who I am — My plans and My character [if we can truly say such a thing], then study My handwriting [i.e. the Torah which I have given]. For one who studies the Torah with a pure mind and with complete faith will attain knowledge of G-d (*Makor Baruch*, cited in *Recollections*, p. 129).

⎰ 558 ⎱

אָסוּר לְאָדָם לְהִסְתַּכֵּל
בְּצֶלֶם דְּמוּת אָדָם רָשָׁע

"A man is forbidden to gaze into the face of a wicked man"
(*Megillah* 28a).

"When Rebbe asked R. Yehoshua b. Korcha, 'In virtue of what have you reached such a good [ripe] old age . . .?' He replied: 'Never in my life have I gazed at the countenance of a wicked man.'"

Maharsha explains that according to the sages of *Kabbalah* the countenance of one's face reflects his character. An unclean spirit rests upon the wicked man, and if one looks directly at his face the evil spirit will also rest upon him.

Reb Eliyahu Lopian, in analyzing this kabbalistic interpretation writes: "Sight is a spiritual property located in the brain that is connected by nerves to the eyes through which vision is transmitted. Hence, if one looks into the face of a wicked man, this harms the spiritual power of sight in the brain, and an unclean spirit will rest upon him. That is why our sages prohibited us from looking into the face of a wicked man.

This is not mere *midath chassidus* [pious behavior] but an actual prohibition. If one transgresses this prohibition he will later notice an evil thought passing through his mind and wonder whence such an evil thought came — such a lustful or arrogant thought. The answer is that the unclean spirit of the wicked man who is lustful or arrogant has clung to him (*Lev Eliyahu*, p. 212).

〽 559 〽 אָסוּר לְאָדָם שֶׁיְּמַלֵּא שְׂחוֹק פִּיו בעוה"ז

"It's forbidden that a man's mouth be filled with laughter in this world" (*Berakoth* 31a).

"Some commentaries assert that the rationale of this prohibition is the destruction of the Holy Temple, for if not for the *Churban* [the Destruction] it would be permissible [to engage in excessive laughter]. This is incorrect, for if that were the case, it [the dictum] should not have said, 'It is forbidden . . . in this world,' but 'From the time of the destruction of the Holy Temple it is forbidden that a man's mouth be filled with laughter.'

"This prohibition has always been in effect, for excessive joy [merriment] is conducive to forgetfulness and laxity in the performance of *mitzvoth*" (*Rabbeinu Yonah, Berakoth, Rif* 21b).

See, however, *Taz, Orach Chaim* 560:7 who distinguishes between a *simchah shel mitzvah* [rejoicing in the merriment of a commandment] in which case "total" joy would have been appropriate had the Holy Temple been in existence, and other "rejoicings" which would never be appropriate.

Cf. *Sotah* 48a, "When the Sanhedrin ceased [to function] song ceased from the place of feasting."

〽 560 〽 אָסְיָא אַסִּי חִיגְרְתָךְ

"Physician, heal your own limp" (*Beraishith Rabbah* 23:4).

Before you correct others, correct yourself. The above midrashic maxim is similar to the talmudic dictum. "First adorn yourself and then adorn others" (*Baba Bathra* 60b) See *Insights*, vol. 1, #469.

Cf. *Va'yikra Rabbah* 5:6, "Shame on the province whose physician is gouty . . . ."

Cf. *Baba Mezia* 59b, "Do not taunt your neighbor with the blemish you yourself have." See #853.

A physician who is an intensive smoker should not counsel others to stop smoking. Similarly, it would be incongruous for an excessively stout physician to lead a diet workshop.

❏ 561 ❏   אַסְתֵּירָא בְּלָגִינָא קִיש קִיש קַרְיָא

"One stone in a pitcher cries out, 'rattle, rattle'" (*Baba Mezia* 85b)

When a pitcher is filled with stones, they have no room for rattling; but when it is empty, one stone makes a great deal of noise. "Empty vessels make the most noise." Empty-headed people advertise the little "scholarship" they possess.

Rabbi Avraham Pam, in one of his "Erev Shabbos talks," tells the story of the Jew who thinks he is a "great scholar" because he knows the proper manner of performing "*hagboh*" [raising the Torah Scroll] after it is read. Whenever this Jew witnesses someone performing *hagboh* improperly, by placing the left side of the scroll above the right side, he cries out, "*Beraishith fon oiben*" [the side commencing with *Beraishith* is placed on top]. He proclaims "*Beraishith fon oiben*" with such authority that it sounds like the pronouncement of an "*halachic* decision" of far-reaching consequences. Rav Pam remarked that whenever he sees someone parading his meager knowledge before others, believing that he is a "great scholar," he is reminded of the man who shouts, "*Beraishith fon oiben*."

English proverb: "Empty vessels make the loudest clatter."

❏ 562 ❏   אֲפִילוּ מַה שֶׁתַּלְמִיד וָתִיק עָתִיד לְהוֹרוֹת
לִפְנֵי רַבּוֹ, כְּבָר נֶאֱמַר לְמשֶׁה בְּסִינַי

"Even that which a competent disciple will in the future expound before his Rebbe, has already been said to Moshe at Sinai"
(*Yerushalmi*, *Pe'ah* 2:4).

Rabbi Shear Yashuv Cohen writes: "This is indeed a revolutionary statement. The *Yerushalmi* explains that this was included in the covenant of G-d with His people at Sinai. The authority of the "competent disciple" to continue the chain of tradition, to suggest and even innovate decisions, but always making sure that he is doing so under the watchful eye of his Rebbe, is derived from the verse, 'Write these words, for after the tenor of these words I have made a covenant with you and with Israel' (Ex. 34:27).

Only a *"talmid vathik"* [a "competent disciple"] can take it upon himself to decide, or instruct — and expect his decisions to be accepted and become part and parcel of Jewish Law. Obviously, all the relevant precedents must be taken into account and dealt with, but the vitality and strength of *chidush* [innovation] is what finally counts" (*Torah From Zion*, pp. 28, 29).

◊ 563 ◊

אֲפִילּוּ נִרְאִים בְּעֵינֶיךָ עַל שְׂמֹאל שֶׁהוּא יָמִין
וְעַל יָמִין שֶׁהוּא שְׂמֹאל, שְׁמַע לָהֶם

"Even if it seems to you [that what the sages tell you] regarding the left, that it is right, or regarding the right, that it is left — listen to them" (*Sifri, Devarim* 17:11).

"Even if you are told that the right is left or the left is right — how much more so if you are told the right is right and left, left" (Rashi).

In commenting on this *Rashi*, Rabbi Yaakov Tzvi Mecklenburg writes: "If in your eyes they seem to have made a wrong decision, nevertheless, follow them; but if you are absolutely certain they are mistaken, the Talmud has already instructed you not to listen to them in the event of their calling the right, left . . . . *Rashi's* words need emending" (*Haksav V'hakabbalah*).

Rabbi Mecklenburg was referring to the *Yerushalmi, Horioth* 1:1, which states: "On the verse, 'You shall not deviate from the thing which they shall tell you, to the right or to the left' [Deut. 17:11] — You might think that if the sages tell you that the right is left or the left is right, that you are to heed them; however, the text reads: 'to the right or to the left' — when they tell you the right is right and the left is left."

See, however, Ramban [Deut. 17:11], "Even if you think in your heart that they [the Sanhedrin] are mistaken and the matter is simple in your eyes, just as you know [the difference] between your right hand and your left hand, you must still do as they command you."

See also *Torah Temima* [ibid.], who reconciles Ramban with the *Yerushalmi* [cited above] that if you are absolutely certain that the sages are mistaken, you are not to listen to them.

Cf. *Rosh Hashanah* 25a, Rabbi Yehoshua was instructed by Rabban Gamliel to come before him with his walking stick on the *Day of Atonement that occurred according to R. Yehoshua's reckoning*. When Rabbi Yehoshua arrived, "Rabban Gamliel stood up and kissed him on the head and said to him: 'Come in peace, my master and my disciple' — 'my master' in wisdom, and 'my disciple' because you accepted my words."

〔 564 〕   אֲפִילוּ רָשָׁע וּבָטוּחַ בַּה' חֶסֶד יְסוֹבְבֶנּוּ

"Even if he is wicked, but he trusts in G-d, he will be surrounded by loving-kindness" (*Yalkut Shimoni, Tehillim*, Sect. 719).

"He who places his trust in G-d will be surrounded by loving-kindness" (Psalms 32:10).

Rabbi Yosef Zundel of Salant, in a letter to his son who was about to embark on a hazardous journey, writes: "Do not worry at all, for this is a unique feature of *bitachon* [trust], that the Almighty fulfills the desire of one who trusts in Him with a perfect heart, providing him with all his needs at every time and place, even if he is not a *tzaddik*" (Rabbi Dov Katz, *Tenuath HaMussar*, vol. 1, p. 124).

The Chafetz Chaim similarly observes: "The trait of *bitachon* does not depend upon [the individual's] merits. Even if he is unworthy, if his trust in G-d is firm, the power of *bitachon* will protect him, and the Almighty will do kindness for him (*Shem Olam*).

Rabbi Yosef Yozel Hurwitz [The Alter of Navardok] writes: "To the extent that the individual draws closer to G-d, to that extent will G-d's protection and His benevolence descend upon the individual" (*Madregas HaAdam*, vol. 1, p. 202).

The above insights are cited by Rabbi Zechariah Fendel, *The Halacha and Beyond* pp. 234-238).

The Vilna Gaon writes: "The man who is steadfast in his confidence in G-d, even though he commits severe sins, is better than the man who is insecure. For as a result of his insecurity, the latter comes to jealousy and hatred, despite the fact that he studies Torah and helps others — which he does solely to acquire a good name" (*Even Sheleimah,* ch. 3:2).

"*Bitachon* involves the belief that there is no coincidence in the world and that every occurrence under the sun is by *Hashem's* proclamation" (*The Chazon Ish,* p. 150).

Cf. Rambam, *Moreh Nevuchim* III chap. 18, "The relation of Divine Providence is not the same to all men; the greater the human perfection a person has attained, the greater the benefit he derives from Divine Protection."

◊ 565 ◊ לא . . . . אַרְבַּע מִדּוֹת בְּהוֹלְכֵי בֵית הַמִּדְרָשׁ
הוֹלֵךְ וְלֹא עוֹשֶׂה רָשָׁע

"There are four types of people who go to the House of Study . . . . One who neither goes nor acts is wicked" (*Aboth* 5:17).

The Baal Shem Tov raises the obvious question. How can the one who does not go to the House of Study be included in the "four types of people who go to the House of Study"?

He explains that evil causes the good to be discerned. If there were no evil, then good would not be recognized. "Light is known to exist because there is darkness; wisdom because of folly; righteousness because of wickedness; pleasure because of pain." [Hence, evil fulfills a purpose in the world and "the fourth type," who neither goes nor acts, strengthens the other three.] (Rabbi Yitzchok Isaac of Komarna, *Notzer Chesed*).

Cf. Aboth 5:16, "There are four attitudes among those who give charity, ... One who neither gives nor wishes others to give is wicked." See *Insights,* vol. 1, #86.

☙ 566 ☙ „אֲשֶׁר יֶחְסַר לוֹ" : אֲפִילוּ סוּס לִרְכּוֹב עָלָיו וְעֶבֶד לָרוּץ לְפָנָיו

"'Sufficient for his needs' [Deut. 15:8] — Even a horse to ride upon and a servant to run before him" (Kethuboth 67b).

"If an impoverished person was accustomed to riding on a horse and having a servant running in front of him, a riding horse and a running servant should be procured for him" (Mishneh Torah, Hil. Matnoth Aniyim 7:3).

Rabbi Menachem Mendel of Kotzk commented: "As far as providing an impoverished person with 'a horse to ride upon,' I can understand perhaps the man is ill or weak and therefore requires a horse. But 'a servant to run before him' — this is nothing but sheer foolishness! Why are we obligated to grant him this desire?" Said the Kotzker: "From this we learn, noch tzugeben ah nar zein shtus is oich a gemilas chesed [to provide a fool with his foolishness is also an act of kindness]" (Emeth MiKotz Titzmach, p. 129).

Charity is to be dispensed according to the psychological as well as the physical needs of each person. When the Tzanzer Rav, Rabbi Chaim Halberstam, was told that the wife of a charity recipient was seen purchasing expensive duck meat, he responded, "I was under the impression that this man's wife was able to manage with a small amount of money. Now that I know that she requires duck meat, I will increase the weekly charitable allowance of that family" (HaAdmor MiTzanz), p. 71).

☙ 567 ☙ אַשְׁרֵי זְקֵנָתֵנוּ שֶׁכִּפְּרָה אֶת יַלְדוּתֵנוּ

"Happy is our old age which has atoned for our youth" (Sukkah 53a).

During the Simchas Bais HaSho'eivah [the rejoicing at the water-drawing in the Temple on the festival of Succoth] the penitents sang: "Happy is our old age . . . ."

Rabbi Yitzchok Hutner analyzes this remarkable shirah [song] at this festive occasion. "For what is *shirah* but the ecstacy of the soul overflowing from joy in the performance of the Will of the Almighty. *Simchas Bais HaSho'eivah* was the one occasion reserved for the song of the repentant sinner. Why?

Rabbeinu Yonah writes: 'The *simchah* associated with having achieved repentance is a special joy that is not extrinsic to *teshuvah*, added to embellish the *mitzvah*, but is an integral part of its inner dynamics. Moreover, the anguish of having sinned can be assuaged only by the joy of having been forgiven — thus *simchah* becomes a fundamental aspect of *teshuvah*' (*Shaarei Teshuvah* 4:8).

The Vilna Gaon suggests that our celebration of *Succoth* does not only commemorate the Clouds of Glory, but also marks their return after their absence since the sin of the Golden Calf. The long *teshuvah* process culminated with the descent of Moshe Rabbeinu from Mount Sinai on *Yom Kippur*, with the evidence of forgiveness in hand — the Second Tablets.

Hence, *Succoth* is the holiday of rebirth and rejuvenation through *teshuvah* . . . . Can there be, then, anything more natural than a song for *ba'alei teshuvah* on *Succoth*? At the lofty moment of *Simchas Bais HaSho'eivah* . . . a song for penitents was inevitable (*Pachad Yitzchok*, adapted by Rabbi Feitman, *Seasons of the Soul*, pp. 92-97).

⟦ 568 ⟧ אַשְׁרֵי מִי שֶׁבָּא לְכָאן וְתַלְמוּדוֹ בְּיָדוֹ

"Praiseworthy is he who enters this place [the World to Come] retaining his studies in his hand" (*Baba Bathra* 10b).

"Note, it does not say, 'retaining his studies in his head,' but 'in his hand,' implying that he enters the World to Come with the learning he acquired through toil and determination. This teaches us that in the Hereafter the yardstick used to measure a person's Torah knowledge is not his intellectual proficiency, but the exertion expended in gaining it" (Rabbi Eliyahu Eliezer Dessler, *Michtav MeEliyahu*, vol. 3, "On Laboring for Torah").

The *Maharsha* comments that this [our dictum] may refer to one who records his *chiddushei Torah* [Torah novellae] thereby leaving a lasting impression.

The *Ksav Sofer*, in commenting on the dictum, "Even if one's parents have left him a Torah Scroll, it is proper that he should write one of his own" (*Sanhedrin* 21b), suggests that a person should not feel satisfied with the Torah knowledge he inherited from his forebears, but should rather toil to seek new insights of his own, that they act as spiritual sustenance for his soul when it leaves his physical self; i.e, he will arrive in the World to Come with his own insights.

ב

⟦ 569 ⟧ בֹּא וּרְאֵה, כַּמָּה גָדוֹל כֹּחָהּ שֶׁל חָמָס, שֶׁהֲרֵי
דּוֹר הַמַּבּוּל עָבְרוּ עַל הַכֹּל וְלֹא נֶחְתַּם גְּזַר
דִּינָם עַד שֶׁפָּשְׁטוּ יְדֵיהֶם בְּגָזֵל

"Come and see how great is the power of robbery, for though the
generation of the flood transgressed all laws, their decree of punishment was sealed only because they stretched out their hands to
rob" (*Sanhedrin* 108a).

Rabbi Joseph Ber Soloveitchik, in commenting on the above dictum, asks:
"Why, indeed, is the 'power of robbery' greater than the power of idolatry,
murder and unchastity, the cardinal sins committed by the 'Generation of
the Flood'?

"Moreover, why is it that at the *Yom Kippur Ne'ilah* service, when we
plead for forgiveness for all our sins, we conclude with the words, '*L'maan
nechdal me'oshek yadeinu*' (that we may cease to engage in robbery)?"

Rav Soloveitchik suggests that "all sinning involves thievery. When we
indulge in what is forbidden we are, in effect, taking that which is not ours.
In our *Selichoth* prayers, we acknowledge that 'the soul is Yours and the
body is Your work.' All that we presumptuously call 'ours' is really 'His.'
We may use G-d's gifts conditionally, only with His concurrence and in
accordance with his stipulations. When we sin, these privileges are forfeited
and nullified. Their continued utilization is larceny" (Rabbi Abraham R.
Besdin, *Reflections of the Rav*, pp. 20, 21).

In a similar vein, the *Sfath Emeth* [Gerer Rebbe] comments on the verse,
"And the earth was filled with thievery" [Gen. 6:11], "All transgressions are
essentially an aspect of thievery since everything comes from the Almighty."

54

☖ 570 ☖ . . . בֹּא וּרְאֵה, כַּמָּה גָדוֹל כֹּחָהּ שֶׁל בּוּשָׁה

"Come and see how potent shame is, for the Holy One, blessed
be He, gave aid to Bar Kamtza and destroyed His Dwelling Place
and burned His Palace" [because a person was shamed]
(*Gittin* 57a).

Just before the destruction of the Second Temple, the episode of Kamtza
and Bar Kamtza took place. This was a pernicious incident in which a certain
host ordered Bar Kamtza to leave his house. Deeply offended, Bar Kamtza
defected to the Roman camp and, by means of a base stratagem, he set in
motion the siege of Jerusalem that culminated in the *Churban* [See ibid. 55a].

Rabbi Yehudah Leib Chasman, in commenting on the above dictum
writes: "And yet, who was Bar Kamtza? The lowest of the low, an oppressor, an informer . . . . When he was filled with wrath, he decided to take
vengeance on all Israel . . . . Our sages tell us that he fell into the category
of the pursuer who is chasing another with intention to kill: Such a man
may be slain, if there is no other way to save his intended victim . . . . But
despite all this, because he was shamed, that shame was the cause of a
boundless indictment and caused the destruction of the *Beis Hamikdash*,
raging famine and death to tens of thousands of Israel, and the terrible Exile.

Every thinking person will ponder, tremble and stand in awe" (*Or Yahel*,
cited by Rabbi Shalom Meir Wallach, *Depths of Judgment*, p. 165).

See *Insights*, vol. 1, #307.

☖ 571 ☖ בָּא חֲבַקּוּק וְהֶעֱמִידָן עַל אַחַת, שֶׁנֶּאֱמַר וְצַדִּיק בֶּאֱמוּנָתוֹ יִחְיֶה

"Havakuk came and based them all [the 613 commandments] on
one [principle] as it is said, 'But the righteous shall live by his
faith'" [Hav. 2:4] (*Makkoth* 24a).

"Havakuk came and emphasized one central *mitzvah* [belief in G-d]. For
he who fulfills this, fulfills the entire Torah, providing he does so properly,

by accepting His G-dliness, His Oneness, and the yoke of His dominions
. . . . Therefore does it say, 'The righteous shall live by his faith,' much as
it says concerning all the *mitzvoth* [Lev. 18:5], 'Which if a man shall do them,
he shall live thereby'" (Rabbeinu Yom Tov b. Avraham Ishbili, *Ritva*, s.v. *bah
Havakuk*).

Rabbi Chaim Shmulevitz explains that the prophet Havakuk singled out
the *mitzvah* of belief in G-d from all the 613 *mitzvoth*, "for it is the foundation
and root which will make it possible for every Jew to attain the entire Torah"
(*Sichoth Mussar, Ma'mar 4, Ahavath HaBriyoth*, p. 12).

In this regard, it should be noted that Rabbi Joseph Ber Soloveitchik
maintains that faith in G-d and ethical conduct are indivisible.

That is the meaning of the words of the *Mechilta* that "the *Ten Commandments* were proclaimed *in one utterance*." There can be no morality without
faith and no faith without morality (Lecture delivered at RCA Convention,
June, 1970).

॥ 572 ॥ בְּאֶחָד בֶּאֱלוּל ראש הַשָּׁנָה לְמַעְשַׂר בְּהֵמָה.
רִ׳ אֶלְעָזָר וּרִ׳ שִׁמְעוֹן אוֹמְרִים בְּאֶחָד בְּתִשְׁרֵי

"The first of Elul is the New Year for the tithe of cattle. R. Eleazar
and R. Shimon say: On the first of Tishrei (*Rosh Hashanah* 2a).

For purposes of tithe it was necessary to specify the year on which cattle
were born, because animals born in one year could not be given as tithe for
animals born in another.

Rebbe Elimelech [the Lizhensker], in a fanciful vein, suggests a moral
interpretation of the above dictum. "Jews who are separated from the
Almighty throughout the year, but on the first of Elul commence to devote
a portion of their time to G-d, are compared to cattle, for they have no sense
to remember the Almighty until the Day of Judgment is a month away.
Rabbi Eleazar and Rabbi Shimon [are more tolerant and] say that those who
arouse themselves a month before *Rosh Hashanah* are still men; those
however, who wait until the first of Tishrei, on the very Day of Judgment
— they are indeed as cattle" (*Ohel Elimelech*, p. 139).

Rabbi Yisrael Salanter would say: "Each person should consider the entire year like the month of *Elul* and *Elul*, of course, is *Elul*" (Shmuel Himelstein).

⎰ 573 ⎱

בָּדְקוּ וְלֹא מָצְאוּ אֶלָּא פַּךְ אֶחָד שֶׁל שֶׁמֶן
שֶׁהָיָה מוּנָח בְּחוֹתָמוֹ שֶׁל כֹּהֵן גָּדוֹל

"They [the *Chashmona'im*] searched and found only one cruse of oil which lay with the seal of the High Priest" (*Shabbath* 21b).

When the [Syrian] Greeks entered the Holy Temple, they defiled all the oils therein, and when the *Chashmona'im* prevailed against and defeated them, they searched and found . . . . (ibid.).

Rabbi Yisroel Alter [the late Gerer Rebbe] comments: "It seemed clear that no pure [undefiled] oil was to be had. Nevertheless, they searched and found! That, too, was one of the eternal lessons of the miracle of Chanukah. There is no room for despair in Jewish life. One must search; and if one seeks, he will find. When effort is expended, results are achieved" (*Beis Yisroel*).

Cf. *Megillah* 60b, "If one says: 'I have labored and not found,' do not believe him." See *Insights*, vol. 1, #72.

⎰ 574 ⎱

בִּזְמַן שֶׁאַתֶּם עוֹשִׂין רְצוֹנוֹ שֶׁל מָקוֹם, אַתֶּם
קְרוּיִים בָּנִים . . .

"When you carry out the desires of G-d, you are called 'children' and when you do not carry out the desires of G-d, you are called 'servants'" (*Bava Bathra* 10a).

Rabbi Eliyahu Lopian once asked: "How can one who does not fulfill the will of G-d be considered a 'servant,' for that implies that he in fact, is serving his Master?" Rabbi Lopian explained that there is a difference between a loyal son and a dutiful servant. Both fulfill their obligations. However, the son does so enthusiastically, while the servant carries out his duties in a perfunctory manner [and that is not the desire of G-d]" (Rabbi

Paysach J. Krohn, *The Maggid Speaks*, p. 245).

"A man in Kotzk was punctuating his prayers with cries of 'Father, Father.' Someone heard him and jokingly remarked, 'Maybe G-d is not his father. We are taught, "When you carry out the desires of G-d you are called 'children' . . . ."'

"Rabbi Menachem Mendel of Kotzk heard this and said: 'When a person cries "Father" often enough, G-d becomes his father'" (*Emeth v'Emunah*, p. 20).

Cf. *Kiddushin* 36a, "In both cases you are called children." This is Rabbi Meir's view. Whether you behave as children or not, you are always called children.

Rabbi Nachman of Breslov comments: "You may think that you have done so much wrong that you are no longer one of G-d's children. Still, you must realize that G-d calls you His child" (*Sichoth HaRan*, 7).

⎨ 575 ⎬ בִּזְמָן שֶׁבֵּית הַמִּקְדָּשׁ קַיָּים מִזְבֵּחַ מְכַפֵּר עַל אָדָם, עַכְשָׁו שֻׁלְחָנוֹ שֶׁל אָדָם מְכַפֵּר עָלָיו

"As long as the Holy Temple stood, the altar used to make atonement for a person, but now a person's table makes atonement for him" (*Hagigah* 27a).

"Through hospitality to wayfarers" (Rashi).

"The table is compared to an altar, and one who eats with Heaven in mind, merits the special blessings the presence of the *Shechinah* brings" (*MeAm Lo'ez*, Deut. 12:18).

Cf. *Berakoth* 55a, "He who prolongs his stay at his table . . . prolongs his days and years."

Rabbeinu Bachya writes: "It was the custom of the *chassidim* in France to have their tables transformed into caskets for burial, thereby signifying that one carries nothing away with him except the *tzedakah* he does in his lifetime and the benevolence he bestows on his table. That is why our sages declare that one who prolongs his stay at his table [by being hospitable to others], his days and years will be prolonged" (*Rabbeinu Bachya Al HaTorah, Terumah*).

Rabbi Elimelech of Lizhensk noted: "Most people exert all their energy in the time of prayer, to direct their heart and to ward off 'foreign thoughts.' But when they eat they make no effort or exertion, since they eat only for their own pleasure . . . . But as for the *tzaddikim*, the sages said: 'The time of eating is a time of war.' The righteous have no need to exert themselves when they pray; then, their minds are always pure and clean. But during the time of eating, that is when they have to use their energy and exert themselves" (*Noam Elimelech*, p. 43).

Cf. *Shabbath* 127a, "Hospitality to wayfarers is greater than welcoming the presence of the *Shechinah*." See *Insights*, vol. 1, #125.

Rabbi Yisrael Salanter once made the following poignant observation. "Many times, I have seen someone passing by a *shul* and the people inside call out to him, '*Kedushah, Kedushah*, please come in and join us!' But I have never seen someone passing by a house where a meal is being eaten, and the people inside call out to him '*seudah, seudah* (a meal, a meal), please come in and join us!'" (Rabbi Dov Katz, *Tenuath HaMussar*).

⟦ 576 ⟧

בִּישִׁיבָה הַלֵּךְ אַחַר חָכְמָה,
בִּמְסִבָּה הַלֵּךְ אַחַר זִקְנָה

"At a 'session' [matters of law] priority is to be given to wisdom; at a festive gathering, age takes precedence" (*Baba Bathra* 120a).

"In matters of Din [law] or other gatherings of Torah, we 'sit' [give a place of honor] to those with greater wisdom before 'sitting' those who are distinguished in old age. At a banquet or at a wedding, age takes precedence over wisdom" (*Rashbam*).

Rabbi Moshe Feinstein was asked whether a younger brother is permitted to get married before his older brother if the latter is *makpid* [has strong feelings against it]. His response was that in a case where both brothers and sisters were "engaged" to be married, then the older sibling has priority, though the younger one is superior in wisdom. However, where [as in the case presented to him] the older brother did not yet find a bride, though he may also be superior in wisdom, we are not required to wait for him to find a mate (*Iggeroth Moshe, Even HaEzer*, part II, #1).

577 בַּיִת אָפֵל, אֵין פּוֹתְחִין בּוֹ חַלּוֹנוֹת לִרְאוֹת אֶת נִגְעוֹ

"The windows of a dark house may not be open to examine its leprosy" (*Negaim* 2:3).

If leprosy breaks out in the walls of a house too dark for a proper survey, the windows must not be opened to allow the light to enter, as it must be examined by its usual light.

Cf. *Sanhedrin* 92a — R. Elazar said: "Be always 'obscure' (humble) and you will endure." Just as the darkness of a house shields it, for it cannot be pronounced "unclean," so too, the obscurity and humility (darkness) in which one envelops himself will shield his life.

"Even though a house may in fact be afflicted with leprosy, yet halachically it is not 'ritually impure.' Since it is dark, neither displaying itself nor publicizing itself, as it were, the priest does not illuminate it in order to reveal its afflictions. So too, the harsh lights of rebuke and judgment will not be trained upon a humble man, though he may be tainted . . . . We must be humble and unassuming, similar to 'an unilluminated house' whose blemishes are not scrutinized" (Rabbi Chaim Shmulevitz, *Reb Chaim's Discourses*, p. 34).

578 „בְּכָל מְאֹדֶךָ," בְּכָל מָמוֹנְךָ

"'With all your might' [means] with all your money" (*Berakoth* 54a).

"And you shall love the L-rd your G-d with all your heart and with all your soul and with all your might" [Deut. 6:4].

"One should forfeit all his money so as not to violate a biblical prohibition" [*Rema, Orach Chaim* 654].

See *Torah Temima* [Deut. 6:5 (24)] who maintains that this only applies to the three cardinal prohibitions (murder, unchastity, idolatry) for which one is required to forfeit his life.

The Chafetz Chaim suggests that "the true meaning of *meodecha* [translated as 'your might'] is not 'your money,' but anything that is very dear to you. It is generally translated 'your money,' for our sages determined that for most people the most precious thing in life is their money and possessions. They, therefore, interpreted 'with all your might' as 'with all your money.'"

In line with this insightful interpretation, the Chafetz Chaim once said to his son-in-law, Reb Tzvi, "For you, money has no value at all, for you cherish nothing but *mitzvoth*. So for you, 'with all your might' means '*your mitzvoth*.' You are commanded to be ready to give away your good deeds for the sake of love of G-d" (*The Chafetz Chaim on the Siddur*, p. 99).

〔 579 〕   בַּל תַּשְׁחִית דְּגוּפָא עָדִיף

"'Thou shalt not destroy,' as applied to one's own person, is
better [is a higher priority] (*Shabbath* 140b).

"We are forbidden to destroy fruit-trees during a siege in order to cause distress and suffering to the inhabitants of the besieged city. 'Thou shalt not destroy the trees . . .' [Deut. 20:19]. All [needless] destruction is included in this prohibition: for instance, whoever burns a garment or breaks a vessel needlessly, contravenes the prohibition of '*Bal Tashchith*' ['Thou shalt not destroy']" (Rambam, *Sefer HaMitzvoth*, Negative Commandment #57). See *Mishneh Torah, Hil. Malachim* 6:10.

The above dictum was uttered in response to R. Chisda who said: "When one can eat barley bread but eats wheaten bread, he violates *Bal Tashchith*"; and in response to R. Papa who said: "When one can drink beer but drinks wine, he violates *Bal Tashchith*." The Talmud concludes that "*Bal Tashchith*, as applied to one's person, is a higher priority." Although some may consider purchasing more expensive food a wasteful extravagance, the consensus is that to consume "better" [more nutritious] food and drink is beneficial and not wasteful.

Cf. *Shabbath* 129a. The Talmud narrates four incidents where sages burned expensive furniture in order to make fire for someone suffering chills. The *Bal Tashchith* of one's health stands higher than the *Bal Tashchith* of property.

Rabbi Don Well comments: "Perhaps, we can understand why Rambam deletes this principle that 'wasting your own body or health is a higher priority' and the *Shulchan Aruch* omits the entire subject of *Bal Tashchith*. Decisions concerning what should be preserved and what should be disposed of are individual decisions that depend on the circumstances" (*Turrets of Silver*, p. 210).

◊ 580 ◊ בְּמָקוֹם שֶׁאֵין אֲנָשִׁים הִשְׁתַּדֵּל לִהְיוֹת אִישׁ
"In a place where there are no men, strive to be a man"
(*Aboth* 2:6).

"In situations where true men are lacking, where the interests of the community suffer for lack of proper leadership . . . it is your duty to strive to become a man qualified to act as a leader and spokesman . . . for under such conditions reticence would not be modest, but downright criminal" (Rabbi Samson Raphael Hirsch).

Cf. *Berakoth* 63a, "'Where there is no man, there be a man.' Abbaye said: 'Understand from this that where there is a man, there you should not be a man. Is this not self-evident! It is only required when both are equal.'"

The dictum above in *Aboth* was voiced by Hillel; the dictum in *Berakoth* was voiced by Bar Kappara. The *Maharsha* suggests the following distinction: Hillel is referring to "the needs of the community," i.e., where there is no man to occupy himself with the needs of the community, you strive to be such a man, even though this entails curtailing somewhat one's Torah studies. Bar Kappara, however, is referring to the responsibility of a *moreh horo'ah* [decisor of halachic questions], i.e., in a place where there is no one who is capable of being a *moreh horo'ah*, you strive to be such a man.

See divergent opinion of Rabbeinu Chananel, *Tosafoth, Sotah* 22b s.v. *B'shavin*.

⟦ 581 ⟧ בֶּן מֵאָה כְּאִלּוּ מֵת וְעָבַר וּבָטֵל מִן הָעוֹלָם

"The man of a hundred is as though already dead and gone,
removed from the world" (*Aboth* 5:24).

"At one hundred, one could not expect new initiatives. The individual is
resting on past achievements and coasting along. He is not expected to
contribute actively to the world and is considered, under normal circumstances, as having passed away from the world" (Rabbi P. Bulka, *As a Tree
by the Waters*, p. 230).

The words *"Avar U'batel"* (gone and removed), in the above maxim, has
unfortunately led to the popular pejorative expression *"ovair botel"* when
referring to someone who is no longer "with it" mentally — an expression
morally degrading (S.W.)

Cf. *Shabbath* 152a, "Torah scholars: the older they grow, the more wisdom
the acquire." See #996.

Cf. *Berakoth* 8b, "Be careful to respect a scholar who has forgotten his
learning through misfortune."

Cf. *Baba Bathra* 14b, "Both the tablets and the fragments of the tablets
were placed in the Ark." See *Insights*, vol. 1, #360.

⟦ 582 ⟧ בְּקָעָה מָצָא וְגָדַר בָּהּ גָּדֵר

"He found an open field and put up a fence around it" (*Erubin*
6a).

The Talmud applies this metaphor to Rav, who imposed additional
halachic restrictions in some localities when he found the inhabitants negligent in certain religious observances. When the people were morally exposed
[like an 'open field'], he instituted preventive regulations [he put up a fence]
in order to keep them away from further transgressions.

Our sages have consistently applied this maxim to the Jewish community.
Witness how far a great Rabbi went in order to counteract the effects of a
negative experience.

Rabbi Yoel Ashkenazi [the Yasser Rav] always took "the fourth *aliyah*" when called to the Torah, rather than *shlishi* or *shishi* [the third or the sixth *aliyah*] which most Rabbis take. This was the reason: He once witnessed a fist fight break out at the *Bima* on Shabbos. It seemed that a man was "embarrassed" and angry that he received "the fourth *aliyah*" rather than a more "respectable" one. Rav Ashkenazi was so startled by this behavior that he vowed to "protect" and save the fourth *aliyah* from embarrassment. So, for the rest of his life, this became his *aliyah* (Rabbi Mordechai Mehlman, *The Jewish Press*, 2/23/90).

⎰ 583 ⎱ בְּרֹאשׁ הַשָּׁנָה כָּל בָּאֵי עוֹלָם עוֹבְרִין לְפָנָיו כִּבְנֵי מָרוֹן

"On *Rosh Hashanah* all mankind passes before Him like a flock of sheep [G-d judges each person individually]" *(Rosh Hashanah* 16a).

How do we reconcile this *mishnaic* declaration that the Almighty judges each person on *Rosh Hashanah*, with the statement uttered by Rabbi Yossi that, "Man is judged every day" [ibid.]?

The Baal Shem Tov explains the two seemingly contradictory statements in this fashion: "On *Rosh Hashanah*, G-d decides how much a person will earn for the entire year — will he be blessed with riches or will he suffer with poverty. Every day, however, G-d decrees in what frame of mind the person will be when he receives his ordained portion. Will it make him happy or will it bring sadness to him? This is part of the reward and punishment that the person's actions have earned for him" (Rabbi Paysach J. Krohn, *The Maggid Speaks*, p. 184).

584

„בָּרוּךְ אַתָּה בָּעִיר . . . " בִּשְׂכַר הַמִּצְוֹת
שֶׁאַתָּה עוֹשֶׂה בָּעִיר

"'Blessed shall you be in the city' [Deut. 28:3] — As a reward for
the *mitzvoth* which you fulfill in the city" (*Devarim Rabbah* 7:5).

"If you will not be embarrassed to observe the commandments even in
the city, i.e., publicly so that all can see, then you will receive the blessings
enumerated in Scripture. For there are Jews who perform *mitzvoth* privately
within the confines of their own home, but are ashamed to practice their
religion in the street — this is not conducive to blessing" (Rabbi Chaim
Sofer, *Divrei Sha'arei Chaim*).

Unfortunately, there are some misguided Jews who follow the philosophy
of Judah Leib Gordon, the secular Hebrew poet, who proclaimed: "Be a Jew
in your tent, and a man outside."

Rabbi Shlomo of Karlin used to say: "He who is a complete Jew at home
is only half a Jew on a journey. He who is half a Jew at home is only a
quarter Jew on a journey" (A. Yellin, *Derech Tzaddikim*).

585

בְּרִית כְּרוּתָה לִשְׁלֹשׁ עֶשְׂרֵה מִדּוֹת: שֶׁאֵינָן
חוֹזְרוֹת רֵיקָם

"A covenant has been struck that the *'Thirteen Attributes'* are never
turned back unanswered" (*Rosh Hashanah* 17b).

Israel will not be turned away empty-handed whenever they recite the
"*Thirteen Attributes*" of G-d: "The L-rd, the L-rd, is a merciful and gracious
G-d, slow to anger and abounding in kindness and truth. He extends
kindness to the thousandth generation, forgives iniquity, transgression and
sin, and clears [the guiltless]" (Ex. 34:6-7).

Rabbi Yitzchak Zev HaLevi Soloveitchik [the Brisker Rav] explains the
nature of this *covenant*. It was as if the Almighty assembled an infinite
supply of mercy, which he promised to withdraw in response to Israel's
invocation of the *Thirteen Attributes* (*Chiddushei Griz HaLevi, Ki Sisa*).

Rabbi Yitzchak Meir Alter [*the Chiddushei HaRim*] taught that the most abundant of all of G-d's treasures is one called *the treasury of free gifts*, which has an endless supply of goodness. One can tap this resource, however, only if he feels sincerely that he has no claim on G-d and that G-d owes him nothing (*Sifsei Tzaddik, Va'eschanan*).

⟦ 586 ⟧   בְּרִית כְּרוּתָה לַשְׂפָתַיִם

"A covenant is made for the lips" (*Moed Katan* 18a).

The manner in which a thing is expressed may foretell a future course or event. "Where is this [concept] found — the notion that lips are subject to a covenant? It is said: 'And Abraham said to his young men, You stay here with the donkey. The boy and I will go there, we will worship and we will return to you'" [Gen. 22:5] — and the words came true so that they both [Abraham and Isaac] came back (ibid.).

The Chasam Sofer insisted that one should not utter anything negative concerning a person's chances of survival, for this would be a violation of "the covenant of the lips." "He had a mystic concept of the power of the spoken word . . . so he did not speak unless he had to" (Rabbi Moses J. Burack, *The Hatam Sofer*, p. 264).

See *Torah Temimah*, Gen. 22:5.

Cf. *Berakoth* 19a, "A man should never speak in such a way as to give an opening to Satan." See *Insights*, vol. 1, #60.

According to *Sfas Emes*, the [above] dictum of not providing an opening for Satan "is based on an awareness that there are forces for evil in the world opposing the forces of good. The believer treats these evil forces with reserve, even though he does not consider them to be invincible. He knows he can dominate them, but only with G-d's help. Thus, he avoids challenging them openly" (Rabbi Elie Munk, *The Call of the Torah*, Va'yikra, p. 153).

⫾ 587 ⫾

בִּשְׁלֹשָׁה דְּבָרִים נִתְּנָה הַתּוֹרָה,
בָּאֵשׁ וּבַמַּיִם וּבַמִּדְבָּר

"The Torah was given to the accompaniment of three things: fire, water, and wilderness" (*Bamidbar Rabbah* 1:7).

"Why was the giving of the Torah marked by these three factors? To indicate that, as these are free to all mankind, so also are the words of the Torah free; as it is said, 'Ho everyone that thirsteth come ye for water'" [Isa. 55:1] (ibid.). ["Water" is a metaphorical term for Torah.]

In commenting on the above *Midrash*, Rabbi Meir Shapiro [the Lubliner Rav] writes: "Through three tests the Jewish people was made the enduring possessor of the Torah. Abraham our father allowed himself to be cast into a fiery furnace for the sake of his faith. He demonstrated that the surrender of life was preferable to renunciation of his faith. But he was a lone individual. Could a whole people pass such a test? Then came the test of water. At the edge of the sea, the entire Jewish nation accepts the Divine command: 'Speak to the Children of Israel and let them journey.' All of Israel leaps into the sea in perfect faith. But, perhaps that was only the result of momentary inspiration. Would an entire people endure in its faith in G-d through the passage of time and its trials? Then came the third test — the wilderness. The forty year stay in the wilderness, of all Israel, was the crucible in which Israel's capacity for enduring faith was tried and forged" ("Reflections of the Lubliner Rav," *The Jewish Observer* 1, no. 2 [October 1963]:25).

⫾ 588 ⫾

בְּשַׁמְתָּא דְּאִית בֵּיהּ גַּאֲוָה
וּבְשַׁמְתָּא דְּלֵית בֵּיהּ . . .

"[A scholar] who possesses [pride] deserves excommunication, and if he does not possess it he deserves excommunication" (*Sotah* 5a).

"A scholar must have some pride so that those who are lightheaded will not take advantage of him, and so that his words will be accepted" (Rashi).

"It is forbidden to be prideful. Only this is permitted — to be afraid of no thing and to have pride that one has a Father in Heaven . . ." (Rabbi Levi Yitzchak of Berditchev, *Kedushath Levi, Vezoth HaBracha*).

The following is a holocaust incident concerning the Jews of Lublin — their pride in "our Father in Heaven" remains long after they and their Nazi oppressors have perished.

"The local Nazi commander had assembled the Jews outside the city limits and had beaten them and assaulted them with his dogs. In the midst of this cruelty, he ordered them to sing a *chassidic* song. No one could sing under those conditions, so he increased his attacks. Suddenly the *chassidim* began to sing, '*Mir velen zey iberleben, iberleben ovinu shebashomayim*' [We will outlive them, outlive them our Father in Heaven]. The *chassidim* danced and sang with an enthusiasm that came from above. The Nazi commander ordered them to stop, but they did not. They paid a heavy price, but the singing and the dancing did not stop" (M. Prager, *Sparks of Glory*, pp. 9-13).

Cf. *Sotah* 5a, "A disciple of the sages should possess an eighth [of pride]." See *Insights*, vol. 1, #496.

⫦ 589 ⫦ בְּשָׁעָה שֶׁהַצַּדִּיקִים יוֹשְׁבִים בְּשַׁלְוָה — הַשָּׂטָן בָּא וּמְקַטְרֵג

"When the righteous dwell in tranquility and wish to dwell in tranquility in this world, Satan comes and accuses them" (*Beraishith Rabbah* 84:3).

He says, "They are not content with what is in store for them in the World to Come, but they wish to dwell at ease even in this world" (ibid.).

Rabbi Judah L. Ginsburg comments: "It is not proper for a righteous person to desire a tranquil life, since most people live desperate lives. The few who are blessed with tranquility arouse envy in the majority who are not so fortunate. The righteous, therefore, should be satisfied with their meager station in life, so as not to arouse envy in others" (*Yalkut Yehuda*, Gen. 37:1).

Rabbi Shmuel Ashkenazi explains the "accusation" against the righteous in the following manner: "The righteous person must always be cognizant of the fact that his stay on earth is similar to a guest staying over at an inn.

He should, therefore, not be overly concerned with the inn. Anxiety and worry over worldly matters will divert the righteous from the service of G-d" (*Yefeh Toar*, B.R. 84:3).

It seems that our sages find fault not so much with the righteous dwelling in tranquility, but rather in their *mevakshim* [searching for] a life of ease. The message is clear. Tranquility and serenity are not qualities that the righteous actively *pursue*. They are rather spiritual dividends that may *accrue* to them if the Almighty so desires.

See #703, "The Patriarch Jacob wished to live at ease in this world, whereupon he was attacked by Joseph's Satan."

See Rabbi Yosef Yozel Hurwitz, *Madreigoth HaAdam, Nekudas HaEmes*, where a distinction is drawn between *shalvah* and *menuchah*.

⌂ 590 ⌂ בְּשָׁעָה שֶׁעָלָה מֹשֶׁה לַמָּרוֹם, מְצָאוֹ לְהַקב"ה שֶׁהָיָה קוֹשֵׁר כְּתָרִים לָאוֹתִיּוֹת

"When Moshe ascended on High he found the Holy One, blessed be He, engaged in affixing crowns to the letters" (*Menakoth* 29b).

These are the *Taggin* [three small strokes written on top of certain letters] of the *Sefer Torah* (Rashi).

"Said Moshe, 'L-rd of the Universe, who requires this of You ["to add to what you have written" — Rashi]?' He answered, 'There will arise a man at the end of many generations, called Akiva ben Yosef, who will derive mountains of *halachoth* from every minute part of each letter'" (ibid.).

Rabbi Moshe Feinstein explained the above passage, saying that the "crowns" allude to *sovereignty* imparted to the letters — the interpretation of the letters was made, to some extent, independent of their Author; and if, despite their best efforts, the sages misinterpret the letters, their misinterpretation becomes *halachah*" (Intro. to *Iggeroth Moshe, Orach Chaim*).

Cf. *Baba Mezia* 59b, "It is not in Heaven — the Torah had already been given at Mount Sinai." See *Insights*, vol. 1, #333.

〔 591 〕 בְּשָׁעָה שֶׁנִּכְנְסוּ עכו״ם לַהֵיכָל, רָאוּ כְּרוּבִים הַמְעוֹרִין זֶה בָּזֶה

"When the heathens entered the Temple [to destroy it], they saw the *cherubim* in embrace" (*Yoma* 54b).

Rabbi Chaim Shmulevitz cites the *Maharsha*, who questions the "embrace of the *cherubim*," which is an expression of G-d's closeness to Israel (*Baba Bathra* 99a), at the moment of severe punishment and destruction. He suggests "that it is *because* Israel was being so severely punished that there had to be this manifestation of utter closeness and love. Only at the moment of embrace could the Almighty decree the destruction of the Temple and Israel's subsequent exile."

Reb Chaim concludes: "We are enjoined to follow in the ways of the Almighty — 'Just as He is compassionate, so you must be compassionate' (*Shabbath* 133b). We should therefore bear in mind that even in instances when we must punish someone, we should not do so out of hate or spite, but out of love and closeness that resembles the embrace of the *cherubim*" (*Reb Chaim's Discourses*, p. 235).

Cf. *Berakoth* 28b, "Is there a man who can formulate the benediction of heretics?" They found *Shmuel HaKatan*, whose motto was "Do not rejoice when your enemy falls and do not be glad in your heart when he stumbles" (Prov. 24:17). See *Aboth* 4:24.

Rabbi Joseph Ber Soloveitchik comments: "Shmuel the humble, who had never tasted the desire to settle accounts with malefactors, who had never complained about insults caused him, was chosen to fulfill this necessary task . . . . This benediction, which cries to G-d for the destruction of evil, grew from the soil of love and *chesed*" (*A Eulogy for Rabbi Chaim Heller*).

〚 592 〛 בִּשְׁעַת יֵצֶר הָרַע לֵית דְּמַדְכַּר לֵיהּ לְיֵצֶר טוֹב

"When the Evil Impulse [gains dominion], none remember the Good Impulse" (*Nedarim* 32b).

Rabbi Mordechai Yosef Leiner of Izbica comments: "In truth, the person who is immersed in desire cannot extricate himself. At that point, it will not help him to remember that it is forbidden. The prohibition does not have the power to separate the person from evil when the Evil Impulse is dominant."

Citing the talmudic dictum which prescribes the proper method for dealing with the Evil Impulse, Rabbi Mordechai Yosef explains: "A man should always incite the Good Impulse to fight against the Evil Impulse . . . . If he subdues it, well and good; if not, let him study Torah . . . (*Berakoth* 5a). The teachings of the Torah help a person extricate himself from indulging in pleasures. In a situation where the Evil Impulse is dominant — then the person is advised to remember that he can find the same good in the Torah, in holiness" (*Mei HaShiloah* I, *Va'yigash*, cited in *All is in the Hands of Heaven*, p. 47).

Cf. *Berakoth* 5a, "A man should always incite the Good Impulse to fight against the Evil Impulse." See *Insights*, vol. 1, #375.

〚 593 〛 בָּת דִּינָא בְּטַל דִּינָא

"If the verdict is postponed overnight, it comes to naught" (*Sanhedrin* 95a).

This maxim has been interpreted by the sages in two diametrically opposite ways. (1) What is not done immediately may never be done. "He who hesitates is lost." (2) If you sleep on a quarrel it will be nullified. "Sleep on it!"

Rabbi Yisrael Salanter considered *zerizuth* [acting with eagerness and swiftness] one of the primary principles of *mussar* [ethical teaching]. One should carry out his decisions swiftly and enthusiastically.

At the same time, one must be cautious in arriving at a decision. "Be deliberate in judgment" (*Aboth* 1:1). "*Zehiruth* [caution] requires that every subject for decision be given adequate thought and consideration . . . . Only then can action be taken . . . . The decision will be cautious and well considered, but the action will be performed with eagerness" (Rabbi Moshe Chaim Luzzatto, *Mesillath Yesharim*).

Cf. *Sanhedrin* 35a, "Declare happy [bless] the judge who makes sour [preserves] his verdict."

◊ 594 ◊ בְּתוֹרָתוֹ שֶׁל רַבִּי מֵאִיר מָצְאוּ כָתוּב:
וְהִנֵּה טוֹב מְאֹד, וְהִנֵּה טוֹב מָוֶת

"In the copy of Rabbi Meir's Torah it was found written: 'And behold it was very good' [Gen. 1:31], and behold it was *tov maveth* [death was good] (*Beraishith Rabbah* 9:5).

"*Tov maveth*" was inserted as a marginal comment in Rabbi Meir's Torah. Rashi comments: "'And behold, death was good' — this is what Scripture says: 'A good name is better than oil, and the day of death than the day of birth'" [*Koheleth* 7:1].

Rabbi Yitzchak ben Moshe Arama writes: "The man who has lived a righteous life and acquires a good name considers his death as the culmination of a life well spent and as a transition to the World to Come" (*Akedath Yitzchak*).

In commenting on the above marginal note, that "*very good* connotes death," Rabbi Yosef Engel suggests a negative connotation. "This is, indeed, a general principle of the Torah — all that is 'very,' all extremes, are 'deadly' with the exceptions of humility and gratitude" (*Otz'roth Yosef*).

Cf. *Beraishith Rabba* 9:7, "'And behold it was very good' — this refers to the Evil Inclination."

See #664.

595

בַּתְּחִילָה הוּא נַעֲשֶׂה אוֹרֵחַ וְאַחַר כָּךְ הוּא
נַעֲשֶׂה כְּבַעַל הַבַּיִת

"At first he is like a guest and then like the master of the house"
(*Beraishith Rabbah* 22:6).

This refers to the *Yetzer Ha'ra* [the Evil Impulse]. At first he has little "authority" over man [he is likened to a guest at another's house]. Once man continues to yield to temptation, the Evil Impulse becomes more "authoritative" and he is then likened to the master of the house.

Similarly, "At first it [the Evil Impulse] is like a spider's web, but eventually it becomes like a ship's rope" [ibid.].

The Vilna Gaon writes: "The way the Evil Inclination entices a man is by first having him study Torah and at the same time having him fulfill his desires. For if it were to persuade him to neglect studying Torah completely, the man would never listen. Once the man has accustomed himself to physical pleasure and enjoyment, he spontaneously ceases to study Torah, for he is constantly occupied with the fulfillment of his desires" (*Even Sheleimah*, ch. 2:11).

Cf. *Sukkah* 52a, "In the time to come, the Holy One, blessed be He, will bring the Evil Impulse and slay it in the presence of the righteous and the wicked. To the righteous it will have the appearance of a towering hill, and to the wicked it will have the appearance of a hair thread . . . . They [the wicked] will weep saying, 'How is it that we were unable to conquer this hair thread.'"

ג

⟦ 596 ⟧ ג' דְּבָרִים מַעֲבִירִין אֶת הָאָדָם עַל דַּעְתּוֹ וְעַל
דַּעַת קוֹנוֹ, וְאֵלּוּ הֵן, עוֹבְדֵי כוֹכָבִים וְרוּחַ
רָעָה וְדִקְדּוּקֵי עֲנִיּוּת

"Three things deprive a man of his senses and of a knowledge of
his Creator, viz., idolaters, an evil spirit and oppressive poverty"
(*Erubin* 41b).

It is extremely difficult to be in control of one's senses and to be aware
of the Creator when one is plagued by the above three evils.

An *"evil spirit,"* according to Rambam, is "any injury that does not come
from man, whatever its cause may be" (*Commentary on the Mishnah, Erubin,*
chap. 4). According to the *Sforno* [Gen. 28:21], "an *evil spirit* is any illness
which causes man to transgress."

"Oppressive poverty" can only be overcome with 'great difficulty,' unlike
the Evil Impulse, which is somewhat easier to subdue" (*Maharsha*).

Rabbi Yaakov Kamenetsky poignantly illustrates the dire consequences of
"oppressive poverty" as related to the Golden Calf incident. He writes: "All
the commentators struggle to understand how such a grave transgression
could have been committed by a people who stood at Mount Sinai! In
reality, we are unable to put ourselves in their place. But imagine for a
moment, such a large multitude of people standing in a desolate desert
without any sustenance of bread or water. Why should we wonder at their
inability to withstand this great trial? They all knew that manna descended
for them only in the merit of Moshe, and when it appeared [through an
optical illusion engineered by Satan] that Moshe was dead, they thought that
manna would no longer descend; there would be no food for their children

who were crying out to them. Indeed, "oppressive poverty" deprives a man of his senses and of a knowledge of his Creator" (*Emeth L'Yaakov*, p. 319).

▯ 597 ▯ גַּבָּאֵי צְדָקָה שֶׁאֵין לָהֶם עֲנִיִּים לְחַלֵּק, פּוֹרְטִין לַאֲחֵרִים וְאֵין פּוֹרְטִין לְעַצְמָן

"Administrators of charity who have no poor to whom to distribute [their funds], must change the copper coins with others, not themselves" (*Pesahim* 13a).

Copper coins were unsuitable for keeping a long time, being liable to tarnish. They would therefore be exchanged for silver ones. One is prohibited, however, to change the coins with one's own money so as to avoid even the appearance of suspicion. "And you shall be guiltless towards the L-rd and towards Israel" (Num. 32:22).

When Rabbi Yosef Chaim Sonnenfeld's impoverished and orphaned granddaughter sought financial assistance from her illustrious grandfather who was in charge of distributing large sums of charity to Jerusalem's poor, he tearfully replied: "My dear granddaughter, please do not beg the impossible of me. You are asking me to breach one of the inviolable principles of my life — not to take anything from charity funds nor to distribute any of the funds under my control to my family . . . . It is precisely *because* you are my granddaughter that I cannot give you any of this money . . . . But please do not despair, G-d has many ways of providing for your needs. I assure you that you will merit children who will be great Torah scholars as compensation for all your hardships . . ." (Rabbi Hillel Danziger, *Guardian of Jerusalem*, p. 154).

Cf. *Yerushalmi, Shekalim* 3:2, "It is man's duty to be free from blame before man as before G-d." See *Insights*, vol. 1, #464.

⟦ 598 ⟧

גָּדוֹל מֵרַב רַבִּי, גָּדוֹל מֵרַבִּי רַבָּן,
גָּדוֹל מֵרַבָּן שְׁמוֹ

"Greater than Rav is Rabbi; greater than Rabbi is Rabban; greater than Rabban is his name [alone]" (*Tosefta, Eduyoth* 3:4).

"Rabbi [Rabbi Yehuda HaNasi] subdivided the standings of the 128 sages mentioned in the *Mishnah* into three levels. All those who were extremely distinguished and were on the highest level he called by their names [only], such as Hillel and Shammai and Shemayah and Avtalion. This is their greatness and the exaltation of their status, because it is impossible to find a title appropriate to honor their name, just as there are no titles for the prophets. Those sages whom he considered somewhat below this level, he designated with the title *Rabban*, such as Rabban Gamliel and Rabban Yochanan ben Zakkai. Those whom he considered to be below this latter level, he called *Rabbi*, such as Rabbi Meir and Rabbi Yehuda. He also gave people on this level the appellation *Abba*, as for example, Abba Shaul" (Rambam, Intro. to *Seder Zeraim, Commentary on the Mishnah*).

⟦ 599 ⟧

גָּדוֹל שָׁלוֹם שֶׁבֵּין אִישׁ לְאִשְׁתּוֹ, שֶׁהֲרֵי אָמְרָה
תּוֹרָה: שְׁמוֹ שֶׁל הַקָּבָּ"ה שֶׁנִּכְתַּב בִּקְדוּשָׁה
יִמָּחֶה עַל הַמָּיִם

"Great is the peace between man and wife, for the Torah has permitted the Name of the Holy One, blessed be He, which is written in holiness, to be erased in the water" (*Hullin* 141a).

Rabbi Yaakov Kamenetsky analyzes the "*Sotah ordeal*" in a psychological manner. He writes: "Human nature is such that once a husband is obsessed with jealousy and suspicion toward his wife, no force on earth can allay these emotions. According to Torah law, the truth on any claim is established on the testimony of two witnesses. Still, such testimony would not satisfy a jealous husband . . . . His doubts can be removed only by one incontrovertible fact — an act of G-d.

"Thus, the Torah ordained that G-d's Name be dissolved in the water that the woman [the suspected adulteress] is then made to drink. Clearly, the entire procedure is not a punishment for any wrongdoing. Rather it is designed to ensure that the innocent wife will be fully accepted as pure in her husband's eyes. Then domestic peace will be restored.

"Our Rabbis summed up this thought: 'Great is peace between man and his wife . . .'" (*Emeth L'Yaakov*, p.239).

🙘 600 🙚   גְּדוֹלָה מִילָה שֶׁנִּכְרְתוּ עָלֶיהָ י"ג בְּרִיתוֹת
"Great is circumcision, for concerning it thirteen covenants were made" (*Nedarim* 31b).

The word *"bris"* [covenant] occurs thirteen times in the scriptural passage dealing with G-d's command to Abraham to circumcise himself.

A basic question arose among the *Rishonim* [early decisors of the law] regarding the *mitzvah* of circumcision. Is its function the removal of a defect [the foreskin being considered a blemish] or does it serve as a positive factor in increasing the sanctity of Israel?

Rabbi Yitzchak ben Moshe Arama maintains that it does both — it removes a defect while it adds sanctity. Our sages proclaim: "Detestable is the foreskin, for with it the wicked are disparaged . . . " — this characterizes the foreskin as a blemish. "Great is circumcision, for concerning it thirteen covenants were made" — this signifies the elevation and sanctification of Israel (*Akedath Yitzchak*).

Rabbi Yosef Dov HaLevi Soloveitchik suggests that the two concepts — removal of a defect and adding sanctity, may be implied in the dual process of the *mitzvah* — *milah* and *periah*. *Milah* is cutting away the foreskin covering the head of the membrum, while *periah* is the uncovering of the tender membrane beneath it. Hence, *milah* serves to remove the defect of the foreskin and *periah* serves to increase the sanctity of Israel (*Beis HaLevi*).

〖 601 〗   גְּדוֹלָה נְקָמָה שֶׁנִּיתְּנָה בֵּין שְׁתֵּי אוֹתִיּוֹת

"Great is vengeance since it has been placed between two Divine Names" (*Berakoth* 33a).

As it is said: "A G-d of vengeance is Hashem" [Psalms 94:1].

"What is the essence of *nekamah* [vengeance]? It is the manifestation and revelation of the enactment of justice in this world. Thus, true *nekamah* can be an unparalleled 'glory of G-d,' showing that there is an ultimate judge, and that justice is eventually carried out" (Rabbi Chaim Shmulevitz, *Reb Chaim's Discourses*, p. 117).

Rabbi Moshe Avigdor Amiel points to the unique nature of *nekamah*. "Regarding other commandments our sages teach us, 'Always should a man occupy himself with Torah and *mitzvoth* even though he performs them not for the sake of Heaven, for ultimately this will lead to their performance for the sake of Heaven. However, with regard to the precept of *nekamah*, this principle certainly does not apply. It is only permissible and constitutes a *mitzvah* if the 'prescribed punishment' is meted out to a transgressor, and it is done without any personal animosity and solely for the sake of Heaven.

"This is the meaning of 'Great is vengeance since it has been placed between two Divine Names,' i.e., both before and after it is perpetrated, vengeance must entail 'proper intention,' unlike other commandments that may initially be performed without proper intention" (*Hegyonoth El-Ami*, vol. 2, p.222). See *Insights*, vol. 1, #374).

Cf. *Berakoth* 28b, "Is there a man who can formulate the benediction of heretics?"

〖 602 〗   גְּדוֹלָה שִׁמּוּשָׁהּ יוֹתֵר מִלִּמּוּדָהּ

"Greater is the service [attending upon a scholar] than the study [of Torah] itself" (*Berakoth* 7b).

Rabbi Chaim Shmulevitz comments on the significance of 'personal service' [*shimush*] as part of the process of acquiring Torah knowledge. He states: "It was as a result of his 'servitude' that Joshua was designated as Moshe's successor, for there were men of greater personal status who could have been selected."

Cf. *Bamidbar Rabbah* 21:14, "'And his attendant Joshua son of Nun was a lad who never left his tent' (Ex. 33:11) — The Holy One, blessed be He, said to Moshe, 'Joshua has served you and honored you greatly . . . he therefore is worthy to serve Israel for he shall receive his rightful reward . . . .'"

See *Makkoth* 10a, "A disciple who has been exiled [to a city of refuge], his teacher is exiled with him, as it says, 'so that he might live,' which implies, provide him with whatever he needs to live.

There is no shortage of books in 'the cities of refuge,' yet without a personal teacher it is not considered a place fit to live" (*Reb Chaim's Discourses*, pp. 159, 268).

According to Rabbi Joseph Ber Soloveitchik, "personal contact with and attendance to Torah scholars is greater than the mastery of their Torah knowledge, for this attachment to outstanding Torah personalities leads to the cultivation of moral sensitivity" (*Chamesh Derashoth*).

I will never forget the *shiur* [Torah lesson] on *Tanach* [Bible} given by the outstanding Gaon, Rabbi Chaim Heller, who was a Rebbe of Rabbi Joseph Ber Soloveitchik. Reb Chaim was sitting behind a desk and Rav Soloveitchik was sitting attentively beside him. Suddenly Reb Chaim's few scribbled notes fell off the desk. Rav Soloveitchik would not allow anyone to retrieve them. He fell on all fours, picked up the notes and lovingly gave them to his Rebbe.

⫯ 603 ⫯ גְּדוֹלִים צַדִּיקִים בְּמִיתָתָן יוֹתֵר מִבְּחַיֵּיהֶן

"The righteous are greater [more powerful] after death than in life" (*Hullin* 7b).

After the death of Rav Nathan Zvi Finkel [*the Alter of Slabodka*], Rabbi Yitzchak Hutner [one of his disciples] wrote the following letter:

"During the past year, the '*Elder of Slabodka*' worked hard to explain several fundamental perspectives which pertain to me personally, but in no way could I assimilate them, could I integrate them into my consciousness.

And now, suddenly, with the death of the 'Elder,' they have all become clear and vivid" (*Pachad Yitzchak, Iggeroth U-Ketuvim*, 159; cited by Hillel Goldberg, *Tradition* 22, no. 4 [Winter 1987]: p. 21).

Cf. *Berakoth* 18a, "The righteous in their death are called living." See *Insights*, vol. 1, #460.

Rabbi Moshe Avigdor Amiel notes that only those portions of the Torah dealing with the death of the righteous have the word *chaim* [life] in their scriptural designation, e.g., *Chayei Sarah* and *Va'yechi Yaakov*.

◊ 604 ◊ גַּמְלָא אֲזַלָא לְמִיבָּעֵי קַרְנֵי, אוּדְנֵי דַּהֲווּ לֵיהּ גְּזִיזַן מִינֵּיהּ

"When the camel went to look for horns [to fight with], they cut off the ears he had" (*Sanhedrin* 106a).

The Vilna Gaon's text reads *chamra* [donkey] instead of *gamla* [camel]. "A donkey once went and got himself a pair of horns. He tied them to his head and, fancying himself now as powerful as a mountain goat, began engaging other animals in combat. His adventure was not successful: not only did he lose the fight, but the other animal's real horns tore off his ears."

The Gaon explains the above parable. "When a Torah student prematurely presumes himself to be an accomplished scholar, and instead of sitting at his teacher's feet, he considers presenting his own insights more important than absorbing those of his teacher's, he is jeopardizing his own development in two ways. First, he wastes precious time that he could have been using to learn true wisdom. Second and worse, by concentrating on impressing others he loses his capacity to accept, even from his own teacher. In terms of the talmudic parable, not only does he make himself ridiculous by pitting his fake horns against the real horns of the mountain goat; he ends up 'losing his ears' — he becomes incapable of listening. Without ears ready to bend to the teacher's words, Torah can never be acquired" (*Perush Al Kamma Aggadoth*, cited by Rabbi Aharon Feldman, *The Juggler and the King*, p. 49.

Cf. *Aboda Zarah* 5b, "One should always see himself in his relations to the words of Torah as an ox to its yoke and a donkey to its load." See #831.

⫯ 605 ⫯

גֵּרִים גְּרוּרִים

"Dragged-in proselytes" (*Aboda Zarah* 3b).

An insincere class of [self-made] converts who Judaize en masse under the impulsion of fear [like the Gibeonites].

"Judaism had always been plagued by *gerim gerurim* who convert for selfish, ulterior motives and become a scourge to the Jewish people. At the very dawn of Jewish history, with the Exodus from Egypt, hundreds of thousands of insincere converts jumped on our triumphant 'bandwagon' . . . . This group, known collectively as the '*Erev Rav*' [the mixed multitude], was the source of all of Israel's woes . . . .

"The Vilna Gaon reveals that all heretics and wicked Jews throughout the ages are the descendants of this group, and they will proliferate and rise to power in the era preceding the Messiah, causing tremendous harm to the righteous" (*Even Shleimah*, ch. 11).

Cf. *Yebamoth* 47b, "Proselytes are as bad for Israel as a sore on the skin." See *Insights*, vol. 1, #470.

Cf. *Yebamoth* 24b, "Proselytes will not be accepted in the days of the Messiah." See #536.

ד

⟦ 606 ⟧ דְּאָכִיל מִן חַבְרֵיהּ בָּהִית מִסְתַּכֵּל בֵּיהּ

"One who eats that which comes from his neighbor is ashamed to look at him [his benefactor]" (*Yerushalmi, Orlah* 1:3).

"The Almighty created His creatures so that He could bestow good upon them. In His sublime wisdom, however, He knew that for this good to be complete it should be received as the fruits of one's labor. For then the recipient would feel himself the proprietor of that good and would not be shamefaced in receiving it, as if he were receiving charity. As it is said: 'One who eats that which comes from his neighbor is ashamed to look at him [his benefactor]'" (Rabbi Moshe Chaim Luzzatto, *Da'ath Tevunoth*).

Rabbi Avraham Yehoshua Heschel [the Apter Rebbe], interpreted the above dictum in a kabbalistic vein. "The main reason why man was created, and his soul sent down to a physical body, was so that he would be able to serve G-d through Torah and *mitzvoth*. As a result of such worship . . . what one eats is then his own, given in return for his worship.

"Such a person does not have to look in the face of his Benefactor. This would not be true if the soul had remained in the highest universe. It would then be 'eating' and receiving sustenance as a free gift, through G-d's love alone. Since this would be given without any 'motivation from below' through Torah and good deeds, it would be the 'bread of shame'" (*Ohev Yisroel*, *Ekev* 82d).

82

∬ 607 ∬ דִּבְרֵי הָרַב וְדִבְרֵי תַּלְמִיד דִּבְרֵי מִי שׁוֹמְעִים?

"[When] the words of the Master and the words of the student
[are in conflict], whose are obeyed?" (*Kiddushin* 41b).

Obviously the master's words are obeyed. This is the rationale for the
talmudic dictum, "There can be no agent for a wrongdoing" [See #539]. Any
wrongful act committed through an agent on the instructions of the principal
is not accounted as an act of the principal but of the agent himself" (Rashi).

See *Teshuvoth Rabbi Akiva Eiger, Yoreh De'ah, Responsum* 210. See also *Sma*
(*Sefer Me'irath Ainayim*) 182.

See *Shach, Choshen Mishpat* 348:6.

Cf. *Kiddushin* 41b, "A man's agent is as himself." See *Insights*, vol. 1,
#485.

∬ 608 ∬ דִּבְרֵי תוֹרָה וְדִבְרֵי חֲכָמִים מֵרוֹעֶה אֶחָד נִתָּנוּ

"The words of the Torah [Written Law] and the words
of the sages [Oral Law] have been given from the same Shepherd"
(*Bamidbar Rabbah* 14:4).

See *Koheleth Rabbah* 12:11, "Shepherd" refers either to the Almighty or to
Moshe, the shepherd of Israel.

The above dictum points to the unity and inseparability of the Written
and Oral Law.

Rabbi Yaakov Zvi Mecklenburg writes: "Quite apart from our faith
concerning the authenticity of the Oral Law, it is incumbent upon us not to
rest . . . until we shall be found worthy of understanding the absolute unity
of the Oral and Written Laws, so that there shall not be the slightest
difference to us between the truth of *peshat* [the literal interpretation of a
scriptural text], or that of a *derash* [its exegetical interpretation]" (Preface to
HaKesav V'HaKabbalah, cited by Rabbi Zechariah Fendel, *Anvil of Sinai*, p.
209).

Cf. *Yerushalmi, Pe'ah* 2:4 (p. 13a), "If you will fulfill the Oral Law and you will fulfill the Written Law, I will make a covenant with you, and if not, I will not make a covenant with you."

⟦ 609 ⟧

דּוֹר שֶׁבֶּן דָּוִד בָּא בּוֹ הָעַזּוּת תִּרְבֶּה

"In the generation of Messiah's coming, impudence will increase"
(*Sanhedrin* 97a).

Rabbi Elchonon Wasserman comments: "One interpretation of this saying of the Rabbis is that by shamelessness will fame be achieved. In bygone times the leaders [of the community] were required to be endowed with Torah, with the fear of G-d in addition to being wise. In the Messianic era, anyone who possesses an adequate amount of shamelessness can be crowned with the title "*Gadol*" [great in Torah scholarship]. The greater the *chutzpah*, the more will he be considered reliable. It is quite evident that the main prerequisite for party-leadership is impudence" (*Epoch of the Messiah*, p. 19).

Cf. *Sanhedrin* 97a, "The face of the generation will be dog-faced." See *Insights*, vol. 1, #455.

Cf. *Sanhedrin* 105a, "Impudence is sovereignty without a crown."

⟦ 610 ⟧

דּוֹרוֹת הָרִאשׁוֹנִים עָשׂוּ תּוֹרָתָן קֶבַע
וּמְלַאכְתָּן עֲרַאי

"The earlier generations made their Torah fixed and their work temporary" (*Berakoth* 35b).

Keva [fixed] in the above dictum, according to the *Meiri*, refers not to the quantity of learning, but to its centrality (ad. loc.).

The Slabodka Rosh Yeshiva, Rav Mordechai Shulman, cites Rabbeinu Yonah's comment on the dictum "*Make of your study of the Torah a fixed practice*" — "One who considers his Torah secondary and his work primary, even if he has committed no transgression and merits *Gan Eden*, will be considered secondary there."

"This implies," says Rav Shulman, "that what is primary [fixed] and what is secondary [temporary] have nothing to do with quantity or quality of learning . . . . Hence making one's Torah the essential in life implies that one's Torah 'fixes' or sets the tone for one's life, implying that all other things are inconsequential" (Rabbi Reuven Grossman, *The Legacy of Slabodka*, p. 84).

Cf. *Aboth* 1:15, "Make of your study of the Torah a fixed practice." See *Insights*, vol. 1, #446.

Cf. *Shabbath* 31a, "Did you establish set times for studying Torah?" See #950.

⌑ 611 ⌑

דְּלָא יָלֵיף קְטָלָא חַיָּיב

"He who does not study [Torah] is deserving of death"
(*Aboth* 1:13).

"He neglects to acquaint himself with the tasks for which he was given life and to acquire the skills and knowledge necessary for their fulfillment" (Rabbi Samson Raphael Hirsch, *Commentary on Aboth*).

"The Chafetz Chaim recounted that he had once been privileged to spend a night in the same hotel in Vilna as Rabbi Yisrael Salanter. Curious to know what the latter would be doing during the night, the Chafetz Chaim pressed his ear against the wall of the adjoining room, which was occupied by Reb Yisrael. He kept hearing Reb Yisrael repeating throughout the night, in a voice trembling with excitement, 'He who does not study is deserving of death'" (Rabbi Moses M. Yoshar, *Dos Leben und Schaffen fon Chafetz Chaim*, p. 335).

Rabbi Yitzchak Eizik of Komarno writes: "This is a warning against foolish *chasiduth*. It is perfectly true that the main thing is to study Torah for its own sake and in order to be in a state of attachment to G-d. But such is on a most elevated plane and it is impossible for a man to arrive all at once to the stage of 'Torah for its own sake.' One is bound to study Torah out of ulterior motives at first, until his character has been sufficiently refined to enable him to take delight in the Torah. But the foolish try all at once to seize hold of this inner light, and since they are unworthy of it, they give

up Torah study entirely . . . . In order to negate this thinking . . . the sage
declares: 'He who does not study . . . .'" (*Notzer Chesed*).

"Rabbi Mendel Kaplan used to say in the name of his Rebbe, Reb
Elchanan Wasserman: 'Learning [Torah] is very hard, but without learning,
living is very hard'" (Yisroel Greenwald, *Reb Mendel and his Wisdom*, p. 91).

⟦ 612 ⟧ דַּע מַה שֶׁתָּשִׁיב לְאֶפִּיקוּרֹס
"Know what to respond to a heretic" (*Aboth* 2:19).

"Three classes of people are called *Epikorsim* [heretics]: He who denies the
reality of prophecy and maintains that there is no knowledge which emanates from the Creator to the human mind; he who denies the prophecy of
Moshe, our teacher; he who asserts that the Creator has no knowledge of
the deeds of men" (Rambam, *Mishneh Torah, Hil. Teshuvah* 3:16).

"One should study Torah in order to know how to respond to the heretic,
for just as it is a *mitzvah* for a man to study and acquire Torah, which is the
'Torah of truth,' so is it important to banish false opinions from the world
in order that the truth be magnified in it" (Maharal miPrague, *Derech Chaim*).

Rabbi Yaakov Emden comments: "You should be aware of the need to
know these matters [i.e., the opinions of the gentiles] as our sages ordained.
What is forbidden is only to study them in depth, as one studies Torah, or
to make them primary. Yet their study is necessary, and the Torah personality should not lack knowledge of these matters. One who believes [in the
Torah] will not be harmed by the noxious fumes" (*Lechem Shamayim*, III:
134a) [*Sanhedrin* 10:1]. Cf. Rabbi Emden, *Etz Aboth* 2:14.

Cf. *Sanhedrin* 38b, "Be diligent to learn the Torah and know what to
respond to a heretic. Rabbi Yochanan commented: They taught this only
with respect to a Gentile *Epikoros* [heretic]; with a Jewish *Epikoros*, it would
only make his heresy more pronounced." With him, therefore, discussion is
not advised since he is deliberate in his negation and not therefore easily
dissuaded (Rashi). See also Rambam, *Comm. on the Mishnah*, Aboth 2:14, "A
Jewish heretic will only become uprooted further . . . ."

Rabbi A. I. Kook writes: "To fully understand the Torah, it is also
necessary to possess worldly knowledge in many areas, especially in order

to be able to respond to the arguments of heretics, which is most urgent in our time" (*Igroth* I, *Letter* 43).

ה

⟦ 613 ⟧   הָאָבוֹת הֵן הֵן הַמֶּרְכָּבָה

"The Patriarchs are [G-d's] Heavenly Chariot" (*Beraishith Rabbah* 47:6).

This conveys the theological doctrine that through Abraham, Isaac and Jacob, the knowledge of G-d was diffused among all peoples.

Cf. Rashi, Gen. 17:22, "The righteous are the Chariot of the Holy One, blessed be He." See *Shnei Luchoth HaBrith* 38b.

Rabbi Shneur Zalman of Liadi writes: "All their [the Patriarchs'] organs were completely holy and detached from mundane matters, and throughout their lives they served as a vehicle for nothing but the Divine Will."

Rabbi Yosef Weinberg comments: "The reason for the sages' designating specifically the Patriarchs as G-d's chariot, although every Jew's body becomes a 'chariot' when he performs a *mitzvah*, is that the Patriarchs' submission to the Divine Will was unique in its power, its scope and its consistency. All their organs were totally surrendered to the Divine Will throughout their lives — whereas with other Jews, only those organs which perform a *mitzvah* are a 'chariot,' and only during the act" (*Lessons in Tanya*, vol. 1, ch. 23, p. 302).

Rabbi Mendel of Vorki comments: This term "*HaMerkavah*" ["The Chariot"] is used because a chariot has no direction of its own and goes whichever way the driver directs it. The Patriarchs had so devoted themselves to the Divine Will that they became its "chariot"; i.e., every fiber in their bodies automatically strove to do the Divine Will (Rabbi Abraham J. Twersky, *Living Each Week*, p. 305).

◊ 614 ◊

הָאוֹהֵב אֶת אִשְׁתּוֹ כְּגוּפוֹ וְהַמְכַבְּדָהּ יוֹתֵר
מִגּוּפוֹ . . . עָלָיו הַכָּתוּב אוֹמֵר: "וְיָדַעְתָּ כִּי
שָׁלוֹם אָהֳלֶךָ"

"He who loves his wife as himself and honors her more than himself . . . concerning him Scripture says: 'You will know that all is
well [shalom] in your tent'" [Job 5:24] (Yebamoth 62b).

"Only concerning honor does it say that one 'honors her *more* than
himself,' but regarding love one is advised to 'love her *as* himself,' for kavod
[honor] pertains to others rather that to oneself" (Maharal miPrague).

When Rabbi Shlomo Zalman Auerbach was in the *cheder yichud* (alone
with his bride for the first time after the *chuppah*) he told her, "If we were
ever to disagree about anything — you are right" (Hanoch Teller, *and from
Jerusalem His Word*, p.114).

When Rabbi Yaakov Yitzchak Ruderman attended an Agudah Convention
in *Eretz Yisrael*, a group of wives of the Rosh HaYeshiva's students felt it
necessary to express their gratitude to him. The wives believed as a group,
that their husbands treated them with greater respect and deference, because
they observed how their *Rebbe* had treated his *Rebbetzin* (*The Torah Profile*,
p. 229).

In commenting on the phrase "he who loves his wife as himself," the
Orach Yesharim points out that one who loves his wife because of her beauty,
in reality only loves her beauty; hence, when she loses that, he despises her.
However, one who loves his wife for he sees in her a portion of his own
self, then even if she loses her beauty he will love her, for he loves himself
regardless of how he looks. Our sages, therefore, advise a husband to love
his wife "as himself" (Rabbi Shmuel Alter, *L'Kutei Bosar L'kutei [Aggadoth]*
vol. 3, p. 222).

Cf. *Baba Metzia* 59a, "A man should always be careful to honor his wife
properly, because all blessings come to the home only through the merit of
the wife."

⟦ 615 ⟧

הָאוֹמֵר עַל קַן צִפּוֹר יַגִּיעוּ רַחֲמֶיךָ —
מְשַׁתְּקִין אוֹתוֹ

"He who says: 'Your mercies extend over the bird's nest' is
silenced" (Berakoth 33b).

"Whoever says in his *tachanunim* [supplications] 'He who dealt mercifully
with a nest of birds, forbidding the taking of the mother-bird together with
the nestlings . . . may He have mercy on us . . .' is silenced, for the precept
['Let the mother (bird) go and take only the young' Deut. 22:6,7] is a
scriptural decree and has not been ordained in a spirit of compassion. Were
this the motive, the slaughtering of all animals would have been forbidden"
(*Mishneh Torah, Hil. Tefillah* 9:7).

In his philosophical treatise, however, Rambam writes: "When the mother
bird is sent away, she does not see the taking of the young ones, and does
not feel any pain . . . . If the Torah provides that such wrong and pain
should not be caused to cattle or birds, how much more careful we must be
not to inflict any pain or cause any worry to human beings" (*Moreh Nevuchim*
3:48).

"There is evidently no conflict between Rambam's words in his philosophical work *Moreh Nevuchim*, where he contends that the consideration for
the animal constitutes the rationale of these commandments, and the *halachic*
statement in *Mishneh Torah*, where he deals with rules of conduct and not
with the motivation behind the laws" (Rabbi B. S. Jacobson, *Binah Bamikra,
Ki Thetze*).

Similarly, Rabbi Joseph B. Soloveitchik asserts that the *mishnaic* dictum
(above) refers to a *sheliach tzibbur* (public reader) who is not permitted to say
"Your mercies extend . . . ." Such manner of formal prayer is not permitted,
"for the assumption that compassion is the reason for the *mitzvah* cannot be
accepted with certainty. It is wrong to render a prayer in behalf of the
community contingent on an uncertain hypothesis" (Rabbi Abraham R.
Besdin, *Man of Faith in the Modern World*, p. 97).

❘ 616 ❘

הָאוֹמֵר סֶלַע זוֹ לִצְדָקָה בִּשְׁבִיל שֶׁיִּחְיֶה בְּנִי
— הֲרֵי זֶה צַדִּיק גָּמוּר

"If one declares, 'This coin be for charity in order that my son
may live . . .' he is a perfect *tzaddik*" (*Pesahim* 8a).

Rashi explains that he performs the *mitzvah* of giving charity in accordance with the Divine Commandment. The fact that he also intends to benefit himself does not imply that his act was performed *shelo lishmah* [not for its own sake].

Rabbi Yaakov Yitzchak, the Chozeh of Lublin, raises the question: "Is not one who gives charity without mentioning a reward a greater *tzaddik*? The answer is, that one is a perfect *tzaddik* when he wishes his son to live so that he may serve G-d wholeheartedly and perform good deeds" (*Niflaoth HaChozeh Lublin*, p. 35).

Cf. *Rosh Hashanah* 4a, "[The above dictum only] applies to Israelites. Heathens are assumed to regret the charitable deed should the attached condition not be realized" (Rashi and Tosaf.).

❘ 617 ❘

הָאוֹמֵר שֶׁלִּי שֶׁלִּי וְשֶׁלְּךָ שֶׁלָּךְ זוֹ מִדָּה בֵּינוֹנִית
וְיֵשׁ אוֹמְרִים זוֹ מִדַּת סְדוֹם

"He who says: 'What is mine is mine, and what is yours is yours,'
is an average character;
some say this is the characteristic of Sodom" (*Aboth* 5:13).

"It would seem that the view that every person should keep that which is his, and that no one else should derive benefit from the property of another, is midway between good and evil. Some, however, feel that it is a most reprehensible attitude, because it would expunge from the human heart and mind that guiding principle of loving-kindness without which man would lose his Divinely-given nobility . . . ." (Rabbi Samson Raphael Hirsch, *Commentary on Aboth*).

Rabbi Moshe Avigdor Amiel distinguishes between individual standards and communal policy, and he interprets the above dictum accordingly. "*Ho'omer*" — "If one says 'mine is mine, and yours is yours,' i.e., if an individual behaves in this manner — that is 'average' or a middle course. If, however, '*Yesh Omrim*,' there are those who say it, i.e., if the community behaves in this manner, then it is a characteristic of Sodom."

〔 618 〕   הָאי מָאן דִּיָהִיר, בַּעַל מוּם הוּא

"An arrogant person is a blemished person" (*Megillah* 29a).

When the Torah was about to be given, Mount Tabor and Mount Carmel presented themselves to the Almighty for consideration as the site for Divine Revelation. They imagined themselves more eligible for this honor than Mount Sinai because of their impressive size. "A Heavenly Voice went forth and said to them: 'Why do you "compete" with Sinai? You are full of *blemishes* [for the Torah refers to you as "hunchbacks" (Psalms 68:17)].'" Said Rav Ashi: "We can learn from this that an arrogant person is a blemished person."

"The very quality which led Mount Tabor and Mount Carmel to believe themselves worthy of being the site for the giving of the Torah — their loftiness — was the cause of their disqualification. Their loftiness led them to pride, and pride rendered them unfit to be associated with Torah.

"The Torah was given on a mountain and not a plain to symbolize that its wisdom stems from a loftier plane than that of ordinary existence. At the same time, it was given on Mount Sinai, the humblest of mountains, to teach mankind the evil of pride" (Vilna Gaon, *Perush Al Kamma Aggadoth*, cited by Rabbi Aharon Feldman, *The Juggler and the King*, p. 50).

It is true, said the Kotzker, that "Our sages teach us that 'A *talmid chacham* [a Torah scholar] should possess an eighth of an eighth of pride' (*Sotah* 5a). The problem is that some *talmidei chachamim* are very poor in mathematics" (Shmuel Himelstein, *Words of Wisdom, Words of Wit*, p. 125).

Rabbi Simcha Zissel of Kelm commented: "Arrogance is a reprehensible trait that is the father of all other negative traits" (*Chochmah Umussar*, vol. 1, p. 231).

R' Yisrael Salanter would often remark, "When I see an arrogant person,

I feel such a revulsion that I almost vomit" (*Tenuath HaMussar*, vol. 1, p. 303)

Cf. *Sotah* 5a, "A person should always strive to emulate the ways of his Maker." See *Insights*, vol. 1, #373.

Cf. *Ta'anith* 7a, "The words of the Torah endure only with him who is meek-minded." See *Insights*, vol. 1, #45.

⌑ 619 ⌑

הַאי צוּרְבָּא מֵרַבָּנַן דְּמִרְחֲמִין לֵיהּ בְּנֵי מָתָא,
לָאו מִשׁוּם דְּמַעֲלֵי טְפֵי אֶלָּא מִשׁוּם דְּלָא
מוֹכַח לְהוּ בְּמִילֵי דִשְׁמַיָּא

"If a scholar is loved by his townspeople, [their love] is not due to his superiority, but [to the fact] that he does not rebuke them for [neglecting] matters of Heaven" (*Kethuboth* 105b).

"Matters of Heaven" is interpreted by many as "*mitzvoth* between man and G-d." It is quite common for people to accept chastisement and rebuke for transgressions committed "between man and his fellow." However, due to lack of understanding, very few people will accept chastisement concerning transgressions "between man and G-d." A rabbi who has the courage of his convictions and admonishes his congregation concerning these "Heavenly" matters, will not win a popularity contest.

Rabbi Chaim ibn Attar comments: "Thus, we see that admonishment will often arouse animosity. Nevertheless, this should not discourage the rabbi from speaking out against wrongdoing. It is wrong for the rabbi to remain silent and say, 'Why do I need this trouble? Why should I create animosity and strife within the Jewish community?' He should have confidence in the basic decency of his people and should say to himself, 'I will chastise them properly and believe that they are honest enough to accept the truth and that they will not hate me'" (*Ohr HaChaim*, Lev. 19:17).

⎨ 620 ⎬

הָאִשָּׁה . . . קוֹנָה אֶת עַצְמָהּ בְּגֵט
וּבְמִיתַת הַבַּעַל

"A woman . . . is released from marriage [in two ways]: by
divorce and by her husband's death (*Kiddushin* 2a).

"During the course of Rabbi Akiva Eiger's travels he came to Warsaw
where the case of a *meshumad* [a convert from Judaism], who refused to issue
his wife a Jewish divorce, was brought to his attention. The *Beth Din*
[rabbinical court] had long since ruled that the man must award his wife a
divorce, but he persisted in ignoring the ruling.

Rabbi Akiva Eiger instructed his attendants to bring this man to him. Reb
Akiva greeted him by saying, 'My friend, let us sit down and learn a
Mishnah together . . . .' He opened up *Mishnayoth Kiddushin* and began to
read, 'A woman is acquired in marriage in three ways . . . . She is released
from marriage by divorce or her husband's death.'

'You see, it is very clear,' said Reb Akiva Eiger, 'You have one of two
options . . . .'

The fellow ridiculed both the *Mishnah* and the Rabbi and left hurriedly.
Just a few steps outside the door he began to feel faint. He subsequently lost
consciousness and within minutes, was dead" (Rabbi Hanoch Teller, *Soul
Survivors*, p. 200).

⎨ 621 ⎬

הֶדְיוֹט קוֹפֵץ בָּרֹאשׁ

"The ordinary [common] man pushes himself in front [lit., he
leaps to the top]" (*Megillah* 12b).

The Vilna Gaon underscores the sharp contrast between Esther and the
other contestants who vied for the royal appointment as Achashveirosh's
queen. The *Megillah* records: "*And when the turn of each maiden and maiden
arrived to come before the King Achashveirosh*" (*Esther* 2:12). The melodic note,
the *trop*, above the words "maiden and maiden" is *kadma v'azla*, which
literally means "they went forth early." Every other girl competed to be the

first to appear before the king. But by pushing to the forefront, they betrayed themselves and revealed the commonality that disqualified them from the throne.

"*And upon the arrival of the turn of Esther bas Avichayil* . . . ." Here, the musical notes are four straight *munach* signs — implying: *rest, rest, rest, rest*. Not only did Esther not push forward, she restrained herself and went with reluctance and calm (Rabbi Avraham Chaim Feuer, *Seasons of the Soul*, p. 187).

〚 **622** 〛 הַדָּן חֲבֵירוֹ לְכַף זְכוּת דָּנִין אוֹתוֹ לִזְכוּת

"He who judges his fellow man favorably, is himself judged favorably (*Shabbath* 127b).

The Almighty will then judge him in a favorable manner. In one of his *Rosh Hashanah shmeussen* [mussar discourses], Reb Chaim Shmulevitz points out that "at first glance, the equating of human judgment with Divine judgment seems incongruous. Human beings can never be sure of the motives of a fellow human being and therefore one must judge another favorably, giving him the benefit of the doubt. But how can we say this concerning Divine justice? Are there any doubts before G-d? . . . The answer is that our sages are not referring to a situation where we are judging a person's actions, but rather his motives [which are unclear]. The requirement 'to judge favorably' means to appraise favorably an action done with mixed motives by emphasizing its positive aspects . . . . It is regarding the evaluation of one's motives that 'judging favorably' is reciprocated by the Divine 'judging favorably.' If a person judges his fellow man from the perspective of his finer and nobler motives, then the Almighty will judge him by the same standards" (*Reb Chaim's Discourses*, p. 35).

In commenting on the above dictum, Rabbi Simcha Zissel Ziv (*The Alter of Kelm*) declared: "This principle is not meant to be applied in all situations. If a person does not censure wrongdoing, it will have a negative influence on him" (*Chochmah Umussar*, vol. 1, p. 269).

Rabbi S. R. Hirsch declared: "Better that a hundred should be judged too favorably than that one should be wronged in judgment" (*Horeb*, v. 1, p. 58).

Cf. *Aboth* 1:6, "Judge every man in the scale of merit." See *Insights*, vol. 1, #159.

〚 623 〛 הֱוֵי מְקַבֵּל אֶת כָּל הָאָדָם בְּסֵבֶר פָּנִים יָפוֹת

"Receive every man with a cheerful countenance" (*Aboth* 1:15).

"What does this mean? It teaches that if a man presents the most precious gifts in the world to his fellow Jew, but gives them with a sullen countenance, Scripture regards him as having presented his friend with nothing. On the other hand, he who receives his fellow with a cheerful countenance, though he give him nothing, Scripture accounts it to him as though he has presented him with the most precious gifts in the world" (*Aboth D'Rabbi Nathan* 13:4).

"Reb Yisroel Salanter met a fellow Jew on *Erev Yom Kippur* who exclaimed in a troubled voice: 'I'm worried about the Day of Judgment we are facing tomorrow!' Reb Yisroel looked at the man's gloomy countenance and said to him: 'Your heart is a *reshus ha'yochid* [private domain]. You can carry within it all you want. However, your face is a *reshus ha'rabim* [public domain] and you have no right to burden others with your problems and fears. The rule in *Pirke Aboth*, "Receive every man with a cheerful countenance," applies even to *Yom Kippur* eve'" (Chaim Shapiro, *The Torah Profile*, p. 52).

Cf. *Aboth* 3:16, "Receive all men happily." See *Insights*, vol. 1, #161.

〚 624 〛 הֱוּ כַעֲבָדִים הַמְשַׁמְּשִׁים אֶת הָרַב שֶׁלֹּא עַל מְנָת לְקַבֵּל פְּרָס

"Be like servants who serve their master without conditioning for a reward" (*Aboth* 1:3).

Do not make your service to the Almighty conditional upon receiving a reward.

In some *mishnaic* editions, the reading is "Be like servants who serve their master *al menas shelo lekabel peras*" [conditioning for no reward].

According to the Baal Shem Tov, both versions are correct and point to different stages of prayer — one lower and one higher. They both refer to those who pray without seeking a reward for themselves. In the lower form of prayer, while the worshipper entreats G-d to satisfy his needs, he acknowledges that G-d may not answer his prayer, i.e., he prays without conditioning for a reward.

In the higher stage of prayer, however, the worshipper "conditions for no reward." He too entreats G-d to satisfy his needs, since he is so obligated to pray, but he does not want his request granted. His real desire is to be in a continual state of need so that he can always come before the Almighty with his requests. The joy of approaching his Creator is his primary interest (Rabbi Moshe Chaim Ephraim of Sudlikov, *Degel Machne Ephraim, Haftorah Ki Thetze*).

"The story is told about the Vilna Gaon, who could not find an *ethrog* for *Succoth* one year. The owner of the only available *ethrog* agreed to sell it to him on condition that the reward for the Gaon's *mitzvah* be credited to the seller. Hearing this, the Gaon joyfully agreed to the condition. When asked as to the cause of his joy, he replied, 'All my life I've looked forward to be able to fulfill the *Mishnah*, "Be as servants serving their master without conditioning for a reward," and now, I finally have the opportunity'" (Rabbi Chaim Shmulevitz, *Reb Chaim's Discourses*, p. 216).

⎰ 625 ⎱   הַיּוֹם קָצֵר וְהַמְּלָאכָה מְרוּבָּה . . . .

"The day is short and the work load is large . . ." (*Aboth* 2:20).

"Life is short and the task that each individual must complete on earth is great; yet men are slow to complete their work" (Rabbi Samson Raphael Hirsch, *Commentary of Aboth*).

"Late one night, Reb Yisrael Salanter happened to pass by the house of a shoemaker, and saw him working by the light of a candle that was almost dying out. 'Why do you work so late,' Reb Yisrael asked him. 'The candle will soon go out, and you won't be able to do any more.' 'That makes no difference,' the shoemaker replied. '*Kol zman de licht brent, ken men noch farichten'* ['as long as the candle keeps burning, one can still make repairs'].

Reb Yisrael was deeply affected by this remark. He reasoned: 'If one should continue working for his material needs as long as the candle burns and its light can be used — then how much more so is the man to work for the needs of his soul as long as the lamp of G-d, which is the soul of man, is still burning, and rectify as much as one possibly can'" (Rabbi Dov Katz, *The Mussar Movement*, vol. 1).

626

הַיּוֹצֵא מִן הַטָּמֵא — טָמֵא
וְהַיּוֹצֵא מִן הַטָּהוֹר — טָהוֹר

"That which goes forth from the *tamei* [unclean] is *tamei* and that which goes forth from the *tahor* [clean] is *tahor*" (*Bekoroth* 5b).

"If an unclean animal has an offspring resembling a clean animal, even if it has cloven hoofs and does chew the cud, and completely resembles an ox or a sheep, it is forbidden for consumption. The rule is that the offspring of an unclean animal is unclean, and the offspring of a clean animal is clean . . ." (*Mishneh Torah, Hil. Ma'acholoth Asuroth* 1:5).

Rabbi Meir Shapiro of Lublin points out that there are two exceptions to the above *mishnaic* ruling, namely, "milk and honey." Milk comes from blood [which is "unclean"], as our sages explain, "The blood [during the nursing period] is 'disturbed' [decomposed] and turns into milk" (*Bekoroth* 6b). Nevertheless, milk is "clean." Similarly honey, which is produced from the "unclean" bee, is "clean" — both are permitted foods.

In a homiletic vein, Rabbi Shapiro compares the Land of Israel to "milk and honey," for it is characterized as "a land flowing with milk and honey (Lev. 20:24). Just as milk and honey have the peculiar distinction of being "clean" although derived from that which is "unclean," so too, the Land of Israel is imbued with the characteristic of transforming that which is "unclean" [an idolatrous nation] to that which is "clean" [The Holy Land] (Menachem Baker, *Parperaot LaTorah*, vol. 3, p. 144).

◊ 627 ◊ הֵיכִי דָמִי רָשָׁע עָרוּם? זֶה הַמַּטְעִים דְּבָרָיו
לַדַּיָּין קוֹדֶם שֶׁיָּבֹא בַּעַל דִּין חֲבֵרוֹ

"What is a cunning rogue [shrewd in his wickedness]? . . . He who explains his case to the judge before the other party to the suit arrives" (Sotah 21b).

"For when he has fixed his claims in the heart of the judge it becomes difficult for the judge to remove them, and this is his cunning" (Rashi).

"The judge believes the person who appears before him first, while the other person's claim will be believed by the judge only after extensive investigation" (Rabbi Levi ben Gershon [Ralbag] on Prov. 18:17).

Rabbi Chaim Shmulevitz comments: "If this is true of a judge, an objective outsider, certainly it holds true of a person's attitude toward his own opinions and statements. Once a human being has stated a position, he becomes inwardly bound to that stand and remains obstinately intransigent and it is difficult for him to admit otherwise" (Reb Chaim's Discourses, p. 204).

◊ 628 ◊ הַיָּרֵא וְרַךְ הַלֵּבָב: זֶה הַמִּתְיָרֵא מִן הָעֲבֵירוֹת
שֶׁבְּיָדוֹ

"'Fearful and faint-hearted' [Deut. 20:8], alludes to one who is afraid of the transgressions he had committed" (Sotah 44a).

An announcement was made before battle that the following people were to return home, for they were exempt from the draft. "One who has built a new home, but has not dedicated it; one who has planted a vineyard, but has not partaken from its fruits; one who has betrothed a wife, but has not married her; and one who is fearful and faint-hearted" (Deut. 20:5-8).

Rabbi Akiva says: "This [last category] is to be understood in its usual sense, i.e., one who is not able to stand in the battle-ranks." Rabbi Yosi Haglili says that this refers to someone who fears that he is unworthy of being saved because of his transgressions. Moreover, this is the reason why the other categories were exempted. For if people were to leave the ranks only because of their sins, they would be publicly humiliated. Now, however, that the other groups were also sent home, no one would know which individuals were leaving because of their sins [*Sotah*, ibid.].

Rabbi Zelig Pliskin comments: "This is truly amazing. A large number of soldiers are sent home in wartime in order to save a sinner from humiliation. We should learn from this that we must do everything possible to protect people from shame" (*Love Your Neighbor*, p. 410).

The Kotzker Rebbe suggested that "the men who were sent home for being fearful because of past sins were in fact virtuous people. Their only fault was that they were obsessed with guilt feelings over a sin they committed long ago. A dispirited person cannot go to war" (*Emeth VeEmunah*).

〚 629 〛   הַכֹּל בִּידֵי שָׁמַיִם חוּץ מִצִּנִּים פַּחִים

"All is Heavenly-directed except [illness through] cold [or] heat"
(*Kethuboth* 30a).

"For it is said: 'Cold [and] heat are in the way of a perverse man; he who values his life will keep far from them'" (Prov. 22:5).

See *Tosaf. Baba Bathra* 144b, s.v. *HaKol*, "This [dictum] is not to be compared to 'All is Heavenly-directed except the fear of Heaven' (*Berakoth* 33b), for that refers to the *middoth* [characteristics] of man, e.g., whether he will be strong or weak, wealthy or poor, etc. . . ., whereas this [dictum] refers to events that occur to an individual."

Rabbi Yechezkel Abramsky related the following story after he was released from a Siberian prison, where he was sentenced to five years of hard labor. "Every morning, in temperatures that often plummeted to 40 degrees below zero, we were forced to take off our shoes and run barefoot in the snow. From this torture alone, men fell like flies. I looked toward Heaven and cried, 'Master of the Universe, You have taught us that "All is Heavenly-directed except cold and heat." Cold and heat are in man's own hands since man can guard himself from the elements by donning a coat or removing a sweater. This reason, however, no longer applies to me, for these iniquitous captors not only fail to provide me with clothes, but force me to remove whatever I am wearing. My obligation to guard my health, therefore, returns to You. So please protect me, O G-d, for I trust in You!'"

Reb Yechezkel concluded: "As a child, my mother always bundled me up warmly due to my frailty and yet, while in the midst of that Siberian cold, I never once took ill or even caught a cold!" (Hanoch Teller, *Sunset*, p. 266).

Cf. *Berakoth* 33b, "All is Heavenly-directed except the fear of Heaven." See *Insights*, vol. 1, #172.

Cf. *Aboth* 3:15, "All is foreseen, but the choice is given."

⎗ 630 ⎗   הַכֹּל הוֹלֵךְ אַחַר הַחִתּוּם

"Everything is determined by the conclusion" (*Berakoth* 12a).

If one commences his benediction in the morning or in the evening service wrongly [changing the morning for the evening formula, or vice versa], but when he is about to conclude the *beracha* he realizes his error and ends with the correct benediction — "he has performed his obligation" (ibid.).

The *Sheloh HaKadosh* applies the above legal dictum in a moralistic fashion pertaining to the "end" of each year. "Everything is determined by the end." "We can make amends for all the days of the year by rectifying the days of the last week of the year.

How one conducts himself on the last Sunday of the year will be considered as he conducted himself all the Sundays throughout the year, etc.

It is especially appropriate to strive to conduct oneself on the last Sabbath of the year in a more perfect manner of Sabbath observance. This will credit all the Sabbaths of the year as having been conducted in like fashion."

Similarly, the *Sifrei Mussar* write that the last *Ma'ariv*, *Shacharis*, and *Minchah* of the year can rectify all such corresponding prayers of the year (Rabbi Aaron Levine, *The New Rosh Hashanah*, pp. 34-36).

〖 631 〗   הַכֹּל צְרִיכִין לְמָרֵי חִטַּיָא

"All require the owner of the wheat" (*Berakoth* 64a).

The Talmud asks: Whom does the world need more, one with a very broad knowledge of Torah law [a "*Sinai*"], or one whose sharp mind enables him to deduce the law [the "uprooter-of-mountains"]? Our sages answer that the person with the broad knowledge is like the one who sells already harvested wheat — all people have a need for such an individual.

In a Kabbalistic vein, Rabbi Nachman of Breslov comments: "There are two aspects to the Torah; the aspect of revealed and the aspect of hidden . . . . The Torah which is revealed corresponds to "*Sinai*" as our sages teach, 'As between "*Sinai*" and an "uprooter-of-mountains," which should have preference?' And they answer, '*Sinai* is preferable, for everyone needs the owner of wheat' — *revealed Torah* is something which everyone needs. As for the *hidden Torah* [uprooting mountains], few are those who need it" (*Zohar* III, p. 73a, cited in *Likutey Moharan*, vol. 1B, #15).

Cf. *Berakoth* 64a, "As between '*Sinai*' and an 'uprooter of mountains,' which should have preference?" See *Insights*, vol. 1, #431.

〖 632 〗 הַכֹּל תָּלוּי בְּמַזָּל, אֲפִילוּ סֵפֶר תּוֹרָה שֶׁבַּהֵיכָל

"Everything depends upon *mazal* even a Torah Scroll in the Temple" (*Zohar* IV, 134a).

Rabbi Yisrael Salanter cited the above dictum in his sharp criticism of some of his contemporaries who were ostensibly G-d fearing and learned, and yet failed to observe the laws of the *Choshen Mishpat* [business ethics] with proper care. "Everything depends upon *mazal*, even a Torah Scroll in the *Aron Kodesh*." "Similarly," he said, "the four divisions of the *Shulchan Aruch* [Code of Jewish Law] have also been subjected to varying fortunes; the *Orach Chaim* and *Yoreh De'ah* were accepted by the masses, while the *Choshen Mishpat* was neglected and forsaken" (Rabbi Dov Katz, *Tenuath HaMussar*, vol. 1).

Rabbi Joseph B. Soloveitchik once quoted the above dictum in reference to the popularity of *Chanukah* observance in America. What *mazal* this Festival has, simply because it occurs in the month of December!

Cf. *Shabbath* 156a, "Israel is immune from *mazal* [planetary influence]." See *Insights*, vol. 1, #43.

Cf. *Shabbath* 31a, "Did you conduct your business affairs with faith?" See #897.

⟦ 633 ⟧ הַלּוֹמֵד יֶלֶד לְמָה הוּא דּוֹמֶה? לִדְיוֹ כְּתוּבָה עַל נְיָיר חָדָשׁ

"He that studies as a child, to what may he be likened? To ink written on fresh paper" (*Aboth* 4:25).

"If one studies as an old man, to what may he be likened? To ink written on erased paper" (ibid.).

Rabbi Chaim of Volozhin comments that, nevertheless, the studies of an old man may leave some trace [even on erased paper] if *better ink* is used. Hence, with extra concentration and devotion to his studies, his Torah learning may also leave a lasting impression on his mind (*Ruach Chaim*, ad. loc.).

The Koritzer, Rabbi Pinchas Shapiro, asks: "Why discourage the older man? The dictum may, however, be interpreted in this fashion: 'One who learns as a child, namely as one who concentrates his thoughts on that which he is learning, and has no foreign thoughts at the time, is like ink written on fresh paper . . . . Thus, even an old man may learn as a child if he displays the necessary concentration" (*Nofeth Tzufim*, p. 58).

⟦ 634 ⟧   ... הֲלָכוֹת הֵן גּוּפָהּ שֶׁל תּוֹרָה
אַגָּדוֹת מוֹשְׁכוֹת לֵב הָאָדָם כַּיַּיִן

"Halachoth are the substance [the body] of the Torah . . . .
Aggadoth draw the heart of man as wine" (*Sifri, Ha'azinu* 32:14).

Rabbi Samuel Belkin writes: "The *halachah* concerns itself primarily with man's daily conduct and the rules of human behavior; it is above all an exposition and clarification of the positive and negative commands. *Aggadah* gives us the spiritual and moral insights of the *halachah*.

"In a sense, the *halachah* is the symbol of the body, for it deals with human actions and responsibilities . . . . The *aggadah* is the symbol of the soul. It appeals to the heart and emotions of man.

"*Halachah* endeavors to bring earth closer to Heaven; *aggadah* endeavors to bring Heaven closer to earth. *Halachah* deals with practice; *aggadah* primarily with theory.

"And yet, *halachah* and *aggadah* cannot stand as two separate and independent fields, just as body and soul cannot possess vitality if they are in separate abodes. The *aggadah* must serve as the soul of the *halachah*, and the two must supplement and complement each other" (*Essays in Traditional Jewish Thought*, p. 106).

⟦ 635 ⟧   הַמַּבְדִּיל עַל הַיַּיִן בְּמוֹצָאֵי שַׁבָּתוֹת [מִנּוּחֲלֵי
הָעוֹלָם הַבָּא]

"One who recites *havdalah* over wine at the termination of the Sabbath [is assured a portion in the World to Come]"
(*Pesahim* 113a).

The Gemara explains that this refers to one "who leaves over [wine] from *kiddush* for *havdalah*."

Rabbi Bernard Berzon offers a magnificent homiletical interpretation of the above talmudic passage. The recitation of *kiddush* which introduces the Sabbath every week, symbolically represents the periods of spiritual exaltation and holiness in our lives, whereas *havdalah* takes us back to the ordinary and routine — the mundane normalcy of our existence. There are numerous occasions in our lives when we catch a glimpse of the sublime, the true and the beautiful . . . . but how long do these moments last? The pity is, that instead of saving some of "the wine" of those extraordinary moments to give lingering flavor to our souls, we allow it to evaporate. If we could only retain a fraction of the joy and inspiration of those rare experiences and incorporate them into our daily routine, how much better off we would be. If we could but cling to those *kiddush* moments and retain a little wine for *havdalah*, how assured of the World to Come we would be! (*RCA Sermon Manual*, 1954 pp. 27–29).

The Maharal of Prague writes: "When a person leaves over [wine] from *kiddush* for *havdalah*, he demonstrates that the sanctity that he pronounces on *Shabbos* at its onset is what necessitates the [*havdalah*] separation at its conclusion. This stresses that *Shabbos* remains sanctified from the onset of its holiness until the end, and is thus *totally apart* [undiluted sanctity]. When a person is drawn to this sort of sanctity, he is worthy of the World to Come, which is *totally apart*" (*Nesivoth Olam, nesiv haTorah*, trans. by Eliakim Willner, p. 228).

〖 636 〗 הַמַּגְבִּיהַּ יָדוֹ עַל חֲבֵירוֹ אַף עַל פִּי שֶׁלֹּא הִכָּהוּ נִקְרָא רָשָׁע

"He who lifts his hand against his neighbor, even if he did not smite him, is called a wicked man" (*Sanhedrin* 58b).

"As it is written, 'And he said to the wicked one, "Why would you strike your fellow?"' [Ex. 2:13]. 'Why *did you* strike' is not said, but 'why would you strike,' showing that though he had not stricken him yet, he was termed a *rasha* [a wicked man]" [ibid.].

Rabbi Yehuda Loew of Prague writes: "Raising of the hand to deliver a blow is the beginning of the devious act against one's fellow . . . . If [however] one journeys far off in order to commit an evil deed — this is not a basic part of the purpose. The mere act of traveling is not intimately associated with deviation and evil. 'Raising of the hand' [on the other hand] to deliver a blow is an intrinsic expression of such deviation and is the essence of evil" (Maharal miPrague, *Gevuroth HaShem*, ch.19).

In this regard, it is interesting to note that in Common Law "an *attempt* to commit a crime may be described as an endeavor to do an act, carried beyond mere preparation but short of execution" (*Black's Law Dictionary*).

॥ 637 ॥ הַמְהַלֵּךְ בְּקוֹמָה זְקוּפָה אֲפִילוּ ד' אַמּוֹת כְּאִלּוּ דּוֹחֵק רַגְלֵי שְׁכִינָה

"He who walks with an upright stature, even a distance of four cubits, is as though he pushed against the feet of the Divine Presence" (*Berakoth* 43b).

Cf., *Kiddushin* 31a, "One is forbidden to walk four cubits with an upright stature."

The Talmud (*Berakoth*) lists as one of the six things which are a *genai* [unbecoming] for a scholar — "*to walk with an upright stature.*" In light of the *Gemara* in *Kiddushin*, why, we may ask, is it merely considered "unbecoming," is it not forbidden?

It is significant to note that on the verse, "And I will walk among you, and will be your G-d, and you shall be My people" (Lev. 26:12), the *Sifra* comments: "I will walk about with you in Paradise as one of you . . . ." The blessing concludes (v. 13), "And I made you walk upright," which the *Sifra* interprets as "*b'komah zekufah*" [with an upright stature]. This implies that when all the blessings will be fulfilled, then you will be able to walk with "an upright stature," for this cannot possibly entail "pushing against the Divine Presence" since the Almighty "will walk about with you" (*Chasam Sofer*).

In light of this explanation, it may be suggested that since the true scholar merits the blessing of "I made you walk upright," his walking with an "upright stature" would not be considered a form of arrogance at all. Nevertheless, since some people may attribute his demeanor to haughtiness, it would be a "*genai*" [unbecoming] for him to walk in this manner (S. W.)

638

הַמַּלְבִּין אֶת פְּנֵי חֲבֵירוֹ בָּרַבִּים אֵין לוֹ חֵלֶק
לעוה"ב

"He who publicly humiliates his fellow man has no portion in the World to Come" (*Baba Mezia* 59b).

"He commits the gravest of all sins against the dignity and nobility inherent in every human being by virtue of the fact that he was made in the image of G-d" (Rabbi Samson Raphael Hirsch, *Commentary on Aboth* 3:15).

Rabbi Yisrael Spira [the Bluzhever Rebbe] once visited a shul where a guest *chazan* began to repeat words of the prayers for the sake of cantorial style. This agitated the congregants, who pounded their fists and shouted that the man stop this practice. When *davening* was over, the *chazan* quickly left the shul. Said the Bluzhever Rebbe to the remaining congregants, "Our sages tell us that one who publicly shames his fellow man has no portion in the World to Come. Nowhere, however, is it said that one forfeits his portion for repeating words of the prayer text. I consider the outburst today a serious mistake" (Rabbi Shimon Finkelman, "The Bluzhever Rebbe," *The Jewish Observer*, 22, no. 10 [Teves 5750]:14-15).

Cf. *Baba Mezia* (ibid.), "He who publicly humiliates his fellow man is as though he shed blood." See *Insights*, vol. 1, #281.

Cf. (ibid.), "Better for a man to cast himself into a fiery furnace rather than shame his fellow in public" — See *Insights*, vol. 1, #423.

Cf. "One who elevates himself at the expense of his friend's degradation has no portion in the World to Come" (*Yerushalmi, Hagigah* 2:1).

⟦ 639 ⟧

הָמָן מִן הַתּוֹרָה מִנַּיִן?
שֶׁנֶּאֱמַר: "הֲמִן הָעֵץ . . .".

"Where is Haman indicated in the Torah? [In the verse] 'Is it
[*Hamin*] from the tree' [whereof I commanded you should not eat,
that you have eaten?]" [Gen. 3:11] (*Hullin* 139b).

The word "*hamin*" can be read *Haman*, and the tree alludes to the tree
upon which *Haman* was hanged" (*Rashi*).

Rabbi M. A. Amiel compares the transgression of eating the fruit of the
"Tree of Knowledge" with the phenomenon of anti-Semitism by utilizing the
talmudic phrase *ipcha mistavra* [the reverse is desirable] as the rationale for
both the "transgression" and anti-Semitism. He raises the obvious question
— how was it possible for Adam to succumb to an ordinary food temptation?
The answer, he suggests, is alluded to in the verse, "*Is it from the tree
whereof I commanded you should not eat* . . . ." Had there been no prohibition concerning this tree, Adam would have no desire to partake of it! Once,
however, the command was given, there stirred within him the perverse
passion of *ipchah mistavrah* — "I will do just the opposite"!

Haman, similarly, adopted this policy of *ipchah mistavrah* in his attitude
towards the Jews. Whatever the life-style of the Jews, Haman would
advocate "the reverse is desirable." Throughout the ages ant-Semitism
utilized this *hamanic* perversion. They always saw in the Jews the exact
opposite of what they deemed desirable. If gentiles were capitalists, the Jews
had to be communists. If they were communists, the Jews were capitalists.

This is alluded to in the dictum, "Where is Haman [the policy of *ipcha
mistavrah*] indicated in the Torah? In the verse '*Hamin ha'etz*' ['Is it from the
tree . . . ']." The root cause of anti-Semitism lies in seeing the Jews as acting
"contrary" [*Derashoth El-Ami*, vol. 3, pp. 148-151].

640

הַמְפַיְּסוֹ בִּדְבָרִים מִתְבָּרֵךְ בְּאַחַת עֶשְׂרֵה
בְּרָכוֹת

"He who addresses to him [a poor man] comforting words obtains eleven blessings" (*Baba Bathra* 9b).

"He who gives a coin to a poor man obtains six blessings" [ibid.].

"Whosoever gives charity to a poor man ill-manneredly and with downcast looks has lost all the merit of his actions, even though he should give him a thousand gold pieces. He should give with good grace and with joy, and should sympathize with him in his plight . . . . He should speak to him words of consolation and sympathy . . ." (*Mishneh Torah, Hil. Matnoth Aniyim* 10:4).

The Chafetz Chaim writes: "If one finds a friend depressed by his poverty or some other trouble, and one is, G-d forbid, unable to help him, it is still a *mitzvah* to speak sympathetically to him to allay his anxieties. All these acts fall in the category of *chesed*" (*Ahavath Chesed*, p. 225).

"A disciple of Rabbi Yisrael Salanter once saw his Rebbe conversing about mundane matters with a certain individual. Later, during a discussion on 'idle speech,' the disciple asked Reb Yisrael about that conversation. In his humility, Reb Yisrael was not offended by the question. He explained that the man with whom he was speaking was depressed and it was a great *chesed* to cheer him up. 'Now, how can I cheer him up? With talk of *mussar* and fear of G-d? The only way was with light, pleasant conversation about worldly matters'" (Rabbi Chaim E. Zaitchik, *HaMeoroth HaGedolim*).

641

הַמַּצְנִיעַ אֶת הַקּוֹץ וְאֶת הַזְּכוֹכִית . . . וְהוּזְּקוּ
בָּהֶן אֲחֵרִים, חַיָּב בְּנִזְקָן

"One who hides thorns or glass . . . and others are injured by them, he is liable for their injury" (*Baba Kamma* 30a).

"He hid them in a public domain" (R. Ovadiah of Bertinoro).

"A certain 'scholar' took a walk with Rabbi Yisrael Salanter and held his cane diagonally under his shoulder letting the bottom protrude. Reb Yisrael pointed out that what he was doing fell into the talmudic category of 'scattering one's thorns in the public domain' for which one is liable as a damaging agent in the category designated as 'pit.' The scholar pulled in the cane and held it vertically. A few minutes later he again placed his cane under his shoulder. Reb Yisrael was extremely provoked. He reproved the man and refused to continue walking with him.

"Similarly, he would reprimand his disciples for bending over their lecterns as they studied, since they would thereby be setting obstacles in a public domain" (Rabbi Dov Katz, *Tenuath HaMussar*, vol. 1).

I remember one of Reb Yaakov Kamenetsky's *shmuessen* in Mesivta Torah Vodaath concerning the prohibition of *bor birshus harabim* [allowing an obstacle to remain in a public place] by not removing a nail head protruding from a lectern in the *beis hamidrash* — an echo of Reb Yisrael Salanter (S. W.).

When Rav Leib Chasid of Kelm was at his *chupah*, after breaking the glass, he bent down to pick up the broken pieces, saying: "It is my obligation to clean up the pieces for I am the maker of this *bor* ['pit']" (*HaMeoroth HaGedolim*, p. 351).

At a wedding where Rabbi Shlomo Zalman Auerbach was officiating, an attendant began to decant a full cup of wine under the *chupah*, but Reb Shlomo Zalman interrupted him saying, "Personally, I don't mind if you are *machmir* [stringent], but you should not be stringent at the expense of the bride's gown" (Hanoch Teller, *and from Jerusalem His Word*, p. 127).

642 הַמַּשְׁמִיעַ קוֹלוֹ בִּתְפִלָּתוֹ הֲרֵי זֶה מִקְּטַנֵּי אֲמָנָה

"He who says his *Tefillah* [*Shemoneh Esrei*] so that it can be heard is of the small of faith" (*Berakoth* 24b).

"He acts as if the Holy One, blessed is He, does not hear prayer uttered in a soft voice" (Rashi).

See Rambam, *Mishneh Torah*, Hil. *Tefillah* 5:9 for exceptions to the above *halachic* ruling.

Rabbi Yehudah Loew b. Bezalel [Maharal miPrague] writes: "A person who prays too loudly has not arrived at the highest realm, the realm of the mystery. He has only a sense for the obvious and apparent, and whatever is apparent is not attached to the highest realm, for what is highest is hidden" (*Nesivoth Olam, nethiv ha'avodah*, ch. 2).

Rabbi Menachem Mendel of Kotzk, in commenting on the Torah given at Sinai amidst thunder and lightning, said: "The masses of the people seemed to be impressed with the externals of thunder and lightning but missed the deep meaning of the Torah . . . 'You may sway your body in prayer and still be removed from Torah'" (*Amud HaEmeth*, p. 24).

At the *Yeshiva* in Kelm, when people entered at certain times, they thought it was empty for there was total silence in the building. Upon further exploration, they saw the entire student body praying *Shemoneh Esrei*, standing straight, motionless, feet together, hands at sides, completely silent — yet praying with great intensity and concentration (Rabbi Hillel Goldberg, *The Fire Within*, p. 66).

The Vilna Gaon warned against crying or raising one's voice more than usual in the *Rosh Hashanah davening*. Both, he felt, were inconsistent with the day's status as a *Yom Tov* (Rabbi Betzalel Landau, *HaGaon HaChassid MiVilna*).

⫟ 643 ⫟

הַמִּתְכַּבֵּד בִּקְלוֹן חֲבֵרוֹ,
אֵין לוֹ חֵלֶק לָעוֹלָם הַבָּא

"One who elevates himself at the expense of his friend's degradation has no portion in the World to Come"
(*Yerushalmi, Hagigah* 2:1).

Cf, *Megillah* 28a, "Rabbi Nehunia b. haKaneh was asked by his disciples, 'In virtue of what have you reached a good old age?' He replied, 'Never in my life have I sought respect through the degradation of my fellow . . . .'"

In light of the above dictum, it may be prohibited for one to disparage his competitor's product, even when no misrepresentation of fact is made. "While a seller has the legitimate right to point out to everyone the fine qualities of his product, he has no right to point to the deficiencies of [lower-priced] rival models. This amounts to 'elevating himself at the expense of his friend's degradation'" (Rabbi Aaron Levine, *Journal of Halacha and Contemporary Society*, vol. 1, no. 2, p. 21).

Cf. *Baba Mezia* 59b, "He who publicly humiliates his fellow man has no portion in the World to Come." See #638.

⎰ 644 ⎱ הַמִּתְפַּלֵּל צָרִיךְ שֶׁיִּרְאֶה עַצְמוֹ כְּאִילוּ שְׁכִינָה כְּנֶגְדּוֹ

"He who prays should regard himself as if the *Shechinah* was before him, as it is written [Psalms 16:8], 'I have set G-d always before me'" (*Sanhedrin* 22a).

"I do not turn my thoughts away from Him, as if He were my right hand, which one does not forget for even the slightest moment" (Rambam, *Moreh Nevuchim*, III, chap. 51).

Rabbi Yitzchak Luria comments: "One should always imagine the letters of the Tetragrammaton ['Yud,' 'Kay,' 'Vav,' 'Kay'] before one's eyes — and this is the mystery of 'I have set G-d always before me'" (*Be'er Hetev, Orach Chaim*, 1:3).

The Baal Shem Tov derives the word "*shivi-si*" [I have set] from "*shaveh*" [equal] — thus *shivi-si* "I have made all things equal." In assessing the events of my life, I accept and appreciate everything which happens to me with complete detachment. It makes no difference whether it is "good" or "bad." Why? Because "*l'negdi thamid*" — "He is always before me" (R. Aaron of Opatov, *Kether Shem Tov*, p. 16b).

Cf. *Megillah* 28a, "He who passes by his measures [overcomes his natural tendencies], all his sins are passed by."

⎮ 645 ⎮

הַמִּתְפַּלֵּל צָרִיךְ שֶׁיִּתֵּן עֵינָיו לְמַטָּה
וְלִבּוֹ לְמַעְלָה

"Let him who prays cast his eyes downward, but his heart upward" (*Yebamoth* 105b).

"One should imagine in his heart that he is standing in Heaven. He must banish from his heart all worldly delights and bodily enjoyments" (Rabbeinu Yonah, *Commentary of Alfasi, Berakoth* 22b).

"This was the practice of the *chassidim* and men of deed. They would meditate and concentrate on their prayers until they reached a level where they divested themselves from the physical" (*Tur, Orach Chaim* 98:1).

Rabbi Yaakov Yosef of Polonoye applied the above dictum to the doctrine of "the descent of the *tzaddik*." He writes: "The *tzaddik* should cast his eyes down and concern himself with the simple folk — for they are downward — to join himself in prayer with them; but during this union he must 'turn his heart upward' in order to raise them . . . for the center of his prayer should not be for himself. Out of compassion, he should join himself to the common people, even though they may not know the meaning of the prayers" (*Kesoneth Pasim* 2c).

⎮ 646 ⎮

הַנִּפְטָר מִן הַמֵּת יֹאמַר לוֹ לֵךְ בְּשָׁלוֹם, הַנִּפְטָר
מִן הַחַי יֹאמַר לוֹ לֵךְ לְשָׁלוֹם

"One bidding farewell to the dead, should say to him, 'Go *in* peace'; one bidding farewell to the living, should say to him, 'Go *towards* peace'" (*Moed Katan* 29a).

Rabbi Moshe Avigdor Amiel explains that there is a semantic difference between the words *l'shalom* and *b'shalom*. "*Lech l'shalom* [go towards peace] connotes the striving towards that ultimate goal of achieving a lasting peace. One must utilize every effort in order to achieve that desired state of *shalom*!

"'*Lech b'shalom*' [go in peace], however, connotes an immediate and present state of peace. 'Peace now' is the cry, without any friction or strife in the process of achieving it. This 'Peace' ideal, in truth, can only be achieved by the dead — not the living" (*Derashoth El-Ami*, vol. 2, p. 210).

⟦ 647 ⟧ הַפִּשְׁתָּנִי הַזֶּה בְּשָׁעָה שֶׁהוּא יוֹדֵעַ שֶׁהַפִּשְׁתָּן
שֶׁלּוֹ יָפֶה, כָּל שֶׁהוּא כוֹתְשָׁהּ הִיא מִשְׁתַּבַּחַת

"When a flax worker knows that his flax is of good quality, the more he beats it the more it improves" (*Beraishith Rabbah* 32:3).

"If it is of inferior quality, he cannot give it one knock without its splitting" (ibid.).

Rabbeinu Yonah ben Avraham of Gerona comments: "G-d brings upon the wicked only afflictions of retribution. Afflictions of trial he brings only upon the righteous, who accept them with love, and improve their deeds. The afflictions are for their own good and benefit to increase their reward, as it is said: 'G-d tests the righteous' [Psalms 11:5]. Our sages of blessed memory have offered an analogy here. 'When a flax worker knows that his flax is of good quality . . . .'"

Ramban explains that G-d tests the righteous in order to extract the latent, potential powers of faith from their inner selves and to bring it forth to fruition. G-d Himself [obviously] knows what strength the righteous possess, but He wishes to let them know for themselves (*Sha'ar Hagmul*).

A perfect example of the above *mamor* is the life of the *Chazon Ish*. He wrote of himself: "Because of my fragile condition and the physical afflictions which have accompanied me from my youth until this day, all my in-depth learning must be accomplished through perseverance over suffering" (Rabbi Shimon Finkelman, *The Chazon Ish*, p. 132).

⎰ 648 ⎱

„הַצְנֵעַ לֶכֶת עִם אֱלֹקֶיךָ", זוֹ הוֹצָאַת הַמֵּת
וְהַכְנָסַת כַּלָּה לַחוּפָּה

"'To walk humbly with your G-d' (*Michah* 6:8), refers to attending
to funerals and dowering a bride for her wedding" (*Sukkah* 49b).

One's help in such matters should be given humbly and in privacy. The
phrase "to walk humbly with your G-d" is translated by Targum Yonathan
ben Uziel, "Be modest in walking with the fear of your G-d."

Rabbeinu Bachya comments: "Now, is this not a *kal v'chomer* [a fortiori]
conclusion? If the Torah tells us 'to walk humbly' in matters which are
ordinarily done overtly, how much more should we covertly perform matters
which are generally done in privacy! [Charity, for example, should be given
to the poor in secrecy so that the poor man should not be embarrassed by
anyone knowing about it.]" (*Kad Hakemach*, *Avel*, trans. by Rabbi C. B.
Chavel, p. 73).

⎰ 649 ⎱

הַקָּבָּ"ה הִנִּיחַ כָּל הָרִים וּגְבָעוֹת וְהִשְׁרָה
שְׁכִינָתוֹ עַל הַר סִינַי

"The Holy One, blessed be He, ignored all the mountains and
heights and caused His *Shechinah* to abide on Mount Sinai"
(*Sotah* 5a).

When the Almighty chose the mountain upon which to give the Torah to
Israel, He selected Mount Sinai, for it was the lowest of the mountains [it
was the most humble].

"If humility and lowliness are such great virtues," asks Rabbi Menachem
Mendel of Kotzk, "why didn't G-d choose a valley in which to give the
Torah?"

Says the Kotzker, "To be considered an 'undistinguished' valley and not
to boast about it, is not a remarkable characteristic. However, if one is
considered a mountain, and possesses the same virtues and distinctions of

which others boast, and yet does not behave with conceit and vainglory —
that is considered extraordinary humility" (Rabbi Ephraim Oratz, . . . *And
Nothing But the Truth*, p. 71).

Cf. *Sotah* 5a, "A man should always strive to emulate the ways of his
Maker." See *Insights*, vol. 1, #373.

See Rabbi Chaim Volozhin, *Ruach Chaim* on *Aboth* 4:1, "A man who has
no [outstanding] qualities at all, cannot be considered a humble person, even
if he humbles himself — for he has nothing to be proud of. On the other
hand, a person endowed with many admirable attributes, who nevertheless
is not aware of his merits, but is meek and unpretentious — that person can
be characterized as humble."

See #527.

⎗ 650 ⎗   הקב"ה מַבִּיט בַּתּוֹרָה וּבוֹרֵא אֶת הָעוֹלָם

"The Holy One, blessed be He, looked into the Torah and
[through its words] created the universe" (*Beraishith Rabbah* 1:1).

Rabbi Aharon Soloveitchik writes: "Just as science is expressive of the
physical laws of the universe, the Torah is the manifestation of the moral
laws of the universe."

He records in the name of his grandfather, Reb Chaim, that the deeper
meaning of the above dictum is "that the principles of the Torah harmonize
with the innate consciousness of every human being . . . . One could say
that when the Creator of the world revealed the Torah to the Jewish people,
He molded it to conform to the laws of nature . . . . But Reb Chaim said this
is incorrect. The Midrash comes to tell us that the reason there is harmony
between the principles of the Torah and human nature is because when G-d
created man, He created the world according to the moral pattern of the
Torah. The moral patterns of the Torah declared this categorical imperative
— 'You must not kill, you must not lead an immoral life, you must not
steal' — and because of that, the Creator of the world molded the human
psyche in accordance with the moral law of the universe. '*Torah kadmoh
l'vrias ha'olam*' or the moral law of the universe preceded the creation of the
world" (*Logic of the Heart, Logic of the Mind*, p. 40).

▯ 651 ▯ הַקָּבָּ"ה מְדַקְדֵּק עִם סְבִיבָיו כְּחוּט הַשַּׂעֲרָה

"The Holy One, blessed be He, deals strictly with those round
about Him even for matters as light as a thread of hair"
(*Baba Kamma* 50a).

"A stain on a precious garment is worse than on ordinary clothing. What
would not be considered a transgression for an ordinary person is considered criminal for a Torah scholar.

"A common person can do all sorts of improper things simply because he
doesn't know or understand, but the scholar knows well enough to beware
. . . In addition, there are many acts that when performed by a simple man
do not profane G-d's Name, while when performed by a scholar become
grave offenses" (Rabbi Sholom Dov Ber Schneersohn, *Kuntres Uma'ayon*).

Cf. *Sotah* 13b, "In accordance with the camel is the load." See *Insights*,
vol. 1, #379.

"The *Chovos HaLevovos* writes that the expectations of a man are relative
to his awareness. The more elevated a man is, the more he can grasp, the
greater the demand that he conduct himself in accordance with his understanding. Thus, there are specific sacrifices in the Torah for a leader who
sins. Because of his loftier conception of the world, his punishment is more
severe" (Rabbi Leib Chasman).

See, however, *Maharsha* (*Yebamoth* 121b) who comments that the
Almighty's apparent strictness is actually the opposite, for it enables punishment to be dispensed in a comparatively mild manner in this world, while
reserving perfect blessings for the World to Come.

⟦ 652 ⟧

„הַקּל קוֹל יַעֲקֹב", בִּזְמָן שֶׁקּוֹלוֹ שֶׁל יַעֲקֹב
מָצוּי בְּבָתֵּי כְנֵסִיּוֹת, אֵין הַיָּדַיִם יְדֵי עֵשָׂו,
וְאִם לָאו, הַיָּדַיִם יְדֵי עֵשָׂו

"'The voice is the voice of Jacob': When the voice of Jacob is heard
in the synagogues, the hands are not the hands of Esau; and
when [they are] not [heard], 'the hands are the hands of Esau'"
(Beraishith Rabbah 65:20).

Rabbi Meir Leibush b. Yechiel Michel comments: "'Hands' — physical
power and strength — was the portion of Esau; while 'voice' — the power
of the soul — was the portion of Jacob. G-d arranged the events [recorded
in the Torah] so that Jacob would also obtain the 'hands of Esau,' i.e.,
through the power of his soul (the voice of Jacob) he would merit physical
strength, wealth, power, and dominion. These benefits would not be derived
from nature, but would come from Divine Providence in merit of 'the voice
of Jacob' and study of the Torah. Hence, 'When the voice of Jacob is heard
in the synagogue, the hands are not the hands of Esau, i.e., then the hands
of Esau belong to Jacob. But when the voice of Jacob pauses through neglect
of Torah, 'the hands of Esau' do belong to Esau. Jacob can only obtain
'hands' through his 'voice' — his studying of the Torah" *(Malbim, HaTorah
VeHamitzvah,* [Gen. 27:22]).

⟦ 653 ⟧

„הַקּל קוֹל יַעֲקֹב", בְּשָׁעָה שֶׁהוּא מְצַפְצֵף
בְּקוֹלוֹ אֵין הַיָּדַיִם יְדֵי עֵשָׂו, אֵין יְדֵי עֵשָׂו
שׁוֹלְטוֹת

"'The voice is the voice of Jacob' — when his voice rings out clearly [with pride in his faith], the hands of Esau have no dominion"
(Beraishith Rabbah 65:20).

"The voice is the voice of Jacob and the hands are the hands of Esau"
[Gen. 27:22]. Says the Vilna Gaon, "At first glance the text would seem to

indicate that the voice of Jacob and the hands of Esau will prevail simultaneously, contrary to the interpretation of the Midrash. However, upon closer
examination, we discover a deeper meaning. In the verse, *KOL* [voice],
appears in the abbreviated form [it is spelled defectively], without a *vav*. As
such, it can also be read as *KAL* [unsteady or timid]. Consequently, it may
be interpreted in accordance with the Midrash. If the voice of Jacob is KAL,
i.e., wavering and half-hearted, then the hand of Esau will prevail. If, on the
other hand, the voice of Jacob is KOL, in its full form, resolute and vigorous,
then the hands of Esau are indeed powerless" (*Adereth Eliyahu*).

〔 654 〕 הַקִּנְאָה וְהַתַּאֲוָה וְהַכָּבוֹד מוֹצִיאִין אֶת הָאָדָם
מִן הָעוֹלָם

"Envy, lust, and thirst for honor remove a man from the world"
(*Aboth* 4:28).

"The vices listed here make selfish interest the sole purpose of him whom
they dominate, and so they cause him to clash with the rest of the world
. . . . Thus he forfeits the destiny for which G-d made him" (Rabbi Samson
Raphael Hirsch, *Chapters of the Fathers*, p. 74).

"Rabbi Yisrael Salanter's unique method of *mussar* study was designed to
elevate himself above all physical propensities. Once, while in Byalistock on
some communal mission, his host became aware that Reb Yisrael had
jumped from bed and had begun walking to and fro while repeating, 'Envy,
lust, and honor remove a man from the world.' Reb Yisrael explained his
conduct. The next day, he would have to go to the house of one of the local,
wealthy residents, to solicit a contribution for a public project. His concern
was that, upon being confronted by the wealth and luxury of the rich man's
house, he might become affected by feelings of envy and desire. Hence he
was studying *mussar* to immunize himself against such influences" (Rabbi
Dov Katz, *Tenuath HaMusar*, vol. 1).

The last words of Rabbi Yisrael Salanter, repeated by his bedside attendant, were, "Our sages say that envy, lust and honor remove *haAdam* (*the
man*) from the world. Do you know why the word 'man' appears with the

definite article, *the*, before it? Because even *the* man, that is the loftiest of men, is liable to fall into the trap of envy, lust and desire" (Rabbi Shalom Meir Wallach).

◊ 655 ◊ הַרְבֵּה לָמַדְתִּי מֵרַבּוֹתַי וּמֵחֲבֵרַי יוֹתֵר מֵרַבּוֹתַי, וּמִתַּלְמִידַי יוֹתֵר מִכּוּלָן

"I have learned much from my teachers, and from my colleagues more than from my teachers, and from my students more than from them all" (*Ta'anith* 7a).

When students ask probing questions, they stimulate the teacher to analyze his subject matter [his prepared lesson] and to search for insightful answers:

Rabbi Shimon Shkop suggested a theological explanation of the above maxim in addition to the above interpretation.

A person is granted wisdom not only for his own benefit, but also for the benefit of others. He is obligated to share his Torah knowledge with others. Hence, if he is a reliable transmitter of this knowledge to others, the Almighty will bestow even greater wisdom upon him, so that he may continue to share it (Intro. to *Sha'arei Yoshor*, cited by Rabbi Zelig Pliskin, *Love Your Neighbor*, p. 387).

◊ 656 ◊ הַרְבֵּה שְׁכֵנִים הָרָעִים עוֹשִׂין

"Bad neighbors do much" (*Sotah* 7a).

When a *Sotah* [a woman suspected by her husband of infidelity] was brought to the Great Court in Jerusalem, the Judges solemnly said to her: "My daughter, wine does much, frivolity does much, youth does much, *bad neighbors do much*" [i.e., there may be some excuse for your behavior — therefore, confess if you are guilty and so make the "ordeal" unnecessary].

"It is natural to be influenced, in sentiments and conduct, by one's neighbors and associates, and observe the customs of one's fellow citizens.

Hence, a person ought constantly to associate with the righteous and frequent the company of the wise, so as to learn from their practices, and shun the wicked who are benighted, so as not to be corrupted by their example" (*Mishneh Torah, Hil. Daioth* 6:1).

"When one finds himself in the company of coarse and lusting people who constantly pursue the wild dictates of their hearts, then he becomes so drawn [to their lifestyle], that he [eventually] becomes desensitized to his spiritual descent . . ." (Rabbi Yosef Yitzchak Schneersohn, *Chassidic Discourses*, vol. 2, p. 245).

Cf. *Aboth* 1:7, "Keep away from an evil neighbor, and do not associate with the wicked." See *Insights*, vol. 1, #191.

⟦ 657 ⟧ הָרוֹצֶה שֶׁיַּחְכִּים יַדְרִים וְשֶׁיַּעֲשִׁיר יַצְפִּין

"He who desires to become wise should turn to the south [while praying], and he who desires to become rich should turn to the north" (*Baba Bathra* 25b).

"The symbol [by which to remember this] is that the *shulchan* [the table in the Sanctuary] was to the north of the altar and the *menorah* [candlestick] to the south" [ibid.].

The *shulchan* is the symbol of wealth, while the *menorah* is the symbol of wisdom.

On the verse, "Awake, O north wind, and come, O south wind; blow [upon] my garden . . . [*Shir HaShirim* 4:16], the Midrash comments: "In the time to come, G-d will drive the two winds [north and south] together so that both will blow [simultaneously] (*Shir HaShirim Rabbah*).

The *Ein Eliyahu* interprets this Midrash in light of the dictum above. In the Messianic era, a debate will ensue between "the north" and "the south" winds regarding the question of ultimate redemption. "The north" [representing wealth] will proclaim, "Zion will be redeemed with justice and *tzedakah*" [Isaiah 1:27], i.e., through wealth distributed to the needy. "The south" [representing wisdom] will proclaim that only through it [Torah study] will redemption occur. The Almighty will then make peace between them and they will act in unison; i.e., both elements are needed for redemption, as the verse implies, "Awake O north wind, and come, O south wind; blow [upon] my garden . . ." (*L'kutei Bosar L'kutei, Chamesh Megilloth*, p. 31).

◊ 658 ◊

הַרְחֵק מִן הַכִּעוּר וּמִן הַדּוֹמֶה לוֹ

"Keep your distance from anything [morally] hideous and from anything that resembles it" (*Hullin* 44b).

Avoid doing anything which may give the appearance of impropriety. Witnesses who testified in a lawsuit concerning a certain article that was in dispute, may not subsequently purchase that article, for it has an appearance of wrongdoing.

Rabbi Eleazar ben Yehudah of Worms [*Baal HaRokeach*] points out that the letters of the word *shochad* [bribe], *shin, ches, daled,* are the same letters of the word *chashad* [suspicion], *ches, shin, daled.* This alludes to the ruling that a judge in Israel must not take *shochad,* a bribe, not only when he is sitting in judgment, but he must always conduct himself in an exemplary and modest manner. In this way, he will never be under *chashad,* suspicion of transgressing the prohibition of "You shall not take *shochad*" [Deut. 16:19]. This is an application of keeping one's distance [not only] from anything hideous, [but also] from whatever seems like it (*Parpera'ot La'Torah,* vol. 5, p. 120).

"When Rabbi Nosson Zvi Finkel (The Alter of Slobodka) felt compelled to accept money from the yeshiva [for the most part he did not draw a salary], he traveled to Brisk to ask Rabbi Chaim Soloveitchik whether he was permitted to accept a stipend, and if so, how much. More than that amount he refused to accept, even if a member of his family needed money for clothing" (Rabbi Chaim E. Zaitchik, *HaMeoroth HaGedolim*).

◊ 659 ◊

הָרָשׁוּת מְקַבֶּרֶת אֶת בְּעָלֶיהָ

"Authority [power] buries those who possess it" (*Yoma* 86b).

This refers to the abuse of authority, not its legitimate use. Rabbi Nachman of Breslov explains: "There are some whose authority extends over their own household. Others have a wider influence — each according to his level. A person must always take care to use his authority and influence, not for his own personal benefit, but for the sake of G-d alone . . . . A person who is negligent about guiding those who are under his influence will be punished because of them . . . . This is what the sages meant when they said, 'Authority buries those who possess it.' But those who use their authority to offer guidance and moral criticism and draw people closer to G-d, will be blessed with long life and vitality" (Rabbi Nathan of Breslov, *Likutei Etzoth*).

Cf. *Pesahim* 87b, "Woe to lordship which buries its possessor."

Cf. *Berakoth* 55a, "One of three things which shorten a man's life is 'one who assumes airs of authority.'" See *Maharsha*, who differentiates between legitimate authority and the illegitimate arrogation of authority upon oneself.

Cf. *Pesikta Rabbthi*, "Whoever assumes *s'rara* [authority] to derive benefit from it, is no better than an adulterer."

⎰ 660 ⎱   הַשּׁוֹנֶה וְאֵינוֹ עָמֵל כְּזוֹרֵעַ וְאֵינוֹ קוֹצֵר

"One who studies [Torah] and does not toil in it, is like one who sows but does not reap" (*Toseftah Ohaloth* 16:4).

"If in My statutes you shall walk . . ." [Lev. 26:3] — "You shall toil in [the study of] the Torah" (*Sifra*).

"Toiling" in the study of Torah applies specifically to the Oral Law, as indicated in the following Midrash. "Israel did not accept the Torah until the Holy One, blessed be He, overturned the mountain upon them like an [inverted] cask" [*Shabbath* 58a]. "You cannot say that G-d overturned the mountain [threatening to destroy them] if they would not accept the Written Law, for as soon as G-d asked them if they would accept the Torah they responded, 'Na'aseh V'Nishmah' [We will do and we will hearken] — because there is no toil and hardship [in the Written Law] and it is brief" (*Midrash Tanchuma, Noach*).

Hence, inasmuch as there is "toil and hardship" in the Oral Law, Israel was reluctant to accept it. The term "*amalus b'Torah*" [toiling in Torah] only applies to the Oral Law.

Cf. *Sanhedrin* 99a, "Whoever studies the Torah and does not review it, is likened to one who sows without reaping."

⧫ 661 ⧫
הַשָּׂח שִׂיחַת חוּלִין עוֹבֵר בַּעֲשֵׂה
"One who engages in casual [lit. profane] conversation transgresses a positive command" (*Yoma* 19b).

"For it is written, 'And you shall speak of them' [Deut. 6:7] 'of them,' but not of other matters" (ibid.).

Cf. *Avodah Zarah* 19b, "Even the casual conversation of scholars demands study." See *Insights*, vol. 1, #83.

"Rabbi Eliyahu Eliezer Dessler relates an anecdote to illustrate this. When his great-grandmother, Esther, was married to the renowned saint, Rav Yisrael Salanter, the groom made the following arrangement for the management of their home. He would have complete authority in spiritual matters while she would dictate all worldly decisions. Grandmother Esther laughed when recalling this suggestion and said that for a holy man of Rav Yisrael's caliber, even the most mundane things are used in the performance of commandments and are thus transformed into spiritual concerns. Thus, Rav Yisrael had the final word over everything!" (Rabbi Avraham Chaim Feuer, *ArtScroll Tehillim*, vol. 1, p. 63. See *Insights*, vol. 1, #83.

וֹ

[] 662 []

וּבָהּ תֶּחֱזֶה

"And through it [the Torah] you will see" (*Aboth* 5:19).

"Turn it this way, turn it that way, everything is in it, *and* through it you will see [ibid.].

Rabbi Shraga Feivel Mendelowitz would constantly emphasize to his students the importance of "Torah spectacles." "The Almighty," he explained, "has given man two modes of study, to observe, meditate, and learn of his Creator: Nature and History. On the one hand, Scripture bids us 'read' nature and discern the Divine hand behind it. 'Lift up your eyes on high and see, who created these?' [Isaiah 40:26]. Similarly, we are bidden to 'read' history. 'Remember the days of old, understand the years of each generation' [Deut. 32:7].

"The tragedy of modern man, however, is that his vision is defective, distorted by a miasma of sin and arrogance. Many examine the sky and see cold empty space; many study history and see only the rule of naked power. Therefore, the Almighty gave man a Torah: *'through it shall you see.'* Once he puts on his 'Torah spectacles,' man can discern the unmistakable hand of a Creator in the starry skies and in human history" (Irving M. Bunim, *Ethics From Sinai*, vol. 3, p. 240).

See *Insights*, vol. 1 #185.

⦗ 663 ⦘

„וֶהְיֵה בְּרָכָה", קְרֵי בֵּהּ בְּרֵכָה —
מַה בְּרֵכָה זוֹ מְטַהֶרֶת אֶת הַטְמֵאִים אַף אַתְּ
מְקָרֵב רְחוֹקִים וּמְטַהֲרָם לַאֲבִיהֶם שֶׁבַּשָּׁמַיִם

"'And you shall be a *berachah* [blessing],' read it *bereichah* [pool]:
just as a pool purifies the unclean, so do you bring near [to Me]
those who are afar and purify them to their Father in Heaven"
(*Beraishis Rabbah* 39:11).

The Almighty assures Abraham: "I will make of you a great nation, and
I will bless you; I will make your name great, and you shall be a blessing"
[Gen. 12:2].

Rabbi Avraham Schreiber comments on the above midrashic rendering of
bereichah for *berachah*. Our sages tell us that it was Abraham's custom to
invite strangers to eat with him and then to give thanks to the Almighty for
His bounty. In this way Abraham was able to gain converts to his belief in
One G-d. This, then, is the meaning of the Midrash — do not read "and you
shall be a blessing," i.e., you shall only be a blessing for others in having
them benefit from your generosity, but through your *chesed* you will ultimately serve as a "a pool" in purifying the unclean — the unbelievers. Hence
his *berachah* will act as a *bereichah* in bringing others closer to the Almighty
(*Ksav Sofer*).

⦗ 664 ⦘

„וְהִנֵּה טוֹב מְאֹד", זֶה יֵצֶר רָע

"'And behold, it was very good' [Gen. 1:31] — this refers to the
Evil Inclination" (*Beraishith Rabbah* 9:7).

"Can then the Evil Inclination be very good? That would be extraordinary!
But for the Evil Inclination, however, no man would build a house, take a
wife and beget children" (ibid.).

The Vilna Gaon comments: "Man is given the Evil Inclination in order to
make it fragrant (to turn bitterness into sweetness). The Evil Inclination is
called 'very good.' Something that was always good is 'good'; but some-

thing which became good from evil is 'very good'" (Rabbi Yissachar Dov Rubin, *Oros Hagra*).

The challenge in confronting the Evil Inclination, in itself, serves as a source for good. This is poignantly illustrated in a letter written by Rabbi Yitzchok Hutner to one of his former students who was "plagued" by his Evil Inclination.

Rabbi Hutner, in affectionate terms, writes to him: "My cherished one, I clasp you to my heart, and whisper in your ear . . . with your letter telling of slumps and falls and obstacles, I say that I have received a very good letter from you. Your spirit is storming as it aspires to greatness. I beg of you, do not portray for yourself great men as being at one with their *Yetzer Tov* [Good Inclination]. Picture rather their greatness in terms of an awesome war with every base and low inclination.

"When you feel the turmoil of the *Yetzer hara* within yourself, know that with that feeling you resemble great men far more than with the feeling of deep peace, which you desire. In those very areas where you feel yourself failing most frequently — particularly in those areas — do you have the greatest potential for serving as an instrument of distinction for the honor of G-d" (*Pachad Yitzchok*).

Cf. *Beraishith Rabbah*, "In the copy of R. Meir's Torah it was found written, 'And behold, it was very good' — and behold *tov maveth* (death was good)." See #594.

◊ 665 ◊

וַוי לָן דְּמִיתְנַן וַוי לָן דְּמִיתְנַן

"Woe to us for we are dying, woe to us for we are dying!"
(*Berakoth* 31a).

This plaintive expression of human mortality was uttered by Rabbi Hamnuna Zuta during a wedding feast.

In commenting on this declaration, Rabbi Moshe Feinstein writes: "At the conclusion of a wedding-feast we vividly sense our mortality. We realize that we are dying every moment and that our bodies are nothing but vanity of vanities, for we know that this great *simcha* [the wedding feast] will not last till tomorrow. Rabbi Hamnuna therefore expresses himself in the present tense, 'We are dying,' implying that all of life is vanity" (*Darash Moshe*, p. 383).

The *Alter of Kelm* (Rav Simcha Zissel Ziv pointed out that an awareness of death can be an exhilarating incentive to realize the spiritual potential in every moment. "That," said the *Alter*, "was why R. Hamnuna Zuti entertained the guests at the wedding feast by singing, 'Woe to us for we are dying . . . .' This chant was not a dirge, but rather a joyous challenge to the couple to enhance their true *simchah*" (Rabbi Zev Leff, *Outlooks and Insights*, p. 37).

Cf. *Erubin* 54a, "The world from which we must depart is like a wedding feast." See *Insights*, vol. 1, #439.

⬇ 666 ⬇

וְוִיתֵּר הַקָּדוֹשׁ בָּרוּךְ הוּא לְיִשְׂרָאֵל עַל עֲבוֹדַת
כּוֹכָבִים וְעַל גִּילוּי עֲרָיוֹת וְעַל שְׁפִיכַת דָּמִים,
עַל מָאֳסָם בַּתּוֹרָה לֹא וִיתֵּר

"The Holy One, blessed be He, overlooked [was tolerant of] idolatry, immorality and bloodshed; but He would not overlook the deliberate neglect of the Torah" (*Yerushalmi, Hagigah* 1:7).

"Why was this sin so much worse? The only reason is that the Torah is an elixir of life for us. Without it, authentic Jewish life is not possible. Whoever draws away from the Torah draws away from life. Is it possible, then, for a father to see his son swallowing poison and he should keep still?

"This is why the Holy One will not overlook or tolerate the neglect of Torah, because that neglect shortens our life" (Chafetz Chaim, *P'ninim Y'karim*).

Rabbi Elchonon Wasserman explained the above dictum by way of a parable: "In war, even a great victory cannot be considered decisive, so long as the losing army still retains its arms. However, when one side has been disarmed, then the war is surely over. There is only one weapon with which to fight the ways and wiles of the Evil Inclination — the Torah. Even if the Jewish people are guilty of serious sins . . . there is still hope that they would repent, as long as they cling to the study of Torah . . . . However, when the study of Torah has been abandoned, the sole weapon against the *Yetzer hara* has been lost."

Reb Elchonon quoted the Chafetz Chaim, "'The *Yetzer hara* does not mind if a Jew fasts and sheds tears and prays all day long — as long as he doesn't study Torah'" (Rabbi Shimon Finkelman, "Reb Elchonon Wasserman," *The Jewish Observer* 24, no. 8 [Kislev 5752]:10).

▯ 667 ▯

„וְחַנֹּתִי אֶת אֲשֶׁר אָחֹן",
אַף עַל פִּי שֶׁאֵינוֹ הָגוּן

"'And I will be gracious to whom I will be gracious' [Ex. 33:19], although he may not deserve it" (*Berakoth* 7a).

"G-d showed Moshe all the treasures in which the rewards of the righteous are stored away . . . . Later he [Moshe] saw a huge treasure and inquired: 'Whose is this great treasure?' G-d said to him . . . 'Unto him who does not have [good deeds to his credit] I supply freely and I help him from this pile . . . '" (*Shemoth Rabbah* 45:6).

Rabbi Moshe Cordovero comments: "There are people who are unworthy and yet the Holy One, blessed be He, has mercy upon them . . . . There is a storehouse of grace from which He graciously dispenses free gifts to them, for He says: 'Their fathers had merit and I have made an oath to the Patriarchs that even when their children will be unworthy, they will be shown grace . . . .'

"So, too, should man behave. Even when he meets with the wicked he should not behave cruelly towards them nor insult them, but he should have mercy upon them, saying: 'Are they not, after all, children of Abraham, Isaac and Jacob? If they are not worthy, their fathers were worthy . . . .' Thus he should conceal their shame and improve them as much as is in his power" (*Tomer Devorah* XII).

▯ 668 ▯

"וַיַּחֲלֹם וְהִנֵּה סֻלָּם", זֶה סִינַי, אוֹתִיּוֹת דְּדֵין
הוּא אוֹתִיּוֹת דְּדֵין

"'And he dreamed, and behold a ladder' [Gen. 28:12] — this is
[symbolizing] *Sinai*, the letters of this [*sulam*-ladder] are [equivalent
to] the letters of this [*Sinai*] (*Beraishis Rabbah 68:12*).

"And he [Jacob] dreamed, and behold a ladder set upon the earth, and
the top of it reaching to heaven . . ." [Gen. 28:12]. The Midrash points to
the same *gematria* [numerical value] of the words *sulam* [ladder] and *Sinai* —
130. The *Baal HaTurim* adds that mamon [money], likewise, has the *gematria*
of 130.

The *Pardes Yosef* comments that the "ladder reaching up to heaven" can
be ascended either through personal and direct involvement in Torah study
[*Sinai*] or by subsidizing, supporting and providing for Torah scholars
[*mamon-tzedakah*]. There is an equation between the Sinai Jew and the *mamon*
Jew as long as they are both motivated by *sulam* — establishing a "metaphysical ladder" on the earth which extends towards heaven (*L'kutei Bosar L'kutei*)
Midrash, vol. 1, p. 183).

▯ 669 ▯

„וַיֵּלְכוּ וַיָּבֹאוּ" . . . מַקִּישׁ הֲלִיכָה לְבִיאָה,
מַה בִּיאָה בְּעֵצָה רָעָה,
אַף הֲלִיכָה בְּעֵצָה רָעָה

"'And they went and came' [Num. 13:26] . . . . It compares the
going to the coming back: as the coming back was with evil
design, so the going was with evil design" (*Sotah* 35a).

When they were first selected, however, the leaders of the tribes [who
were subsequently designated as the *meraglim* (spies) in a pejorative sense]
were distinguished and honorable men . . . . See Rashi, Num. 13:3, "At that
time they were all *kosher* [honorable]." But something happened as soon as
they arrived in the Promised Land. What was it that caused them to speak

evil about the Land?

Rabbi Yosef Chaim Sonnenfeld explains: "When these great men came to *Eretz Yisrael*, a spirit of prophecy rested upon them, and they peered into the future and saw all the generations that were destined to live there. In their vision, they also saw all those generations that would sin . . . and they were shaken by what they saw. 'If so,' they reasoned, 'it would be better to remain in the wilderness and not enter Israel.' That is the meaning of their statement, 'It is a land that consumes its inhabitants' [Num. 13:32]. For the holiness of the land cannot tolerate those who violate the precepts of holiness, and the land will ultimately expel them . . . . If so, better not to enter the Land.

"To this, Joshua and Caleb responded: 'The Land is exceedingly good . . . we will surely go up and take possession of it.' In spite of everything, it is incumbent upon us to go up and take possession of the Land and to withstand all tests . . . . Thus, the sin of the spies was that they should not have allowed their reasoning to contradict G-d's command and promise" (Rabbi Hillel Dansinger, *Guardian of Jerusalem*, p. 234).

❏ 670 ❏

„וּלְעָבְדוֹ בְּכָל לְבַבְכֶם, " אֵיזוֹ הִיא עֲבוֹדָה
שֶׁהִיא בַּלֵּב, הֲוֵי אוֹמֵר זוֹ תְּפִלָּה

"'To serve Him with all your heart.' What is Service of the Heart?
You must say, it is 'Prayer'" (*Ta'anith* 2a).

"Prayer" specifically refers to the *Shemoneh Esrei*. This is designated as "Service of the Heart," although the central core of this prayer contains thirteen personal requests. Rabbi Yaakov Lorberbaum of Lisa explains: "We have created a universal liturgy so that all Jews will *daven* from essentially the same *siddur*. The only thing that will differentiate between them is the intent of the heart. The egocentric person who lives to serve his own needs will read these thirteen requests and think only of his personal welfare. However, the Jew who views Divine service as his *raison d'etre* will arouse his heart to inject deeper meaning into the words of his prayer. He will, for example, ask G-d to heal his ailments so that he may serve his Master vigorously, in robust health. He will plead with G-d for a livelihood, so that he will have the financial security to fully observe His commandments. Prayer is called 'Service of the Heart' because in his heart the supplicant's attitude should be to serve G-d, not himself" (*Emes L'Yaakov; Aggadoth, Rosh Hashanah,* cited by Rabbi Avraham Chaim Feuer, *Shemoneh Esrei,* p. 89).

⟦ 671 ⟧

„וּלְצִיּוֹן יֵאָמַר אִישׁ וְאִישׁ יֻלַּד בָּהּ" . . . .
אֶחָד הַנּוֹלָד בָּהּ וְאֶחָד הַמְצַפֶּה לִרְאוֹתָהּ

"'But of Zion it can be said, man and man was born there' . . . [Psalms 87:5]. Both he who was born there and he who looks forward to seeing it" (*Kethuboth* 75a).

"Two types of people can be called Children of Zion: both the person who was actually born there and the non-native who always yearned to live there.

"At the time of the British mandate over Palestine, the authorities were very strict about illegal immigration. However, if a Jew declared that he had been born in Palestine, then he would be given permission for reentry.

"A group of desperate Jews contacted Rav Yosef Chaim Sonnenfeld. They were foreign born, but the only way for them to enter *Eretz Yisroel* was by declaring themselves to be born there. Rav Sonnenfeld permitted them to make their declaration, and he explained: 'The Talmud teaches that both the man born in Zion and the man who yearns to live there, equally deserve to be called Children of Zion [both are designated as being "born there"]'" (*Ha'ish al HaChomah,* vol. II, p. 154; ArtScroll, *Tehillim,* vol. 4, p. 1087).

In commenting on the above dictum, Rabbi Aharon Soloveitchik writes: "That concept is the moral basis for *hok ha-shvut,* the Law of Return. How is it that the Law of Return in Israel, to the effect that every Jew is entitled to enter Israel and settle there, is not considered chauvinistic, even though it discriminates between Jew and non-Jew? The answer is implicit in the *halacha* of '*ulTzion ye'amar ish v'ish*' [of Zion it shall be said, this man and that . . .]. In succinct terms, there are two kinds of people in Zion who are recognized as *benei Tzion* [citizens of Zion]: one who is actually born there, and the other who yearns to see it" (*The State of Israel: A Torah Perspective*).

❘ 672 ❘ „וְנִקְּתָה וְנִזְרְעָה זָרַע," מְלַמֵּד שֶׁאִם הָיְתָה
עֲקָרָה נִפְקֶדֶת

"'She will remain unharmed and shall conceive seed' [Num. 5:28]
— this teaches that if she had been barren, she now conceives"
(*Berakoth* 31b).

In the chapter concerning the *sotah* [the suspected adulteress], we read:
If the woman is pure and has not been defiled to her husband, she will
remain unharmed and shall conceive seed [will become pregnant]." One of
our sages comments, "If she had been barren, she now conceives." Another
sage maintains that this verse teaches that "if she usually gave birth in pain,
she will now give birth with ease." See also *Sotah* 26a.

Rabbi Eliyahu Lopian comments, "At any rate, both [R. Yishmael and R.
Akiva] agree that the *sotah* profited from the experience. The question arises,
'Why does she deserve a reward? We have here a woman whose husband
warned her not to be alone with a certain man. Paying no attention to his
warning, she secluded herself with him and behaved in a licentious manner.
Why, then, does an immodest woman, as she is, deserve a reward?'

"For a correct understanding we must view this woman's actions from a
different perspective. By secluding herself with this man in defiance of her
husband's warning, we must conclude that she was compelled by an uncon-
trollable erotic drive. This being so, why did she not commit the sinful act
itself? There can be only one explanation. That in the final moment she
overcame her passion 'and remained pure'! It is for subduing her inclination
that she merited a heavenly reward" (*Lev Eliyahu*, chap. 53).

〖 673 〗

„וְעָשִׂיתִי לְךָ שֵׁם גָּדוֹל כְּשֵׁם הַגְּדוֹלִים" . . .
זֶהוּ שֶׁאוֹמְרִים "מָגֵן דָּוִד"

"'And I shall make you a great name, equal to the names of the
greatest . . .' [II Sam. 7:9], this is why we say 'Magen David'"
[Shield of David] (Pesahim 117b).

We conclude the blessings of the Haftarah with the words "Magen David."
Magen David is popularly known as "the Star of David" and is regarded
as a symbol of Judaism, although there is no mention of this symbol in any
authoritative Jewish source. Nonetheless, Rabbi Moshe Feinstein believes
that the source for this sign as a symbol of Judaism is David himself. He
states: "It is clear that David did not find security in battle from any armor
or shield. Only in G-d did he find himself securely enveloped from every
side — above and below, east, west, north, south — six directions in all.
Thus the six-pointed symbol stands for David's true shield — G-d! For this
reason, this symbol — hallowed by centuries of traditional usage — should
be respected, because it is meant to symbolize the eternal Jewish faith in G-d
no matter what the adversity" (Igroth Moshe, Orach Chaim, vol. 3, Res. 15).

〖 674 〗

וְצִוָּנוּ עַל הָעֲרָיוֹת וְאָסַר לָנוּ אֶת הָאֲרוּסוֹת
וְהִתִּיר לָנוּ אֶת הַנְּשׂוּאוֹת עַל יְדֵי חוּפָּה
וְקִידּוּשִׁין

". . . And has commanded us regarding forbidden unions; Who
forbade betrothed women to us and permitted women who are
married to us through chuppah and kiddushin" (Kethuboth 7b).

This is the central portion of the birkath erussin [the blessing recited at the
marriage ceremony].
Rabbi Asher ben Yechiel [Rosh] writes: "Some people raise the question
concerning the formula of this blessing. Why don't we say, instead, '. . .
who has commanded us with His commandments and commanded us

l'kadesh [to consecrate] a wife'? Moreover, where do we find such a blessing [as the above] pertaining to what the Almighty has forbidden us? We do not recite a blessing, '. . . who has forbidden us to eat the limb of a live animal and has permitted us to eat meat from an animal slaughtered by means of *shechitah.*' Furthermore, why mention forbidden unions at such an occasion?"

Says the Rosh: "This blessing was not instituted for the fulfillment of a mitzvah — for the fulfillment of the mitzvah [of marriage] is in *'being fruitful and multiplying.'* This is proven by the fact that this blessing is recited even at the wedding of a couple that is past child-bearing age . . . . This blessing was instituted in order to give praise to G-d, Who sanctified us with His *mitzvoth* and separated us from the other nations, and commanded us to consecrate a woman whom we are permitted to marry and not one who is forbidden to us" (*Kethuboth* 1:12).

675

‎„וְרָאִיתָ אֶת אֲחֹרָי" . . . . מְלַמֵּד שֶׁהֶרְאָה
‎הַקָּדוֹשׁ בָּרוּךְ הוּא לְמֹשֶׁה קֶשֶׁר שֶׁל תְּפִילִין

"'And you shall see My back' [Ex. 33:23]; this teaches that the Holy One, blessed be He, showed Moshe the knot of the *tefillin*" (*Berakoth* 7a).

See *Berakoth* 6a for the theological significance of G-d's *tefillin*.

Rabbi Avraham Chaim of Zlotchov interprets "My back" as "what is behind Me," i.e., the Almighty imparted to Moshe this most important message, that even if Israel descends to the status of being "behind Me" [alienated from Me], My love for them will always be "tightly bound" [thus the reference to the "knot" of His *tefillin*].

The Chasam Sofer comments, that we can understand the true purpose of historical events only after they take place. This is implied in the verse, "And you shall see My back" [lit. *after Me*] (*Torath Moshe*, Ex. 33:23).

This may be illustrated by the following incident. A young man came to the Chafetz Chaim requesting a *bracha* [blessing] so that he would be exempted from the draft in Czarist Russia. The Chafetz Chaim [uncharacteristically] refused the request and said: "*Siz git tzu kenen shison*" [It's good to know how to shoot]. The young man was aghast at this response and, indeed, was drafted into the army. Thirty years later, this "young man" escaped from the Warsaw Ghetto and was captured by Russian partisans in the forest who intended to shoot him. He told them that he could help them fight the Germans. The partisans laughed and said they were not interested in training some Jew how to shoot — He told them that he was already trained and showed them that he knew how to use a rifle. With G-d's help he survived the war, always remembering the prophetic words of the Chafetz Chaim, "Siz git tzu kenen shison" (Rabbi Fischel Schecter).

The knot of G-d's *tefillin* signifies our eternal attachment to the Almighty, though we may not perceive His Providential involvement in our lives until much later on.

⌠ 676 ⌡

עֲשׂוּ . . . . "וּשְׁמַרְתֶּם אֶת מִשְׁמַרְתִּי״
מִשְׁמֶרֶת לְמִשְׁמַרְתִּי

"'You shall keep My charge' [Lev. 18:30]; provide a charge to My charge" (*Yebamoth* 21a).

Protect yourselves from anything that might cause you to neglect your duty to guard the Law against violation.

Rabbi Samson Raphael Hirsch explains: "This means that we are urged to be most punctilious to shun not only any act forbidden by the Law, but also any act that, because of its similarity to — or other association with — a forbidden act, could bring us to commit the violation itself . . . . This is the Jewish concept of punctilious observance, which is subsumed under the rabbinic terms *geder* [fence] and *se'yag* [hedge], making a fence or a hedge around the law, and which is expressed by the formula: 'Keep your distance from anything [morally] hideous and from anything that resembles it' (*Hullin* 44b), or as it is stated in *Shabbath* 13a: 'Take a circuitous route, O Nazirite, do not come close to the vineyard.'

"Thus, when the sages, in their profound insight into human nature . . . were led to enact such *gezeiroth* in order to safeguard the observance of the laws, they were simply enacting into law precautions which any sensible, conscientious Jew should adopt on his own as a habit to govern his personal life" (*The Pentateuch*, Lev. 18:30, p. 450).

Cf. *Aboth* 1:1, "Make a hedge about the Torah." See *Insights*, vol. 1, #447. See #658.

ז

⎰ 677 ⎱ זוּזָה לְעָלְלָא לָא שְׁכִיחָא לִתְלֵיתָא שְׁכִיחַ

"Money for purchasing grain is not to be found. [Money]
'suspended' can be found" (*Hagigah* 5a).

Help rendered when needed for ordinary affairs is generally not provided.
It is only *"tilesah"* — "suspended," i.e., food is suspended in a basket — only
for an emergency (*Rashi*).

Tosafoth translates *"tilesah"* — "when one is about to be hanged," i.e., a
man is threatened with execution unless he offers a ransom; being poor, a
small ransom would be accepted. But now the arrangement of a mortgage
is offered him; this serves only to aggravate his misfortune, for the ransom
price is raised.

It is a sad commentary that many of us are not motivated to maintain and
support Yeshivoth until there is an emergency which threatens the very life
of these noble institutions. These financial crises very often could have been
avoided had we provided the necessary day to day provisions to maintain
our citadels of Torah.

▯ 678 ▯

„זֶה סֵפֶר תּוֹלְדוֹת אָדָם", מְלַמֵּד שֶׁהֶרְאָהוּ
הַקָּדוֹשׁ בָּרוּךְ הוּא דּוֹר דּוֹר וְדוֹרְשָׁיו,
דּוֹר דּוֹר וַחֲכָמָיו

"'This is the book of the generations of Adam . . .' — this teaches
us that the Holy One, blessed be He, showed him [Adam] every
generation and its leaders, every generation and its sages"
(*Sanhedrin* 38b).

When Rabbi Naftali Linsker was invited by the town of Ropshitz to be its
Rav, he said: "We are told that the Almighty showed Adam every generation and its leaders . . . . This seems strange — why did the Almighty feel
it necessary to show Adam not only its leaders, but also the people of the
generation?"

Said the Ropshitzer: "Had *Hashem* shown Adam that Naftali was acting
as a Rav of a congregation, Adam would have fainted away. However, G-d
first showed Adam the generation, and for such a generation, even Naftali
can be a Rav and leader" (Shmuel Himmelstein, *A Touch of Wisdom, A Touch
of Wit*, p. 164).

Cf. *Arakhin* 17a, "As the leader, so the generation." See *Insights*, vol. 1,
#140.

Cf. *Rosh Hashanah* 25b, "Yiftach in his generation was like Shmuel in his
generation." See #708.

▯ 679 ▯

זְרוֹק חֲטְרָא לַאֲוִירָא וְעַל עִקָּרָה הוּא קָאֵם

"Throw a stick in the air and it will fall back to its source"
(*Beraishith Rabbah* 53:15).

Thus, Hagar [Sarah's handmaid] did not take a wife for her son Ishmael
from the house of Abraham [where she lived], but from a faraway land —
in Egypt — for she was, after all, an Egyptian.

Rabbi Eliyahu Lopian cites the question raised in *Pirke de Rabbi Eliezer* concerning the whereabouts of the descendants of Eliezer of Damascus [Abraham's faithful servant] — what happened to them? The Talmud tells us that Eliezer ruled over [controlled] the Torah of his master [Abraham] and he "drew and gave drink to others of his master's teachings" [*Yoma* 28b]. The answer given is, "If you throw a stick in the air, it falls back to its source." Just as when one throws a stick up in the air [regardless of how great the propelling force is] it will eventually descend, so too, the people who rose to "great spiritual heights" as a result of Abraham's thrust — once Abraham died and his spiritual force could no longer be felt by the masses, they descended — they "reverted to their source" (*Lev Eliyahu al HaTorah*, vol. 2, p. 51).

Cf. *Sanhedrin* 94a, "Before a proselyte, even unto the tenth generation, insult not an Aramean." See *Insights*, vol. 1, #130.

ח

⟦ 680 ⟧

חָבִיב מֹשֶׁה מִנֹּחַ

"Moshe is more beloved than Noah" (*Beraishith Rabbah* 36:3).

"At first, Noah is described as 'a righteous man' [Gen. 6:9], but in the end he is called 'a man of the soil' [Gen. 9:20]. Moshe, on the other hand, at first is called 'an Egyptian' [Ex. 2:19], but ultimately the Torah describes him as 'a man of G-d' [Deut. 33:1]" (ibid.).

Rabbi Aharon Kotler explains: "It is G-d's will for man to grow ceaselessly, never to be content with his spiritual achievements no matter how lofty they may be, but to continually ascend to ever higher levels.

Noah is called 'a man of the soil' as an admonition for planting a vineyard. Having attained such levels of spiritual elevation and piety as to make him worthy of saving the world from extinction, he is chided for taking up the mundane labor of tilling the soil. Moshe, by contrast, after performing all the great miracles and ascending to Heaven to receive the Torah from G-d, never ceased to reach for more exalted spheres. He always viewed himself as standing on the lowest rung of an endless ladder" (*Mishnath Rabbi Aharon*, vol. 1 — essay entitled, "Moshe, a Man of G-d").

Cf. *Shabbath* 21b, "We promote in matters of sanctity but we do not reduce." See #871.

681

חַדְּשׁוּ מַעֲשֵׂיכֶם, שַׁפְּרוּ מַעֲשֵׂיכֶם

"Renew your actions; improve your actions" (*Midrash Tehillim* 81:4).

This is the midrashic interpretation of "Sound at the *chodesh* [new month] a *shofar*, at the time designated for our holiday" (Psalms 81:4).

Rabbi Yosef Dov Ber Soloveitchik [the Brisker Rav] comments: "The midrash is disturbed by the phrase, 'Sound at the *chodesh* a *shofar*.' Proper syntax would require that the verse read, 'Sound a *shofar* at the *chodesh*.' Instead, the phrasing draws our attention to the word *chodesh*, thereby teaching us a lesson about *teshuvah* [repentance]: when a sinner begins to repent, he should immediately start doing good deeds and desist from evil, even though his thoughts have not yet been purified and he cannot perform *mitzvoth* with the loftiest intentions. For if he waits passively until his thoughts are pure, he will never attain his goal.

"Thus, the verse tells us, the first step is *chadshu* [renew] your actions; i.e., start a new pattern of activity unlike that of the past. Then 'improve your actions' — enhance them and make them more acceptable" (*Beis HaLevi, Beraishith*, trans. by Yisrael Herczeg, p. 23).

682

חוּמְרָא סַכַּנְתָּא מֵאִיסּוּרָא

"Regulations concerning danger to life are more stringent than ritual prohibitions" (*Hullin* 10a).

The above dictum accounts for Rabbi Yisrael Salanter's rulings in matters pertaining to health and danger to life. "From here stemmed his audacious granting permission to perform acts otherwise forbidden on the Sabbath, and to eat on *Yom Kippur* during the outbreak of the cholera epidemic in Vilna . . . .

"From here stemmed his lenient ruling on his own conduct where others might thereby suffer hardship. When praying alone Saturday nights or at the end of fast days, Reb Yisrael would defer his *Tefillah* till an hour or more after dark. When he prayed with a congregation that would wait for him to finish, however, he would be among the first, 'so as not to burden the public'" (Rabbi Dov Katz, *Tenuath HaMussar*, trans. by Rabbi Leonard Oschry, *The Mussar Movement*, p. 252, p. 224).

"Two students always attended Rabbi Nosson Zvi Finkel (*The Alter of Slobodka*) when he lay sick in bed in Jerusalem. *Shabbos* evening, one of the students told R' Nosson Zvi that in their hotel a *minyan* had gathered for *Ma'ariv*. The student was told to go, but after he returned, R' Nosson Zvi rebuked him. 'How can you leave a sick man and go to pray? The *Rambam* states: "Whoever visits the sick takes away part of his sickness . . . If he does not visit the sick it is as if he sheds blood." If so, was your prayer considered a *mitzvah*? It is bloodshed!'" (Rabbi Chaim E. Zaitchik, *Sparks of Mussar*, p. 160).

Cf. *Shabbath* 132a, "The saving of life supersedes the Sabbath." See *Insights*, vol. 1, #458.

〚 683 〛 חֲזָקָה אֵין אָדָם מֵעִיז פָּנָיו בִּפְנֵי בַּעַל חוֹבוֹ

"There is a presumption that no one is that insolent in the presence of his creditor [to deny his debt in toto]" (*Baba Mezia* 3a).

"Rabbah said: The reason the Torah has declared that he who admits part of his opponent's claim must take an oath, is the presumption that no one is that insolent . . . . [The one who admits part of the claim] would have liked to give a complete denial, but he has not done so because he has not been able to adopt such an insolent attitude" (ibid.).

The Lubavitcher Rebbe applies the above talmudic presumption in a theological vein: "It is impossible for a Jew to deny G-d altogether, because he has a soul which 'remains faithful to Him, blessed be He, even at a time of sinning' [*Tanya*]. The soul has a constant vision of Divinity — it is in the presence of its Creditor. Even the most frivolous is not that insolent to deny the whole claim, alleging that it is 'my power and the strength of my hand [that brought me success]'" (Rabbi Menachem M. Schneerson, *Likutei Sichoth*, vol. 1, *Beraishith*, p. 77).

⎰ 684 ⎱ חֲזָקָה עַל חָבֵר שֶׁאֵין מוֹצִיא מִתַּחַת יָדוֹ דָּבָר שֶׁאֵינוֹ מְתוּקָן

"There is a presumption concerning a scholar, that he does not let anything untithed [lit., unprepared] pass out from under his hand" (*Pesahim* 9a).

"Consequently, if a *chaver* [scholar] dies and leaves a storehouse full of produce [crops], even if they are but one day old, they stand in the presumption of having been tithed" [ibid.].

This presumption is utilized quite often today regarding Torah books and articles. There is a presumption that manuscripts published by Torah "scholars" are proper and reliable. Hence, many *Gedolim* [Torah giants] will often give their approbation to *sefarim* based on the above presumption.

⎰ 685 ⎱ חַיֵּי בָּנֵי וּמְזוֹנֵי לָא בִּזְכוּתָא תַּלְיָא מִילְּתָא אֶלָּא בְּמַזְּלָא תַּלְיָא מִילְּתָא

"[Length of] life, children, and sustenance depend not on merit, but [rather on] *mazal*" (*Mo'ed Katan* 28a).

Maimonides alludes to the above dictum in his *Epistle to the Jews of Marseilles* and asserts that it is only allegorical. He denounces astrology as an irrational illusion of fools.

Rabbi Elimelech of Lizhensk, however, suggests that the term *"mazal"* [in the above dictum] has nothing to do with planetary movements, but refers to *zechuth avoth* [the merit of the fathers]. In other words, it is not our own merit which determines "duration of life, children, and sustenance," but the "merit of the fathers" (*Noam Elimelech, Ekev*).

The Gaon of Vilna points out that the aspect of *hashgachah pratis* [Divine Providence] that conducts the destiny of the universe is designated as "mazal," for in most cases man does not fathom what appears to him as a random disposition of human affairs. Nevertheless, the Divine plan is present at all times, and the length of one's life, children, and sustenance is often not determined by the merit of his deeds, but by how he fits into the overall picture of historical events.

See, however, *Sforno*, Deut. 8:1, "By observing the commandments you shall attain [length of days, children and wealth].

⟦ 686 ⟧

חַיָּב אָדָם לוֹמַר מָתַי יַגִּיעוּ מַעֲשַׂי
לְמַעֲשֵׂי אֲבוֹתַי

"A man has the duty to say, 'When shall my deeds reach those of my fathers?'" (*Tanna d'vei Eliyahu Rabbah*, ch. 25).

"Every Jew has the potential to say, 'When will my deeds reach those of my forefathers, Abraham, Isaac and Jacob?' There are no limitations, boundaries or obstacles in drawing closer to G-d" (Rabbi Joseph Isaac Schneersohn, *Bosi L'Gani*, p. 14).

Rabbi Chaim Mordechai Katz comments: "Aspiration to achieve greatness in Torah and G-dliness is a duty. One must strive to reach the pinnacle of greatness, i.e., the level of the Patriarchs."

Rabbi Katz bemoans the fact that in America, the drive for great Torah achievement is missing and people are spiritually complacent. "It is hard to find young men who dream of 'greatness in Torah.' In European *yeshivoth* we saw a keen competition in the study of Torah. But here, there is no such problem — no competition, no jealousy . . . . There are precious few who are at all ashamed of their ignorance of Torah" ("Aspiration for Torah," *The Jewish Observer*, 2, no. 3 [December 1964]:12-14).

The above was adapted from an essay written by the late Telsher Rosh HaYeshiva, Rav Katz, *before* the proliferation of *yeshivoth* and the intensification of talmudic study throughout America (S.W.).

Cf. *Baba Bathra* 21a, "The jealousy of scribes increase wisdom." See *Insights*, vol. 1, #467.

〖 687 〗

חַיָּיב אָדָם לְמַשְׁמֵשׁ בְּבִגְדּוֹ
עֶרֶב שַׁבָּת עִם חֲשֵׁכָה

"One must examine his garments on Sabbath eve before nightfall"
(*Shabbath* 12a).

As a general rule, steps must be taken before the Sabbath to avoid its
desecration. Hence, one must examine his garments to see whether there is
anything in them, for this may ultimately lead to Sabbath desecration.

The *Orach Yesharim* suggests a homiletical interpretation of this halachic
ruling. Sabbath eve, traditionally, is one of the designated periods for self-
examination and repentance. One is required to review his deeds and
activities of the entire week. "One must examine *b'gadov* [his garments]
before the Sabbath." *B'gadov* may also be translated as "his betrayals," i.e.,
one should determine before the onset of the Sabbath the extent of "his
betrayals" before the Almighty [the transgressions committed during the
week], and repent his sins before G-d (Rabbi Samuel Alter, *L'kutei Bosar
L'kutei* [*Aggadoth*], vol. 1, p. 189).

For fifteen years, Rabbi Yisrael Salanter was heard confessing: "My sin is
before my eyes always" for having once forgotten to check his pockets before
Shabbos, and for having once forgotten to check for *chometz* before *Pesach* in
the place where salt was kept (Rabbi Chaim E. Zaitchik, *HaMeoroth
HaGedolim*).

〖 688 〗

חָכָם עָדִיף מִנָּבִיא

"A wise man is superior to a prophet" (*Baba Bathra* 12a).

Rabbi Yitzchak Arama writes: "The prophet, by reason of being privy to
the king, overhears many palace secrets. Unless, however, this prophet is
specifically informed concerning details, his knowledge will remain very
sketchy, and he will not know the causes for the events concerning which
he has foreknowledge.

"The wise man, on the other hand, has calculated by means of his intellect that certain events ought to occur at certain times and places. Since, however, he cannot be sure that the king is aware of the causes for such events, he has no idea if the king intends to act . . ." (*Akedath Yitzchak*, *Chukath*, trans. Eliyahu Munk, vol. 2, p. 779).

When the *Chasam Sofer* was asked how he was able to answer certain questions so quickly, he replied: "G-d appoints one person in every generation to guide the people and to reply to questions. Since so many people query me, it appears that Heaven concurs [with my decisions]" (Yehudah Nachshoni, *Rabbeinu Moshe Sofer*, p. 147).

Rabbi E. E. Dessler referred to the *Chazon Ish* as "the *Urim V'Tumim* (vehicle of Heavenly responses) of his generation" (*The Chazon Ish*, p. 199).

"With all its fiery arsenal, prophecy was unable to eradicate idolatry and base degeneration, oppression and violence, murder and immorality, the pursuit after bribery and unjust gain from Israel. Instead, this transformation was effected by the sages, by their dissemination of Torah learning, by raising up many disciples and by inculcating the observance of the individual laws and their details" (*Orot Yisrael*, p. 101).

Cf. *Zohar* III 23a, "The 'wise' is he who, by the power of his own contemplation, attains to the perception of profound mysteries which cannot be expressed in words."

Cf. *Baba Bathra* 12a, "Since the day when the Temple was destroyed, prophecy has been taken from the prophets and given to the wise."

⦙ 689 ⦙   חַמְרָא לְמָרֵיהּ טִיבוּתָא לְשָׁקְיֵהּ

"Though the wine belong to the owner, thanks are given to the waiter" (*Baba Kamma* 92b).

As it says, "'And he [Moshe] laid his hands upon him [Joshua]' [Num. 27:23]. The wisdom and greatness of Joshua are considered as if they were given to him by Moshe — in fact they came from G-d" (Rashi).

In commenting on the above dictum, Rabbi Chaim Shmulevitz said: "The lesson here is that since the wine belongs to the king, no one can possibly take any himself; rather, one is dependent on the waiter to bring it from the wine cellar and serve him. So, too, the wisdom of the Torah is G-d's, but no one can partake of it without a *Rebbe* to serve it to him. Thus the *Rebbe* is indispensable, and one is indebted to him, although the wisdom came from the Almighty" (*Reb Chaim's Discourses*, p. 158).

Cf. *Aboth* 1:6, "Provide yourself with a teacher." See *Insights*, vol. 1, #444.

〖 690 〗   חָשׁ בְּרֹאשׁוֹ יַעֲסוֹק בַּתּוֹרָה

"If he aches in his head, let him engage in the study of the Torah" (*Erubin* 54a).

Rabbi Eliyahu Lopian cites the *Shevet Mussar* who explains that this dictum is not to be interpreted to mean that if you have a headache and seek "relief," then occupy yourself with the study of Torah. It is to be understood in the following manner: "Even if you have a headache and it is difficult for you to study, you are nevertheless obligated to engage in Torah study."

This is the Rambam's source for the halacha that "Every Israelite is under an obligation to study Torah, whether he is rich or poor, in sound health or ailing, in the vigor of youth or very old and feeble . . ." [*Mishneh Torah, Hil. Talmud Torah* 1:8] (*Lev Eliyahu, Shevive Lev* 176).

In a moralistic vein, we may interpret the above dictum to read, "*Chosh B'rosho*," if one is deeply hurt by not being selected to be the *rosh* — the leader in the community, synagogue, etc. . . then "*ya'asok baTorah*," let him engage in Torah study, for he will come to realize that all such worldly ambitions are vanity of vanities (S.W.).

Cf. *Shabbath* 11a, "Rather any illness, but not illness of the bowels; any pain, but not heart pain; any ache, but not headache . . . ." See #764.

ט

〔 691 〕 טוֹב לַשָּׁמַיִם וְלַבְּרִיּוֹת זֶהוּ צַדִּיק טוֹב

"He who is good to Heaven and good to man is a righteous man who is good" (*Kiddushin* 40a).

A truly righteous man is one who fulfills both "the *mitzvoth* between man and G-d" and "the *mitzvoth* between man and his fellow."

Rabbi Levi Yitzchak of Berditchev comments: "There are two types of *tzaddikim* who serve G-d. One who serves G-d with great enthusiasm, but does so alone. He is not involved with the wicked [who do not serve the Almighty]. The other *tzaddik* not only serves G-d, but also influences the wicked to serve Him. This righteous person emulates Abraham, who converted people to the worship of the one true G-d.

One who is "good to Heaven and good to man," therefore, refers to this righteous person. He is called "good to Heaven" for he serves G-d, and "good to man" for he enables others to do likewise (*Kedushath Levi, Noach*, p. 8).

〔 692 〕 טוֹבָה צִפּוֹרְנָן שֶׁל רִאשׁוֹנִים מִכְּרֵיסוֹ שֶׁל אַחֲרוֹנִים

"The fingernails of the first [earlier generations] are better than the belly of the later [generations] (*Yoma* 9b).

The "first" refers to the generations immediately preceding the destruction of the First Temple, while the "later" refers to the generations causing the

149

destruction of the Second Temple.

A homiletical interpretation of the above maxim was suggested by Rabbi Gershom Zev Damesek: "The transgressions of the first generations [although cardinal sins] were openly revealed, similar to fingernails that scratch and create open wounds for all to see. The transgressions of the later generations, however, were hidden. Outwardly, people ate, drank, and 'filled their stomachs' in a friendly, congenial atmosphere — while inwardly they conspired to destroy each other. This was the sin of *sinas chinom* [causeless hatred] which ultimately led to the destruction of the Second Temple" (*L'ohr HaAggadah*, p. 128).

In commenting on the sin of "causeless hatred," Rabbi Eliyahu E. Dessler writes: "It is the irrational hatred which cannot abide the other person's *being there*. It's origin is that boundless arrogance which characterizes Esau, or Edom. Since the Jews of that time tended — in however attenuated a form — towards this terrible failing, the enemy sent against them was in fact Edom [measure for measure], in the form of the Roman Empire" (*Michtav Me-Eliyahu*, vol. 2, p. 51).

⟦ 693 ⟧   טוֹבָה קְלָלָה שֶׁקִּיּל אֲחִיָּה הַשִּׁילוֹנִי אֶת יִשְׂרָאֵל יוֹתֵר מִבְּרָכָה שֶׁבֵּירְכָן בִּלְעָם הָרָשָׁע

"Better is the curse which Achiyah the Shilonite pronounced on Israel, than the blessings with which Balaam the wicked blessed them" (*Ta'anith* 20a).

See the talmudic analysis on the above dictum (ibid.). Rabbi Yaakov Yosef of Polonoye explains that this statement reflects Achiyah the Shilonite's constructive purpose in exposing the failings of his generation. "The preacher who criticizes in order to prod people to mend their ways is a true prophet; the hypocrites and flatterers who only sing the praises of their contemporaries are false prophets" (*Toledoth Yaakov Yosef, Balak*).

"True criticism," said Rabbi Yehudah Halevi, "is such that you reprove with the intent to improve the object of your remonstrations" (*The Kuzari* 5:20).

Cf. *Beraishith Rabbah* 54:3, "Love unaccompanied by reproof is not love."

See *Insights*, vol. 1, #256.

Cf. *Sotah* 41b, "Whoever flatters another will ultimately fall into his hands." See #739.

Cf. *Arakhin* 16b, "I wonder if there is one in this generation who accepts reproof — who knows how to reprove." See *Insights*, vol. 1, #498.

⫟ 694 ⫟

טוּמְאָה דְּחוּיָה בְּצִיבּוּר

"Impurity [*tumah*] is overridden in the case of a community"
(*Pesahim* 80a).

When the whole community is "ritually impure," the defilement is suspended on account of communal need. See *Mishneh Torah, Hil. Biath HaMikdash* 4:15.

In commenting on the miracle of Chanukah in "finding a flask of pure oil," the Lubavitcher Rebbe asserts: "By Torah-law, it would have been permissible to light the *menorah* [in the Sanctuary] even with oils that had been defiled, for 'impurity is overridden' — or permitted [*hutrah*] in the case of the community. Nevertheless, to manifest His love for Israel, the Almighty performed a miracle which not only made it possible to begin anew the observance of the *mitzvah* [of lighting the *menorah*], but also enabled it to be in the most ideal manner without recourse to legal allowances, not even such as are fully consistent with the *Shulchan Aruch*" (Rabbi Menachem M. Schneerson, *Likkutei Sichot*, vol. 1, *Beraishith*, p. 158).

ר

695

יי״ג דְּבָרִים נֶאֶמְרוּ בְּפַת שַׁחֲרִית

"Thirteen things were said of the morning bread" (*Baba Mezia* 107b).

"It is an antidote against heat and cold, wind and demons; instills wisdom into the simple, causes one to triumph in a lawsuit, enables one to study and teach the Torah, to have his words heeded, and retain scholarship; he does not perspire, lives with his wife and does not desire another woman; and it kills the worms in one's intestines" (ibid.).

It was reported in the name of Rabbi Yaakov Yitzchak, "the Jew" of Przyscha, that in the study of the Torah every morning were encompassed all the virtues enumerated in the *Gemara* concerning *pas shachris* [the morning bread]. An allusion to this is to be found in the gematriah — *pas* has the same numerical value as *talmud* — 480 (*Siach Sarfei Kodesh*, vol. 2, no. 253).

696

יְהִי רָצוֹן שֶׁיָּכוֹפוּ עֶלְיוֹנִים אֶת הַתַּחְתּוֹנִים

"May it be the will [of the Almighty] that the [immortals] above overpower the [mortals] below" (*Kethuboth* 104a).

On the day when Rebbe [Rabbi Yehudah HaNasi] was dying, the Rabbis decreed a public fast and offered prayers for heavenly mercy . . . . When Rebbe's maidservant witnessed his suffering and agony due to his inability to don his *tefillin*, she prayed, "May it be the will of the Almighty that the immortals [the angels who desired Rebbe to join them] above, overpower the

152

mortals [who desired Rebbe to remain with them] below" (ibid.).

Cf. *Ran, Nedarim* 40a, "There are times when one is required to pray for mercy that a patient should die, i.e., when the patient suffers a great deal and it is impossible for him to recover."

Rabbi Yechiel Michel Epstein follows the ruling of the *Ran* in *Nedarim* (*Aruch HaShulchan, Yoreh De'ah* 335:3).

Rabbi Eliezer Waldenberg argues from the silence of the other codifiers of Jewish Law that they would disagree with the *Ran*, for they side with the Rabbis who prayed for Rabbi Yehudah HaNasi to live. Rabbi Waldenberg insists that under no circumstances should the immediate members of the patient's family pray for his demise (*Tzitz Eliezer*, vol. VII, no. 49).

Rabbi Moshe Feinstein writes: "We cannot use this source [the *Ran*] to justify praying for a patient's death" (*Iggeroth Moshe, Choshen Mishpat*, part II, Responsum 74).

⎰ 697 ⎰

יִהְיוּ מְזוֹנוֹתַי מְרוּרִין כַּזַּיִת וּמְסוּרִין בְּיָדְךָ
וְאַל יִהְיוּ מְתוּקִין כַּדְּבַשׁ
וּתְלוּיִין בְּיַד בָּשָׂר וָדָם

"May my food be as bitter as the olive but entrusted to Your hand rather than sweet as honey but dependent on the hands of flesh and blood" (*Erubin* 18b).

When Noah sent a dove from the Ark to see if the waters of the flood had receded, it returned with an olive branch in its mouth, symbolically containing the above message, "May my food be as bitter as the olive . . . ."

Rabbi A. Henach Leibowitz, the Rosh Ha'yeshiva of Chafetz Chaim comments: "We may readily appreciate the sentiments expressed by this dove. Surely we are all aware of the humiliation of having to ask another person for help. Yet there is a deeper meaning. This dove received its sustenance from Noah. It is beyond our capacity to appreciate the hardship Noah must have faced in caring for all the animals in the Ark . . . . Would we think for an instant that the beneficiary of such genuine assistance would be humbled or hurt? Yet despite the warmth of Noah's kindness, the dove felt pain in being dependent on him.

This broadens the dimension of our conception of *chesed*. It is not enough to engage in charity. We must be aware that another human being is deeply hurt when asking for our help, and we must strive to relieve him by acting as genuinely and sincerely as we can . . . . To do less would be to ignore the suffering of a fellow human being" ("Chochmas HaMussar," *Building Jewish Ethical Character*, p. 58).

〔 698 〕

יוֹדְעִין רְשָׁעִים שֶׁדַּרְכָּם לְמִיתָה
וְיֵשׁ לָהֶם חֵלֶב עַל כִּסְלָם

"The wicked know that their way leads to death, but their loins are covered with fat" (*Shabbath* 31b).

The wicked may know that their actions are self-destructive, nevertheless, their "understanding," their loins, are covered with lust [with fat]. Their passions master their reason so that they cannot control themselves.

Cf. *Beraishith Rabbah* 57:8, "'And Esau said in his heart . . . I will slay Jacob my brother' (Gen. 27:41). The wicked are controlled by their hearts [passions]."

Although Esau believed in the existence of G-d who created and administers the universe, he was dominated by the desires of his heart.

Rabbi Eliyahu Lopian comments: "We are obliged to conclude that anyone who desires to merit this world and the World to Come must labor to eradicate and nullify his desires and passions . . . so that no other desire remains but to do the Will of the Creator" (*Lev Eliyahu*, p. 114).

Cf. *Erubin* 19a, "The wicked do not repent even at the entrance to Gehinom." See *Insights*, vol. 1, #479.

⟦ 699 ⟧

יוֹתֵר מִשֶּׁהָאִישׁ רוֹצֶה לִישָׂא
אִשָּׁה רוֹצָה לְהִנָּשֵׂא

"More than the man desires to marry, the woman desires to be
married" (*Yebamoth* 113a).

A recent psychological study indicates that women suffer more often than
men upon the dissolution of a marriage. "88% of women [compared with
74% of men] suffered physical effects — insomnia, overeating, loss of
appetite, chest pains or headaches — if their partner initiated the breakup.
Even when they were the "breakers," 50% of the women reported physical
symptoms, compared with only 26% of the men" (Robin Akert, cited in *The
Book of Health Secrets*, p. 127).

Cf. *Megillah* 14b, "While a woman talks she spins." This alludes to single
women who have the thought of marriage in the back of their minds.

Cf. *Yebamoth* 63a, "Any man who has no wife is no man." See *Insights*,
vol. 1, #252.

Cf. *Gittin* 90b, "If a man divorces his first wife, even the altar sheds
tears." See *Insights*, vol. 1, #273.

⟦ 700 ⟧

יָחִיד וְרַבִּים הֲלָכָה כְּרַבִּים

"Where there is a controversy between an individual and the
many [a group], the *halachah* is with the many" (*Berakoth* 9a).

Rabbi Yoel Teitelbaum [the Satmarer Rebbe] questioned the talmudic
formulation "*Yachid ve'rabbim halachah ke'rabbim*," why not simply state
halachah ke'rabbim [the law is with the many]? He suggests that *yachid* refers
not to a single person, but to *Yechido Shel Olam*, to the One and Only of the
universe. Hence, says the Satmarer Rebbe, one should follow the *rabbim* [the
many] only when you know that the *Yachid* [G-d] is with the rabbim;
otherwise, hold out, even against the whole world.

See the Kotzker's interpretation of "He that repeated his chapter a
hundred times is not to be compared with him who repeated it a hundred

and *one* times" (*Hagigah* 9b, *Emeth V'Emunah*, par. 780; cited in *Insights*, vol. 1, #55).

"*Sefer HaChinuch* sees an assurance for Jewish survival in the obligation to accept the opinion of the majority of sages. We are forbidden to stray from their opinion, even if they are wrong. In such instances, they will be responsible for their error [*Horayoth* 2a], but the unity of Israel will not be jeopardize" (Rabbi Elie Munk, *The Call of the Torah*, Shemos, p. 330).

▯ 701 ▯

יֵיתֵי וְלָא אִיחְמִינֵיה

"Let him [the Messiah] come, but let me not see him"
(*Sanhedrin* 98b).

This was the declaration of a number of talmudic sages who feared "*chevlei moshiach*" [the birth pangs preceding the advent of the Messiah].

The *Zohar*, in commenting on Balaam's "blessing" [Num. 24:23] writes: "*Who will survive the time of the Yishmaelites?*" In their savagery, they will be the ones to wage the final battles against the Jews. Happy are those who will not be witness to the birth pangs of the Messiah. This confrontation will ultimately lead to the destruction of Yishmael and Rome (*Parshas Balak*).

When the chassidic Rabbi of Grodzhisk was led, together with thousands of Jews — men, women and children — to the gas chambers in one of the Nazi extermination camps, he asked permission to address a few farewell words to the mass of inmates.

"My brothers and sisters! In talmudic times, one of our sages declared: 'Let the Messiah come, but let me not see him.' That sage dreaded to witness the enormous sufferings that Israel would endure prior to the advent of the redeemer — during the 'birth pangs of the Messiah.' He could have permitted himself such a request. In his time, redemption was still very far off. Now, however, when we stand at the very threshold of actual redemption — now, at this time when we are cleansing with our very blood the path that lies ahead of the Messiah, it is our duty to look upon ourselves as privileged. It has fallen in our lot to pave the way before the redeemer as he continues to approach, and to accept our martyrdom, the sanctification of His Name, may He be blessed in love. Come, then, my fellow Jews. Let us recite the *Shema* with joy. Come, let us sing *Ani Ma'amin*" (Dov Rosen, *Shema Yisrael*, vol. 1, p. 8).

⎨ 702 ⎬   יַעֲקֹב אָבִינוּ לֹא מֵת

"Jacob our father did not die" (*Ta'anith* 5b).

The word "death" is not stated regarding him. Our Rabbis therefore said, 'Jacob our father did not die' (Rashi).

"The above remark, which of course cannot be taken in a literal sense, as the commentators tell us, has a more general meaning.

Why was this distinction attributed to Jacob and not to the other patriarchs? Rabbeinu Bachya reminds us that in his lifetime Jacob achieved the harmonious union of those virtues which each of his ancestors only possessed singly: Abraham's infinite love of G-d and man, and the spirit of obedience and unconditional discipline which characterized Isaac. While Abraham incarnated the principle of *chesed* [love] and Isaac that of *din* [law and legality], Jacob took the royal path, the happy medium *tifereth* = *rachamim*, of love tempering justice. This way is the way of harmony and truth. And while throughout the course of history, love and justice experience periods of eclipse and defeat, and carry in them the seeds of their opposition, the way of harmonious union — 'love in justice' [*rachamim b'din*] — asserts itself at all times and in all places. It is everlasting and does not fade or decay. This principle of Jacob overcomes death" (Rabbi Elie Munk, *The Call of the Torah*, vol. 2, p. 1070).

⎨ 703 ⎬   יַעֲקֹב אָבִינוּ עַל יְדֵי שֶׁבִּקֵּשׁ לֵישֵׁב בְּשַׁלְוָה
בָּעוֹלָם הַזֶּה נִזְדַּוֵּג לוֹ שְׂטָנוֹ שֶׁל יוֹסֵף

"Jacob our father wished to live at ease in this world, whereupon he was attacked by Joseph's Satan" (*Beraishith Rabbah*, 84:3).

The patriarch Jacob was shaken out of his tranquility by his troubles with his son Joseph. What, indeed, was so terrible for Jacob to desire a life of tranquility and serenity?

Rabbi Yeruchem Levovitz explains that our purpose in this world is to elevate ourselves and to grow spiritually from every life situation. It was therefore improper for Jacob to focus on a life of ease and tranquility.

Reb Yeruchem concludes: "Every occurrence in this world can make you a better person. If you have this awareness, then you will have a positive attitude towards everything that happens to you. Before, during or after every incident that occurs, reflect on your behavior and reactions. Ask yourself, 'What type of person am I after this incident? How did I do on the test? Did I pass it in an elevated manner?'" (*Daas Torah, Beraishith*, pp. 222-3, cited by Rabbi Zelig Pliskin, *Growth Through Torah*, p. 102).

See #589, "When the righteous dwell in tranquility and wish to dwell in this world, Satan comes and accuses them."

॥ 704 ॥ יָפָה שָׁעָה אַחַת בִּתְשׁוּבָה וּמַעֲשִׂים טוֹבִים בָּעוֹלָם הַזֶּה מִכָּל חַיֵּי הָעוֹלָם הַבָּא

"Far better an hour of repentance and good deeds in this world than a lifetime in the World to Come" (*Aboth* 4:22).

Rabbi Chaim Shmulevitz explains that the pleasure of the World to Come consists of the closeness to the Almighty which is attained in this world. Although the enjoyment in *Olam Haba* is infinite, its scope is limited to that which is achieved in this world.

"This is the understanding of the well-known story of the Vilna Gaon's weeping on his death bed. Those with him asked him the reason for his tears. He held his *tzitzis* in his hand and replied, 'I am leaving a world where for but a few pennies one can perform such wonderful *mitzvoth*, while in the World to Come the opportunity no longer exists'" (*Reb Chaim's Discourses*, p. 109).

The "hour" [in the above dictum], says the Kotzker Rebbe, refers to the very last hour of Shabbos, when all the feeble candles have long died out. In the grip of the inescapable darkness one is finally confronted with the grim reality of one's self. The man who knows himself cannot fail to repent (Rabbi Avraham Chaim Feuer, *Seasons of the Soul*, p. 152).

〔 705 〕 יָפֶה תַּלְמוּד תּוֹרָה עִם דֶּרֶךְ אֶרֶץ שֶׁיְּגִיעַת שְׁנֵיהֶם מַשְׁכַּחַת עָוֹן

"The study of Torah combined with an occupation is an excellent thing, for the wearying labor of both keeps sin forgotten" (*Aboth* 2:2).

"Only a way of life devoted to the pursuit of study as well as of economic independence can take up our time to such a degree, that there will be no unoccupied hours during which we could indulge in thoughts that . . . could make us drift away from the path of goodness" (Rabbi Samson Raphael Hirsch, *Comm. on Aboth*).

Rav Chaim of Volozhin views "occupation" as being inextricably linked with Torah. "Even during one's occupation, one should meditate upon the words of the Torah" (*Ruach Chaim* 2:2).

Rabbi Menachem Mendel of Kotzk in commenting on the verse, "If you eat [the product] of the labor of your hands, you are fortunate and all is well with you," [Psalms 128:2] said: "Eat of the labor of your *hands*, but not of your heart and soul . . . Even as you toil with your hands, concentrate your thoughts upon lofty spiritual goals" (Rabbi A. C. Feuer, *Tehillim Treasury*, p. 67).

Reb Levi Yitzchak of Berditchev comments: "If one does not engage in evil thoughts or dishonest declarations in the course of his occupation — for he is mindful of the Torah prohibition — he is wonderfully infusing his occupation with the study of Torah."

Rabbi S. R. Hirsch's slogan for his educational system, *Torah im Derech Eretz*, was based on the above dictum. Samson Raphael Levy [a great grandson of Rabbi Hirsch] writes concerning this slogan: "Rabbi Hirsch apparently took it to mean that there need be no objection to the study of any science or general subject that might possibly be of help to us in learning, understanding and observing Torah. He consequently included in the curriculum of the school which he founded in Frankfurt, an integration of Torah studies with 'general' subjects. There are those who see in this the basis for the present-day institution of the 'Yeshiva Secondary School' and for the engagement of Orthodox Jews in 'liberal' professions" (*Jewish Studies* 34

160

[Summer 1990]:39).
Cf. *Torath Kohanim*, Va'yikra 18:4, note 141. See #815.

〖 706 〗 יָפָה תְּפִלַּת הַחוֹלֶה לְעַצְמוֹ יוֹתֵר מִכֹּל

"A sick person's prayers on his own behalf are more efficacious
than those of anyone else" (*Beraishith Rabbah* 53:14).

This is derived from Ishmael [Abraham's son], who prayed to the
Almighty after Sarah had sent him [and his mother Hagar] away. The Torah
states: "G-d had heard the voice of the lad [Ishmael] where he is" [Gen.
21:17]. This implies that his prayers were accepted for his own [and not for
Abraham's] sake.

The *Yefeh Toar* [Rabbi Shmuel Yaffe] comments: "It is best when one
prays for his own suffering because 'G-d is close to those broken in heart'
[Psalms 34:19].

The above midrashic dictum is not inconsistent with the talmudic maxim
that "A prisoner cannot release himself from the house of detention"
(*Berakoth* 5b), for "the only time one cannot release himself is when he
cannot concentrate on his prayers. If he can, however, his own prayers are
best" (Rabbi Eliyahu Mizrachi, Comm. ad loc.).

See #532, "A prisoner cannot release himself . . . ."

Cf. *Baba Bathra* 116a, "Whosoever has a sick person in his house should
go to a sage who will invoke [Heavenly] mercy for him." See #782.

〖 707 〗 יָפְיוּתוֹ שֶׁל יֶפֶת יְהֵא בְּאָהֳלֵי שֵׁם

"The beauty of Yefeth shall reside in the tents of Shem" (*Megillah*
9b).

This is based on the verse [describing Noah's blessing for his son Yefeth],
"G-d will *yaft* [expand] for Yefeth and he will dwell in the tents of Shem"
[Gen. 9:27]. The word "*yaft*" also means "beauty," hence the talmudic play
on words — "Let the beauty of Yefeth dwell in the tents of Shem."

Our sages applied this blessing specifically to the use of Greek to translate the Torah since it was "the most beautiful language of the descendants of Yefeth" (Rashi).

"[Our sages] investigated and found that the Torah cannot be properly translated into any language except Greek" (*Yerushalmi, Megillah* 1:9).

Rabbi Avraham Pam commented that from this *Yerushalmi* we see that the *"beauty"* inherent in the Greek language lies only in its ability to accurately translate the Torah. Hence, says Rav Pam, when one is looking for a *shiduch* [marriage partner] he should look for "beauty" that is Torah translatable (Erev Shabbos Shiurim).

Regarding Greek philosophy, however, Rabbi Yehudah HaLevi writes: "Let not Greek wisdom lead you astray, since it produces only flowers but no fruit."

The prohibition of "wisdom of Greek" [See *Sotah* 49b] is explained by Rashi [ad loc.] as "A subtle language used by courtiers which other people do not understand."

However, *Rashba* only forbids studying Greek wisdom in one's youth, before one learns the wisdom of the Talmud (*Teshuvoth HaRashba* 1:414).

When *Rema* (Rabbi Moshe Isserles) was criticized by *Maharshal* (Rabbi Shlomo Luria) for quoting from "the wisdom of Aristotle," *Rema* wrote the following in his defense. "Although I have quoted some of the words of Aristotle, I bring heaven and earth as witnesses that in my entire life I never had anything to do with any of his [Aristotle's] books, besides what I read in *Moreh Nevuchim* and other books . . . written by *talmidei chachamim* [Torah scholars]" (Yaakov D. Shulman, *The Rema*, pp. 178-180).

Rabbi Elie Munk writes: "Retrospectively, we see that Yefeth, the ancestor of the Greeks, developed the cult of beauty and oriented man toward an esthetic culture. On the other hand, thanks to the tents of Shem, the great religious ideas were spread throughout the world" (*The Call of the Torah*, vol. 1, p. 224).

708

יִפְתָּח בְּדוֹרוֹ כִּשְׁמוּאֵל בְּדוֹרוֹ

"Yiftach in his generation was like Shmuel [the prophet] in his
generation" *(Rosh Hashanah 25b).*

"Do not presume that since the present leaders are not comparable to
those in previous generations, one should only heed the former leaders and
not the latter ones. One should not go to anyone except the judge in his
days" *(Tosafoth ad loc.).*

Rabbi Chaim Shmulevitz comments: "This means that the leaders of each
generation are those most suited to its needs. This is evident from the
Midrash which states that if Aharon would have been alive during Yehoyada
or Tzaddok's generation [both of whom were High Priests], the latter would
have been greater than Aharon [*Koheleth Rabbah* 1:8]. In the absolute sense,
Aharon was certainly greater. However, they were more suited to the needs
of their specific generation" *(Reb Chaim's Discourses,* p. 271).

The Gerer Rebbe, R' Yitzchak Meir, would say: "The weaker the genera-
tion, the greater the Torah leaders it needs. To what may this be compared?
To sickness. The sicker the patient, the greater the doctor he requires"
(Shmuel Himmelstein).

Cf. *Arakhin* 17a, "As the leader, so the generation." See *Insights,* vol. 1,
#140.

Cf. *Baba Bathra* 75a, "The countenance of Moshe was like that of the sun,
the countenance of Joshua was like that of the moon." See *Insights,* vol. 1,
#456.

709

יְצַעֵר אָדָם עִם הַצִּבּוּר

"A man should share in the distress of the community"
(Ta'anith 11a).

This is derived from the conduct of Moshe Rabbeinu, who shared the
distress of the Israelites in their battle against Amalek. See Ex. 17:12.

"In the days after 'the great fire' which broke out in Brisk, Rav Chaim

Soloveitchik did not sleep at home, but on the floor of the sloping hallway of the synagogue. All the entreaties of his family that he rest at home in his bed were to no avail. 'I cannot sleep on a bed,' he exclaimed, 'when so many Jews have no roof over their heads'" (Rabbi Aharon Surasky, *Giants of Jewry*, vol. 1, p. 177).

Similarly, the Chafetz Chaim, during World War I, denied himself any kind of comfort, and he would place his pillow on the floor. "When Jews are lying in bunkers," he would explain, "I am not able to sleep on a pillow" (Rabbi Reuven Grossman, *The Legacy of Slabodka*, p. 27).

Rabbi Yehudah Zev Segal comments: "If one hears that a neighbor's child has been stricken by illness, he must immediately ask himself, 'How would I feel were it my child?'" (*Yirah VaDaas*).

〔 710 〕 יֵצֶר הָרַע דּוֹמֶה לִזְבוּב

"The Evil Inclination resembles a fly" (*Berakoth* 61a).

Rabbi Eliyahu Lopian suggests the following similarity between the fly and the Evil Inclination. "A fly will flit away from a clean place and attach itself to filth and dirt. Similarly, when the Evil Inclination finds a stain of sin in a person, that is where it will choose to attach itself" (*Lev Eliyahu, Shevive Lev* 174).

The Vilna Gaon interpreted the Evil Inclination in this case to refer to one who speaks *lashon hara* (evil speech). Just as a fly typically alights on that which is decayed and rotting, so one who speaks *lashon hara* is constantly looking for the faults in others.

Secondly, just as a fly that falls into fine oil spoils all the oil in the vessel, so one who habitually speaks *lashon hara* causes all the Torah that he possesses to smell (Rabbi Betzalel Landau, *HaGaon HaChassid MiVilna*).

"The Chafetz Chaim explained that when swatted at, a fly will find another spot upon which to settle. Similarly, when the Evil Inclination loses a battle, it returns to test the individual in some other way" (Rabbi Shimon Finkelman, *Inspiration and Insight*, vol. 2, p. 245).

〖 711 〗   יֵצֶר הָרַע רֹאשׁוֹ מָתוֹק וְסוֹפוֹ מַר

"The Evil Inclination is initially sweet but ultimately bitter"
(*Yerushalmi, Shabbath* 14:3).

"The Evil Inclination begins 'sweetening' the transgression for him: 'See this money — how desirable it is! This harlot — how beautiful she is! This sin — how sweet it is! Who are you afraid of? No one sees you. No one will "tell" on you' . . . He continues enticing him in this manner until the other transgresses and forfeits his life in the world" (Rabbeinu Yechiel, *Ma'aloth Hamiddoth*, trans. by Rabbi Shraga Silverstein, *The Book of Middoth*, p. 220).

Cf. *Koheleth Rabbah* 3:3, "The beginning of a sin is sweet, but its end is bitter."

This talmudic dictum coincides with Rabbi Chaim of Volozhin's interpretation of the "Tree of Knowledge of Good and Evil." Reb Chaim suggests that the *"eitz hada'ath tov v'ra"* should be translated as "the tree *joining* good and evil," for the word *da'ath* [knowledge] connotes the conjunction of two things. Hence, the result of man's first sin was that good and evil became mixed together.

"Indeed, many things in life contain both good and bad elements, and it is our task to separate the two. How often do people fight for their principles until the strife they cause is far the worse evil! How many wars have been fought because each party insists on its own prerogatives and mixes righteous indignation with unrighteous wrath! How many individuals make life miserable for themselves and others on the same account; and even in the worship of G-d, how much pettiness can result when worshippers contend for the same honor or privilege. Unfortunately, this is no more than a pious *yetzer hara* [Evil Inclination]" (*Ruach Chaim, Comm. on Aboth* 3:3; Rabbi M. Miller *Shabbath Shiurim* [second series], p. 22).

▌712 ▐

יְשִׁיבַת כְּרַכִּים קָשָׁה
"Dwelling in cities is difficult" (*Kethuboth* 110b).

Owing to overcrowding; lack of pure country air; and an insufficiency of park and open spaces (Rashi).

Rabbi Berel Wein, in his book on modern Jewish history, writes: "Urbanization has always been an unsettling experience. The Talmud characterizes urban living as 'difficult,' spiritually and physically debilitating. New surroundings, crowded living conditions, the spiritual squalor and accepted immorality of life in the big city, the more hurried pace and frantic activity of the metropolis — all combine to erode the old faith and its value system and lifestyle. The city has always been the place for the young, the new, the experimental, and even the deviant side of life.

"Traditional Jewry suffered mightily from the transition from the rural world of the village to the new mores of the city. Family bonds were loosened; the *kehillah* was weakened; the opportunity to stray was now more available; and the new secular way proved attractive, exciting, and more in tune with city life" (*Triumph of Survival*, p. 185).

▌713 ▐ יִשְׂרָאֵל מוֹנִין לַלְּבָנָה וְעוֹבְדֵי כוֹכָבִים לַחַמָּה
"Israel reckon by the moon and idolaters by the sun" (*Sukkah* 29a).

Jews use a lunar calendar while the nations of the world use a solar calendar. Says the Gerer Rebbe [Rabbi Yehuda Leib Alter], this symbolizes the existential difference between them. The non-Jews can survive only as long as "the light" shines upon them — when their environment is "sunny." When their sun sets, however, so do their empires — they perish and disappear from the scene of history. In contradistinction to the nations, the Jews live and survive even in darkness — like the moon they shine even through the darkest night, even when persecuted and humiliated. They illuminate even when the sun is not shining (*Sefath Emeth*).

Rabbi Nachman of Breslov proclaimed: "*Mitzvah gedolah lihyoth b'simchah*

000000000000000000

tamid" [It is a great mitzvah always to be happy] (*Likutei Moharan, Tanina* 24).

During the Second World War, Breslover chassidim put up a sign on the gate to their ghetto: *"Yidden zeit zich nisht m'yaesh"* [Jews, do not despair!]. See *Insights*, vol. 1, #230, *"yiush shelo midaas."*

〚 714 〛   יִשְׂרָאֵל קְדוֹשִׁים הֵן: יֵשׁ רוֹצֶה וְאֵין לוֹ, וְיֵשׁ שֶׁיֵּשׁ לוֹ וְאֵינוֹ רוֹצֶה

"The people of Israel are holy: There are some who desire [to invite others to dine with them] but have not the means, while others have the means but have not the desire" (*Hullin* 7b).

Why are those who "have the means but have not the desire" considered holy? *Tosafoth* comments: "They are called holy for although they do not have the desire, they nevertheless invite others to dine with them because of embarrassment."

The *Yalkut HaGershuni* explains: The fact that one Jew invites another to eat with him because he is "embarrassed into it" — that in itself testifies to the holiness of Israel. The people of Israel are compassionate, and even if there is an individual who is miserly [by nature], he overcomes this negative inborn trait by a positive "sense of embarrassment" (*L'kutei Bosar L'kutei* [*Aggadoth*], vol. 5, p. 216).

כ

⟦ 715 ⟧

כָּאן יָשַׁנְנוּ, כָּאן הוּקַרְנוּ,
כָּאן חָשַׁשְׁתָּ אֶת רֹאשֶׁךָ

"Here we slept; here we caught cold; here you had a headache"
(*Midrash Tanchuma, Masai* 3).

On the verse, "These are the journeys of the Children of Israel" (Num. 33:1), the Midrash cites the following parable: "There was once a king who took his ailing son on a long journey in search of a cure. On their way home, the father enumerated all their travels. 'Here we slept ι . . .' In the same way, G-d told Moshe, 'Enumerate to them all the places at which they angered Me.'"

"Rabbi Avraham Mordechai Alter [the *Imrei Emeth*] asks: 'What is the relationship between the parable and the journeys of Israel? Should they not have slept? etc. . . .' He proceeds to explain each of the [above] three phrases allegorically.

'Here we slept' refers to the shameful way in which the Israelites, instead of being wakeful and eager to receive the Torah at Mount Sinai, had to be awakened by Moshe.

'Here we caught cold': Amalek cooled down the ardor of Israel in their Divine service. See Rashi on Deut. 25:18.

'Here you had a headache' alludes to the sin of the Golden Calf. The Hebrew phrase reads '*kahn chashashta es roshecha*' which, if interpreted homiletically, means 'here you entertained doubts [*chashashta*] concerning your head [*roshecha*] Moshe Rabbeinu — doubts concerning the very foundations of our faith'" (Rabbi A. Y. Bromberg, *Rebbes of Ger*, p. 292).

167

⟦ 716 ⟧   כְּדֵי לְחַבְּבָה עַל בַּעֲלָה

"In order to make her beloved to her husband" (*Baba Mezia* 87a).

"The Ministering Angels knew that our mother Sarah was in the tent [nevertheless they asked Abraham about her whereabouts] . . . in order to make her beloved to her husband" (ibid.).

"To make known to him that she was more modest than her companions, for she was not seen, and it was necessary to inquire concerning her whereabouts" (Rashi).

Rabbi Chaim Shmulevitz comments: "Abraham and Sarah were both very old and had been married for many years. Nevertheless, the angels felt it appropriate to point out Sarah's good qualities to her husband. An important lesson about married couples can be learned from this. Regardless of a couple's age and the length of time they have been married, it is always worthwhile to endear one to the other and to be careful not to say anything derogatory about a husband to a wife, or vice versa" (Rabbi Zelig Pliskin, *Love Your Neighbor*, p. 72).

⟦ 717 ⟧   כּוֹלָא מְחַנְּפִים לְמַלְכָּא

"Everyone flatters the king" (*Bamidbar Rabbah* 10:4).

"On the very same night that King Solomon completed the work on the Holy Temple he married Bathiah, the daughter of Pharaoh, and there was great jubilation on account of the Temple, and jubilation on account of Pharaoh's daughter; and this jubilation . . . exceeded that of the Temple — as the proverb says: 'Everyone flatters the king'" (ibid.).

See, however, *Yerushalmi Sanhedrin*, "The righteous know their Master is true and they do not flatter Him."

Rabbi Meir Premishlaner comments: "When it appears that there is a 'dispute' between Israel and the Almighty, the *tzaddikim* would always be on the side of Jewry. G-d neither needs nor desires flattery, and doesn't need anyone to defend Him."

Regarding the recent attempts to explain the Holocaust, Rabbi Chaim Shapiro writes: "To my knowledge, the various *Gedolim* [great spiritual leaders] that I met never attempted to deal with the *Churban*. The wound was too fresh, the pain too deep, their *Ahavas Yisroel* [love of Jews] too great. They always sided with the 'community of Israel' (*The Jewish Observer*, vol. 22, no. 5, p. 14).

Cf. *Sotah* 42a, "Four classes will not receive the presence of the *Shechinah*: the class of scoffers; the class of flatterers; the class of liars; and the class of slanderers."

⫛ 718 ⫛

כֹּחַ דְּהֶתֵּירָא עָדִיף

"The power of the *heter* [lenient ruling] is superior" (*Bezah* 2b).

"It is better to accept a lenient interpretation based on a definite tradition one has received than a stringent interpretation, for anyone can assume a more stringent view" (Rashi).

"The more lenient view of necessity brings evidence to support it, whereas the more stringent one may be an imposition on oneself" (Tosafoth).

The *SheLah HaKodesh* [Rabbi Isaiah Horowitz] writes: "If there is no reason for stringency, but for lack of knowledge one adopts a stringent ruling for himself, then he is a *chassid shoteh* [a foolish pious man]" (*Shney Luchoth HaBrith*, 1, p. 184b).

Rabbi Shabbasai HaCohen offers the following directive for ritual decisions: "Just as it is wrong to permit what is forbidden, so is it wrong to forbid what is permitted . . . . Such prohibition may eventually result in an unjustified leniency . . ." (*Shach, Yoreh De'ah* 442, *Kitzur minhagoth horaoth issur veheter*, 9).

Rabbi Yitzchak Elchanan offered the following prayer for the recovery of his son who was seriously ill: "Master of the Universe, before Thee it is well known that numerous questions came to me concerning *agunoth* [women whose husbands are nowhere to be found] . . . . In all cases, I labored earnestly to find a *heter* [legal permission] for these unfortunate people . . . . Therefore, have mercy on me and my son . . . ."

In time of tribulation, Rabbi Yitzchak Elchanan prayed to the Almighty to remember the virtue of *heterim* (Rabbi Yaakov Lifschitz, *Toledoth Yitzchak*, p. 16).

〔 719 〕

כִּי מָחִית לְינוּקָא,
לָא תִימְחֵי אֶלָּא בְּעַרְקְתָא דִמְסַנָּא

"When you strike a child [a pupil], do not strike him with anything but a shoelace [lit., the string of a shoe] (*Baba Bathra* 21a).

Punish him with a light stroke which can do no harm (Rashi).

"A teacher may punish his students to instil awe in them, but he may not strike them with enmity or cruelty. He may, therefore, not whip them with a scourge or a stick, but with a little strap" (*Mishneh Torah, Hil. Talmud Torah* 2:2).

Rabbi Samson Raphael Hirsch writes: "A good teacher, of course, will be able to avoid physical punishment during the normal school life with its usual incidents. Yet if the child is beaten at home, if he is trained to realize his mistakes only when corporal punishment is meted out, if he obeys only when the stick threatens in the background — then the home merely succeeds in dulling the child's sense of moral values and he hardly can be expected to pay appropriate heed to the teacher's constructive criticism" (*Timeless Torah*, trans. of *Gesammelte Schriften*, 518).

See *Sotah* 47a, "One should thrust aside a child with his left hand, and draw him near with his right hand. In educating children, we discipline with the 'left hand' [indirect restrictions] while we draw them close with our 'right hand' [with love and respect]."

Cf. *Aboth* 4:15, "Let the honor of your student be as dear to you as your own." See *Insights*, vol. 1, #231.

∬ 720 ∬

כִּי סַיֵּים מְסָאנֵיה לֵימָא
"בָּרוּךְ שֶׁעָשָׂה לִי כָּל צָרְכִּי"

"When he ties his shoes he should say: 'Blessed is He who has provided me with all my needs'" (*Berakoth* 60b).

"Why does one recite this blessing only when he wears shoes and not when he dons other garments?

"We find that shoes are a symbol of '*histapkuth*' [contentment].

"When a woman refuses to be betrothed to a husband who is 'of higher caste,' she says, 'I do not want a shoe too large for my foot' (*Kiddushin* 49a). Hence, one who possesses the trait of *histapkuth* — who is content with what he has and is happy with his lot — is able to give thanks to the Almighty, Who has supplied him with all his needs. 'His shoe fits' — and he is able to recite the *bracha*, 'Blessed is He who has provided me with all my needs'" (Rabbi Aaron Levin, *Hadrash Veha'iyun*, Gen. mamor 188).

∬ 721 ∬

כִּי קָאֵי רַבִּי בְּהָא מַסֶּכְתָּא לָא תִּשַׁיְילֵיה
בְּמַסֶּכְתָּא אַחֲרִיתִי

"When Rebbe is engaged [in the study of a particular] tractate, one should not question him about another tractate" (*Shabbath* 3b).

"Lest he not be conversant with it" (ibid.). Both Rashi and Rambam explain that the above ruling serves to protect the teacher from embarrassment. See *Mishneh Torah, Hil. Talmud Torah* 4:6.

Rabbi Yitzchak Hutner notes that from the Rishonim, just the opposite emphasis is suggested. "That is, the rule manifests the great stature of a Rebbe, rather than his limitations. Torah study requires total concentration. The sage who learns Torah is involved in his pursuit with every fiber of his essence. Any questions extraneous to his present subject matter is a distraction. The greater the sage, the more total is the isolation of his thinking process. The ability to respond to other matters means that the Rebbe has not yet achieved fusion with his present tractate" (*Pachad Yitzchak, Shevuoth,*

Ma'amar 9, cited by Rabbi J. Simcha Cohen, *Timely Jewish Questions, Timeless Answers*, p. 88).

An excellent example of total immersion in one's current subject matter — to the exclusion of all else — was the Rosh Yeshivah of Mir, Rabbi Nochum Percowiz.

"One Chanukah someone came to relate a thought connected to the Chanukah holiday, and Reb Nochum, as always, listened attentively. He offered a warm compliment but excused himself for not delving into the matter for 'I simply cannot tear myself away from *Baba Kamma'"* (Hanoch Teller, *Sunset*, p. 32).

⎰ 722 ⎱   כֵּיוָן שֶׁמֵּת אָדָם נַעֲשֶׂה חָפְשִׁי מִן הַמִּצְוֹת

"As soon as a man dies he is free from the commandments" (*Niddah* 61b).

Rabbi Chaim ben Attar comments: "Ordinarily, a person has no opportunity to serve G-d after death, as our sages taught: 'For the dead there is freedom' [Psalms 88:6], meaning that after a person dies he is free of the obligation of *mitzvoth*. However, those who passionately yearn to serve G-d in their lifetime, will be designated as G-d's ministering angels in the future and will serve Him for eternity" (*Ohr HaChaim*, Ex. 21:5).

Just before the passing of the Vilna Gaon, he grasped his *tzitzis* in his hand and said: "How difficult it is to leave this world. In this world, for a few *kopeks*, a person can purchase *tzitzis*, and as a reward for that simple *mitzvah* he merits to experience the Divine Presence in the World to Come. But in the Upper World, he can no longer earn anything, even if he exerts all his energies" (*HaGaon HaChassid MiVilna*).

〖 723 〗

כֵּיוָן שֶׁנָּשָׂא אָדָם אִשָּׁה עֲוֹנוֹתָיו מִתְפַּקְּקִין

"As soon as a man takes a wife, his sins are stopped up"
(*Yebamoth* 63b).

"The groom and bride should sanctify themselves as they prepare to enter the *chuppah*, for our sages have said, 'G-d forgives them their sins.' They should therefore repent on the day before their wedding and resolve from that day onward to serve the Almighty in truth and total commitment" (Rabbi Isaiah Horowitz, *Shelah*).

Cf. *Ta'anith* 26b, "Israel had no days as festive as the Fifteenth of Av and *Yom Kippur* . . . ."

Rabbi Yaakov Yitzchok of Parsischa, the Yud HaKadosh, comments: "The reason that the Talmud compares the Fifteenth of Av to *Yom Kippur* is as follows: The 15th day of Av commemorates the granting of permission for marriage between the various tribes of Israel, and the sins of the groom and bride are forgiven on a wedding day as on *Yom Kippur*" (J. K. K. Rakotz, *Niflaoth HaYehudi*, p. 67).

〖 724 〗

כִּיחֲלָה וּפִירְכְּסָה אֵין לָה מְזוֹנוֹת

"If she painted her eyes and dyed her hair, she is not entitled to maintenance" (*Kethuboth* 54a).

A widow is supported from the inheritance of the orphans only as long she remains a widow. Once she begins to use cosmetics, she forfeits this support since she thereby demonstrates that she is no longer concerned with the memory of her late husband and intends to remarry.

When Rabbi Yosef Dov Soloveitchik [the *Beis HaLevi*] was informed that many of the Jews of Slutsk were sending their children to secular schools, he publicly reprimanded the parents for their apathy toward their children's spiritual welfare. He cited the above dictum and exclaimed: "The Jewish nation in exile is like a widow whose needs are provided by the Almighty. But, the instant Jewry adorns herself with the cosmetics of a gentile culture, she indicates her intent to follow the gentiles, and thereby forfeits all her privileges. No longer is Jewry justified in asking G-d to have pity on her" (Rabbi Aharon Surasky, *Giants of Jewry*, vol. 1, p. 48).

◊ 725 ◊

כָּךְ הִיא דַּרְכָּהּ שֶׁל תּוֹרָה,
פַּת בְּמֶלַח תֹּאכֵל . . . .

"This is the way of the Torah: To eat bread with salt . . ."
(*Aboth* 6:4).

". . . to drink water by ration, to sleep upon the ground, to live a life of hardship, and to toil in the Torah . . ." (ibid.).

"Even if you find yourself in the extremes of poverty . . . and your life is a life of privation, even then toil in the Torah" (R. Joseph b. Joseph Nahmias, *Comm. on Aboth*).

Rabbi Meir Shapiro of Lublin comments: "I explain this [the above dictum] not as statements, but as questions. 'Is this the way of Torah? Is it proper to abandon one who learns Torah? Should he eat bread with salt and no more? And should he sleep on the ground? No, that is not the way of Torah!"

At the national convention of the Polish Agudah (1929), Rabbi Meir Shapiro warned of the degradation of Torah and announced: "In my yeshiva (of Lublin), no student will be made to feel inferior, he will not . . . be forced to eat in various homes like a beggar going from door to door. Rather, he will enjoy living conditions in keeping with his status — that of a prince" (Rabbi Aharon Surasky, *Great Chassidic Leaders*, pp. 142, 143).

◊ 726 ◊ כָּל אָדָם שֶׁיֵּשׁ בּוֹ תּוֹרָה וְאֵין בּוֹ יִרְאַת שָׁמַיִם
דּוֹמֶה לְגִזְבָּר שֶׁמָּסְרוּ לוֹ מַפְתְּחוֹת הַפְּנִימִיּוֹת,
וּמַפְתְּחוֹת הַחִיצוֹנוֹת לֹא מָסְרוּ לוֹ, בְּהֵי עָיֵיל

"Every man who possesses Torah study without the fear of Heaven, is like a treasurer who is entrusted with the inner keys but not with the outer keys: How is he to enter?" (*Shabbath* 31a).

Der alter of Novhardok [Rav Yosef Yozel Horowitz] comments: "Everything in life, both material and spiritual matters, can only be understood through Torah study. However, if one should acquire Torah knowledge without 'fear of Heaven,' then he is as 'one who carries books' — it is extraneous to him. The Torah cannot influence him, for his evil characteristics act as an iron curtain. Hence, his Torah remains external to him" (*Madregath HaAdam*, intro.).

"G-d declares in plain words that it is the object of all religious acts to produce in man fear of Heaven and obedience to His word" (Maimonides, *Moreh Nevuchim*, III, 52).

◊ 727 ◊   כָּל אֶחָד וְאֶחָד חַיָּיב לוֹמַר
בִּשְׁבִילִי נִבְרָא הָעוֹלָם

"Every single person is obliged to say: 'The world was created for my sake'" (*Sanhedrin*, 37a).

Rabbi Simchah Bunim of Peshischa suggested that every person carry in his pocket two cards. On one card he should inscribe the verse, "I am but dust and ashes" [Gen. 18:27], and on the other card the words, "The world was created for my sake" (*Siach Sarfei Kodesh*).

Rabbi Joseph Isaac Schneersohn comments: "The Hebrew word for world, *Olam*, has the same root as the word for 'hiding.' The world hides and does not reveal G-dliness. The meaning of our sages' statement [above] is that each person has to realize that the creation of the *world*, i.e., of the *hiding* of

G-dliness, was for him — so that he could refine and elevate it" (*Bosi L'Gani*, p. 22).

Rabbi Isaac Hutner philosophizes: "Is it not obvious that the fact of death must seem to contradict the truth that 'The world was created for my sake.' The world continues to exist even after the death of a man. Only out of the faith that ultimately the decree of death is but contingent and transient . . . and that death is thus a temporary phenomenon, while the law of life is an eternal one — only out of this faith can a man ready himself for the truth that 'The world was created for my sake'" (*Pachad Yitzchak*, vol. 3, Lecture 2.).

◊ 728 ◊   כָּל דְּאַלִּים גְּבַר

"Whoever is stronger prevails" (*Baba Bathra* 34b).

"If there are two claimants to a property [real or personal] and one says, 'It belonged to my father,' while the other says 'To my father' [without either of them bringing any evidence], Rabbi Nachman says, 'That which is stronger prevails' [whether by argument or force]" (ibid.).

The *Rosh* [R. Asher ben Yechiel] maintains that "power" establishes a right in the contested property. Hence, the loser may not subsequently exercise force to retrieve it for himself, for it is not logical to believe that we would allow contesting parties to engage in perpetual strife. The successful use of force in the first instance is some "evidence" that right is on the side of the victor, for "the rightful owner will 'sacrifice himself' for his property, more than anyone else will in order to steal it."

"For this reason, Rav Chaim Volozhiner told an officer in Napoleon's army that although the French forces might actually be stronger than the Russians, since the Russians were fighting for their own land, they would demonstrate greater *mesiras nefesh* (sacrifice) than the French and would therefore emerge victorious" (Rabbi Aharon Soloveitchik, *The Warmth and the Light*, p. 35).

Rabbi Amiel comments: "From here [the reasoning of the *Rosh*] we see the trust [our sages] place in the victory of *hatzedek hamusari* [ethical justice]" (*Hatzedek Hasotziali Vehatzedek Hamishpat Vehamusari Shelanu*).

See, however, the *Shitah Mekubezeth* [R. Bezalel Ashkenazi], who maintains that "power" cannot establish a right. Consequently, he who was defeated in a contest of power may subsequently use his strength to wrest the object form the initial victor.

⟦ 729 ⟧   כָּל דְּאָסַר לָן רַחְמָנָא, שָׁרָא לָן כַּוָּתֵיהּ

"For everything that the Torah has forbidden us, it has permitted us an equivalent" (*Hullin* 109b).

"It has forbidden us blood, but it has permitted us liver . . . it has forbidden us the fat of cattle, but it has permitted us the fat of wild beasts; it has forbidden us pig's flesh, but it has permitted us the brain of *shibbuta* [a certain fish which tastes like pig] . . . (ibid.).

The *Maharsha* comments: "A person should not say that we do not eat blood because it is repulsive, but simply because the Torah forbade it. For if the reason were its repulsiveness, the Torah would never have allowed us to eat liver, which has the taste of blood."

Cf. *Sifra, Va'yikra* 20:26, "A person should not say, 'I loathe swine's flesh' . . . but he should say, 'I do desire it, yet what can I do, since my Father in Heaven has decreed upon me.'" See *Insights*, vol. 1, #58.

Rabbi Eliyahu Dessler writes: "The idea behind this [our dictum] is that the Torah wishes to undermine that insatiable curiosity which insists on tasting everything and enjoying everything. By allowing a person to 'taste' the 'prohibition' in a permitted way, the sting is taken out of the curiosity" (*Michtav Me-Eliyahu*, vol. 1, p. 263).

〚 730 〛

כָּל דַּיָּין שֶׁדָּן דִּין אֱמֶת לַאֲמִיתּוֹ
מַשְׁרֶה שְׁכִינָה בְּיִשְׂרָאֵל

"Every judge who judges a true judgment according to its truth,
causes the Shechinah to dwell in Israel" (*Sanhedrin* 7a).

Why the double expression of truth — "*emeth la'amitoh*" [true judgment according to its truth]?

"There are two kinds of truth — but one is more *true* than the other. (a) When a judge issues a judgment based on *pesharoh* [compromise] — it is a judgment, but it is nonetheless not in accordance with the Attribute of Justice. (b) When the judge issues a judgment in accordance with strict *Din* [Justice], then it is truly just — it is absolutely true" (Rabbi Isaiah Horowitz, *Shney Luchoth HaBrith* II, 270a).

See *Baba Bathra* 8b, *Tosaf.* s.v. "*Din*," An absolutely true verdict can be arrived at by the judge if he endeavors to find out the truth himself, and does not rely only on the evidence.

Nonetheless, a judge is required to recommend *pesharoh* to the litigants before the case is heard, for the sake of "peace" between the parties.

Cf. *Shabbath* 10a, "Every judge who judges a true judgment according to its truth, it is as though he had become a partner to the Holy One, blessed be He, in the creation." See *Insights*, vol. 1, #258.

Cf. *Pirke de Rabbi Eliezer* 21, "Man is compared to a tree." See *Insights*, vol. 1, #5.

〚 731 〛

כָּל הָאוֹמֵר הַקָּדוֹשׁ בָּרוּךְ הוּא וַתְּרָן
יִוָּתְרוּ חַיָּיו

"Whosoever says that the Holy One, blessed be He, waives [is lax in the execution of justice], his life shall be waived" (*Baba Kamma* 50a).

He forfeits his life, for he teaches [or encourages] others to sin (Rashi).
Rabbi Chaim of Volozhin comments: "A strange dictum, on the face of it.

Even among men, the kind ones deal generously with others. But the meaning of this saying is that punishment for sin is not some kind of revenge, G-d forbid! Rather, 'evil pursues the sinners' [Prov. 12:21]; sin is its own punishment. At the time of Creation, G-d fixed all the rules by which the Worlds are regulated in such a manner that they should depend upon the good or evil deeds of man . . . . Man is obliged to accept judgment according to the type and importance of the infringement, at the hands of those very forces of uncleanliness which he strengthened by his deeds. By the acceptance of this judgment, the perfection of his own soul and that of the World is automatically effected" (*Nefesh HaChaim*, ch. 12).

⎕ 732 ⎕ כָּל הָאוֹמֵר „תְּהִלָּה לְדָוִד" בְּכָל יוֹם שָׁלֹשׁ פְּעָמִים מוּבְטָח לוֹ שֶׁהוּא בֶּן הָעוֹלָם הַבָּא

"Whoever recites [the psalm] *tehillah l'David* [*Ashrei*, Psalms 145] three times daily, is sure to inherit the World to Come" (*Berakoth* 4b).

The Chasam Sofer once met an errant Jew who boasted that he was so busy, that he had no time to study Torah or to perform *mitzvoth*. The Rabbi asked him, "So what are you doing to insure yourself a place in the World to Come?" The fellow replied confidently, "I have no fear on that account, because the one thing I do perform religiously is the recitation of *Ashrei*, and our Rabbis have taught that whoever recites *Ashrei* thrice daily is assured of a place in the World to Come."

Meanwhile a young yeshiva student entered the Chasam Sofer's study and complained of a terrible cold. When asked if he was taking medicine, the student said, "Yes." The Chasam Sofer then asked the boy where he boarded and he answered, "In a cold, damp cellar!" Upon hearing this, the Chasam Sofer exclaimed, "If so, then all the pills in the world will not help you, for you are in a place which breeds sickness anew every day!"

The Chasam Sofer then turned to the visitor. "*Ashrei* is like medicine," he explained. "If you practice everything incumbent upon a Jew, but err slightly and catch a touch of spiritual illness, then *Ashrei* can save you. But if you don't study Torah, and neglect all the *mitzvoth*, then you are terminally ill and you are in an environment which perpetually breeds sickness. You can say *Ashrei* as many times as you wish, but you will not merit a portion in the Hereafter" (*ArtScroll, Tehillim*, vol. 5, p. 1700).

Cf. "Whoever walks four cubits in the Land of Israel is assured of a place in the World to Come." See #737.

𝄆 733 𝄇

כָּל הַדָּר בְּחוּצָה לָאָרֶץ דּוֹמֶה כְּמִי
שֶׁאֵין לוֹ אֱלוֹ-הַ

"Whoever lives outside the Land [of Israel] may be regarded as one who has no G-d" (*Kethuboth* 110b).

"He may be regarded as one who worships idols" (ibid.).

Rabbi Chaim ben Bezalel [the Maharal's brother] writes: "This refers to one who has, in his state of mind, *permanently established* his residence in the Diaspora to the extent that he has no thoughts of the redemption, no thoughts of *Moshiach*, and no thoughts of the Holy Land" (*Sefer HaChaim*, sec. *Geulah Ve'Shuah*).

The Lubavitcher Rebbe comments: "The hearts of the people of Israel, though scattered over the globe, are all turned to one point — Jerusalem. Whenever a Jew prays, he turns to the Holy City; thus, even in those places that are physically outside the boundaries of the Land of Israel, spiritually Jerusalem is *there*!" (Rabbi Menachem Mendel Schneerson, *A Thought for the Week*, vol. 8, p. 86).

In Ramban's critical notes to Rambam's Sefer HaMitzvoth, he points to the statement in the *Talmud*: "*Whoever leaves the Land and settles outside of it, consider him as if he was an idol-worshiper.*" Ramban sees settling the Land as a formal positive command, part of the 613 commandments and valid for all generations.

Cf. *Kethuboth* 75a, "But of Zion it can be said, 'man and man was born there . . .' [Psalms 87:5]. Both he who was born there and he who looks forward to seeing her." See #671.

See #1000.

734

כָּל הַכּוֹפֵר בְּטוֹבָתוֹ שֶׁל חֲבֵרוֹ, לִבְסוֹף כּוֹפֵר
בְּטוֹבָתוֹ שֶׁל הַקָּדוֹשׁ בָּרוּךְ הוּא

"Whoever is ungrateful for good done to him by his friend will eventually prove ungrateful for the good done to him by the Holy One, blessed be He" (*Midrash HaGadol, Shemoth* 1:8).

Rabbi Nahum Velvel Sieff of Kelm comments: "A person's behavior depends on his character. If he is of an irritable nature, he will react irritably to whatever interferes with his desires; and so with arrogance, kindness and indifference. One cannot borrow character traits for special purposes and discard them at will. A person who is by nature ungrateful will be ungrateful not only in his relations with his fellow man, but also in his relations with his Creator. Once this trait is ingrained in his character, it will take charge of all his behavior and permeate all his attitudes, even when standing before the Almighty" (Rabbi Eliyahu E. Dessler, *Michtav Me-Eliyahu*, vol. 1, p. 50).

Cf. *Mishnath R. Eliezer*, 137 — "Why did Scripture prescribe punishment especially for those who are ungrateful? Because it is akin to denying the Holy One, blessed be He. This man shows no gratitude now for his neighbor's kindness; tomorrow he will be ungrateful for his Maker's kindness."

Cf. *Abodah Zarah* 5a, "Ungrateful ones, children of ungrateful ones." See *Insights*, vol. 1, #326.

735

כָּל הַלָּן שִׁבְעַת יָמִים בְּלֹא חֲלוֹם נִקְרָא רַע

"He who sleeps seven days without a dream is called evil"
(*Berakoth* 14a).

The Vilna Gaon explains the above enigmatic dictum in the following metaphorical manner. "Our whole life is but a 'fleeting dream,' but owing to the toils and cares of life, man is unable to perceive its inherent nothingness. Whereas one can find an excuse for his lack of perception during the six working days, when he has no opportunity for reflection — the same excuse is no longer valid on the Sabbath, when he rests from his toils and the cares of his life. Hence, he who sleeps for seven days — one of which must be the Sabbath — without perceiving that the world is but a dream and that all he seems to hear, taste, see and feel is but imaginary, he is called evil; it is evidence of the evil of his heart" (Rabbi Moshe Avigdor Amiel, *Derashos El-Ami*, vol. 1, p. 70).

⎡ 736 ⎤ כָּל הַמְגַדֵּל יָתוֹם וִיתוֹמָה בְּתוֹךְ בֵּיתוֹ מַעֲלֶה עָלָיו הַכָּתוּב כְּאִילוּ יְלָדוֹ

"Anyone who brings up an orphan boy or girl in his house, Scripture accounts it *as if* he had begotten him" (*Megillah* 13a).

Rabbi Shlomo Kluger wonders whether the above dictum should be taken literally. Is one who raises an orphan in his house virtually like the one who fathers a child, in that he fulfills thereby the precept of "be fruitful and multiply"? The answer to this question, Rabbi Kluger believes, is dependent upon the semantic dispute between the *Derishah* and the *Taz* in *Yoreh De'ah* 242.

The *Derishah* maintains that wherever the term *k'illu* [as if] is used by the sages, it is not to be taken literally. Hence, raising an orphan is not like fathering a child, and one cannot thereby fulfill his obligation of *pru ur'vu* ["be fruitful and multiply"] in this fashion. The *Taz*, however, maintains that *k'illu* means that they are indeed "*shaveh mamash*" [exactly alike]. Hence, raising an orphan in one's house is in fulfillment of the first commandment (*Chochmath Shlomo*, *Even HaEzer* 1:1).

Cf. *Shabbath* 31a, "Did you engage in procreation?" See #922.

⦚ 737 ⦚

כָּל הַמְהַלֵּךְ אַרְבַּע אַמּוֹת בְּאֶרֶץ יִשְׂרָאֵל
מוּבְטָח לוֹ שֶׁהוּא בֶּן הָעוֹלָם הַבָּא

"Whoever walks four cubits in the Land of Israel is assured of a place in the World to Come" (*Kethuboth* 111a).

How is it possible to achieve immortality for merely walking four cubits in the Land of Israel? Rabbi Nachman of Breslov explains: "The motive for making the journey to Israel must be purely spiritual, to draw closer to G-d. Hence, merely by stepping foot on the Land, one becomes merged with it and transformed by its sacred character. That is why even one who walks a short distance in Israel will assuredly inherit the World to Come.

On the other hand, if a person's motive has nothing to do with devotion to G-d and cleansing himself of his evil, then what help will the Land be to him? The Land will vomit him out . . ." (Rabbi Nathan of Breslov, *Likutey Etzoth*).

Cf. *Berakoth* 4b, "Whoever recites '*tehillah l'David*' three times daily, is sure to inherit the World to Come." See #732.

⦚ 738 ⦚

כָּל הַמּוֹסֵר עַצְמוֹ לַמָּוֶת עַל דִּבְרֵי תוֹרָה,
אֵין אוֹמְרִים דְּבַר הֲלָכָה מִשְׁמוֹ

"Whosoever places himself in deadly peril for words of the Torah, no *halachic* matter may be reported in his name" (*Baba Kamma* 61a).

The *Maharsha* explains: "Whoever reports a saying in the name of its originator brings deliverance to the world" [*Aboth* 6:6] (See *Insights*, vol. 1, #263). However, one who embarks upon an extremely dangerous [Torah] mission, relying upon a miracle to save him, is not worthy of bringing deliverance and redemption ["One may not rely on a miracle," *Yerushalmi*, *Yoma* 1:4. See *Insights*, vol. 1, #51].

Although "those sent to perform a *mitzvah* do not suffer harm" [*Pesahim* 8b; see *Insights*, vol. 1, #486], where harm is highly probable [*shechicha hezeka*] this principle does not apply."

The Maharal miPrague comments "This [the above dictum] does not in any way contradict the dictum which states: 'The words of the Torah are firmly held by one who kills himself for it' [*Berakoth* 63b], for that statement refers to one who studies Torah amidst great difficulties and suffering, i.e., 'he kills himself for it.' However, one is forbidden to place himself in deadly peril for 'the words of Torah,' for the Torah is 'life' itself. Consequently, one who surrenders himself to the 'negation' of life for the sake of Torah, his Torah should not be quoted."

See *Insights*, vol. 1, #34.

〔 739 〕　　כָּל הַמַּחֲנִיף לַחֲבֵרוֹ, סוֹף נוֹפֵל בְּיָדוֹ

"Whosoever flatters another will ultimately fall into his hands" (*Sotah* 41b).

Rabbi Menachem Mendel Schneerson, the Lubavitcher Rebbe, believes that our present troubles started from "Whoever flatters another . . . ." He writes: "In recent years we have seen how all those who once adopted a philosophy of compromise, thinking it would attract the youth, have in fact lost the very youth they sought to guide on the path of compromise."

Moreover, they also weakened those young people under their influence who had regarded themselves as thoroughly religious. On the other hand, those who years ago followed the principle of not yielding even a detail, particularly in education, have been successful" (*Likkutei Sichot*, vol. 1, *Beraishith*, p. 163).

Cf. *Beraishith Rabbah* 54:3, "Love unaccompanied by reproof is not love." See *Insights*, vol. 1, #256.

◊ 740 ◊   כָּל הַמַּלְוֶה בְּרִיבִּית כּוֹפֵר בָּעִיקָּר

"Whoever charges interest on loans is a 'denier of the fundamental principle' [the existence of G-d] (*Yerushalmi, Baba Mezia* 5:8).

"The giving up of the perfectly justified demand for interest on loans is ordained to show that we are to consider G-d as the real Owner and Master of our property. Hence, the Torah concludes [the prohibition of interest] with the words: 'I am the L-rd your G-d, who brought you out of the land of Egypt, to be your G-d" (Rabbi Samson Raphael Hirsch, *Pentateuch*, Ex. 22:24).

Similarly, the Alshich HaKadosh writes: "Payment of interest implies that the person who pays feels that the sum he had borrowed 'had belonged' to the lender. The fact is that the lender loaned G-d's money. We are only administering this money on behalf of its true Owner" (*Torath Moshe, Behar*).

Essentially, charging and paying interest on loans is not an ethical, but a theological offense. Hence, it is codified not in *Choshen Mishpat* [Civil Laws] where we would expect to find it, but in *Yoreh De'ah* [Ritual Laws]. It is an infraction of the mitzvoth that pertain "between man and G-d."

◊ 741 ◊   כָּל הַמְלַמֵּד אֶת בֶּן חֲבֵירוֹ תּוֹרָה זוֹכֶה וְיוֹשֵׁב בִּישִׁיבָה שֶׁל מַעְלָה

"He who teaches Torah to his neighbor's son will be privileged to sit in the Heavenly Academy" (*Baba Mezia* 85a).

In an address to Day School teachers concerning the vital importance of *Kiruv* [outreach to non-affiliated Jews], Rabbi Yitzchak Hutner, cited the above dictum.

It is significant to note, in this regard, that when Rabbi Pinchas Stolper [the Executive Director of UOJCA] spoke to Rabbi Hutner many years ago about his dream of organizing a national outreach youth movement called NCSY [National Conference of Synagogue Youth], Rav Hutner responded, "I envy you your portion in the World to Come."

Cf. *Sanhedrin* 19b and 99b, "He who teaches the son of his neighbor Torah, Scripture ascribes it to him as if he had begotten him" . . . "as though he fashioned him." See *Insights*, vol. 1, #282, 283.

〚 742 〛

כָּל הַמְסַפֵּר לְשׁוֹן הָרָע . . .
רָאוּי לְהַשְׁלִיכוֹ לַכְּלָבִים

"Whosoever spreads evil tales . . . deserves to be cast to the dogs" (*Pesahim* 118a).

The Chafetz Chaim explains that our dictum underscores the "measure for measure" principle. It is quite natural for a dog to bark at, to frighten, and sometimes even to bite, those who walk past him and pay him no concern. Similarly, the gossip-monger injures everyone with his voice — he finds something derogatory to say about everyone. Hence, it is but fitting to cast him before the dogs who will likewise frighten and bite him (Chafetz Chaim, *Shmiras HaLashon*, part 1, ch. 2).

Cf. *Arakhin* 15b, "Whoever spreads evil talk, is as if he denies the very existence of G-d." See *Insights*, vol. 1, #284.

See Vilna Gaon's interpretation of "The Evil Inclination resembles a fly" (*Berakoth* 61a) in #710.

〚 743 〛

כָּל הַמַּעֲבִיר עַל מִדּוֹתָיו
מַעֲבִירִין לוֹ עַל כָּל פְּשָׁעָיו

"He who passes by his measures [overcomes his natural tendencies], all his sins are passed by [forgiven]" (*Rosh Hashanah* 17a).

Rashi explains the term *ma'avir al midosov* to mean that one refrains from 'measuring out' a corresponding response to those who have caused him hurt. "For this," says *Rashi*, "the Attribute of Justice [responds in kind] by not scrutinizing this person's deeds; rather, it lets him be."

Rabbi Aryeh Kaplan asserts that "the Talmud clearly states that those who attain this level of stoicism [overcoming natural tendencies] are able to radiate spirituality. He relates this talmudic principle with the kabbalistic concept know as 'hishtavus,' a term derived from the root *shaveh* meaning 'equal.' This denotes making all things equal for oneself, and can be translated as equanimity, or more accurately as 'stoicism.' It involves total indifference to all outside influences, good or bad."

In speaking of *hishtavus* [stoicism], the Baal Shem Tov states that this is the intent of the verse *"Shivi'si Hashem l'negdi tamid"* [generally translated as "I have set G-d before me at all times" [Psalms 16:8]. According to the Baal Shem, the word *shivi'si* should be translated "I have been stoic [*shaveh*]." Hence the verse reads, "I have been stoic, G-d is before me at all times" (*Meditation and Kabbalah*, p. 140).

Cf, *Sanhedrin* 22a, "He who prays should regard himself as if the *Shechinah* was before him . . . . See #644.

⟦ 744 ⟧

כָּל הַמְעַנֵּג אֶת הַשַּׁבָּת
נוֹתְנִין לוֹ מִשְׁאֲלוֹת לִבּוֹ

"Whoever makes the Sabbath delightful is granted his heart's desire" (*Shabbath* 118b).

"For it is said: 'Take delight in the L-rd, that He may grant you the desire of your heart' [Psalms 37:4]. 'Delight' refers to the Sabbath, as it is said, 'And you shall call the Sabbath a delight' [Isa. 58:13].

What is the link between 'Sabbath delight' and the heart of man [as implied in the above dictum]? The Maharal explains that the Sabbath relates to the days of the week as the heart relates to the organs of the body. The Sabbath is the sanctity of days and the heart is the vitality of the body" (*Perushei Maharal MiPrague*).

In commenting on the wording of our dictum, the Vilna Gaon suggests that it does not say *"ha'me'aneg es atzmo"* [he delights himself], but *"ha'me'aneg es haShabbath"* [he makes the Sabbath delightful]. The focus is on the Sabbath becoming "a delight" rather than on his finding delight on the Sabbath.

In a similar vein, Rabbi Eliyahu Lopian writes: "If the sole intention was that we eat tastier foods on the Sabbath, surely we could have the same pleasure if such foods were placed before us on any day of the week. This is not honoring the Sabbath, but honoring oneself on the Sabbath" (*Lev Eliyahu*, p. 49).

Reb Yisrael Salanter poignantly remarked [regarding how one eats on the Sabbath], "*meh ken oifessen dem gantzen Shabbos in de tzimmes*" [the entire Sabbath may be "consumed" in the eating of *tzimmes*]. This would be honoring oneself, not honoring the Sabbath!

⦊ 745 ⦉

כָּל הַמְעַנֵּג אֶת הַשַּׁבָּת נוֹתְנִין לוֹ
נַחֲלָה בְּלִי מְצָרִים

"Whoever makes the Sabbath delightful will be granted a heritage that has no limitations" (*Shabbath* 118a).

Rabbi Akiva's dictum, "Treat your Sabbath as a weekday rather than be dependent on men" [ibid.], refers to those individuals whose poverty precludes buying special food to enjoy on the Sabbath. See *Insights*, vol. 1, #445. But if at all possible, one should honor the Sabbath according to one's means (Rabbi Yaakov Baal Haturim, *Orach Chaim, Hil. Shabbath* 242:1).

Rabbi Eliyahu E. Dessler writes: "The mitzvah of *Oneg Shabbath* is to bring the spirit of the holy Sabbath into all one's physical pleasures and so sanctify them, that it softens their materialistic aspects. The Sabbath can then cast its influence over the whole week, drive out physical desires and destroy them" (*Michtav Me-Eliyahu*, vol. 1, p. 230).

"The peace and serenity that are an integral ingredient of the Sabbath should become part of a person's nature the entire week. The inner peace that one experiences on the Sabbath should be internalized so that its positive effect would be noticeable in one's relationship with family and friends" (Rabbi Chaim E. Zaitchik, *Maayanei HaChaim*, vol. 3, p. 313).

INSIGHTS: A TALMUDIC TREASURY 189

ֆ 746 ֆ

כָּל הַמְקַבֵּל עָלָיו מִצְוָה אַחַת בֶּאֱמוּנָה, כְּדַאי
הוּא שֶׁתִּשְׁרֶה עָלָיו רוּחַ הַקּוֹדֶשׁ

"Whosoever accepts even one single commandment with true faith
is deserving of having the Holy Spirit rest upon him" (*Mechilta*,
Ex. 14:31).

"This is one of the fundamental principles of faith in the Torah. When
one fulfills one of the 613 commandments properly and sincerely, without
any worldly or personal motivation, but only for its own sake and out of
love — he will merit life in the World to Come" (Rambam, *Commentary on the
Mishnah, Makkoth* 23b).

Cf. *Kiddushin* 39b, "He who performs one mitzvah, good is done to him,
his days are prolonged and he inherits the 'Land' [the future world]." See
Yerushalmi, Kiddushin 1:9, [This refers to] "one who sets apart one mitzvah
never to transgress [deviate from it] all the days of his life."

Rabbeinu Saadiah Gaon comments: "The reward of one good deed will
be infinite" (*Emunoth V'daioth, Reward and Punishment*).

ֆ 747 ֆ

כָּל הַמְקַיֵּים אֶת הַתּוֹרָה מֵעוֹנִי
סוֹפוֹ לְקַיְּמָהּ מֵעוֹשֶׁר

"Whoever fulfills the Torah amid poverty, in the end will fulfill it
amid wealth" (*Aboth* 4:11).

"A man who, while poor and destitute, takes upon himself the extra
hardship of occupying himself with Torah, will finally occupy himself with
Torah in wealth, when nothing will disturb his studies" (Maimonides,
Commentary on Aboth).

When Rabbi Yisrael Salanter met Rabbi Shmuel Strashun, Reb Shmuel
said to him: "I have been told that your Rebbetzin bought a lottery ticket,
and that when you became aware of it, you called her before two witnesses
and said, 'I have no claim upon your estates, their produce, and the produce

of their produce forever.' Does this imply that you hold that it is forbidden
to be a wealthy man?"

"No," answered Rabbi Yisrael. "Why should it be forbidden to be a
wealthy man if one utilizes his money properly, as ordained in the Torah?
. . . The reason I renounced any share in the lottery ticket was because I feel
that buying a lottery ticket and depending on such sources is in itself a
manifestation of lack of faith. We are obligated to believe that the L-rd will
bless us in a manner of His choosing. But to risk money in anything where
the loss [the cost of the lottery ticket] is immediate, and the reward [the
prize] distant and far-fetched, or to speculate in order to become wealthy,
this is something which one who has faith in G-d should not do" (Zalman
Aryeh Hilsenrad, *My Soul Thirsts*, p. 184).

Cf. *Sifri, Devarim* 18:13, "'Be wholehearted with the L-rd your G-d' —
when you are wholehearted, your portion will be with the L-rd your G-d."
See #997.

⎰ 748 ⎱   כָּל הַמְקַיֵּים דִּבְרֵי חֲכָמִים נִקְרָא קָדוֹשׁ

"Whosoever acts in accordance with the rulings of the sages is
called a holy person" (*Yebamoth* 20a).

The *Baale HaMussar* [ethical moralists] explain that the term *kadosh* [holy]
may more appropriately be applied to one who fulfills the words of the sages
than to one who fulfills the words of Scripture. The Evil Inclination initially
entices an individual to transgress rabbinic rulings, thereby making it easier
for him to later violate the graver pentateuchal commandments. Consequently, one who stands firm at the outset against a rabbinic breach of the Torah
is designated a *kadosh* (*Orach Yesharim, L'kutei Bosar L'kutei*, [*Aggadoth*], vol.
3, p. 9).

Cf. *Yebamoth* ibid., "Sanctify yourself by that which is permitted to you."
See *Insights*, vol. 1, #466.

⟦ 749 ⟧

כָּל הַמְשַׁמֵּר שַׁבָּת כְּהִלְכָתוֹ אֲפִילוּ עוֹבֵד
עֲבוֹדָה זָרָה . . . מוֹחֲלִין לוֹ

"Whoever observes the Sabbath in accordance with its laws, even
if he worshiped idols . . . [his sins] will be forgiven"
(*Shabbath* 118b).

"For the Sabbath to atone [for our sins] it must be observed properly
. . . . R. Eliezer Rokeach of Worms explains why the Sabbath had no *korban
chatas* [sin offering] as part of the *Musaf* offering in the *Beis HaMikdash* [as
opposed to *Yom Tov*]. The reason for this, according to Rokeach, is that the
very essence of the Sabbath atones; there is no need for sacrificial atonement
. . . .

A *ben Torah* must be ever mindful that he utilize the Sabbath as would be
expected of one who is immersed day and night in Torah study. This
thought lies at the very words of the talmudic passage cited above: 'Whoever
observes the Sabbath *in accordance with its laws*,' which can be understood
homiletically. Whoever keeps the Sabbath in accordance with his personal
dictates [*ke'hilchatho*], i.e., in accordance with his own spiritual level . . . .

With this approach, one will surely merit atonement of sins through his
Sabbath observance" (Rabbi Yehudah Zev Segal, *Yirah VeDa'as*, trans. Rabbi
Shimon Finkelman, *Inspiration and Insight*, pp. 146-150).

⟦ 750 ⟧

כָּל הַמַּשְׁפִּיל עַצְמוֹ הַקָּדוֹשׁ בָּרוּךְ הוּא
מַגְבִּיהוֹ, וְכָל הַמַּגְבִּיהַּ עַצְמוֹ הַקָּדוֹשׁ בָּרוּךְ
הוּא מַשְׁפִּילוֹ

"He who humbles himself is lifted up by G-d; he who holds himself in high esteem is cast down by G-d" (*Erubin* 13b).

"Meritorious is he who humbles himself in this world; how greatly
exalted is he in that world [in the World to Come]" (*Zohar* III, 168a).
Rabbi Joseph Schneersohn of Lubavitch commented in a chassidic dis-

course: "Herein lies the difference between the holy and the unholy: The holy is always in a state of *bittul* [self nullification], while the unholy is always in an egotistical state. Concerning holy service, it is written, 'And you shall love your fellow as yourself' [Lev. 19:18], and the Alter Rebbe [R. Shneur Zalman of Liadi] notes that to 'love your fellow as yourself' is the vessel through which one may fulfill the commandment, 'And you shall love G-d your L-rd'" (*On Ahavas Yisrael*).

Cf. *Erubin* 13b, "He who seeks greatness, greatness flees from him, but he who flees from greatness, greatness follows him." See *Insights*, vol. 1, #276.

⟦ 751 ⟧

כָּל הַמְשַׁתֵּף שֵׁם שָׁמַיִם בְּצַעֲרוֹ
כּוֹפְלִין לוֹ פַּרְנָסָתוֹ

"Whoever associates the Name of Heaven with his suffering will have his sustenance doubled" (*Berakoth* 63a).

"By blessing the Almighty as a *'True Judge'* when evil occurs or by praying to Him for mercy" (*Rashi*).

Why would one receive a "double reward" for associating the name of G-d with his suffering? Rabbi Chaim of Volozhin explains that, in effect, he is rewarded "measure for measure" for seeking to remove the "double suffering" he has inflicted upon the Almighty. "When a Jew sins, he causes the Almighty double pain. First, by sinning he inflicts injury upon himself, which causes pain to our Father in Heaven. Secondly, he must now be punished so that his suffering will atone for his sin. This, too, causes G-d sorrow. When a Jew prays, his primary concern should not be to alleviate his personal woes, but to remove the pain he has caused G-d. If that is his primary purpose in praying, then certainly, he will receive a "double reward," "measure for measure" (*Nefesh HaChaim* II:12).

Cf. *Sanhedrin* 46a, "When man suffers what expression does the *Shechinah* use? My head is too heavy for Me! My arm is too heavy for Me."

The Ropshitzer Rebbe maintains that one's primary *kavanah* [concentration] during prayer should not be his own personal needs but the needs of the Almighty; the fact that He is in pain [so to speak] and suffering with us in our exile. When a Jew prays in this manner it is certain that his prayers will be answered (*Zerah Kodesh*, cited by Rabbi Peretz Zutler).

〚 752 〛   כָּל הַמְשַׁתֵּף שֵׁם שָׁמַיִם וְדָבָר אַחֵר
נֶעֱקַר מִן הָעוֹלָם

"Whoever associates the Heavenly Name with anything else is
eradicated from the world" (*Sanhedrin* 63a).

"It is forbidden to associate His Name with anything else while taking an oath. And whoever associates the Name of the Holy One, blessed be He, with anything else in taking an oath, is eradicated from the world" (*Mishneh Torah, Hil. Shevuoth* 11:2).

Cf. *Sanhedrin* 63b, "One may not enter into a business partnership with an idolater, lest the latter be obliged to take an oath [in connection with a business dispute] and he swears by his idol, whilst the Torah has said: 'Neither let it be heard through your mouth.'" See *Tosafoth* s.v. *Asur*, where Rabbeinu Tam maintains that the prohibition to take G-d's name in partnership with something else does not apply to a non-Jew, i.e., as long as a non-Jew believes in G-d, he may also accept another being as a deity or mediator. See also *Tosaf. Bekhoroth* 2b, s.v. *Shema*.

There are, however, many authorities who maintain that the prohibition against idolatry forbids even a non-Jew to believe in a mediator between G-d and man (*Teshuvoth Noda BeYehudah, Yoreh De'ah*, 2:148; *Teshuvoth Meil Tzedakah* 22; *Teshuvoth Shaar Ephraim* 24; Chasam Sofer on *Orach Chaim* 156:1).

Some authorities suggest that non-Jews are only forbidden to make use of a mediator in the Land of Israel. See Ramban on Lev. 18:25; Rabbi Yaakov Emden, *Mor U'Ketziah* 224.

On the general question whether *Notzrim* [Christians] are considered idolaters, see Shabse Frankel's edition of Rambam's *Mishneh Torah, Hil. Ma'acholoth Asuroth* 11:7.

☐ 753 ☐   כָּל הַמִּתְלוֹצֵץ מְזוֹנוֹתָיו מִתְמַעֲטִין

"He who scoffs, his sustenance will be reduced"
(*Abodah Zarah* 18b).

As it is said, "He withdraws His hand in the case of scoffers" [Hosea 7:5]. "The Holy One, blessed be He, who opens His hand to feed all, withdraws His hand from those who engage in mockery" (Rashi).

In the Blessing of the New Month we petition the Almighty for "*Chaim shel parnosah*" [a life of sustenance]. Says the Chafetz Chaim, "The factor which truly robs us of our daily bread are the books and writings of heretical, faithless authors, and vile periodicals filled with scornful mockery and indecency. All this evil we bring into our homes. Not only does it poison the home, but it is the main cause for our sustenance being withheld" (*The Chafetz Chaim on the Siddur*, p. 247).

☐ 754 ☐   כָּל הַמִּתְפַּלֵּל בְּעֶרֶב שַׁבָּת וְאוֹמֵר „וַיְכוּלוּ"

מַעֲלֶה עָלָיו הַכָּתוּב כְּאִילוּ נַעֲשָׂה שׁוּתָּף
להקב"ה בְּמַעֲשֵׂה בְרֵאשִׁית

"He who prays Erev *Shabbath* and recites *Va'yechulu* [verses pertaining to Creation], Scripture treats him as though he had become a partner with the Holy One, blessed be He, in the Creation" (*Shabbath* 119b).

Rabbi Yeruchem Levovitz notes that on various occasions the Talmud refers to the person who lives according to the dictates of G-d as "one who is a partner in the creation of the world." A partner, he explains, is not a employee, but an owner. A partner has a right to express an opinion on the operations of a business. His opinion may be overruled, but unlike a hired worker, he can insist that his opinion be heard.

The reason the great *tzaddikim* were able to make things happen with their prayers was because they had achieved a status of being "partners with G-d" in the operation of the world. As partners, they had an authoritative position" (Rabbi Avraham Chaim Feuer, *Shemoneh Esrei*, p. 87).

Cf. *Shabbath* 10a, "Every judge who judges a true judgment according to its truth, it is as though he had become a partner to the Holy One, blessed be He, in the creation." See *Insights*, vol. 1, #258.

⎰ **755** ⎰ כָּל הַנְּבִיאִים כּוּלָן לֹא נִתְנַבְּאוּ אֶלָּא לִימוֹת
הַמָּשִׁיחַ אֲבָל לָעוֹלָם הַבָּא עַיִן לֹא רָאָתָה
אֱלֹקִים זוּלָתְךָ

"All the prophets prophesied only for the days of the Messiah, but as for the World to Come, 'No eye has seen [them], O G-d, but You' [Isa. 64:3]" (*Berakoth* 34b).

"The ancient sages taught us that a clear comprehension of the bliss in the life hereafter is unattainable to any man. None but G-d knows its grandeur, beauty and power. All the boons which the prophets prophesied to Israel only refer to material things that Israel will enjoy in the days of King Moshiach, when sovereignty will be restored to Israel" (*Mishneh Torah, Hil. Teshuvah* 8:7).

Rabbi Yehuda Loew of Prague explains why the prophets could not prophecy regarding the World to Come. "Since the prophet requires empirical contact with the object of the prophetic vision, he can only perceive the messianic world, which is something related to this world, but not the World to Come, which is completely *nivdal* [set apart] from this world. The prophet cannot 'see' that which no eye can possibly 'see'" (*Maharal miPrague, Gevuroth HaShem*, intro.).

‖ 756 ‖

כָּל הַנְּבִיאִים נִסְתַּכְּלוּ בְּאַסְפַּקְקַלַרְיָא שֶׁאֵינָה
מְאִירָה מֹשֶׁה רַבֵּינוּ נִסְתַּכֵּל בְּאַסְפַּקְקַלַרְיָא
הַמְאִירָה

"All other prophets saw through a dull lens, while Moshe our
Teacher saw through a clear lens" (*Yebamoth* 49b).

"It was no allegory that was revealed to Moshe, but he realized the
prophetic message clearly, without riddle and without parable . . . . He had
a clear and lucid vision . . . (*Mishneh Torah, Hil. Yesodei HaTorah* 7:6).

Rabbi Aryeh Kaplan writes: "In the case of every prophet, something of
his own mind, his own ego, enters the prophecy. This is a very important
point. The prophecy is being reflected through his mind. You are not
actually seeing the spiritual impact itself. All you are really seeing is what
his mind interprets. This is the non-shining *Ispaklaria* the Talmud refers to
as the medium through which all the prophets received their visions. Moshe,
on the other hand, saw through a shining *Ispaklaria*.

Rabbi Moshe Chaim Luzzatto states that a shining *Ispaklaria* is a lens,
while a non-shining *Ispaklaria* is a mirror (*Adir BaMarom*, p. 78a). In other
words, Moshe saw through a clear glass while all the other prophets saw a
reflection in a mirror" (*Inner Space*, p. 136).

Cf. *Va'yikra Rabbah* 1:14, "What difference is there between Moshe and all
the other prophets? Rabbi Yehudah said: 'All other prophets looked through
nine lenses, but Moshe looked through only one.'"

‖ 757 ‖

כָּל הַנְּגָעִים אָדָם רוֹאֶה חוּץ מִנִּגְעֵי עַצְמוֹ

"A man [a priest] may inspect all the leprosy symptoms, save his
own [which must be examined by another priest]" (*Nega'im* 2:5).

A man sees all the faults [defects] of others, but he never sees his own.
This may be illustrated by the story told concerning the *Shach* [Rabbi Shabse
HaKohen], who became involved in a *Din Torah* [civil suit] with another

individual. "When the *Beis Din* decided against the *Shach*, he respectfully asked the court why his position was rejected. One of the judges explained that he found arguments refuting the *Shach's* position in a recently published work of high repute. When he was shown the *Sifsei Kohen* on the *Choshen Mishpat*, the Shach's own work, he immediately acknowledged that in the attempt to vindicate himself he had not approached the problem objectively, and had therefore completely overlooked the decision which he had arrived at in his own halachic commentary" (Rabbi Zechariah Fendel, *The Halacha and Beyond*, p. 51).

In a secular vein, "Any experienced proofreader will be quick to tell you: *Don't proofread your own copy!* It's difficult to look at your own creative work with a critical or unbiased eye. You will see only what you expect to see" (L. K. Anderson, *Handbook for Proofreading*, p. 1).

Cf. *Minchah Chadashah*, "The hunchback does not see his hump." *We are blind to our own faults.*

⟦ 758 ⟧   כָּל הָעוֹבֵר עַל דִּבְרֵי חֲכָמִים חַיָּיב מִיתָה

"Whoever transgresses the words of the sages deserves to die"
(*Berakoth* 4b).

Rabbeinu Yonah comments: "Now, of course, an explanation is required as to why the death penalty is more in order for one who transgresses the words of the sages than for one who transgresses a positive or a negative commandment. The explanation follows: One who transgresses the words of the sages does so out of the presumption of his heart, as a result of his holding their *mitzvoth* lightly; not because of his evil inclination's overpowering him, but because of his eyes having been blinded to the radiance of their words, and his not having walked by the light of faith. He does not bind himself by their restrictions; nor does he put forth any effort to fulfill their behests, because of their not having been written in the Torah.

"In this respect, he differs from one who transgresses the words of Torah. The latter's soul is bitter to him and he is loathsome in his eyes. He is frightened and aggrieved because his Evil Inclination has incited him to sin.

"The judgment, therefore, of one who casts aside any of their good words is death, for it is as if he said, 'Let us tear our bonds'" (*Sha'arei Teshuvah, Sha'ar Shlishi,* #5).

Cf. *Yebamoth* 20a, "Whosoever acts in accordance with the rulings of the sages is called a holy person." See #748.

▯ 759 ▯

כָּל הָעוֹלָם כּוּלוֹ נִיזּוֹן
בִּשְׁבִיל חֲנִינָא בְּנִי . . . .

"The whole world draws its sustenance because [of the merit] of Chanina, My son . . ." (*Ta'anith* 24b).

"Every day a *Bath Kol* [Heavenly Voice] is heard declaring: 'The whole world draws its sustenance . . . and Chanina My son suffices himself with a *kab* [small measure] of carobs from one Sabbath eve to another'" (ibid.).

Reb Maerl Premishlaner asks: "Do you know why this is so? Because Chanina is satisfied with only a small measure of carob for the entire week. This is the merit of a *tzaddik* who has the power to provide blessings for others. If he is satisfied with very little, and is completely removed from the pleasures of this world, he loves only a spiritual life, then G-d will fulfill his request and bless others" (*Reb Maerl Premishlaner,* p. 459).

When Rabbi Shlomo Kluger delivered the *hesped* [eulogy] for Reb Maerl Premishlaner, he cited the above maxim and said: "Since Reb Maerl despised owning money, and gave all the money he received as *pidyon* [charity] to the poor, he showed G-d that he agrees to have all his wealth shared by others. We all had *parnoso* [sustenance] only because Reb Maerl didn't need all that G-d wanted to give him" (*Meir Einei Chachamim*).

Rabbi Yaakov Yosef of Polonoye said in the name of the Baal Shem Tov that the above dictum should be translated as follows: "The whole world draws its sustenance *through the pathway* that Chanina My son prepared." This exegesis is based on reading *bashvil* [in the path] instead of *bishvil* [because of].

When Chanina ben Dosa revealed a secret, it became easier for other people to understand it.

Similarly, we find that Rabbi Yosef Karo would often have difficulty at first in understanding a cryptic saying, yet afterwards when he figured out its meaning, he heard the same explanation mouthed by several unlearned people. When he asked the *Ari HaKadosh* to explain this phenomenon, the *Ari* simply said: "Since you opened the channel, it is now easier for everyone to understand. And this is what is meant by: 'Had I not lifted up the shard, would you have found the pearl beneath it?'" [*Yebamoth* 92b] (*Shivchei HaBesht*).

See *Insights*, vol. 1, #16.

◊ 760 ◊   כָּל הָעוֹסֵק בַּתּוֹרָה בַּלַּיְלָה, שְׁכִינָה כְּנֶגְדּוֹ

"If one studies Torah at night, the *Shechinah* faces him" (*Tamid* 32b).

"One who studies during the day, although the *Shechinah* may also be with him [see *Berakoth* 6a], he is not aware of it. One who studies at night, however, since he is immersed in Torah, denying sleep to his eyes, he is rewarded in that the *Shechinah* is before him" (Rabbi Moshe Teitelbaum, *Yismach Moshe, Kedoshim*).

In a homiletical vein, this dictum may be applied to a period when "darkness" prevails in the Jewish community. "If one studies at 'night' [when people characterize the 'light' of Torah as 'darkness'] — study during such a period for the sake of Heaven will merit for him the reward of the *Shechinah* facing him" (*Yalkut Eliezer, L'kutei Bosar L'kutei* [*Aggadoth*] vol. 5, p. 279).

Rabbi Meir Simcha of Dvinsk suggests that "night" represents the unseen, the hidden, the non-publicized. The praises lavished by our sages on "one who studies Torah at night" are in fact praises for one who studies for no ulterior motive.

If one studies Torah with an ulterior motive, then his act will bring joy only when that motive is achieved . . . . However, if one studies at night — privately and modestly, then he will "cry out [with joy] at night" (*Eichoh* 2:19) — at the very moment of his learning (*Meshech Chochmah, Va'yikra* 3:2).

Cf. *Menakoth* 110a, "Scholars who devote themselves to the study of the Torah at night, Scripture accounts it to them as though they were occupied with the Temple service."

Cf. *Abodah Zarah* 3b, "Whoever occupies himself with Torah at night, the Holy One, blessed be He, draws over him a chord of lovingkindness by day." See *Insights*, vol. 1, #293.

⎰ 761 ⎰ כָּל הַקּוֹרֵא לְאַבְרָהָם אַבְרָם עוֹבֵר בַּעֲשֵׂה

"Whoever calls Abraham, Abram, transgresses a positive precept"
(*Berakoth* 13a).

"Since it says, 'Your name shall be Abraham' [Gen. 17:5] . . . . He transgresses a negative command, since it says, 'You shall no longer be called Abram'" (ibid.).

Rabbi Chaim ben Attar comments: "Ishmael was born while Abraham was still called Abram . . . . When Abram was elevated and given the name Abraham, he severed his relationship with the lowly Ishmael and he was no longer considered Abraham's son. Later, the L-rd told Abraham to heed the directions of Sarah to drive Hagar and Ishmael from his home, 'since through Isaac [only] will children be considered as yours' [Gen. 21:12]. This is not merely a promise; it is tantamount to a positive commandment. Thus, he who persists in referring to Abraham as Abram, implies that he still retains his former status as Ishmael's father, and thereby the person transgresses the commandment that Abraham is to be considered the father of Isaac only" (*Ohr HaChaim*, 21:12).

Rabbi Baruch HaLevi Epstein, however, maintains that the above dictum is an *asmakta b'alma* [a scriptural text used as support for a rabbinical enactment]. Similarly, the dictum in *Yoma* 19b, "One who engages in idle talk transgresses *a positive command*," and the dictum in *Sanhedrin* 110a, "He who perpetuates strife violates *a negative command*" are merely *asmakta b'alma* (*Torah Temimah*, Gen. 17:5).

See *Insights*, vol. 1, #44, #193.

❪ 762 ❫

כָּל הַשּׁוֹנֶה הֲלָכוֹת בְּכָל יוֹם, מוּבְטָח לוֹ
שֶׁהוּא בֶּן עוֹלָם הַבָּא

"Whoever repeats *halachoth* every day may rest assured that he is destined for the World to Come" (*Niddah* 73a).

Rabbi Moshe Feinstein accentuates the word *shoneh* [repeats] in the above dictum. Only one who studies and is fearful that he may forget that which he learned, and also yearns to fulfill the Divine command to study Torah — only such a person has the assurance of the World to Come.

Knowledge of the *halachoth* in and of itself may lead one to arrogantly assume that the reasons for their enactment do not apply to him. Only one who "repeats" *halachoth* every day in his desire to do the Will of G-d will merit eternal life" (*Dorash Moshe*, p. 374).

Cf. ."Whoever recites '*tehilla l'David*' three times daily is sure to inherit the World to Come." See #732.

Cf. "Whoever walks four cubits in the Land of Israel is assured of a place in the World to Come." See #737.

❪ 763 ❫

כָּל זוֹנָה שֶׁנִּשְׂכֶּרֶת לְבַסּוֹף הִיא שׂוֹכֶרֶת

"Every harlot who allows herself to be hired will in the end have to hire" (*Abodah Zarah* 17a).

The prostitute first does evil only for a fee, but ultimately she squanders her own money on licentiousness.

Rabbi Yosef Dov Ber Soloveitchik explains that this dictum sheds some light on the Evil Inclination and its temptations, and the extent to which sin blocks man's heart. "Our sages chose as an analogy the sin of licentiousness, for its depravity is known to all. Even the harlot herself would admit that it is disgraceful and that she submits to it only to support herself.

"But this is only true at the outset, when the heart is not yet obstructed and the Evil Impulse must tempt man with more than just the pleasure of the sinful act itself. Once man makes a habit of sin, however, it becomes an end in itself. Thus, the harlot will eventually squander all her money on the very same abominable act that she herself was once disgusted by and consented to perform only as a means to an end.

"This is the way of the Evil Inclination. If it initially tempted man with sin itself, it would surely fail. Instead it entices him with the wages of sin, such as financial profit and other 'legitimate' objectives. Only then does man heap impurity upon impurity and come to desire the sin itself so passionately, that he will sacrifice these very objectives just to indulge in it" (*Beis HaLevi, Beraishith*, trans. by Yisrael Isser Zvi Herczeg).

⟦ 764 ⟧   כָּל חוֹלִי וְלֹא חוֹלִי מֵעַיִם, כָּל כְּאֵב וְלֹא כְּאֵב לֵב, כָּל מֵיחוּשׁ וְלֹא מֵיחוּשׁ רֹאשׁ

"Rather any illness, but no illness of the bowels; any pain, but not heart pain; any ache, but not headache" (*Shabbath* 11a).

Interpreted metaphorically, the above maxim alludes to various defects or deficiencies in life. "Illness of the bowels" signifies a defect in physical well-being through overeating or the consumption of harmful foods. "Heart pain" points to a defect in one's relationship to the needy and less privileged, i.e., not being a compassionate and sympathetic person. "Headache" symbolizes a distorted mental attitude towards the Almighty — harboring heretical ideas (*Yalkut Yehoshua*, cited in *L'kutei Bosar L'kutei* [*Aggadoth*], vol. 1, p. 188).

Rabbi Yaakov Yosef of Austria interprets "any ache, but not headache" in the following manner. "One may be bothered about any 'ache' or disappointment in life, but one should never be concerned about a 'head' ache, i.e., that he was not chosen to be the head or leader [of an institution] for, in reality, 'thirst for honor takes a man out of the world' (*Aboth* 4:28). On the contrary, he should rejoice that he was not selected to be 'the head'" (*Biurei HaChassidus L'shass*, p. 76).

𝄵 765 𝄵

כָּל יִשְׂרָאֵל הָיוּ עֲסוּקִים בְּכֶסֶף וְזָהָב וּמֹשֶׁה
הָיָה עָסוּק בְּעַצְמוֹת יוֹסֵף

"All the Israelites were occupied in collecting silver and gold, and Moshe was occupied in collecting the bones of Joseph (*Shemoth Rabbah* 20:19).

This was in fulfillment of the oath which Joseph had imposed upon the Israelites before his death — "When G-d will take notice of you, you shall carry up my bones from here" [Gen. 50:25].

For forty years, Moshe carried the bones of Joseph with him in the wilderness. Moshe was the leader of all Israel — why didn't he delegate this "communal" responsibility to others? Why did he have to do it himself?

Perhaps an answer to this question may be found in one of the verses of the *Shira* [the song at the Red Sea]. The Israelites, together with Moshe, triumphantly shout, "This is my G-d and I will glorify Him, my father's G-d, and I will exalt Him" [Ex. 15:2]. On the phrase "my father's G-d," Rashi comments: "I am not the first graced with His holiness, but the holiness had been possessed and has remained with me . . . from the days of my fathers."

Moshe proclaims that this covenantal relationship with the Almighty was not initiated at the Exodus from Egypt, but was established many hundreds of years before the Egyptian bondage — with the patriarchs of our people. And if you want tangible evidence of the patriarchs [who were long buried in Canaan], then look at the "bones of Joseph," the son of Jacob, the grandson of Isaac, the great-grandson of Abraham.

Moshe was "compelled" to carry the bones of Joseph with him as a constant reminder to the Israelites of their spiritual linkage between them and their patriarchal forbears (S.W.).

In a homiletical vein, Rabbi Moshe Feinstein writes that "perhaps Moshe learned his humility from Joseph. Our sages declare that '*Moshe took the bones of Joseph with him*' — '*with him*,' i.e., Moshe took Joseph's *atzmoos emo* his '*essence*,' meaning his humility, 'with him,' to be a part of his own character, and indeed to surpass Joseph in this trait" (*Darash Moshe*, p. 49).

766

כָּל מַה שֶׁבָּרָא הַקָּדוֹשׁ בָּרוּךְ הוּא בְּעוֹלָמוֹ
בָּרָא בָּאָדָם

"All that the Holy One, blessed be He, created in His world, He created in man" (*Aboth D'Rabbi Nathan*, 31:3).

Rabbi Yitzchak Hutner comments: "All that exists in the world finds a corresponding feature in man. And the opposite is also true: all that exists in man finds a corresponding feature in the world. Now, in the mind of man there exists the power of imagination, with which man can describe a reality that in fact does not exist in the world. It is a reality only by the power of imagination. Since this kind of power exists in man, it certainly has a corresponding counterpart in the world — the creatures whom we call demons. That is to say, demons are reality-nonreality. Hence, when we speak about something as a figment of the imagination, we mean that such a thing has no demonstrative reality.

"When Maimonides writes that demons have no existence in reality [*Commentary on the Mishnah, Abodah Zarah* ch. 4], this in no way contradicts all the talmudic passages pointing to the reality of demons" (Rabbi Yitzchak Hutner, *Zichronoth*, 74).

767

כָּל מַה שֶׁבָּרָא הַקָּדוֹשׁ בָּרוּךְ הוּא בְּעוֹלָמוֹ לֹא
בָּרָא דָּבָר אֶחָד לְבַטָּלָה

"Of all that the Holy One, blessed be He, created in His world, He did not create a single thing without purpose" (*Shabbath* 77b).

"No intelligent person can assume that any of the actions of G-d can be in vain, purposeless or unimportant . . . (Rambam, *Moreh Nevuchim*, part 3, ch. 25).

After citing the above dictum, Rabbi Joseph B. Soloveitchik concluded: "I feel that there is nothing in Israel's history that is in vain; and if on Friday, the fifth of *Iyar* 5708, G-d said: 'Let there be a State of Israel,' His word is not in vain . . . .

"True, I cannot prove my assumption, but even if it is unprovable, it yet has warrant . . . . It is a generally accepted rule in *halachah* that when the hater attacks some principle of Judaism, it is a sign that the principle is of the utmost importance . . . . In ancient times they poured out their wrath on the Temple, on the Sabbath, on circumcision and especially against Torah study [of the Oral Law] . . . . We can assuredly rely upon our enemies when it comes to axiomatic evaluation of Jewish principles. They are most authoritative.

"When we see how all those who hate our people concentrate their anger and wrath upon the State of Israel . . . there can be no better indication that the State embodies great symbolic powers and that in it, despite the layer of secular dust that covers it, inheres an inner sanctity that springs from the eternal sanctity of *Kenesseth Yisrael*" (*The Rav Speaks*, pp. 171-172).

768

כָּל מַה שֶׁהַגְּדוֹלִים עוֹשִׂים הַדּוֹר עוֹשֶׂה

"Whatever the leaders do, the generation does" (*Devarim Rabbah* 2:19).

Rabbi Yechiel Michel HaLevi Epstein [the *Aruch HaShulchan*] bemoaned the fact that in his generation, there were a number of Rabbis who were negligent in their personal religious observances while remaining faithful to the Torah in their public observances. He cited the following parable in his criticism of their actions.

"People traveling on a train are permitted to do what they wish . . . . In contrast, the conductor must subdue all his emotions and concentrate all his feelings, and [focus his] intelligence on controlling every aspect of running the train . . . . The Rabbi of a community is, in fact, driving the spiritual train for the people in his congregation. All their eyes are lifted to him, searching in every public and private act for guidelines in how to run their lives. Thus, if he is lax, he can cause a tragic breakdown in the whole spiritual life of the community" (Rabbi Baruch HaLevi Epstein, *Makor Baruch, Recollections* (trans.), p. 111).

∬ 769 ∬   כָּל מִי שֶׁאֵין בּוֹ דֵּעָה אָסוּר לְרַחֵם עָלָיו

"If one does not have knowledge, it is forbidden to have mercy on him" (*Berakoth* 33a).

This dictum is extremely difficult to understand. Simply because one is not blessed with knowledge, we are forbidden to show him compassion? "The intent of our sages," says Rabbi Yaakov Landau, "focuses on the tendency to exonerate a transgressor simply because of his 'ignorance of the law.' This then is the interpretation of the above ruling. Since everyone is obligated to perform *mitzvoth*, if one does not have knowledge (of how to fulfill the commandments), we should not exonerate him by arguing that he did not commit a willful wrong. The question to be raised is, why didn't he study and learn what G-d requires of him. In the secular society we find a similar principle — 'Ignorance of the law is no excuse'" (*Kavod Chachamim*, p. 52).

"When Balaam said to G-d's angel, 'I have sinned, for I did not know that you were standing on the road before me . . .' [Num. 22:34], the implication is that a person is held liable for failing to be aware of something that he could have known . . . . Ignorance is no excuse. Balaam should have concluded that there must be a reason for his donkey's peculiar behavior . . ." (Rabbi Isaiah Horowitz, *Shney Luchoth HaBrith*).

∬ 770 ∬   כָּל מִי שֶׁאֵין מְבַקֵּר חוֹלִים כְּאִילוּ שׁוֹפֵךְ דָּמִים

"He who does not visit the sick is like a shedder of blood" (*Nedarim* 40a).

The Chafetz Chaim writes: "The visitors who attend to the needs of the sick may know of some remedy or medical attention which might hasten his cure . . . . If a poor man is not visited, his very life may be jeopardized. Usually he cannot afford the food he needs in his illness. He has no one to consult with concerning his condition. Sometimes he cannot even afford to call a doctor or to buy medicine. His worries increase when he realizes that he has lain in bed for several days and no one has opened the door to care for him or to revive him. All these factors weaken his resistance and reinforce his illness, and this might cause his death" (*Ahavath Chesed*, III, 3).

◊ 771 ◊ כָּל מִי שֶׁהוּא צָרִיךְ לִיטוֹל וְאֵינוֹ נוֹטֵל הֲרֵי זֶה
שׁוֹפֵךְ דָּמִים

"He who needs to take but does not take, is as if had shed blood"
(*Yerushalmi*, Pe'ah 8:8).

Rabbi Samson Raphael Hirsch comments: "In Judaism, *tzedakah* does not shame the recipient who is in need of it. Indeed, in the spirit of this law, anyone who is unable to work or is destitute but who, out of misplaced pride, deprives himself and his family of the necessities of life rather than turn to the *tzedakah* to which he is entitled, bears a heavy burden of responsibility.

Yet, the spirit of this same Law attaches great importance also to the preservation of personal independence. An individual should be prepared to restrict himself to the barest necessities of life and accept any work, even that considered most menial in the eyes of a thoughtless world, in order to avoid having to appeal to the charity of his fellow men. In no society is honest toil for an independent living held in such high esteem, as it was among the Jews of old" (*The Pentateuch*, Deut. 15:11).

Cf. *Pesahim* 113a, "Skin a carcass in the marketplace and earn wages, and do not say, 'I am a *kohen* and a great man, and it is beneath my dignity.'"
See #940.

772

כָּל מִי שֶׁיֵּשׁ לוֹ בֵּית הַכְּנֶסֶת בְּעִירוֹ וְאֵינוֹ
נִכְנָס שָׁם לְהִתְפַּלֵּל נִקְרָא שָׁכֵן רַע . . . .
וְלֹא עוֹד אֶלָּא שֶׁגּוֹרֵם גָּלוּת לוֹ וּלְבָנָיו

"Whoever has a Synagogue in his town and does not enter it to pray, is called an 'evil neighbor' . . . . And more than that, he causes exile to come upon himself and his children" (Berakoth 8a).

Rabbi Baruch Moshe Feivelzohn asks: "Why is this so terrible? Why is one who does not enter the Synagogue in his home town deserving of such a severe punishment — causing exile upon himself and his children?

"However, if we analyze this man's attitude towards his 'own' house, the above dictum is understandable. One who considers himself a true Baal HaBayis [Master of the house] of the home in which he dwells, i.e., he considers it his 'permanent abode,' then he will look upon the Beis HaKnesses [the Synagogue] as a 'temporary dwelling.' He begins to rationalize — why do I need a Synagogue when I already have a luxurious home? And so, he forsakes the 'House of Prayer' for the comforts of 'his' home!

"Consequently, he is repaid 'measure for measure.' He is told, in effect, 'Go out of what you may consider to be "your" house and go into exile . . . not only you, but also your children for whom you intended to leave your house'" (Birchoth Moshe, p. 69).

773

כָּל מִי שֶׁיֵּשׁ לוֹ פַּת בְּסַלּוֹ וְאוֹמֵר מַה אוֹכַל
לְמָחָר, אֵינוֹ אֶלָּא מִקְּטַנֵּי אֱמוּנָה

"Whoever has a piece of bread in his basket and says, 'What shall I eat tomorrow?' — belongs to those who have little faith" (Sotah 48b).

The Midrash cites Hagar as an example of one who "was lacking in faith." She worried about her supply of water and filled up her gourd with more water than she needed for immediate use (Beraishith Rabbah 53:14).

Rabbi Menachem Mendel of Kotzk was in the habit of saying: "Torah is only given to people who do not worry about tomorrow."

Rabbi Yechezkail Levenstein comments that [our dictum] "applies only to one who is working on his own attributes. When it comes to other people, be concerned about what they will eat tomorrow and for many days to come" (*Ohr Yechezkail*, vol. 4, p. 22).

The Brisker Rav, Rabbi Yitzchak Zev HaLevi Soloveitchik, lived by the above dictum. He never missed an opportunity to speak about absolute *bitachon* [trust in G-d] to his children. When his son Rabbi Yoshe Ber Soloveitchik was sitting *shiva* he related that his departed father had once asked him, "Have you ever seen me worry even once?" (*Peninei HaGriz*, p. 88).

Rabbi Chaim Shmulevitz commented: "It is incumbent upon every person to fulfill his life's mission while taking from this world only as much as necessary" (*Reb Chaim's Discourses*, p. 85).

Cf. *Midrash Tanchuma, Beshalach* 20, "The Torah was given to expound upon, only to those who ate the *manna*." See #807.

⟦ 774 ⟧

כָּל מִי שֶׁנַּעֲשָׂה רַחְמָן בִּמְקוֹם אַכְזָרִי,
סוֹף שֶׁנַּעֲשָׂה אַכְזָרִי בִּמְקוֹם רַחְמָן

"He who is compassionate when he should be cruel [severe] ends up by being cruel when he should be compassionate"
(*Koheleth Rabbah* 7:16).

Rabbi Eliyahu Meir Bloch comments: "Every trait must be used appropriately. There is a positive aspect to compassion as well as a negative aspect" (*Shiurei Daas*, p. 83).

Similarly, Rabbi Moshe Feinstein points out that "each person must realize that every personality trait can be used both for good and evil. One must be guided by the Torah for knowledge about how to utilize each trait properly" (*Bastion of Faith*, p. 22).

◊ 775 ◊ כָּל סְעוּדָּה שֶׁאֵינָה שֶׁל מִצְוָה אֵין תַּלְמִיד
חָכָם רַשַּׁאי לֵהָנוֹת מִמֶּנָּה

"Every feast which is not in connection with a religious deed, a
scholar must derive no enjoyment thereof (*Pesahim* 49a).

"A Torah scholar must be particularly careful not to eat at places that are
not fitting for a person of his stature. The Talmud [ibid.] uses the strongest
terms to admonish any Torah scholar who is careless about his eating habits,
because he can bring disrepute and shame to the Torah through his conduct" (*MeAm Lo'ez*, Deut. 12:18).

Rabbi Yosef Dov Soloveitchik [the *Beis HaLevi*] was forced to leave the city
of Slutsk as a result of a clash with the powerful and wealthy in town. "It
seems that a rich man, who was far removed from Torah, was preparing a
lavish celebration for his son's *bar-mitzvah*. He invited the Rav to join in the
celebration, and hired a private coach to bring him to the hall. When the
man arrived at the Rav's house to take him to the *simcha*, Rav Yoshe Ber
asked nonchalantly, 'What *drosha* [Torah speech] will the *bar-mitzvah* boy
say?' The man shrugged his shoulders and said: 'Rebbe, you must realize
that times have changed. Today's youth do not address the assembled with
words of Torah.' Rav Yoshe Ber replied, 'A celebration at which the *bar-
mitzvah* does not speak words of Torah is a session of scoffers. I will not
attend'" (Rabbi Aharon Surasky, *Giants of Jewry*, vol. 1, p. 133).

◊ 776 ◊ כָּל פְּסוּקָא דְּלָא פְּסַקֵיהּ מֹשֶׁה
אֲנַן לָא פָּסְקִינַן לֵיהּ

"Any verse which was not divided by Moshe, we may not divide"
(*Megillah* 22a).

It is forbidden to recite an incomplete verse while reading the Torah or
while praying.

When the Torah is raised [*Hagbah*] after the scriptural reading, we recite
the following declaration [in most synagogues]: "This is the Torah that

Moshe placed before the Children of Israel," [Deut. 4:44] "upon the command of *Hashem*, through Moshe's hand" [Num. 9:23]. Rabbi Baruch HaLevi Epstein is perplexed by this custom, for it appears to be in violation of our dictum. It is a combination of one complete verse and a [concluding] incomplete verse, namely: ". . . upon the command of *Hashem* through Moshe's hand."

Rabbi Elie Munk explains: "In the edition of a *Siddur* which was published in Jerusalem with the commentary of the Vilna Gaon, the *entire* verse in Num. 9:23 is recited. In our editions, by some error, only the end of the verse was retained" (*The World of Prayer*, vol. 1, p. 175).

In many yeshivoth and in some synagogues today, only the first half of the above declaration is recited, namely, "This is the Torah that Moshe placed before the Children of Israel."

Similarly, the custom that many have during the Sabbath morning Kiddush, to preface the blessing over wine with the chanting of the verse, "*Al kain bairach*" [Ex. 20:11], [according to the *Mishnah Berurah*,] violates the rule that prohibits citing partial verses of the Bible [*Orach Chaim* 289:2]. See, however, *Aruch HaShulchan, Orach Chaim* 289:3, who contends that there is no violation.

See also R. Aaron Walkin [*Birchoth Aaron, Berakoth, Maamar* 108], who contends that the prohibition relates only to *Keriath HaTorah* and the *Shema*, i.e, during the Torah Reading, one may not read only a part of a verse.

⟦ 777 ⟧   — כָּל פְּעֻלּוֹת וּמַחֲשָׁבוֹת שֶׁפָּעַלְתָּ אֵלֵינוּ בִּשְׁבִילֵנוּ

"All the works and thoughts which You have done, have been towards us, for our sake" (*Beraishith Rabbah* 65:8).

"Thus, why did Isaac's eyes grow dim? So that Jacob might come and receive the blessings" (ibid.). The Almighty's concern for the ultimate success of Israel is the guiding force behind all events in history, even those which initially seemed detrimental.

Rabbi Simcha Zissel Ziv commented on the above dictum: "It was a great joy for me to find this Midrash, almost as much as one would feel if he

found a great treasure. Unfortunately, I am not tolerant. On one level, my
suffering bothers me because I am unable to study and pray properly. But
I suspect the truth is, my suffering bothers me because I lack a sufficient
amount of acceptance" (*Chochmah Umussar*, vol. 1, p. 347).

Cf. *Berakoth* 5a, "Sufferings wash away all the sins of a man." See
Insights, vol. 1, #236.

Cf. *Berakoth* 60b, "Whatever the All-Merciful does is for good." See
Insights, vol. 1, #260.

Cf. *Taanith* 21a, "This is also for the best." See *Insights*, vol. 1, #131.

⟦ 778 ⟧ כָּל צְדָקָה וָחֶסֶד שֶׁאוּמוֹת עוֹבְדֵי כּוֹכָבִים
עוֹשִׂין, חֵטְא הוּא לָהֶם

"All the charity and kindness done by the idolatrous nations is [in
reality] a transgression" (*Baba Bathra* 10b).

"Why is it considered a transgression?" asks Rabbi Moshe Feinstein.
"True, their *tzedakah* and *chesed* cannot be considered a *mitzvah* for it is done
with ulterior motives [to magnify themselves], but why should it be characterized as a transgression — is it any worse than doing nothing?"

"The truth is," says Reb Moshe, "that their *tzedakah* erroneously leads us
to consider them as men of principle whom we can trust. In reality, however, they are totally wicked people whose *tzedakah* is contemptible, and which
therefore constitutes a grave transgression. (*Dorash Moshe*, p. 348).

Cf. *Mishlei* 14:34, "The *chesed* of the peoples is a transgression." See
Insights, vol. 1, #219.

Cf. *Yebamoth* 103a, "All the favors of the wicked are evil for the righteous."

॥ 779 ॥ כָּל צָרוֹת שֶׁאֵרַע לְיוֹסֵף אֵרַע לְצִיּוֹן

"Every distress that occurred to Joseph occurred to Zion"
(*Midrash Tanchuma, Vayigash*).

Concerning Joseph, the Torah records: "And his brothers saw him from afar, and before he came near to them, they conspired against him to kill him [Gen. 37:18]. This was the tragedy! His brothers saw him from afar — they had grievances against Joseph, some real, some imagined — but they always saw him "from afar." They never sat down with him to air their grievances, to confront him with the evil report of them which he brought to their father.

Rabbi Moshe Avigdor Amiel, in reflecting on this fraternal enmity, comments: "They quarrelled over vain words, over matters without reality. Hatred exists first, then comes the explanation and justification.

Indeed, the distress that occurred to Joseph as a result of this unwarranted hatred occurred to Zion — both from her enemies without and enemies within. Our greatest enemies have always been those who 'see us from afar' and not up front. They conspire to destroy us before we have a chance to get close, to establish harmonious relations with them" (*Hegyonoth El-Ami*, p. 228).

Cf. *Yoma* 9b, "Jerusalem was destroyed because of groundless hatred."

In comparing the experiences of Joseph with the historical experience of the Jew, Rabbi Leo Jung writes: "Throughout antiquity and the Middle Ages, and into our own years, the Jew has gone on dreaming for others . . . . Like Joseph, so did he fare. When the chief butlers and kings of history had been liberated, they promptly did not remember the Jew and forgot Joseph" (*Between Man and Man*, p. 253).

⎰ 780 ⎱

כָּל שֶׁאֵינוֹ מְחוּיָּיב בַּדָּבָר אֵינוֹ מוֹצִיא אֶת
הָרַבִּים יְדֵי חוֹבָתָן

"Whoever is not obligated in a matter [a *mitzvah*] cannot discharge
the obligation of many" *(Rosh Hashanah* 29a).

The Talmud explains that this general rule pertains only to one upon
whom there never was an obligation to perform the *mitzvah*. However, one
who was obligated, but has discharged his obligation, can nevertheless
discharge the obligation of others [ibid.].

The above mishnaic principle has been interpreted homiletically. "One
who is *not himself guilty* [of a transgression] cannot help remove the guilt of
others . . . . When the leader of the generation who is 'perfect' wishes to
'bind himself' to the common man, he must find in himself some small
transgression — an aspect of worldly sin by means of which a bond can be
formed" (Rabbi Yaakov Yosef of Polonoye, *Toledoth Yaakov Yosef*, p. 66a).

"The Baal Shem Tov once remarked to a *tzaddik* who was given to
preaching sermons of chastisement: 'What do you know about chastising?
You yourself have remained unacquainted with sin all the days of your life,
and you have nothing to do with the people around you — how could you
know what their sinning is?'" (R. Binyamin b. Aaron, *Amtachath Binyamin*,
pp. 1-2).

Cf. *Yoma* 22b, "One should not appoint an administrator of a community
unless he carries a basket of reptiles on his back." See *Insights*, vol. 1, #47.

⎰ 781 ⎱

כָּל שֶׁבַּיָּם טָהוֹר חוּץ מִכֶּלֶב הַמַּיִם, מִפְּנֵי
שֶׁהוּא בּוֹרֵחַ לַיַּבָּשָׁה

"All [items made from creatures] in the sea cannot be rendered
ritually impure except [what is made] from a sea lion, because it
flees to dry land" *(Kelim* 17:13).

Since the sea lion [seal] flees to dry land when it is in danger, this proves
that it is basically a land animal despite its habitation in the sea.

"Reb Tzaddok HaKohein of Lublin draws an incisive moral lesson from this Mishnah. If we want to determine someone's true character, we must observe him in a time of crisis. People may preach loyalty to Torah and absolute belief in *Hashem*, but even they cannot know how sincere their preachments are until they are challenged by events. What happens to the honesty of a businessman when he perceives truth as costing him dearly . . . does he put Torah imperatives above expediency and profit? What happens to the faith of the observant Jew when a dear one is deathly ill — does he hang only onto his doctor's word, or does he know that his *Tehillim* [recitation of Psalms] is more potent than the prescription pad?" (Rabbi Nosson Scherman, *The Jewish Observer* 24, no. 2 [March 1991]:12-13).

◊ 782 ◊ כָּל שֶׁיֵּשׁ לוֹ חוֹלֶה בְּתוֹךְ בֵּיתוֹ, יֵלֵךְ אֵצֶל חָכָם
וִיבַקֵּשׁ עָלָיו רַחֲמִים

"Whosoever has a sick person in his house should go to a sage who will invoke [Heavenly] mercy for him" (*Baba Bathra* 116a).

The *Nimukei Yosef* comments: "It is the custom in France that when a person is sick, the Rabbi who heads the Yeshiva is asked to bless him."

"This appears to be the source of the custom in all our lands to bless the sick in the Synagogue, and to pray for them" (Rabbi Moshe Isserless, *Darkei Moshe, Yoreh De'ah,* 335:2).

See, however, *Meiri* [on our dictum] who explains that one should go to a sage in order to learn the ways of prayer, so that he himself can ask mercy for his sick relative. The ideal is not that the sage pray in one's place, but that one learn from the sage how to pray.

In keeping with the strict interpretation of our dictum, Rabbi Chaim Soloveitchik [the Brisker Rav] maintained that it is even permissible to send a telegram on Shabbos to a *tzaddik* so that he may pray for a critically ill person. He considered this to be a *safek pikuach nefesh* [a possibility of saving a life] (Rabbi Herchel Schachter, *Nefesh HaRav,* p. 167).

Cf. *Beraishith Rabbah* 53:14, "A sick person's prayers on his own behalf are more efficacious than those of anyone else." See #706.

◊ 783 ◊   כָּל תַּלְמִיד חָכָם שֶׁאֵין תּוֹכוֹ כְּבָרוֹ אֵינוֹ
תַּלְמִיד חָכָם

"Any Torah scholar whose inside is not like his outside, is no
Torah scholar" (Yoma 72b).

Just as the Holy Ark was overlaid with gold inside as well as outside, so
must a scholar have a sterling golden character.

Cf. Berakoth 28a, "No disciple whose character does not correspond to his
exterior may enter the Beth haMidrash. See Insights, vol. 1, #319.

This dictum implies that there are some scholars who may outwardly give
the appearance of Torah scholarship, but who inwardly are deficient in piety
and spirituality.

Rabbi Avraham Pam believes that this indeed was the case in the time of
Rabban Gamliel, when as Nasi he would not allow any disciple in the
Academy if "his inside is not like his outside." Today, however, Rav Pam
suggests, it is just the opposite. We frequently find a ben-Torah who possesses noble character traits and is G-d fearing, but outwardly he does not
manifest Kavod haTorah — he may not have a dignified demeanor. Every
yeshiva student should realize that he is a ben melech [a prince] and as such,
he should behave with "royal dignity" so that his outer behavior will
manifest his inner spirituality (Adapted from Rav Pam's Shiurim).

◊ 784 ◊   כָּל תַּלְמִיד חָכָם שֶׁאֵינוֹ נוֹקֵם וְנוֹטֵר כַּנָּחָשׁ
אֵינוֹ תַּלְמִיד חָכָם

"Any scholar who does not avenge himself and retain anger like a
serpent is not a [real] scholar" (Yoma 22b).

The Maharsha explains this dictum in accordance with the verse, "And I
will put enmity between you and the woman, and between your seed and
her seed; they shall bruise your head and you shall bruise their heel" [Gen.
3:15]. Man will endeavor to crush the serpent so as to deprive it of its life,
whereas the serpent will not inflict fatal wounds, but just bruise the heel.

Thus, serpent-like, the scholar should retaliate in a moderate manner even when great wrongs were done to him.

Rabbi Zalman Sorotzkin comments: "The explanation of this dictum is that the Torah scholar avenges the honor of G-d and the holy Torah, without deriving any personal benefit. This may be compared to a snake, which does not benefit from injecting its venom but merely carries out the mission assigned to him by Heaven [*Va'yikra Rabba, parashah* 22]. Therefore the words of the Torah scholar are neither considered to be taking revenge nor bearing a grudge, but are rather a form of reproval" (*Oznayim LaTorah, Va'yikra*).

Cf. *Shabbath* 63a, "If a scholar is vengeful and retains anger like a serpent, gird him to your loins" ["cleave to him, for eventually you will benefit by his scholarship" — Rashi].

Cf. *Ta'anith* 4a, "A scholar who is not as hard as iron is not a [real] scholar." See next *mamor*.

⟦ 785 ⟧ כָּל תַּלְמִיד חָכָם שֶׁאֵינוֹ קָשֶׁה כְּבַרְזֶל אֵינוֹ תַּלְמִיד חָכָם

"A Torah scholar who is not as hard as iron is not a [real] scholar"
(*Ta'anith* 4a).

In commenting on the above maxim, Rabbi Leo Jung writes: "Hardness of speech or attitude is permissible when it reflects the speaker's righteous indignation and upright character, and especially when it is meant to prevent moral flabbiness or irresponsibility of the disciple.

A true scholar will be sharp when the need arises, but never destructive in his criticism" (*Three Problem Makers*).

The *Tzemach Tzedek* [Rabbi Menachem Mendel Schneersohn] was accustomed to restrain an angry rebuke until he had investigated the *Shulchan Aruch* [Code of Jewish Law] to learn whether anger was permissible in that particular instance.

Cf. *Yoma* 22b, "Any scholar who does not avenge himself and retain anger like a serpent is not a [real] scholar." See previous *mamor*.

Cf. *Ta'anith* 20a, "A man should always be gentle as the reed and never unyielding as the cedar. "See *Insights*, vol. 1, #372.

Rabbi Mendel Kaplan reconciles this statement with the above maxim as follows: "Internally one must be as strong as steel, but in one's relationship with others one must be as pliant and yielding as a reed. A person has to be like a subway door; the door itself is made of steel, but the part that comes in contact with people is made of rubber" (Yisroel Greenwald, *Reb Mendel and his Wisdom*, p. 148).

⎰ 786 ⎱ כְּלוּם יֵשׁ אָדָם שֶׁיּוֹדֵעַ לְתַקֵּן בִּרְכַּת הַמִּינִים

"Is there a man who can formulate the benediction of heretics?"
(*Berakoth* 28b).

Rabban Gamliel, as *Nasi*, posed this question before the sages of Israel. Rambam explains the reason for his concern. "In Rabban Gamliel's days, the number of heretics in Israel increased. They were wont to vex the Israelites and induce them to turn away from G-d" (*Mishneh Torah, Hil. Tefillah* 2:1).

In response to Rabban Gamliel's question, the Talmud tells us: "*Shmuel HaKatan* stood up and formulated it" (ibid.).

Rabbi Joseph B. Soloveitchik, in commenting on the above Gemara, explains that "until the age of Rabban Gamliel, the sages of Israel tended to ignore evil, hoping that it would cease of itself. Then came the *Churban* [the destruction of Jerusalem] and many apostates made peace with the foreign oppressor, spread malice against the people, and plotted its spiritual and physical death . . . .

"A determination, with weighty consequences, was proclaimed by Rabban Gamliel: '*Rabbosai*, the time has come to formulate a "benediction" for heretics. (True, the idea of prayer stems from *chesed* [lovingkindness] and *rachamim* [mercy]; but these two are at war with evil!) Who is the man who has the power to formulate such a benediction? . . .'

"They found *Shmuel HaKatan*, whose motto was: 'Do not rejoice when your enemy falls, and do not be glad in your heart when he stumbles' (*Aboth* 4:19). Shmuel the humble, who had never tasted the desire to settle accounts with malefactors, who had never complained about insults caused him, was chosen to fulfill the necessary task . . . . This benediction, which

cries to G-d for the destruction of evil, grew from the soil of love and *chesed"*
(*A Eulogy for Rabbi Chaim Heller*).
Cf. *Pnei Yehoshua* on *Berakoth* 28b.

⌇ 787 ⌇ בַּמָּה טַפְּשָׁאֵי שְׁאָר אִינְשֵׁי דְּקָיְימֵי מִקַּמֵּי סֵפֶר
תּוֹרָה וְלָא קָיְימֵי מִקַּמֵּי גַּבְרָא רַבָּה

"How foolish are those people who stand up [in deference] to the
Torah Scroll, but do not stand up to a great personage"
(*Makkoth* 22b).

"Because, while in the Torah Scroll forty lashes are prescribed, the Rabbis
came and [by interpretation] reduced them by one [so that only 39 lashes
may be given for violating a biblical prohibition]" (ibid.).

In commenting on the term *"gavra rabbah"* [great personage] in the above
dictum, the Ostrovtzer Rebbe, R. Meir Yechiel HaLevi once said: "If the
Talmud meant that a *gavra rabbah* was merely one who could change what
it seemingly says in the Torah [modifying 40 lashes to 39], then the Talmud
could have used a different source. Regarding 'the counting of the Omer,'
the Torah states that fifty days should be counted. Yet our sages said that
one only counts 49 — the Talmud did not cite that source for one who is a
'great personage,' since one who changes 50 days to 49 days is merely
making a fine talmudic distinction. However, one who minimizes the pain
and suffering of a fellow Jew by reducing 40 lashes to 39, so that he doesn't
get smitten that one extra blow, that indeed is a 'great personage'" (Rabbi
Paysach J. Krohn, *Around the Maggid's Table*, p. 266).

Rabbi Shlomo Kluger asks, "What creates the sanctity of a Torah Scroll?
Is it not the quality of the person who wrote it? Without the input of a
human scribe, Hebrew letters on parchment do not establish a status of
kedushah for a scroll . . . . Now, if a human can establish the holiness of a
parchment scroll, surely he can create a posture of *kedushah* for himself. This
shows the foolishness of the custom cited above. The 'fools' mentioned in
the Talmud recognize the power of man to sanctify a scroll of parchment . . .
but do not comprehend the ability of man to transform himself into a vehicle
of sanctity by mastering the Torah" (Rabbi J. Simcha Cohen, *The 613th*

Commandment, p. 14).

When R' Yisrael, the Rizhiner Rebbe, once dropped his *gartel* [special belt worn around the waist in preparation for prayer], the Apter Rav, Rabbi A. Y. Heshel, picked up the *gartel* and girded it around the much younger Rebbe.

He explained to his disciples who stood in amazement: "I did it because I wanted to fulfill a *mitzvah* of *gelilah* on a *Sefer Torah* [wrapping the *gartel* around a Torah scroll]" (Rabbi Paysach J. Krohn, *In the Footsteps of the Maggid,* p. 180).

See *Insights,* vol. 1, #324.

Cf. *Sanhedrin* 99b, "He who dishonors a Torah scholar is termed 'insolent toward the Torah'" (because a Torah scholar is *actual Torah* — Maharal).

◻ 788 ◻ כַּמָּה יְגִיעוֹת יָגַע אָדָם הָרִאשׁוֹן עַד שֶׁמָּצָא פַּת לֶאֱכֹל

"How much labor the first man Adam must have expended before he obtained bread to eat" (*Berakoth* 58a).

"He ploughed sowed, reaped, piled up sheaves, threshed, winnowed, selected [the ears], ground, sifted [the flour], kneaded and baked, and after that he ate; whereas I get up and find all these things prepared for me" (ibid.).

R' Zelig Pliskin comments: "This type of thinking is especially important for someone who finds himself easily annoyed with other people. Without others, life would be unimaginably difficult. The annoyance they cause you is the price you pay for the benefits you gain . . . . Learn to appreciate things which are usually taken for granted" (*Gateway to Happiness,* p. 42).

◊ 789 ◊

כֵּן דֶּרֶךְ הַתַּגָּרִין עוֹשִׂין, מַרְאִין אֶת הַפְּסוֹלֶת
תְּחִילָה וְאַחֲרֵי כֵן מַרְאִין אֶת הַשֶּׁבַח

"This is the way merchants operate: they show [their] bad wares
first, and afterwards they show the better wares"
(*Midrash Tanchuma, Shelach* 6).

When Rabbi Baruch Ber Leibowitz delivered his first *shiur* [lecture] in
Slobodka, his students, who expected to hear a "profound" [pilpulistic]
lecture, were extremely disappointed. They registered their complaint with
the former dean of the yeshiva, Rav Danishevski. The Rav went directly to
Reb Baruch with the students' complaint.

In total innocence, Reb Baruch Ber replied: "I don't understand. Do you
expect me to violate the *halacha* which states quite clearly that a merchant
should not display the better quality merchandise up front while hiding the
goods of lesser quality underneath? You surely do not expect me to cheat
the public!" (Rabbi Chaim Shapiro, "Rabbi Baruch Ber Leibowitz," *The Jewish
Observer*, [Kislev 5750]: vol. 22, no. 9, p. 15).

◊ 790 ◊

כְּנֶסֶת יִשְׂרָאֵל הִיא בֶּן זוּגֵךְ

"The Community of Israel is your mate" (*Beraishith Rabbah* 11:8).

"The Sabbath pleaded with the Holy One, blessed be He: 'All [days] have
a mate [the first day of the week has the second; the third, the fourth; the
fifth, the sixth], while I have no mate [no partner].' The Almighty replied:
'The Community of Israel is your mate'" (ibid.).

Israel [is the only nation who] observes the Sabbath. They utter the
blessings which sanctify *Shabbath* and recite *Kiddush* and *Havdallah* [a
fulfillment of "Remember the Sabbath day to keep it holy"] (Rabbi Zev Wolf
Einhorn, *M'harzav*).

This metaphysical dialogue between the Sabbath and the Almighty has
been interpreted in the following homiletical manner. The greater the value
of an object, the fewer the connoisseurs who truly appreciate its worth.

Thus, precious stones and diamonds are not discernible by the masses. This was bothering the Sabbath — "Who will be my mate? Who will truly appreciate me? Yes, the Almighty blessed me above all days, but who will acknowledge my greatness and holiness so that I will be honored properly?"

"The Community of Israel is your mate," the Almighty replies, "for her fate is no better than yours. Although Israel is an 'Am Segulah' [a treasured people] and the entire world was created for her sake, she is nevertheless treated by the nations of the world as an intruder. They do not appreciate her greatness. Hence, Israel will be a suitable mate for you" (Siach Yitzchok, cited in L'kutei Bosar L'kutei, Midrash, vol. 1, p. 24).

〔 791 〕

כֶּסֶף מְטַהֵר מַמְזֵרִים

"Money purifies mamzerim" (Kiddushin 71a).

By means of their wealth, mamzerim intermarry with Israel. Having thus mingled, they will not be separated in the future by the Almighty, since they have attached themselves to a great many families in Israel (Rashi).

Cf. Alfasi for another interpretation of "Money purifies . . . ."

This maxim has often been cited as an illustration of the abusive power of wealth. It can even purify the most illegitimate person or project. An illustration of this corruptive power may be seen in the following historical incident.

"During the reign of Czar Nikolas I, Jewish communities were forced to provide the Russian army with young Jewish boys for twenty-five year terms of service. Jewish communities consequently passed regulations to ensure that as long as there was a family from which no children had been taken, they would not conscript a second child from any family. Once, when visiting a certain city, Rabbi Yisrael Salanter met a poor widow, who was sobbing bitterly. When asked to explain her sorrow, she told the Rabbi that she had just been informed that her second son was to be drafted because of the illegal intervention of a wealthy leader of the community who wished to ensure that none of his children be taken. The rest of the community had acquiesced and decided to draft the widow's second son instead.

"Reb Yisrael went that afternoon to the local synagogue and, when one man rose to lead the Service, the Rabbi yelled at him, 'It is forbidden for you to lead us in prayer for you are not a believer in G-d and Torah.' A replacement was sent and Rabbi Salanter shouted the same thing at the second man. This happened a third time. Finally, the congregants asked Reb Yisrael to explain his behavior. 'The fact that you pray does not prove that you are believers,' he answered. 'You pray because your fathers prayed. But you are obviously not believers in the Torah. How do I know this? If you believed in the Torah, sincerely believing that it was the Voice of G-d commanding you, then how would you dare ignore the Torah laws which forbid you to oppress a widow, or to favor prominent people in judgment? That you are willing to ignore such laws shows that you do not really believe in G-d and His Torah.'" (Cited by Dennis Prager and Joseph Telushkin, *The Nine Questions People Ask About Judaism*, pp. 70, 71).

◊ 792 ◊ כְּעוֹבֵד כּוֹכָבִים נִדְמֶה לוֹ . . . כְּתַלְמִיד חָכָם נִדְמֶה לוֹ

"He appeared to him as a heathen . . . . He appeared to him as a *Torah scholar*" (*Hullin* 91a).

On the verse, "And Jacob was left alone, and there wrestled a man with him, until the breaking of dawn" [Gen. 32:25], the *Midrash* comments: "This was the guardian prince [angel] of Esau" (*Beraishith Rabbah* 77:2). The Talmud explains that the spirit of Esau appears to Jacob [Israel] in different guises — "He appears as a heathen . . . ."

"Throughout the long night of our wanderings we have had to wrestle with the 'spirit of Esau,' who has met us in combat in different forms . . . . He appears to us in the form of a pagan, luring us with the prospect of a pagan life, free from the bonds of prohibition and observances, holding out to us the advantages of assimilation with him . . . . Occasionally, he assumes the role of a *talmid chacham* [a "*Torah scholar*"], the role of the pious soul-saver [a missionary]. Under the guise of religion, he tries to undermine Israel's religious foundations. Love the Jew? Of course. It is because of his love for his poor deluded brother, because of his anxiety to save his soul from perdition that he preaches perversion to the Jew" (Rabbi Isaiah

Raffalovich, *Our Inheritance*, p. 46).

⫿ 793 ⫿

כִּקְרִיעַת יַם סוּף

"As the division of the Red Sea" (*Pesahim* 118a).

There are a number of things which the Talmud deems to be as "difficult" for G-d to do as splitting the sea for the Jewish people soon after their exodus for Egypt.

Rabbi Menachem M. Schneerson, the Lubavitcher Rebbe, asks: "Why was splitting the sea considered to be difficult for G-d? The sages explain that the difficulty was not so much in the actual splitting of the sea, but in a related matter. At that moment, two opposites came to pass simultaneously — the Egyptians were smitten and the Jews were saved. This was done notwithstanding the fact that the Attribute of Justice then complained: 'What difference is there between the two [nations]? Both are idolatrous! [See *Zohar* II 170b, 'It is difficult for Him to resist the Attribute of Justice.']

"Treating the Jewish people preferentially and the Egyptians harshly, by completely ignoring the protestations of the Attribute of Justice — which generally is given credence — is considered to be 'difficult' for G-d" (*The Chassidic Discourse*, p. 27).

Rabbi Yaakov Kamenetsky suggests that the "difficulty" for G-d pertains to the division of the sea itself. "The 'division of water' is considered the most difficult of miracles, for water is one of the three spheres of creation, namely: heaven, earth and water. Each sphere is a unique creation with its own set of boundaries. Hence a miracle was needed not only to change the nature of water, but also the foundation of creation" (*Iyunim Bamikra*, p. 158).

Cf. *Sotah* 2a, "It is as difficult to pair them [man and woman] as the division of the Red Sea."

Cf. *Pesahim* 118a, "A man's sustenance is as difficult [to provide] as the division of the Red Sea." See *Insights*, vol. 1, #473.

⦊ 794 ⦉

כַּרְכּוּשְׁתָּא וְשׁוּנְרָא עֲבַדוּ הִלּוּלָא מִתַּרְבָּא
דְּבִישׁ גַּדָּא

"The weasel and the cat had a feast on the fat of the luckless"
(*Sanhedrin* 105a).

Although the weasel and the cat are natural enemies who do not get along with each other, nevertheless, when they come upon a helpless prey they jointly devour it.

Similarly, there never was peace between Midian and Moab, yet they became good friends to conspire against and to attack the Israelites. See Numbers 22:7, "And the elders of Moab and the elders of Midian departed" (ibid.).

The truth of the above maxim is painfully obvious in the Middle East. The Arab nations are like weasels and cats — always at each other's throat, fighting amongst themselves. Yet they have openly declared their united animosity towards Israel, and their diabolical intention to march together against Jerusalem.

As in the past, with Divine assistance, all their evil designs will come to naught!

⦊ 795 ⦉

כְּשֵׁם שֶׁאָסוּר לְטַהֵר אֶת הַטָּמֵא, כַּךְ אָסוּר
לְטַמֵּא אֶת הַטָּהוֹר

"Just as it is forbidden to declare pure that which is impure, so, too, is it forbidden to declare impure that which is pure"
(*Yerushalmi, Terumoth* 5, end).

Cf, *Yalkut Shimoni* on Malachi 2:6, "'The law of truth was in his mouth' — He did not render impure that which was pure, and did not render pure that which was impure."

"It is apparent that one who errs on the side of leniency has only transgressed against G-d while one who errs on the side of *chumra* [stringency] is guilty of a dual transgression: (a) a transgression against G-d by misinterpreting the words of the Torah; and (b) a transgression against his fellow to whom he causes a loss — and the transgression of depriving another of his property applies, irrespective of the amount involved. Thus, he who declares as forbidden that which is actually permitted is guilty of the more serious offense" (*Aley Tamar* . . . on *Yerushalmi, Berakoth* 4:2).

"Just as we may not permit the forbidden, so, too, must we not forbid that which is permitted . . . . In most instances, we find that this will eventually lead to an unwarranted leniency. And even if this course of events is not apparent, it is forbidden, nonetheless, because after a long chain of events, a leniency may result" (*Shach, Kitzur BeHanhagath Hora'ath Isur VeHeter*).

◊ 796 ◊ כְּשֵׁם שֶׁנִּכְנַס לַבְּרִית כָּךְ יִכָּנֵס לַתּוֹרָה לְחוּפָּה וּלְמַעֲשִׂים טוֹבִים

"As he has entered into the Covenant, so may he enter into Torah, the marriage canopy, and good deeds" (*Shabbath* 137b).

In response to the father's *bracha*, ". . . Who has sanctified us with His commandments and has commanded us to lead him into the covenant of our father Abraham," the participants at a *brith* exclaim: 'As he has entered into the Covenant . . . .'"

Rabbi Meir Premishlaner comments: "It is this blessing with which we bless the child. Just as he enters into this covenant today [in total innocence], with no ulterior motives or any purpose other than to keep G-d's covenant and to perpetuate the pact between him and the Jewish people, so shall he continue to serve the Almighty with a pure heart for the rest of his life, in Torah, when he gets married, and as he does deeds of kindness" (Uri Auerbach, *Reb Maerl Premishlaner*, p. 179).

ל

‖ 797 ‖   לָא אִיבְרִי סִיהֲרָא אֶלָּא לְגִירְסָא

"The moon was created only for [the facilitation of] Torah study"
(*Erubin* 65a).

"While it is a duty to study by day and by night, most of one's knowledge is acquired by night. Accordingly, when one aspires to win the crown of the Torah, he should be especially heedful of all his nights and not waste a single one of them in sleep, eating, drinking, idle talk, and so forth, but devote all of them to study of the Torah and words of wisdom . . . . And whoever occupies himself with the study of the Torah by night — a mark of [spiritual] grace distinguishes him by day (*Mishneh Torah, Hil. Talmud Torah* 3:13).

Cf. *Shemoth Rabbah*, 47:5, "The melody of Torah beats only at night." See the Maharal's *Nesivoth Olam, Nesiv HaTorah*, ch. 4; ch. 9 on the specific advantages of nocturnal Torah study.

Since there are few interruptions when one engages in Torah study at night, Torah scholars acquire most of their Torah knowledge at night (*Ksav Sofer*).

Rabbi Yaakov Kamenetsky asserted that our sages' statement that G-d grants a special favor to one who learns at night, is undoubtedly true. But that *does not mean* that if one must choose between studying with a *chavrusa* [study partner] in a full *beis midrash* [study hall] during the day and learning alone at night, one should learn alone at night!

Cf. *Abodah Zarah* 3b, "Whoever occupies himself with [the study of] Torah by night, the Holy One, blessed be He, extends over him a mark of grace by day." See *Insights*, vol. 1, #293.

227

Cf. *Tamid* 32b, "If one studies Torah at night, the *Shechinah* faces him."
See #760.

798

לָא אִבְרִי עָלְמָא אֶלָּא לְדָוִד . . . . לְמשֶׁה

[Rav said] "The world was created on David's account." [Shmuel
said] "On Moshe's account" (*Sanhedrin* 98b).

"On David's account" — in the merit of David who would in the future
recite many songs and praises [to the Almighty].

"On Moshe's account" — for the sake of Moshe who would in the future
receive the Torah (Rashi).

"Rabbi Moshe Avigdor Amiel interprets this debate as expressing a
difference in emphasis: where is the focal point of the ultimate religious
experience? One sees it in Torah, in the exercise of the unique characteristic
of being human, the intellect, in serving G-d by grasping and comprehend-
ing His law, His blueprint for the spiritual dimensions of reality. The other
sees it in the existential experiencing of G-d, in worship, in love, through
the joyous song of exaltation.

Rabbi Amiel develops this contrast by using *Chassidim* and *Misnagdim* as
a starting point and working his way back, all the way to Moshe and David
(*Derashoth El-Ami*, vol. II, ch. 24, cited by Rabbi Joseph Grunblatt, *Exile and
Redemption*, p. 98).

799

לָא בְּסַבֵּי טַעְמָא וְלָא בְּדַרְדְּקֵי עֵצָה

"There is no reason in old men, and no counsel in children"
(*Shabbath* 89b).

"In the future the Holy One, blessed be He, will say to Abraham [and
later to Jacob], 'Your children have sinned against Me.' [They] shall answer
Him, 'Sovereign of the Universe, let them be wiped out for the sanctification
of Your Name.' The Almighty will retort, 'There is no reason in old men
[Abraham, the oldest patriarch] and no counsel in children [Jacob, the

youngest patriarch].' Only Isaac will have the wisdom to argue in defense of Israel" (ibid.).

Reb Maerl Premishlaner explains why Isaac will defend his children more than the other patriarchs. "Isaac had a son, Esau, who was less than good. Still he loved him and even blessed him. He realized that Jacob was the one who followed in his footsteps, but he didn't want to lose Esau altogether, and therefore he showed him his love. Consequently, Isaac was the one who could demand of G-d that He too should overlook the iniquities of His children and forgive them" (Uri Auerbach, *Reb Maerl Premishlaner*, p. 443).

The maxim, "There is no counsel in children," was applied by the *Sforno* to Joseph in his early relationship with his brothers. Commenting on the phrase "And he was a lad" [Gen. 37:2], he writes: "Because he was only a lad, he sinned by telling tales about his brothers, for he was inexperienced and could not foresee where this would lead, even though he was very intelligent and would soon thereafter counsel the elders of Egypt" (*Sforno, Commentary on the Torah*).

⫟ 800 ⫟

לֹא דּוֹמֶה שׁוֹמֵעַ לְרוֹאֶה

"Hearing cannot be compared to seeing" (*Mechilta, Shemoth* 19:9).

This maxim is popularly quoted as *"einoh domeh sh'miah l'riah."*

When the Israelites worshipped the Golden Calf, Scripture records: "As soon as Moshe came near the camp and saw the Calf and the dancing, he became enraged" [Ex. 32:19].

"We see that Moshe had not been thoroughly impressed [with the grave transgression] until he had become an eye-witness [of the event]. Hearing about it, both from G-d Himself as well as from Joshua, was not enough evidence for him to engage in any action. Only 'when he saw,' did he become enraged.

Similarly, the friends of Job were not hit by the full impact of his suffering, until they looked and failed to recognize him [Job 2:3]. Only then did they rend their garments and grieved with their friend" (Rabbi Moshe b. Chaim Alshich, *Toras Moshe*).

See *Maharsha* (*Yebamoth* 62a), who explains why an event perceived through one's own senses evokes a stronger reaction than one learned second hand, even though the information is trusted and beyond any doubt.

"One reason why witnesses whose testimony convicts someone of a capital offense are required to perform the execution themselves, is the principle 'hearing cannot be compared to seeing.' Anyone other than an eyewitness knows what happened only through hearsay, but the witnesses have actually seen the crime take place . . . . Therefore they should be the ones to take action" (Rabbi David Feinstein, *Kol Dodi on the Torah*, p. 275).

〚 801 〛   לֹא יִקְרָא לְאוֹר הַנֵּר

"One must not read [on the Sabbath] by the light of a lamp" (*Shabbath* 11a).

The Talmud gives a reason for the above *mishnaic* ruling. "One must not read by the light of a lamp lest he tilt it [if the light flickers, he may tilt the lamp so that the oil should flow more freely]. Said R. Ishmael b. Elisha, 'I will read and will not tilt.' Yet, once he read and wished to tilt . . . . 'How great are the words of the sages,' he exclaimed, 'who said, One must not read by the light of a lamp'" (ibid. 12a).

The Vilna Gaon suggests that when R. Ishmael exclaimed, "How great are the words of the sages," he was not referring to the Talmud which cites the reason for the prohibition, "lest he tilt it," for that led him to believe that he could guard himself so as not to violate the Sabbath. He was referring to the Mishnah [the above dictum] which does not give any reason for the prohibition.

The fact that no reason is cited points to the greatness of the words of the sages of the Mishnah, for there is no longer any danger of circumventing the prohibition by insisting that "the reason" does not apply.

⦅ 802 ⦆

לֹא יֵרֵד בְּנִי עִמָּכֶם

"My son shall not go down with you" (*Beraishith Rabbah* 91:9).

This scriptural phrase uttered by Jacob has become a midrashic idiom pertaining to one who utters a nonsensical argument. When Reuben urges his father Jacob to allow Benjamin to travel to Egypt together with his older brothers, Reuben says: "You may kill my two sons if I do not bring him back to you" [Gen. 42:37]. Jacob responds, "My son shall not go down with you" [i.e., your words are totally senseless].

Rabbi Tarfon was in the habit of saying, *"Lo yairaid beni imachem"* to anyone who spoke sheer nonsense.

The Hebrew word *"beni"* [my son] is similar to the word *"binah"* [understanding]. Hence, "my understanding does not agree with you."

⦅ 803 ⦆

לֹא יִשְׂמַח אָדָם בֵּין הַבּוֹכִים
וְלֹא יִבְכֶּה בֵּין הַשְּׂמֵחִים

"A man should not rejoice when among people who weep, nor weep when among those who rejoice" (*Derech Eretz Rabbah* 7).

"This is the general rule: A man should not deviate from the custom of his companions nor from society" (ibid.).

See, however, *Seder Eliyahu Zuta*, ch. 16, "Shmuel HaKatan said: 'Do not cry with him who cries, neither search with him who searches, nor fear with him who fears . . . lest he be a fool and you find yourself co m i n g t o folly.'"

This does not contradict the above dictum, for Shmuel HaKatan advises us not to follow the ways of the foolish, those who cry in vain, and search without cause, etc. . . . lest we be led into the ways of folly. Whereas the above dictum teaches us not to act differently from the accepted ways of the community.

Cf. *Beraishith Rabbah* 48:14, "When you enter a town, follow its customs." See *Insights*, vol. 1, #440.

Cf. *Baba Mezia* 86b, "One should never change from the [accepted] custom." See #826.

⟦ 804 ⟧   לֹא כָּל הָרוֹצֶה לִיטוֹל אֶת הַשֵּׁם יִטוֹל

"Not everyone who wants 'to assume distinction' may do so"
(*Berakoth* 16b).

One should not emulate the excessive piety found amongst our great Torah authorities [the *Gedolim*], unless his general behavior is such that it would warrant added stringencies.

Cf. *Hullin* 105a, "Mar Ukba said: 'In this matter I am as vinegar is to wine, compared with my father [i.e., I am inferior to my father]. For if my father were to eat meat now, he would not eat cheese until this very hour tomorrow, whereas I do not eat [cheese] in the same meal, but I do eat it in my next meal."

Rabbi Dovid Shelomo Eibeshvetz comments: "If Mar Ukba had such longings for his father's piety, who prevented him from behaving in a similar manner? The answer is, 'Not every one who wants to assume distinction may do so'" (*Arvei Nachal, Ekev*).

⟦ 805 ⟧   לֹא כָּרַת הַקָּדוֹשׁ בָּרוּךְ הוּא בְּרִית עִם יִשְׂרָאֵל אֶלָּא בִשְׁבִיל דְּבָרִים שֶׁבְּעַל פֶּה

"The Holy One, blessed be He, made a covenant with Israel only for the sake of that which was transmitted orally" (*Gittin* 60b).

"As it says, 'For by the *mouth* of these words I have made a covenant with you and with Israel' [Ex. 34:27]" (ibid.).

In order to prevent the other nations from copying it, the *Oral Law* was revealed to Moshe on Mt. Sinai, but was not permitted to be written down (*Tosaf.* ad loc.). See *Midrash Tanchuma, Ki Thisa* 34.

Cf. *Berakoth* 54a, "*Eis la'asoth l'Shem.*" See *Insights*, vol. 1, #449.

Rabbi Samson Raphael Hirsch translates the scriptural phrase "*ke al pe ha'devarim ha'elah"* as "for according to *the live content* of these words." He writes: "It is not merely the fixed written words, as they stand before our eyes, on which our covenant with G-d is to be established, but the full living meaning and spirit of the words . . . . This, the full comprehensive understanding of the meaning and spirit of the Torah, is what the covenant was built on" *(The Pentateuch,* vol. II, p. 662).

The Chafetz Chaim, in an essay entitled, "The Torah Way," admonishes parents not to neglect the Oral Law when teaching Torah to their children. He writes: "Well-meaning parents do not stop to realize that when they tear their children away from Torah before they comprehend the Oral Law, they are literally tearing them away from their source of life" *(Chomas Hadas).*

⟦ 806 ⟧

לָא מִינַהּ וְלָא מִקְצָתַהּ

"None of it [pride] and not part of it" *(Sotah* 5a).

This is Rabbi Nachman b. Yitzchok's view regarding pride or haughtiness. It should not exist even in the smallest degree. [Rava, however, held that "A disciple of the sages should possess an eighth of an eighth [of pride]." See *Insights,* vol. 1, #496.]

Rambam follows Rabbi Nachman's view. "Under a ban be he who is proud, even in part of it" *(Mishneh Torah, Hil. Daioth* 2:3).

So also the *Rosh,* who writes: "One should distance oneself from haughtiness to the infinite degree of remoteness" *(Orchoth Chaim).*

The *Tzemach Tzedek* [R. Menachem M. Schneersohn] once heard from Reb Levi Yitzchak of Berditchev, that if the Torah would not have written about the character trait of *ga'avah* [arrogance], he would not have believed that this trait could possibly be found in the world. It was impossible for him to imagine how a person could be foolish enough to possess even the slightest amount of arrogance. After all, a man's entire fortune can change overnight, so why should he be proud of his accomplishments? He could not understand the talmudic dictum that, "A disciple of the sages should possess an eighth of an eighth [of pride]." (Rabbi Baruch HaLevi Epstein, *Mekor Baruch,* cited in *Recollections,* p. 135).

807

לֹא נִתְּנָה תּוֹרָה לִדְרוֹשׁ אֶלָּא לְאוֹכְלֵי הַמָּן

"The Torah was given to expound upon only to those who ate the
manna" (*Midrash Tanchuma, Beshalach* 20).

Torah and faith can only be acquired by those who have the spiritual
qualities that existed among those who ate the manna. They only had food
for one day, and did not worry about the next day. Torah is only given to
people who do not worry about tomorrow (Rabbi Menachem Mendel of
Kotzk).

In commenting on Jacob's prayerful request for "bread to eat and clothes
to wear" [Gen. 28:20], Rabbeinu Bachya writes: "This is what the righteous
ask of G-d — not luxuries, but only what is necessary and essential, that
without which a person cannot live . . . . One who fears G-d should be
happy with what he has and be content with less, and should not desire
luxuries" (*Rabbeinu Bachya al HaTorah, Va'yetzei*).

The uniqueness of the manna consisted in its total absorption in the body,
without waste or excretion. Similarly, the Torah's uniqueness is that in *every
word* there is spiritual nourishment for those who recognize its Divine source
(S. W.).

Since the manna had the taste of whatever food the person was thinking
of — what taste did it have if the person was not thinking of any food at all?
The Chofetz Chaim answered: "*Az men tracht nit hott es kein ta'am nisht.* If
you don't think, it has no taste."

The Chofetz Chaim continued, "What can be more tasty than a piece of
Gemara? It is so sweet, but only if you think. If you don't, it has no flavor
at all" (Rabbi Shimon Finkelman, *For Love of Torah*, p. 107).

Cf. *Sotah* 48b, "Whoever has a piece of bread in his basket and says,
'What shall I eat tomorrow?' — belongs to those who have little faith."

See #773.

〚 808 〛

לָא קָאֲרֵי לִיהֲוֵי צַוְותָּא לְחַבְרֵיה

"[If a student] is inattentive [lit., does not read], put him next to a diligent one" (*Baba Bathra* 21a).

"You should not unduly punish [the inattentive] pupil, nor expel him, but simply let him sit in the company of others, and in the end he will 'give heart'" (Rashi).

See, however, *Maharsha*, who maintains that the poor student should be placed in the company of the good student in order to spur the good student to even greater effort, for otherwise the good student will also lose interest and become idle.

In commenting on the above *Maharsha*, it was suggested that "by putting the poor student next to the good one, the latter will try to teach him and, in the process, will inevitably profit by becoming an even better student. As the talmudic adage puts it: 'I have learned much from my teachers, and from my colleagues more than from my teachers, but from my disciples more than from them all' [*Ta'anith* 7a]" (Zalman Aryeh Hilsenrad, *My Soul Thirsts*, p. 197). See #655.

〚 809 〛

לָא שְׁקַל יְדָא מִן כִּיסָא דְּסָבַר דְּילְמָא אָתֵי
עָנִי בַּר טוֹבִים . . . .

"He [R. Chana bar Chanilai] never took his hand from his purse, thinking that perhaps a respectable poor man might come [and while he was getting his purse, he would be put to shame]" (*Berakoth* 58b).

Rabbi Yehudah Zev Segal cites this talmudic passage as an illustration of what he calls *"chesed shel Torah,"* the Torah's brand of kindness. "R. Chana bar Chanilai always walked with his hand in his purse so that if he chanced upon a beggar, the man would be spared the few seconds of shame it would have taken for him to reach into his purse for some coins.

Chesed shel Torah demands that a benefactor ask himself, 'Were I to be in need of this kindness, what would I hope to receive from those who sought to help me? What would be my fears and apprehensions, my needs and aspirations?' Only when one endeavors to feel the pain of another can he be inspired to help him in the most desired manner" (*Yirah VeDa'as*, trans. by Rabbi Shimon Finkelman, *Inspiration and Insight*, pp. 105-106).

Cf. *Kethuboth* 67b, "Sufficient for his needs [Deut. 15:8] — Even a horse to ride upon and a servant to run before him." See #566.

▯ 810 ▯   לֹא תָּלוּשׁ אֶלָּא בְּמַיִם שֶׁלָּנוּ

"[A woman] should knead [unleavened bread] only with water that was kept overnight" (*Pesahim* 42a).

"In [the month of] *Nisan* the water in the wells is warm [which hastens fermentation]. Therefore it must be drawn the evening before it is required, so that it can cool off" (Rashi).

The Talmud records: "Rav Mattenah taught this [in a public lecture] at Papunia. On the morrow, all brought their containers to him and said to him, 'Give us water.' Said he to them, 'I meant with water kept overnight.'"

The inhabitants of Papunia misinterpreted the Rabbi's directions, believing that "*mayim she'lanu*" meant "our water," i.e., the Rabbi's special kind of water. He explained to them that the term *mayim she'lanu* means "water kept overnight."

Rabbi Avraham Bornstein comments on the moral implications of this talmudic tale. "The incident shows us how even the ignorant masses of the olden days respected the sages. If a Rabbi in our day were to announce that his congregation could only use 'our water' for the baking of *matzoth*, the entire community would rise up in indignation and demand why the Rabbi's water should be any holier than ordinary water, and they would suspect him of all sorts of impure and mercenary motives. Not so in talmudic times. When they thought that their Rabbi directed them to use 'our water,' they asked no questions.

This humorous incident is an illustration of the faith which all Jews in those days had in their sages and spiritual leaders" (*Avnei Nezer*, cited in *Wellsprings of Torah*, p. 453).

〖 811 〗   לָבַשׁ שְׁמוּאֵל חֲלוּקָן שֶׁל יִשְׂרָאֵל

"Shmuel clothed himself with the garment of Israel" (*Yerushalmi Ta'anith* 2:7).

The Jerusalem Talmud paraphrases the scriptural verse, "And they said there, we have sinned against the L-rd" [I Samuel 7:6] to read, "*And Shmuel said*, we have sinned against the L-rd," i.e., he put on "clothes of filth."

Rabbi Yaakov Yosef of Polonoye comments: "Since Shmuel is without sin, how can it be said that he deliberately clothed himself with the garment of all Israel? But just as 'Moshe was the most faithful in all His House' [Num. 12:7] and nevertheless, when Israel sinned, Moshe also came into sin — for Moshe was the source of Israel — so it is with each generation and its leaders. Through the sin of Israel, a portion of sin also reached Shmuel. It was *as if* he sinned the same sin which the people committed" (*Toledoth Yaakov Yosef*, 130d).

Me'iri writes: "Moral instruction and admonishment to others must be given 'sensibly,' as we find regarding Moshe Rabbeinu when he said to Israel, 'You shall not do as *we* do here today' [Deut. 12:8]: he included himself in his rebuke. And so did Ezra, 'We rebelled . . . .' [Ezra 10:2]" (Cited in *Me'am Loez, Prov.* 1:3).

Rabbi Yisrael Salanter extended this trait to everyone [not only to the leaders in each generation]. On the verse, "*hocheiach tochiach es amisecha*" ("You shall surely rebuke your neighbor" (Lev. 19:17), Reb Yisrael said the word "*es*" is used in order to include yourself.

〖 812 〗   לִיבָּא וְעֵינָא תְּרֵין סִרְסוּרִין דְּחַטָּאָה

"The heart and the eyes are two agents of sin" (*Yerushalmi, Berakoth,* 1:5).

"As it is written '. . . and that you go not about after your heart and after your eyes'" [Numbers 15:39] (see *Midrash Tanchuma, Shelach*).

"The heart and the eyes are the spies of the body, they are the agents for it in sins; the eye sees and the heart desires, and the body commits the sin" (Rashi, Num. 15:39).

Rabbeinu Yonah b. Avraham of Gerona writes: "The sins of the heart are atoned for by the bitterness and sighing of the sinner, by the breaking of his heart, as it is written, 'A broken and contrite heart, O G-d, You will not despise' [Psalms 51:19]. There is an analogy here to the cleansing of unclean vessels through their being broken . . . .

"The sin of the eyes is atoned for by tears, as it is said, 'Mine eyes run down with rivers of water because they observe not Your Law' [Psalms 119:136]" (Sha'arei Teshuvah, Sha'ar Rishon #15).

"The functions of the soul are knowledge, intelligence, speech, humility, fear and hope, and other good qualities. But when lust is mingled with the soul, it destroys all of these good qualities; just as extraneous juices destroy the structure of the body, so does the mixture of lust destroy the work of the soul" (Sefer Ha'yashar, ch. 6).

⟰ 813 ⟰

לִיגְמַר אִינִישׁ וַהֲדַר לִיסְבַּר

"A man should study and subsequently he will understand"
(Shabbath 63a).

Even if at first one does not fully understand all that he learns from his Rebbe, he should nevertheless study; understanding will eventually come (Rashi).

Rabbi Nachman of Breslov comments: "You should read the words [of Torah] even if you do not completely understand them . . . . When you study quickly you will absorb a great quantity. You will be able to review each volume many times. What you do not understand at first will appear simple the second or third time. You will eventually understand all that is possible.

"A person who is overly precise can become very confused. Often he will abandon his studies completely and end up with nothing" (Rabbi Nathan of Nemirov, Sichos HaRan).

〔 814 〕

לְךָ לְאוֹת וְלֹא לַאֲחֵרִים לְאוֹת

"It shall be to you for a sign, and not a sign for others"
(*Menakoth* 37b).

"And it shall be to you for a sign upon your hand and for a memorial between your eyes . . ." [Ex. 13:16].

Our sages derive from the former part of this verse that the *tefillin* worn on the hand must be covered, for the Torah states "it shall be *to you* for a sign." It must consequently be put high up on the arm, on the part which is usually covered with the sleeve.

"And for a memorial between your eyes" — "He who sees them bound between the eyes, will recall the miracle and speak of it" (Rashi, ad.loc.).

Rabbi Moshe Feinstein comments: "We must understand why this differentiation is necessary, i.e., that the *tefillin* of the hand be a 'sign' solely for the individual wearing them, whereas the *tefillin* of the head be a 'memorial' to all who see them.

It would appear that both of these aspects are necessary and, in fact, complement each other. In order to inspire others to remember the miracle of the exodus from Egypt, the person himself must remember this incident and be cognizant of its everlasting significance. One cannot 'preach' to others what he does not 'practice,' and hope to be successful . . . . After the person will himself see the 'sign' of the *tefillin* of the hand and act accordingly, he will then influence others to follow his lead, without having to utter any speeches but rather only by letting them see his tefillin on the head . . ." (Rabbi Abraham Fishelis, *Bastion of Faith*, p. 79).

〚 815 〛

„לָלֶכֶת בָּהֶם, " עֲשֵׂם עִיקָר
וְאַל תַּעֲשֵׂם טְפֵלָה

"'To walk in them' [Lev. 18:4] — make them [the laws of the
Torah] primary, and do not make them secondary"
(*Torath Kohanim, Va'yikrah* 18:4, note 141).

"'To walk in them' — all your creative activities should be motivated
exclusively by them without the added mixture of any foreign substance.
Thus, you may not say: 'I have studied Jewish wisdom, I will now go and
study the wisdom of other nations' . . . . Therefore it says: 'To walk in
them,' you may not move outside their sphere" (ibid.).

Rabbi S. R. Hirsch comments: "If we interpret these words correctly, the
introductory remark 'make them primary and not secondary' opposes the
contention that the ensuing sentences might imply the complete exclusion
of any knowledge and science gained and applied in non-Jewish circles and
not directly connected with the realm of Torah. The prescription of 'make
them primary and not secondary' presupposes the validity of the study of
other fields of human culture. What it does mean is that we must make
absolutely certain that the science of Torah and the knowledge emanating
from it remain the central, firm and supremely unchangeable entity. Secular
cultures may be studied only as an auxiliary force, and only inasmuch as
they truly help to promote the study of Torah wisdom, subordinating
themselves as the 'secondary' to the 'principle.' Torah and its eternal truths
must be everywhere and at all times the supreme measure and judge of any
knowledge flowing from other sciences" (*The Pentateuch*, Lev. 18:4).

"The name of Samson Raphael Hirsch has become synonymous with the
precept of '*Torah im Derech Eretz*,' which has suffered more misinterpretation
than any other epoch-making ideology of recent Jewish history" (Rabbi
Joseph Breuer, *A Time to Build*, vol. 3, p. 50).

Cf. *Aboth* 2:2, "The study of Torah combined with an occupation is an
excellent thing, for the wearying labor of both keeps sin forgotten."

See #705.

〔 816 〕 לִלְמוֹד וּלְלַמֵּד לִשְׁמוֹר וְלַעֲשׂוֹת, הֲרֵי אַרְבַּע

"To learn, to teach, to guard and to observe, there are four [duties associated with each commandment]" (*Sotah* 37a).

For each *mitzvah* of the Torah, there were four covenants relating to four aspects of the commandments: to learn, to teach, to guard, and to observe.

Rabbi Yitzchak Zev Soloveitchik notes that the third aspect [to guard] requires definition. What, he asks, is the distinction between guarding Torah and observing Torah? Since the latter clause [to observe — *la'asoth*] relates to both positive and negative commandments, guarding Torah must have a specific application. He therefore suggests that the commitment "to guard Torah" [*lishmor*] refers to the need to preserve the purity of the *Mesorah*. It is, therefore, an obligation not only to learn Torah and observe Torah and *mitzvoth*, but also to sustain the purity of the transmission of the Torah.

In commenting on the Brisker Rav's definition of *lishmor* as "guarding the purity of Torah transmission," Rabbi J. Simcha Cohen writes: "It may, therefore, be conjectured that *Keriath HaTorah* [the public reading of the Torah] was established not merely as a format for the public teaching of Torah, but specifically to emphasize the purity and accuracy of Torah as exemplified by the *Sefer Torah*. The teaching of Torah must be based upon *Torath Moshe* — the *Sefer Torah* itself — to preserve Torah for future generations" (*The 613th Commandment*, p. 48).

〔 817 〕 לָמַד וְלִימֵּד וְשָׁמַר וְעָשָׂה, וְהָיְתָה סַפִּיקָה בְּיָדוֹ לְהַחֲזִיק וְלֹא הֶחֱזִיק, הֲרֵי זֶה בִּכְלַל אָרוּר

"If one has learned and taught [the Torah], kept and performed [its precepts], but he had the opportunity to strengthen [its observance by others] and did not do so, he is included in the scope of the curse" (*Yerushalmi*, *Sotah* 7:4).

He is included in the imprecation of "Cursed be he who does not uphold the words of this Torah" [Deut. 27:26].

The Chafetz Chaim would often point out that there are two distinct *mitzvoth*: to study the Torah and to "uphold the Torah." A Jew has no right to be satisfied and smug with his personal spiritual gains and achievements.

"Consider," the Chafetz Chaim would say: "The sacred Torah has ordered a human being to care for his fellow-man's property . . . [Deut. 22:1]. How great, then, should your concern be about your brother's character, to aid him spiritually . . . . If the Torah demands of a person that he care for his fellow-man's material problems, how much more must he treat another's spiritual needs with care and concern" (Rabbi Moses M. Yosher, *The Chafetz Chaim*, vol. 1, p. 114).

See *Midrash Shmuel* on *Aboth* 2:9, "If you have learned much Torah, do not pride yourself on 'it' — *'but rather bestow some of this goodness on others* [i.e., by inspiring them in the pursuit of Torah and mitzvoth].'"

Do not be like the one who, when he is cold, wraps himself up in fur while the others in the room continue to freeze. This is a *"tzaddik in peltz"* [a righteous man in a fur coat] who is concerned only about his own Torah study, not caring whether those around him are "warmed" by the fire of Judaism (Rabbi Simcha Bunim of Peshischa).

⫿ 818 ⫿   לִמְּדָה תּוֹרָה דֶּרֶךְ אֶרֶץ שֶׁלֹּא יֹאכַל אָדָם בָּשָׂר אֶלָּא לְתֵאָבוֹן

"The Torah teaches a rule of conduct, that a person should not eat meat unless he has an appetite for it" (*Hullin* 84a).

"If one has an appetite for meat, he may eat it provided he studies Torah which is inscribed on parchment of animals that are fit for consumption . . . .

"The reason for permitting the eating of meat to those who engage in Torah study and don *tefillin* is this: The Torah scroll and the material of the *tefillin* are formed from the hide and sinews of the animal, and after we have used parts of the animal in order to fulfill the *mitzvah*, we may justify using the rest of the animal for the eating of meat" (*Sefer HaChasidim*, sec. 303, 1082).

Rabbi Chaim Yosef David Azulai writes: "Our Rabbis taught us 'proper conduct' that one should not eat meat except in certain circumstances — if he is not strong and healthy" (Chida, *Chaim Sha'al*, 40:6).

Cf. *Pesahim* 49b, "An *am ha'aretz* may not eat the flesh of cattle, for it is said, 'This is the law [Torah] of the beast and the fowl' [Lev. 11:46], whoever engages in [the study of] Torah may eat the flesh of beast and fowl . . . ."

⟦ 819 ⟧   לָמָה נִקְרָא שְׁמָה בֵּית שׁוֹאֵבָה, שֶׁמִּשָּׁם שׁוֹאֲבִים רוּחַ הַקּוֹדֶשׁ

"Why was it [the ceremony of the *Water Drawing*] called *Sho'evah* [Drawing]? Because from there they would draw the Holy Spirit" (*Yerushalmi, Succoth* 5:1).

"As it is written: 'You shall draw water with joy from the springs of salvation'" (Isaiah 12:3).

Rabbi Yehudah Aryeh Alter (the Gerer Rebbe) comments: "It is called *Simchath Beith HaSho'evah* [Joy of the Water Drawing], because from there, from 'joy,' emanates the Holy Spirit . . . . Moreover, only regarding the Festival of Succoth [when the Water Drawing ceremony took place] does Scripture state, 'You shall observe it for seven days *in the year* . . .' [Lev. 23:14], implying that these seven days [of joy] constitute a vessel of *simcha* radiating joy throughout the year" (*Sfath Emeth, Devarim*, p. 182).

Similarly, the *Sfath Emeth* points out that in our *Kiddush* on *Yom Tov*, we refer to our Festivals as *Mo'adim L'simchah* [appointed times *for* rejoicing] rather than *Mo'adim B'simcha* [appointed times *of* rejoicing], which teaches us that our Festivals are not only days of rejoicing, but storehouses of joy and gladness for the remainder of the year.

The Vilna Gaon was asked which of the 613 *mitzvoth* he considered the most difficult to observe. He answered that it was *Succoth*, because for seven consecutive days a person must be in constant joy. Regardless of what might occur during these days that might make it difficult for a person to feel happy, the *mitzvah* to rejoice requires him to overcome all obstacles to joy (Rabbi Abraham J. Twersky, *Growing Each Day*, p. 22).

Cf. *Shabbath* 30b, "The Divine Presence rests only upon one who performs a commandment in a joyous spirit." See *Insights*, vol. 1, #40.

⦗ 820 ⦘

לָמָה קָדְמָה פָּרָשַׁת שְׁמַע לִוְהָיָה אִם
שָׁמוֹעַ . . . .

"Why does the section of *Shema* ['Hear O Israel'] precede *V'ha'yah im shamoah* ['If you will hearken'] . . . ? (*Berakoth* 13a).

"To indicate that one should first subject himself to the yoke of the kingdom of Heaven, and afterwards subject himself to the yoke of the commandments" (ibid.).

"One should cleave to the commandments and distance himself from transgressions solely because of the King's decree. This, then, is what the [above] dictum suggests. First, one should accept upon himself the yoke of the Heavenly Kingdom — a total commitment to the royal decree, and thereafter accept the yoke of the commandments — whether he feels comfortable with them or not" (Rabbi Gershon Zev Damesek, *L'ohr HaAggadah*, p. 29).

Cf. *Sifra, Va'yikrah* 20:26, "A person should not say, 'I loathe swine's flesh' . . . but he should say, 'I do desire it, yet what can I do, since my Father in Heaven has decreed upon me." See *Insights*, vol. 1, #58.

⦗ 821 ⦘

לָמָה תוֹקְעִין בְּרֹאשׁ הַשָּׁנָה, לָמָה תוֹקְעִין
רַחֲמָנָא אָמַר תִּקְעוּ

"Why do we blow the shofar on *Rosh Hashanah?* Why do we blow it? The All-Merciful has told us: 'Blow the shofar'" (*Rosh Hashanah* 16a).

See *Pnei Yehoshua* who explains that the Gemara's question is not, why do we perform the mitzvah of blowing shofar, but simply, why is the sound of the *tekia* made?

"Although the statutes in the Law are all of them Divine decrees . . . it is nevertheless fitting to reflect upon them and to offer reasons for them whenever possible" (*Mishneh Torah, Hil. Terumah* 4:13).

"It is fitting for man to meditate upon the laws of the holy Torah and to comprehend their full meaning to the extent of his ability. Nevertheless, a law for which he finds no reason and understands no cause, should not be trivial in his eyes . . ." (*Mishneh Torah, Hil. Me'ilah* 8:8).

The mitzvah of *Parah Aduma* [Red Heifer] represents that which is totally paradoxical in the Torah. While a "defiled person" is ritually cleansed through the sprinkling of ashes upon him, all participants in the arrangement of this purification rite are rendered "impure."

"Scripture terms it a *chuka* [implying that] it is a decree from before Me, you have no right to criticize it" (Rashi, Num. 19:2).

Rabbi Yaakov Kamenetsky deduces from this that "the essence of the mitzvah of *Parah Aduma* is the adherence to the Divine decree. This commandment was enacted just to teach us that basic to the observance of all commandments is the [unquestioned] obedience to the Voice of G-d" (*Emeth L'Yaakov*, p. 250).

⏍ 822 ⏍ לְמַיְּימִינִים בָּה סַמָּא דְּחַיֵּי לְמַשְׂמְאִילִים בָּה
סַמָּא דְּמוֹתָא

"To those who go to the right hand thereof [the words of the Torah], it is a medicine of life; to those who go to the left thereof, it is a deadly poison" (*Shabbath* 88b).

"The very Torah that is life-giving to one person becomes a deadly poison to one who is lazy in its study" (Rabbi Chaim Shmulevitz, *Reb Chaim's Discourse*, p. 71).

The Alter of Novardok (Rav Yosef Yozel Hurwitz) once said: "One who studies Torah only for material gain is like a snake who, even when served the food of kings, only tastes dirt. He is unaware of the other flavors" (Rabbi Dov Katz, *Tenuath Ha'Mussar*).

Cf. *Shabbath* 63a, "To those who go to the right hand thereof, there is length of days . . . but for those that go to the left thereof, there is riches and honor, but not length of days." See Proverbs 3:16.

There is a vast difference between "those who go to the left thereof," thereby permeating the atmosphere with a deadly poison, and "those who go to the left thereof," thereby being rewarded with "riches and honor."

See *Tosaf. Berakoth* 17a s.v. *Haoseh shlo lishma* who describes two types of studying Torah "not for its own sake." (1) One who studies Torah in order to vex others by making himself disagreeable. (2) One who studies Torah so that others will honor and praise him.

For the first category, Torah is indeed a deadly poison, whereas the second, "innocuous," category may in fact lead to a reward of "riches and honor."

Cf. *Pesahim* 50b, "Always should a man occupy himself with Torah and mitzvoth even though it be not for their own sake . . . ." See *Insights*, vol. 1, #374.

Cf. *Yoma* 72b, "If he is meritorious it becomes for him a medicine of life; if not, it becomes a deadly poison." See *Insights*, vol. 1, #205.

⏐ 823 ⏐ לְעוֹלָם אֵין הַקָּדוֹשׁ בָּרוּךְ הוּא מְיַחֵד שְׁמוֹ עַל הָרָעָה אֶלָּא עַל הַטּוֹבָה

"The Holy One, blessed be He, does not link His Name with evil, but only with good" (*Beraishith Rabbah* 3:6).

"Thus it is not written, 'And G-d called the light Day, and the darkness G-d called Night,' but 'and the darkness *He* called Night'" (ibid.).

"With regard to good, G-d is considered its actual cause. With regard to evil, G-d is the indirect cause, since it is the absence of G-d's Light and the concealment of His Presence . . . . Regarding this source of evil, Scripture states [Isaiah 45:7], '[G-d] forms light and creates darkness, makes peace and creates evil.' [The word 'create' always refers to the creation of 'something out of nothing,' and therefore, the fact that the verse says 'creates evil' indicates that it is not something that existed previously in G-d]" (Rabbi Moshe Chaim Luzzato, *Derech HaShem*).

⫿ 824 ⫿   לְעוֹלָם אַל יוֹצִיא אָדָם דָּבָר מְגוּנֶּה מִפִּיו

"One should not utter a gross expression with his mouth"
(Pesahim 3a).

"For Scripture employs a circumlocution of eight letters [uses eight letters more than is necessary] rather than utter a gross expression, for it is said [in listing the animals that Noach was to bring in the Ark], '. . . and of the beasts *that are not clean'* [Gen. 7:2] [*asher einenah tehorah* — 13 letters] instead of 'unclean' [*ha'tmeah* — 5 letters]" (ibid.).

"Why is it," asks Rabbi Elchanan Wasserman, "that the Torah does not employ a similar circumlocution in listing the categories of forbidden foods? The term *tamei* [unclean or defiled] is invariably used, and not the expression '[animals] that are not clean.'" "The answer is," says Reb Elchanan, "that when the Torah is dealing with *halacha l'ma'aseh* [practical application], it is important to be clear and precise so that no one should have any doubt as to that which is permitted and that which is prohibited. However, at the time of Noach, when the animal listing was not a *halacha l'ma'aseh* concern [which animals may be eaten and which are forbidden], but only a question concerning the survival of the species — there it wasn't proper to utilize a gross expression" (Elchanan Josef Hertzman, *Malchuth Satmar*, p. 69).

⫿ 825 ⫿   לְעוֹלָם אַל יְשַׁנֶּה אָדָם בְּנוֹ בֵּין הַבָּנִים

"A man should never distinguish one son among his other sons"
(Shabbath 10b).

"For on account of the two *sela's* weight of fine silk, which Jacob gave Joseph in excess of his other sons, his brothers became jealous of him and the matter resulted in our forefather's descent into Egypt" (ibid.).

Cf. *Tosafoth* [loc. cit.] who asked, "Had not 400 years of exile and servitude been decreed for them anyway?" ["Know for a certainty that your offspring shall be aliens in a land not their own, they will serve them, and they will oppress them four hundred years" [Gen. 15:13].

See the explanation suggested by *Tosafoth*.

Rabbi Zalman Sorotzkin interprets the above puzzling verse in the following fashion: "This decree includes three periods. The first, that of being 'alien,' lasted Isaac's whole life and part of Jacob's. The second, exile to 'a land not their own,' began when Jacob fled to Aram, and especially once he descended to Egypt. The third, 'servitude and oppression,' lasted from the death of Jacob's sons until the Exodus.

Taken together, the three periods lasted 400 years, but G-d did not define a precise duration for each one. Had Jacob's children not sinned, they would have remained in the Land almost the whole time, and would have suffered only a short exile and servitude. But those last two stages would begin immediately if they should sin. In fact, Jacob and his sons were not exiled until the sin of bitter squabbling broke out among his children.

If not for the fraternal hatred which caused Joseph to be sold, the period of exile and servitude would have been shortened to a few years" (*Oznayim LaTorah*).

The two *sela's* worth of fine silk that Jacob gave Joseph beyond what he gave his other sons led to hatred between the brothers, which ultimately brought about a *premature* descent to Egypt.

826

לְעוֹלָם אַל יְשַׁנֶּה מִן הַמִּנְהָג

"One should never change from the [accepted] custom" (*Baba Mezia* 86b).

When Moshe ascended on High [to receive the Torah] he did not eat for forty days and nights [acting like heavenly beings]. When the Ministering Angels descended below [to visit with Abraham] they ate bread [acting like earthly beings] (ibid.).

Rabbeinu Sherira Gaon writes: "From where do we know that custom is an important matter? For it is written, 'Do not move your neighbor's border — that which the ancients have partitioned . . .' [Deut. 19:14]. This is to be interpreted not only in its literal sense, but also with relation to generally accepted norms of behavior" (*Sha'arei Tzedek* part 4, 1:20).

A custom instituted by the *Beis Din* [Rabbinical Court] of any generation is included in the scriptural admonition "You shall not deviate from the matter they [the Rabbis] impart to you . . ." [Deut. 17:11].

Cf. *Beraishith Rabbah* 48:14, "When you enter a town, follow its customs." See *Insights*, vol. 1, #440.

Cf. *Derech Eretz Rabbah* 7, "A man should not rejoice when among people who weep, or weep when among those who rejoice." See #803.

Cf. *Yerushalmi*, *Yebamoth* ch. 12:1, "A *minhag* annuls the *halacha*." See *Insights*, vol. 1, #411.

◊ 827 ◊ לְעוֹלָם יָדוּר אָדָם בְּאֶרֶץ יִשְׂרָאֵל אֲפִילוּ בְּעִיר שֶׁרוּבָּהּ עוֹבְדֵי כּוֹכָבִים

"One should always live in the Land of Israel, even in a town most of whose inhabitants are idolaters" (*Kethuboth* 110b).

On the verse, "And you shall take possession of the Land and settle in it, for I have assigned the Land to you to possess" [Num. 33:53], Ramban writes: "In my opinion, this is a positive commandment in which He is commanding them to dwell in the Land and inherit it."

Rambam, however, does not include "dwelling in Israel" in his *Sefer HaMitzvoth* [listing the 613 commandments of the Torah].

Rabbi Yitzchak de Leon maintains that Rambam did not include this mitzvah, for he held that the duty to dwell in Israel lapsed after the destruction of the Holy Temple (*Megillath Esther*, *Comm. on Sefer HaMitzvoth*). See Rabbi Yaakov Weisberg, "The theory of *Megillath Esther* regarding the mitzvah of dwelling in the Land of Israel," (HaMa'ayon, [Tishrei 5752]: 35:42).

See also Rabbeinu Chaim Kohen, *Tosafoth*, *Kethuboth* 110b, s.v. *Hu omair la'aloth*. He maintains that it is no longer obligatory to dwell in Israel, for it is extremely difficult to observe "the mitzvoth that are dependent on the Land."

Rabbi Moshe Feinstein suggests that even according to Ramban, dwelling in Israel is only a voluntary fulfillment of a mitzvah, rather than the discharge of an obligation (*Iggroth Moshe, Even haEzer* I, no. 102).

Rabbi Ovadiah Yosef, however, sharply dissents from this view, for he holds that this mitzvah constitutes "a definite obligation upon all who fear the Word of G-d and His commandment to ascend to the Land of Israel" (*Torah She-be'al Peh*, 5729).

∏ 828 ∏

לְעוֹלָם יְהֵא אָדָם זָהִיר בִּתְפִלַּת הַמִּנְחָה
שֶׁהֲרֵי אֵלִיָּהוּ לֹא נַעֲנָה אֶלָּא בִּתְפִלַּת הַמִּנְחָה

"One should always be meticulous in observing the *Minchah* [afternoon] prayer, because it was at *Minchah* that Eliyahu [the prophet] was answered" (*Berakoth* 6b).

"Adam was created in the afternoon just before the Sabbath, and it was at this time that he uttered the world's first prayer. This is the reason why one must be especially careful during the *Minchah* Service" (Rabbi Chaim Yosef David Azulai, *Chida*, *Midbar Kedemoth*, Tav 4).

Rabbi Yosef Yitzchak Schneersohn of Lubavitch explained that the time for the *Minchah* prayer is in the afternoon, at the height of the day, amidst intense activity. To interrupt business activities to make time for *Minchah* is indeed a great mitzvah and a sign of deep commitment.

In a similar vein, Rabbi Joseph B. Soloveitchik refers to the prayer of *Minchah* as "*tefillath hafsek*" [prayer of interruption]. "In the middle of the day, amidst our mundane activities, we must stop, break away, discontinue our affairs and retreat to *daven Minchah*."

Rabbi Zalman Sorotzkin writes: "Of the three prayers, *Minchah* is the most effectual. The reason for this is that when a man is successful, he has difficulty concentrating on prayer (i.e., *Shacharis* — symbolic of shining success). Once trouble strikes it deprives one of the peace of mind to pray properly (i.e., *Maariv* — when the sun has set). But when the sun is setting on good fortune, but the darkness is not yet total — then our prayers are most powerful. Then one is neither bedazzled by success nor distraught with grief, and he can concentrate on his prayer" (*Oznayim LaTorah*).

Cf. *Berakoth* 26b, "The *tefilloth* were instituted by the patriarchs." See *Insights*, vol. 1, #500.

❘ 829 ❘ לְעוֹלָם יְהֵא אָדָם עַנְוְותָן כְּהִלֵּל

"A man should always be gentle like Hillel" (*Shabbath* 30b).

See talmudic account of Hillel's gentleness and extraordinary control over his temper (ibid. 31a).

"Anger is an exceedingly bad passion, and one should avoid it to the last extreme. One should train oneself not to be angry even for something that would justify anger" (*Mishneh Torah, Hil. Daioth* 2:3).

In the ethical will that Rabbi Moshe Bick left his family, he writes: "The way of the Almighty is to be soft towards others. Our sages long ago said: 'A person should always be gentle as a reed' (*Ta'anith* 20a), and should certainly not be short-tempered. [Since it says that one should not be short-tempered like Shammai,] it appears that even for the sake of Heaven, one should not be a *kapdan* [an impatient person]" (Shmuel Kessner, "Rabbi Moshe Zvi Aryeh Bick," *The Jewish Observer* 23, no. 10 [Jan. 1991]:24).

Cf. *Ta'anith* 20a, "A man should always be gentle as a reed and never unyielding as the cedar." See *Insights*, vol. 1, #372.

❘ 830 ❘ לְעוֹלָם יִמְכּוֹר אָדָם כָּל מַה שֶּׁיֵּשׁ לוֹ וְיִשָּׂא בַּת תַּלְמִיד חָכָם

"Let a man sell all that he has and marry the daughter of a Torah scholar" (*Pesahim* 49b).

"He should not marry the daughter of an *am ha'aretz* [an unlearned man]" (ibid.).

"Let him marry the daughter of a Torah scholar, for if he should die or go into exile his sons will be Torah scholars" (*Mishneh Torah, Hil. Isurei Biah* 21:32).

"'One should not marry the daughter of an *am ha'aretz*' applies only in a case where the 'unlearned man' is not scrupulous in the observance of *mitzvoth*" (*Rema, Even HaEzer* 2:6).

Rabbi Avraham Danzig writes: "It is better for one to marry the daughter of a G-d fearing person although he is an *am ha'aretz* than a Torah scholar with great *yichus* [genealogy] but who is not G-d fearing" (*Chochmas Adam, Hil. Ishus* 123:10).

Rabbi David HaLevi comments: "A woman who appreciates the value of Torah is not in the category of a 'daughter of an *am ha'aretz*, even if her father is one" (*Taz, Even HaEzer* 2(3)).

⎾ 831 ⏋

לְעוֹלָם יָשִׂים אָדָם עַצְמוֹ עַל דִּבְרֵי תוֹרָה
כְּשׁוֹר לָעוֹל וְכַחֲמוֹר לְמַשָּׂאוֹי

"One should always consider himself in his relation to the words of Torah as an ox to its yoke and a donkey to its load"
(*Abodah Zara* 5b).

In order to study the words of Torah, one must cultivate the habit of the ox for bearing a yoke and of the donkey for carrying burdens.

The Chafetz Chaim explains this peculiar analogy. An ox is created with great strength to enable it to plough the earth, so that after it is sowed, the earth will bear fruit and provide grain. The donkey's mission is to carry the harvested grain to its destination, so that it may be fit for consumption.

In a similar manner, when one engages in Torah study, he must labor arduously in order to comprehend the words of Torah. Once he acquires knowledge of the Torah, it is essential that he "carry" this knowledge with him and apply it in life, as it is said, "And these words which I command you this day shall be in your heart" [Deut. 6:6] (*Shem Olam*, part 1, ch. 9).

"The Torah student directs all his efforts towards mastering the wisdom of his teachers, and this he can do in two ways: one, by delving into the depths of their wisdom ['as an ox to its yoke'], and two, by toiling to memorize and retain all the voluminous material they have taught him ['a donkey carrying the load']" (Vilna Gaon, *Perush Al Kamma Aggadoth*).

◊ 832 ◊ לְעוֹלָם לִישַׁתֵּף אֱינָשׁ נַפְשֵׁיהּ בַּהֲדֵי צְבוּרָא

"A person should always associate himself with the community"
(*Berakoth* 30a).

One's prayers should be in the plural form rather than in the singular (Rashi). Rabbi Chaim Shmulevitz comments: "By praying for the public welfare, one is automatically included with them and does not need personal merits in order to benefit from one's prayers. The reason for this is that the community is not seen as a mere collection of individuals, but rather as a new entity exceeding the combination of the merits and strengths of the individuals of which it is composed."

Reb Chaim illustrates this concept by citing the Ran [*Drashos* 1], who points out that Moshe was punished for calling the Children of Israel "*the rebellious people.*" "He explains that although as individuals each one of them deserved to be called 'rebellious,' the people as a whole did not deserve to be described as such. Accordingly, Moshe was unjustified in so labeling them" (*Reb Chaim's Discourses*, p. 195).

◊ 833 ◊ לְעוֹלָם אַל יַעֲמוֹד אָדָם בִּמְקוֹם סַכָּנָה לוֹמַר שֶׁעוֹשִׂין לוֹ נֵס

"A man should never stand in a place of danger and say that a miracle will be done for him . . . (*Shabbath* 32a).

Rabbi Avraham Yeshayahu Karelitz writes: "If this is true with regard to physical dangers, how much more so is this true with regard to spiritual dangers. We must be careful not to place ourselves in a situation where our souls are in danger" (Chazon Ish, *Emunah U'bitochon* 4:9).

Similarly, Rabbi Chaim Shmulevitz comments: "Keep as far as possible from potential temptation to do something improper. Do not intentionally put yourself in a dangerous situation in order to do battle with your Evil Inclination" (*Sichos Mussar*, 1971, essay 6).

Cf. *Yerushalmi Yoma* 1:4, "One may not rely on a miracle." See *Insights*, vol. 1, #51.

Cf. *Pesahim* 8b, "Those sent to perform a mitzvah do not suffer harm."
See *Insights*, vol. 1, #486.

⫾ 834 ⫾   לֶעָתִיד לָבוֹא כָּל הַקָּרְבָּנוֹת בְּטֵלִין וְקָרְבַּן
                       תּוֹדָה אֵינוֹ בָטֵל

"In the Time to Come (Messianic era), all forms of sacrifice are
destined to be annulled with the exception of the thank-offering"
(*Va'yikra Rabbah* 9:7).

Gratitude is so essential to Judaism that it can never be annulled. Our
sages believed that ingratitude displayed towards man is indicative of one's
negative attitude towards G-d. Thus we find the *midrashic* query: "Why did
Scripture prescribe punishment especially for those who are ungrateful?
Because it is akin to denying the Holy One, blessed be He. This man shows
no gratitude now for his neighbor's kindness, [and so] tomorrow he will be
ungrateful for his Maker's kindness" (*Mishnath R. Eliezer*, 137).

The classical talmudic maxim on 'gratitude,' "Cast no mud into the well
from which you have drunk" (*Baba Kamma* 92b), applies to everyone and
anything. Never repay a kindness with a wrong.

Rabbi Joseph B. Soloveitchik was heard to apply this maxim to a spiritual
well. When a student of a particular yeshiva criticized that institution, he
admonished him not to throw verbal stones at the well from which he
drank.

Rabbi Chaim Shmulevitz would be eternally grateful to everyone for the
slightest favor he received. At the last *shiur* [lesson] of the *zman* [semester],
he would invariably thank his students for giving him the opportunity to
deliver his *shiurim*.

The last *shmuess* [moral discourse] of his life, on *Yom Kippur* [5739], dealt
with the profound debt of gratitude a man owes his wife. "There is no one
to whom one is so beholden as to his wife."

Cf. *Va'yikra Rabbah* 9:7, "In the Time to Come . . . all prayers will be
annulled, but (that of) thanksgiving will not be annulled."

See *Insights*, vol. 1, #378 and #101.

835

לֶעָתִיד לָבֹא מְבִיאוֹ הַקָּדוֹשׁ בָּרוּךְ הוּא לְיֵצֶר
הָרַע וְשׁוֹחֲטוֹ

"In the time to come the Holy One, blessed be He, will bring the
Evil Inclination and slay it" (Sukkah 52a).

The commentaries explain that killing or slaughtering the Evil Inclination
means "bittul kocho" [diluting its strength]. This is, in effect, slaughtering and
killing it (Maharsha).

The Baal Shem Tov notes that the Talmud says that G-d will bring the
Evil Inclination "le'shocto," employing the term normally used for ritual
slaughter of kosher animals [instead of "le'horgo" — to kill it]. He concludes
that just as shechita [ritual slaughter] renders an animal kosher, so too, will
"slaughtering" the Evil Inclination render it "kosher" — that is, it will
transform it into an angel of good (Rabbi Yaakov Yosef of Polonoye, Toledoth
Yaakov Yosef, Kedoshim).

836

לִפְנֵי סוּמָא בְּדָבָר . . . אַל תִּתֵּן לוֹ עֵצָה
שֶׁאֵינָהּ הוֹגֶנֶת לוֹ

"Before one who is blind in a [certain] matter, do not give him
counsel that is not suitable for him" (Sifra, Va'yikra 19:14).

This is the standard halachic interpretation of the scriptural prohibition,
"You shall not place a stumbling block before the blind" [Lev. 19:14].

"Anyone who misdirects a person, blind on any subject, by giving him
advice, or by strengthening the hands of a transgressor who is 'blind' and
cannot see the way of truth . . . is transgressing a prohibitive command, as
it is written: 'You shall not place a stumbling block before the blind . . .'"
(Mishneh Torah, Hil. Rozeach 12:14).

It is significant to note that, according to the Minchath Chinuch, the actual
placing of a rock — a stumbling block in front of one who is truly blind —
would not be a violation of the above commandment. He writes: "'You shall
not place a stumbling block' is interpreted figuratively only. The actual

placing of a stumbling block. . . however, would be prohibited by many other commandments in the Torah" (*Negative Commandment* 232:4).

See, also, *Mishneh LaMelech, Malveh* 4:6, s.v. *Kathav.*

However, some say that it is also to be taken in its literal sense, that it is forbidden to place something on the ground where it will cause damage (*Ralbag; Sforno*).

⫿ 837 ⫿

לְקָרֵב אֲבָל לֹא לְרַחֵק

"[Elijah will come] to bring close but not to divide (*Eduyoth* 8:7).

Rabbi Yehuda maintains that the prophet Elijah will come before the advent of *Moshiach* in order "to bring close but not to divide."

Rabbi Ralph Pelcovitz comments: "Homiletically, this has been interpreted in the following intriguing manner. The Hebrew word for truth is *emeth*, comprised of three letters, separated by the total spectrum of the Hebrew alphabet — an *aleph* and *tof*, the first and last letters, with a *mem* in the center — the middle of the alphabet. The Hebrew for falsehood is *sheker*, composed of three letters that are next to each other in the alphabet, *shin*, *kuf* and *resh*.

"This strange variance implies that the forces of *sheker*, who distort Judaism, are usually united, whereas those who champion authentic *Yiddishkeit* are hopelessly divided. Now, there are two solutions to this problem. One is to divide and thereby conquer the forces of *sheker*; the other is to unify the camps of Torah. Which of these will Elijah choose? Rabbi Yehuda maintains that the solution is not *l'rachek*, to separate the closely knit ranks of *sheker* and disrupt the united front of the heterodox [secular] camp, but rather *l'karev*, to bring together the *aleph, mem* and *tof* of *emeth*, the various factions within the camp of Torah-true Jewry" (*Danger and Opportunity*, p. 37).

In this regard, the words of the *Sfas Emes* are most significant. "The Egyptians met their end as a fragmented people, not as a proud and united nation, while the Jews crossed the Sea of Reeds and sang the Song in perfect unison. Thus the *Zohar* describes the forces of evil: '*They begin with unity and end in dispersion*'" (*The Three Festivals*, p. 131).

⟦ 838 ⟧ לְשָׁנָה אַחֶרֶת קְבָעוּם וַעֲשָׂאוּם יָמִים טוֹבִים בְּהַלֵּל וְהוֹדָאָה

"The following year these [days] were appointed a Festival with [the recital of] *Hallel* and thanksgiving" (*Shabbath* 21b).

The Rabbis instituted the observance of Chanukah one year after the miracles occurred. Rabbi Yehudah Aryeh Alter of Ger raises an obvious question. Why did the Rabbis wait a full year before requesting our people to observe this great event with thanksgiving and praise?

The truth is, that human beings often do not recognize the immediate danger of a spiritual threat that surrounds them. Nor are they able to realize the greatness of the rescue when it does come. They might well exclaim: Where and what is the danger? What was this great act of salvation? What were we saved from? The sages of that period were fearful of just such a reaction, were they to immediately demand proper recognition of the miraculous rescue.

When a full year had passed by, when our people came to realize retrospectively what had happened to thousands of Jewish youths, when the stark brutal truth was finally brought home to them, then, and only then, were they in a position to evaluate both the extent of the danger that they had faced, and the great significance of their rescue (*Sfas Emeth*, vol. 1, LeChanukah, p. 207).

מ

839

מַאי חָזֵית דְּדָמָא דִּידָךְ סוּמָק טְפֵי דִּילְמָא
דָּמָא דְּהַהוּא גַּבְרָא סוּמָק טְפֵי

"What [reason] do you see [for thinking] that your blood is redder? Perhaps his blood is redder" (*Pesahim* 25b).

This is the rationale for the ruling that in the case of murder [if one is ordered to kill or be killed], one must allow himself to be killed rather than kill.

Rabbi Simcha Bunim of Peshischa deduced from the above maxim that "No Jew, however learned and pious, may consider himself an iota better than a fellow-Jew, however ignorant or irreligious the latter may be. For if a learned and pious Jew were commanded to slay the ignorant and impious one or be himself slain, he must accept death rather than kill the other, for no one can tell whose blood is redder and whose life is more important in the eyes of G-d. If a man in this crucial moment has no right to deem himself superior to another, what right can he possibly have to do so on less critical occasions" (Rabbi Yisroel Berger, *Simchoth Yisroel*, p. 46).

840

מַאי שׁוֹחַד שֶׁהוּא חַד

"What is [the meaning of] *shochad* [a bribe]? *shehu chad* that he [the recipient] is one [with the donor]" (*Kethuboth* 105b).

The one who gives the bribe and the one who receives it merge into one heart (Rashi).

Rabbi Isaac Unterman suggests that *shehu chad* may be translated *"he is alone,"* i.e., the recipient of a bribe remains "alone." This is based on the talmudic dictum, "Every judge who judges a true judgment according to its truth, it is as though he had become a partner to the Holy One, blessed be He, in the creation" (*Shabbath* 10a). If a judge accepts a bribe, he is indeed "alone" in that he is no longer a partner with the Almighty.

Concerning the dictum of a judge becoming a partner with G-d, Rabbi Yechezkail Landau writes: "Every judge who renders a true judgment . . ." renders his decision with *Siatto Dishmaya* [Divine Assistance], and in that manner he is a partner with the Almighty.

See *Insights*, vol. 1, #258.

Cf. *Kethuboth* 105b, "A bribe of words [or 'acts'] is also forbidden." See #975.

Cf. *Kethuboth*, ibid., "No man sees anything to his disadvantage." See *Insights*, vol. 1, #29.

⟦ 841 ⟧ מֵאִיגָּרָא רָם לְבֵירָא עֲמִיקְתָּא

"From a high roof to a deep pit" (*Hagigah* 5b).

"Rebbe was holding the Book of Lamentations and read from it. When he reached the verse, 'He has thrown [Israel] from the Heavens to the earth' [Lam. 2:1], it fell from his hands. He exclaimed, 'Indeed [they have fallen] from a high roof to a deep pit'" (ibid.).

After having raised the Jews to the spiritual elevation of the uppermost heavens, the Almighty cast them down to the nethermost depths — not gradually, but in one thrust.

Rabbi Chaim Shmulevitz asks: "What did Rebbe see in the fall of the book that enlightened his understanding of the verse? The answer is that he realized that the place of the book in his hand or on the floor was irrelevant to its condition. It was the fall itself which damaged the book. So, too, the tragedy of Israel is not so much in its present lowly condition, but rather the downfall and shock of the abrupt decline that has battered Israel terribly. This is the true understanding of the verse, 'He has thrown [Israel] from the Heavens to the earth.' It is not the change of position from Heaven to earth which has so profoundly affected Israel, as much as the fall itself."

Reb Chaim concludes: "A person must be constantly on guard, when he feels himself undergoing a period of spiritual descent, not to lose himself entirely. The plunge in itself is usually far more damaging than the level to which one has descended. If a person does take hold of himself, not losing his self control under any circumstances, he will succeed in regaining his former stature, perhaps even being lifted by his trying experience" (*Reb Chaim's Discourses*, p. 47).

◊ 842 ◊

מְבַטְּלִין תַּלְמוּד תּוֹרָה לְהוֹצָאַת הַמֵּת
וּלְהַכְנָסַת הַכַּלָּה

"The study of Torah may be suspended for taking out the dead [to the cemetery] and for bringing in the bride [to the canopy]"
(*Megillah* 29a).

Rabbi Moshe of Kutov was asked the following [kabbalistic] question while he was presiding over a *Get* [religious divorce]: "The main intent of all commandments is, 'In all your ways *know* Him' [Prov. 3:6]. This implies that one must bring about unification within each thing — [to 'know' implies to 'unify']. This being so, how can one bring about a unification through a divorce, which is a separation rather than a union?"

He replied by quoting the talmudic dictum [above] and asked: "What relationship is there between a bride and the dead, that both are mentioned in the same breath?" He then explained that before one can bring about a union, one must first remove the *husk* [of evil]. One must first "take out the dead," removing the *husk*. Only then can he bring about a union, "bringing in the bride."

Divorce also involves removing the *husks* and divorcing oneself from them. One can then marry his proper mate and bring about a perfect unification" (Rabbi Yaakov Yosef of Polonoye, *Toledoth Yaakov Yosef, Tazria* p. 315, cited in *Chassidic Masters*, p. 26).

[843]

מֵבִין דָּבָר מִתּוֹךְ דָּבָר

"Understand [how to deduce] one thing from another"
(*Sanhedrin* 93b).

Rabbi Samson Raphael Hirsch writes: "*Binah* is insight, or better, distinguishing sight. True insight, the ability to get at the actual nature of things, is something that no mortal can have, but the distinguishing ability, i.e., to recognize the result of at least two given factors, the deductive faculty, is the real operation which the human mind is to exercise with its given power, its intellect" (*The Pentateuch*, Gen. 41:33).

Rabbi Aryeh Kaplan points out that "the relationship between *Chochmah* [wisdom] and *Binah* [understanding] can be grasped in terms of the relationship between male and female. [In *Kabbalah*, *Chochmah* is seen as the father, while *Binah* is the mother.] In a human relationship, the male provides the sperm and the female takes it, holds it in her womb for nine months, after which she delivers a fully developed child. In the same way, *Chochmah* is a series of facts which we can put into the womb of *Binah* in order to develop an entire logical structure" (*Inner Space*, p. 58).

[844]

מֵה' אִשָּׁה לְאִישׁ

"A woman is [destined] to a man by G-d" (*Moed Katan* 18b).

Rabbi Moshe Avigdor Amiel raises the following question concerning the formulation of the above dictum: "Why does it say, 'A woman is [destined] to a man by G-d' and not, 'A man [is destined] to a woman . . .'? Moreover, we are told, 'Forty days before the creation of a child, a *Bath Kol* [Heavenly Voice] issues forth and proclaims: "The daughter of this person is for this person" [*Sotah* 2a]' There also, the proclamation refers to the daughter and not to the son — why?"

In answering this question, Rabbi Amiel cites Maimonides, who writes: "Men are very often prone to err in supposing that many of their actions . . . are forced upon them as for instance, marrying a certain woman . . . . Such a supposition is untrue. If a man espouses and marries a woman legally, then she becomes his lawful wife, and by marrying her he has [begun to] fulfill the Divine command to increase and multiply, and G-d does not decree the fulfillment of a commandment [it's an exercise of one's free will] (*Shemonah Perokim*, ch. 8).

Perhaps this is the reason our sages emphasize, 'The daughter of this person for this person.' The proclamation only refers to her and not to him, because women were not commanded to 'increase and multiply.' Since marriage for a woman is optional, it rightfully says, 'A woman is [destined] to a man'" (*Hegyonoth El-Ami*, part 2, p. 125).

Cf. *Sotah* 2a, "Forty days before the creation of a child . . . ." See *Insights*, vol. 1, #88.

⫿ 845 ⫿

מַה הַכְּלָבִים אֶחָד נוֹבֵחַ וְכֻלָּם מִתְקַבְּצִים
וְנוֹבְחִים עַל חִנָּם, אֲבָל אַתֶּם לֹא תִהְיוּ כֵן
מִפְּנֵי שֶׁאַתֶּם אַנְשֵׁי קוֹדֶשׁ

"Regarding dogs, if one barks, all the others gather round and bark for no purpose — but you must not be so, for you are holy men" (*Shemoth Rabbah* 31:9).

This is based on the verse, "and holy men shall you be unto Me . . ." [Ex. 22:30]. The above dictum is an admonition against idle hatred, talebearing and fomenting quarrels, i.e., "barking" at others for no good purpose.

In his commentary on the above midrash, Rabbi Avraham Schreiber points out that *baalei machlokes* [contentious people], upon witnessing a man quarreling with his neighbor, will often get involved in the "strife," not in order to decrease it, but to intensify it. This is a *canine* trait, for the nature of dogs is such that when one dog barks at an individual, all other dogs join in the barking for no purpose at all.

"But you, Israel," [the Midrash declares,] "must not behave in this canine fashion, for you are a holy people" (*Ksav Sofer*, Ex. 22:30).

〚 846 〛 מַה יַעֲשֶׂה אָדָם וְיִנָּצֵל מֵחֶבְלוֹ שֶׁל מָשִׁיחַ

"What must a man do to be spared the birth pangs of *Moshiach*?"
(*Sanhedrin* 98b)

Let him engage in Torah study and in deeds of loving-kindness" (ibid.).

The period before *Moshiach's* arrival may be compared to the pangs before childbirth. The nearer the birth, the more intense the pain. Similarly, the closer we get to *Moshiach's* arrival, the more difficult the times become. In the same way, however, as the woman knows that her suffering is worthwhile because afterwards she will have a child, so we know that all our troubles are a fair price to pay for our final redemption (Vilna Gaon).

〚 847 〛 מַה יָּפִית בְּמִילָה וּמַה נָּעַמְתְּ בִּפְרִיעָה

"How beautiful you are with *milah* and how pleasant you are with *periah*" (*Shir HaShirim Rabbah* 7:7).

Rav Yosef Dov Ber Soloveitchik writes: "The early commentators ask: is circumcision essentially the removal of a defect [the foreskin], or the attainment of greater sanctity, as is the case with all positive commandments?" Rav Soloveitchik explains, "the mitzvah in fact encompasses both elements, as the *Ba'al HaAkeidah* has proven conclusively.

"In speaking to Abraham, the Almighty alludes to both these elements: '. . . walk before Me and be perfect . . .,' i.e., by removing the impurity of the foreskin, you will be perfect. 'And I will place My covenant between Me and you . . .,' for through this mitzvah you will gain sanctity and stature
. . . .

"These two aspects of circumcision — perfection and sanctity — are manifest in the first two steps of the circumcision process. The removal of the foreskin separates us from non-Jews, who are referred to as *areilim* [uncircumcised]. *Periah*, the peeling back of the exposed membrane, is a sign of national bonding and sanctification.

"This duality is the basis of the [above] Midrash. 'How beautiful you are with *milah'* [the removal of the foreskin] which is essentially the removal of a blemish; 'How pleasant you are with *periah'* — which represents the sanctity of the covenant" (*Beis HaLevi; Lech Lecha*, trans. by Yisrael I. Z. Herczeg, p. 71).

Cf. *Shabbath* 137b, "If one circumcised but did not perform *periah*, it is as if he did not circumcise." See #865.

⟦ 848 ⟧

מַה כְּלֵי זְכוּכִית שֶׁעֲמָלָן בְּרוּחַ בָּשָׂר וָדָם
נִשְׁבְּרוּ יֵשׁ לָהֶן תַּקָּנָה, בָּשָׂר וָדָם שֶׁבְּרוּחוֹ שֶׁל
הקב"ה עַל אַחַת כַּמָּה וְכַמָּה

"If glassware, which, though made by the breath of human beings, can be repaired when broken, then how much more so man,
created by the Breath of the Holy One, blessed be He"
(*Sanhedrin* 91a).

Glassware, which is made by man's "blowing of glass," can be mended when broken by being melted down again (Rashi).

Rabbi Chaim of Volozhin writes: "The Rabbis, of blessed memory, have compared the inspiration of living breath in man at the time of resurrection with the making of a glass vessel. [The above] saying contains an exact comparison. When we examine the blowing of a craftsman making glass, we discern three stages: The first stage is when the breath is still in the mouth of the craftsman, before it enters the blowpipe. At this stage it can properly be called *breath* [*neshimah*]. The second stage is when the breath is already in the blowpipe, and extends throughout its length, in a straight line. It is then called *ruach* [wind]. The third and lowest stage is when the vapor leaves the blowpipe, enters the glass, and expands within it until the glass takes the shape desired by the craftsman. This is the final stage, called *nefesh*, which can be interpreted as a ceasing from activity, or a state of rest.

"The three categories — *nefesh, ruach, neshamah* — can be distinguished in the breath of *His Holy Mouth*, as it were, by this analogy. *Nefesh* is the lowest, because it is entirely within man. *Ruach* is a spilling over of Divine influence. Its upper end is attached above to the category of *Neshamah* . . ."

(*Nefesh HaChaim*, #15).

〚 849 〛

מַה עִנְיַן שָׁאוֹל אֵצֶל רֶחֶם אֶלָּא לוֹמַר לְךָ מַה
רֶחֶם מַכְנִיס וּמוֹצִיא אַף שָׁאוֹל מַכְנִיס וּמוֹצִיא

"What is the connection between 'the grave' and 'the womb'? It is
to tell you that as the womb receives and yields up, so the grave
receives and yields up" (*Berakoth* 15b).

. This is the talmudic explanation of the scriptural juxtaposition of the
words, "The grave and the barren womb . . ." (Prov. 30:15).

An allegorical interpretation of this dictum is found in the *Gesher
HaChaim*: "Imagine unborn twins in the mother's womb who were specu-
lating on their fate to be after they leave the womb. One twin has faith and
claims knowledge of a future life after leaving the mother, while the other
is a skeptic, believing only what his senses and mind can perceive — only
in 'this world.'

"The first argues: 'I have faith — sustained by a long tradition passed on
to me — that on leaving the womb, we will enter a new life of much broader
dimensions.' But the other twin scoffs at this simpleton: 'Only a fool can
believe in all those fairy tales!'

"As they talked, the womb opened. The 'believing' twin departs first. The
'rational' twin, still inside, grieves and wails over his brother's 'death.' At
the same time there is rejoicing and festivity in the home of the newborn —
'mazal-tov, a son is born to us.'

"The exit from the womb is the birth of the body; and the exit from the
body is the real birth of the soul" (Y. M. Tucatzinski, *Gesher HaChaim*, part
3, cited by Rabbi Immanuel Jakobovitz, *Journal of a Rabbi*, pp. 293-294).

◊ 850 ◊

מַה רַךְ פָּסַל אֶת הַקָּשֶׁה דִּבְרֵי תוֹרָה שֶׁקָּשֶׁה
כְּבַרְזֶל, עַל אַחַת כַּמָּה וְכַמָּה שֶׁיְּחַקְקוּ אֶת
לִבִּי שֶׁהוּא בָּשָׂר וָדָם

"If the soft [water] can wear away the hard [stone], how much
more can the words of the Torah, which are hard as iron, carve a
way into my heart, which is of flesh and blood"
(*Aboth D'Rabbi Nathan* 6:2).

"What was the beginning of Rabbi Akiva . . . ? He was forty years old
and had not learned a thing. Once he stood at the mouth of a well and said:
'Who hollowed this stone?' They told him, 'Is it not the water which
constantly falls on it day after day?' Rabbi Akiva immediately reasoned, 'If
the soft can wear away the hard . . . '" (ibid.).

From the above reasoning, Rabbi Yisrael Salanter found support for his
mussar discipline. "The waters," said Reb Yisrael, "carved the stone, only
because it fell drop after drop for years, without a pause. Had all that
accumulated water been poured in a powerful stream at one given instant,
it would have slipped off the rock without leaving a trace . . . .

"Fervent study of *mussar* once a week assures results . . . . Constant
repetition of ideas will cause these ideas to be implanted in the subcon-
scious" (*Or Yisrael*, cited by Rabbi Meir Wallach, *Depth of Judgment*, p. 22).

◊ 851 ◊

מוּם שֶׁבְּךָ אַל תֹּאמַר לַחֲבֵרְךָ

"Do not taunt your neighbor with the blemish you yourself have"
(*Baba Mezia* 59b).

"You shall not oppress a stranger, for you know the feelings of the
stranger, having yourselves been strangers in the land of Egypt" (Ex. 23:9).
"Remember that you were a slave in Egypt and the L-rd your G-d redeemed you from there; therefore do I command you to observe this
commandment" (Deut. 24:18).
The above talmudic maxim is self-explanatory — do not wrong others by

taunting them with being strangers to the Jewish people, seeing that you yourselves were strangers in Egypt.

Rabbi Louis Rabinowitz, however, suggests that the Torah may be alluding to a perverse trait of human nature. He therefore suggests the following novel interpretation: "The sad but undoubted fact is that when the stranger [or anyone in a position of dependence] appeals for help to a man who was once in a similar position, the man appealed to may be inclined to say, 'Did I get any help or sympathy from my fellowman when I was in trouble?' The memory of his subservient position may well induce a spirit of harshness and revenge; hence, the Almighty sternly commands: 'It is because you were in bondage that *I commanded you* — suppress these ignoble, if natural, feelings. Rise above them!'" (*Sparks From the Anvil*, p. 215).

〚 852 〛   מוּתָּר לוֹ לְאָדָם לְשַׁנּוֹת בִּדְבַר הַשָּׁלוֹם

"One may modify a statement in the interests of peace"
(*Yebamoth* 65b).

"For it is said: 'Your father gave an order before his death, say this to Joseph: "Please forgive your brother's guilt and their sin, for they have done you harm . . ."' [Gen. 50:16,17]. In the interests of peace, they [Joseph's brothers] altered Jacob's words, for he had never given such a command, for he did not suspect that Joseph would harbor resentment towards his brothers" (Rashi on Gen. 50:16).

Cf. *Beraishith Rabbah* 100:8, "Great is peace, for even the tribal ancestors resorted to a fabrication in order to make peace between Joseph and themselves."

"A restriction to this [dictum] is brought down in *Sefer Chassidim* (426): 'If a Jew or non-Jew comes to you for a loan and you do not want to give him the money for fear that he will not repay it, you do not have the right to lie and say that you do not have the means, for permission to tell a "white lie" in the interests of peace applies only to cases which have already happened, but not to events that are in the future'" (Rabbi Elie Munk, *The Call of the Torah*, vol. 2, p. 1084).

Similarly, Rabbi Yosef Shaul Natansohn suggests that one is permitted to alter the truth only when it applies to the past, but not to the future (*Divrei Shaul*). See *Magen Avraham, Orach Chaim* 156:2.

See, however, *Orchoth Chaim* 156, who cites many authorities who do not make this distinction.

Cf. *Yebamoth* 65b, "Great is peace, seeing that the Holy One, blessed be He, modified a statement for its sake." See *Insights*, vol. 1, #124.

Cf. *Kethuboth* 17a, "Always should the disposition of man be pleasant with people." See *Insights*, vol. 1, #377.

⫼ 853 ⫼   מֵחֶלְבֵיהֶן, מִשַּׁמְנֵיהֶן

"'Of the fat thereof' [that means] of their fat ones [the best]
(*Zebahim* 116a).

This is the talmudic exegesis of the scriptural verse: "And Abel, he also brought of the firstlings of his flock and of the fat thereof . . ." (Gen. 4:4).

Rambam codifies this as a general halachic principle. "This applies to everything which is done for the sake of the good G-d; namely, that it be of the finest and the best. If one builds a house of prayer, it should be finer than his private dwelling. If he feeds the hungry, he should give him of the best and the sweetest of his table. If he clothes the naked, he should give him of the finest of his garments. Hence, if he consecrated something to G-d, he ought to give of the best of his possessions" (*Mishneh Torah, Hil. Isurei Mizbeiach* 7:11).

Rabbi Zelig Pliskin comments on our obligation to provide clothes for the needy. "Ideally, one should give the finest quality clothing to the poor. However, before one discards used clothes, one should consider the possibility that a poor person would prefer used clothes to none at all. (Rabbi Eliezer Papu, *Pele Yoatz*, sec. *halbosho*). Great care must be taken not to embarrass the recipient, since a person may feel humiliated when offered used clothing" (*Love Your Neighbor*, p. 30).

Cf. *Menachoth* 83b, "All meal offerings must be offered only from the choicest [produce]."

Cf. *Sifri*, "Only the best should be brought [to the sanctuary]."

∬ 854 ∬

מַחֲשָׁבָה טוֹבָה מְצָרְפָהּ לְמַעֲשֶׂה

"A good intention is combined with deed" (*Kiddushin* 40a).

"If one thinks of performing a mitzvah but is 'prevented,' Scripture ascribes it to him as though he performed it" (ibid.).

In the Musaf service for *Rosh Hashanah* and *Yom Kippur*, we recite the prayer *"b'ain meilitz yosher"* — "When there is no advocate [angel] to defend us against the one who reports our sins, may You [G-d] testify for the sake of 'Jacob's offspring' regarding [their observance of Your] decrees and ordinances, and declare us righteous in judgment, O King of judgment."

How do we understand this puzzling petition to the Almighty? Because we have no advocates to defend us, we ask G-d to vindicate us!

The following insightful interpretation was suggested: "On the Day of Judgment we declare to the Supreme Judge, 'It is true we have no one to defend us, no one who can account for our greater number of good deeds over evil deeds. However You, G-d, know that our innermost thoughts desire to do good. Therefore, You judge our good intentions combined with our good deeds and rule in our favor, for "good intentions are combined with good deeds"'" (Rabbi Bernard Maza, *Insights Into the Sidra of the Week*, vol. II, pp. 145-147).

Cf. *Kiddushin* 40a, "Evil intention, the Holy One, blessed be He, does not combine with deed." See *Insights*, vol. 1, #393.

∬ 855 ∬

מַחֲשָׁבָה מוֹעֶלֶת אֲפִילוּ לְדִבְרֵי תוֹרָה

"Thought helps even for the study of Torah" (*Sanhedrin* 26b).

"Anxiety about one's livelihood [adversely] affects [one's] study of Torah" (Rashi).

Rabbi Nachman of Breslov interprets this dictum literally. "Human thought has tremendous potential . . . . You can concentrate on something so strongly that it comes true . . . . For example, you can concentrate on your intense desire to complete the study of the Code of Jewish Law

[*Shulchan Aruch*] in a single year . . . . If your desire is strong and your concentration intense enough, your plans will be fulfilled."

Rabbi Nathan of Nemirov comments: "Rashi might interpret this talmudic passage differently, but the Rebbe's [R. Nachman's] interpretation is also certainly true" (*Sichos HaRan*).

⦙ 856 ⦙   מִי גִילָה לְבָנַי רָז זֶה שֶׁמַּלְאֲכֵי הַשָּׁרֵת
מִשְׁתַּמְּשִׁין בּוֹ

"Who revealed to My children this secret, which is employed by the Ministering Angels?" (*Shabbath* 88a)

"When the Israelites gave precedence to *na'aseh* [we will do] to *nishma* [we will hear], a Heavenly Voice went forth and exclaimed to them, 'Who revealed to My children . . .'" (ibid.).

Rabbi Yitzchak Hutner explained the *Bas Kol* [Heavenly Voice] in the following fashion: "That the angels place *na'aseh* before *nishma* in their [Divine] service is comprehensible because their hearing [understanding] is not the cause of their performance of G-d's Will. The very existence of *malochim* [angels] is their fulfillment of their Creator's Will. Their very name is indicative of their essence: *maloch* means 'emissary.' These divine beings are called *malochim* because, outside of their mission, they have no other function.

This, then, was the new creation that came down in the world at the time of the Sinaitic Revelation, i.e., a creature whose very existence [likewise] is solely to perform its Creator's Will. The name of this creature is Israel" (*Am HaTorah*, vol. 1, no. 1).

◊ 857 ◊

מִי כְּתִיב חוֹטְאִים, חַטָּאִים כְּתִיב

"Is it written *chotim* [sinners]? It is written *chatta'im* [sins]"
(*Berakoth* 10a).

"There were some highwaymen in the neighborhood of Rabbi Meir who
vexed him sorely, and Rabbi Meir wanted to pray for their death. His wife
Beruriah said to him, 'How do you justify such a prayer? Do you think
Scripture [Psalms 104:35] says *chotim* will cease? The verse actually says
chata'im, which can also mean "*sins will cease.*" . . . Rather pray for them that
they should repent, and they will no more be wicked.' He did pray for them
and they repented" (ibid.).

On the verse, "Abraham came forward and said, 'Will You wipe out the
righteous with the wicked?'" (Gen. 18:23), Rabbi Nosson Tzvi Finkel of
Slobodka comments: "It would stand to reason that the impending destruction of Sodom would be a source of joy to Abraham. Yet, he does not
rejoice. Instead, he fervently prays to have the decree annulled. What
motivated Abraham? Taking delight in the downfall of Sodom would in itself
be a manifestation of a Sodomite character trait, whereas it was Abraham's
mission in life to eradicate every trace of wickedness. He prayed for the
people of Sodom because it was his desire that *sin* — not the *sinners* — be
eliminated from the face of the earth. This corresponds with the talmudic
interpretation of Psalm 104:35, which our sages render homiletically, 'Let
sins cease to be perpetrated on the earth, then the wicked will be no more
— for everyone will be righteous'" (*Ohr Hatzafun*).

◊ 858 ◊

מִי שֶׁלֹּא רָאָה יְרוּשָׁלַיִם בְּתִפְאַרְתָּהּ לֹא רָאָה
כְּרַךְ נֶחְמָד מֵעוֹלָם

"He who has not seen Jerusalem in her splendor has never seen a
desirable city in his life" (*Sukkah* 51b).

Rabbi Avrohom Chaim Feuer writes: "Undoubtedly, Jerusalem in her
glory was a model of architectural brilliance and aesthetic perfection . . . .

The real beauty of Jerusalem, however, was that she beautified her inhabitants and visitors, and afforded spiritual revitalization.

"On the verse, 'Fairest of sites, joy of all the earth, Mount Zion . . .'
[Psalms 45:3], Rashi comments: 'Any man who arrived in the city downcast
and deeply troubled by the burden of his sins, went to the Temple. There,
he sacrificed a *sin* or a *guilt* offering, absolving him of his sins, and left
feeling cleansed and brimming with joy.'

"Moreover, no melancholy or depressed spirits were tolerated in the City
of Joy. The Midrash [*Shemoth Rabbah* 52:5] relates that outside of Jerusalem
was a large rock called '*Kippah Shel Cheshbonoth*.' Whenever a person needed
to analyze his financial affairs, he would have to leave the city and make his
computations at this rock, lest his account prove unfavorable, causing him
anguish, which cannot be tolerated in Jerusalem, 'joy of all the earth'"
(*Shemoneh Esrei*, p. 203).

Cf. *Kiddushin* 49b, "Ten measures of beauty were allotted to the world.
Jerusalem took nine, leaving one for the rest of the world."

⦙ 859 ⦙ מִי שֶׁלֹּא רָאָה שִׂמְחַת בֵּית הַשּׁוֹאֵבָה לֹא
רָאָה שִׂמְחָה מִיָּמָיו

"He who has not seen the rejoicing at the place of water-drawing
has never seen rejoicing in his life" (*Sukkah* 51a).

Rabbi Menachem M. Schneerson [the Lubavitcher Rebbe] analyzes the
distinction between the joy at the water-libation [during Succoth] and the joy
of the standard wine-libation that accompanied various sacrifices offered
throughout the year.

"Wine is indicative of joy, for which reason our sages say, 'Songs of
praise [to G-d] are sung only when accompanied by wine' [*Berakoth* 35a].
However, the joy associated with wine-offerings was bound up with man's
nature . . . . As such, it was not pure and unadulterated spiritual joy.

Water, on the other hand, being flavorless and devoid of any alcoholic
content, does not, in and of itself, bring a man to a state of joy . . . . This
joy was completely spiritual in nature, emanating solely from G-d's command that 'You shall draw water with joy from the wellsprings of deliver-

ance' [Isaiah 12:3].

The joy associated with wine-offerings, coming as it did from something — wine — whose joy had a natural basis, was constricted by the confines of nature. The joy accompanying the water-offering, however, resulted solely from G-d's command. Since He is infinite, the joy was boundless as well" (Rabbi Shalom B. Wineberg, *The Chassidic Dimension*, p. 270).

⟦ 860 ⟧

מִי שֶׁפָּרַע מֵאַנְשֵׁי דוֹר הַמַבּוּל . . . הוּא עָתִיד
לִיפָּרַע מִמִּי שֶׁאֵינוֹ עוֹמֵד בְּדִיבּוּרוֹ

"He who punished the Generation of the Flood . . . He will exact vengeance of him who does not stand by his word."
(*Baba Mezia* 48a).

"If one has paid another [for a movable object] but has not 'drawn' the article, so that the title to the article has not been acquired thereby . . . he who retracts, whether the purchaser or the seller, has committed an act not befitting an Israelite and must submit to *Me She'parah* [the curse expressed in the formula], 'He who punished . . .'" (*Mishneh Torah, Hil. Mechirah* 7:1).

Rabbi Yitzchak Meir Alter, the *Chiddushei HaRim*, comments on the talmudic comparison between "the Generation of the Flood" and "one who does not stand by his word." He asks: "Since according to law, stealing something which has less than the value of a *perutah* [smallest coin] is not legally considered theft, why then, was the 'Generation of the Flood' punished for this sin?" See *Yerushalmi, Baba Mezia* 4:2 and *Beraishith Rabbah* 31:5.

"He suggests that they were punished not for legal sins, but for moral transgressions. One who steals from his fellow something that does not have the value of a *perutah* may be compared to one who does not stand by his word, for both individuals are deficient in basic humanity. Although they are not legally culpable, they are morally corrupt" (Rabbi Shabsi Weiss, *Me'otzar HaMachshova shel HaChasidus*, p. 24).

See *Torah Temimah, Beraishith* 6:13 (20).

861

מִיּוֹם שֶׁבָּרָא הקב״ה אֶת הָעוֹלָם
לֹא הָיָה אָדָם שֶׁקְּרָאוֹ אָדוֹן
עַד שֶׁבָּא אַבְרָהָם וּקְרָאוֹ אָדוֹן

"From the day that the Holy One, blessed be He, created the
world, there was no man that called Him *Adon* [Master] until
Abraham came and called Him *Adon*" (*Berakoth* 7b).

"Someone once asked the Vilna Gaon for a letter of approbation for a
commentary he wrote on the *Siddur*. The Gaon read the opening pages and
found an explanation as to why the order of the *Shachrith* prayers begins
with *Adon Olam* . . . . It read: 'Since we know that Abraham initiated the
Shachrith service, it is fitting and proper that this service be opened with the
Divine appellation *Adon*, which Abraham was the first to use.'

"The Vilna Gaon exclaimed that the publication of the *Siddur* would be
worthwhile if only for this one commentary" (*Kanfei Yonah*, intro.).

In commenting on the Divine appellation *Adon*, Rabbi Joseph Ber
Soloveitchik asserts that "All sinning emanates from a denial of G-d's *adnuth*
[mastery or ownership of the world], His right to restrict and deny. Modern
man, in particular, insists that he is free, that indeed, all restrictions are
repressions and do harm. *Adnuth*, however, insists that man be humbled
before G-d, that he recognize the Master who bestows all gifts . . . .

"When Abraham asked for a child and for the assurance of a national
territory for his descendants, he understood that such gifts are bestowed by
G-d. They are not to be taken freely, but reverently to be beseeched. It was
Abraham, therefore, who introduced the name *aleph, daled, nun, yud* [AD-
NY], and thereby enunciated the basic Jewish *hashkafah* of G-d as *Adon*"
(Rabbi Abraham R. Besdin, *Reflections of the Rav*, p. 21).

⟦ 862 ⟧ מַיִם גְּנוּבִים יִמְתָּקוּ

"Stolen waters are sweet . . . " [Mishlei 9:17] (Nedarim 91b).

This scriptural phrase is employed as a talmudic concept to the effect that what is forbidden becomes dangerously attractive. See Sotah 7a.

"In 1885, in the city of Kovno, there was a meeting of Rabbis at which one prominent leader asked that the community ostracize anyone who studied Darwin's theories. Attending that meeting, among others, were Rabbi Yitzchak Elchanan Spector and Rabbi Alexander Moshe Lapides. Both of these great leaders opposed any harsh measures on the grounds of 'mayim genuvim yimtaku,' the stolen waters of Darwin's theories would only be sweetened for the hostile youth of that time. These men argued that drastic measures and punishment would only promote further rebellion against the Rabbinic establishment" (Rabbi Aharon Soloveitchik, Logic of the Heart, Logic of the Mind, p. 55).

⟦ 863 ⟧ מִיָּמַי לֹא אָמַרְתִּי דָּבָר וְחָזַרְתִּי לַאֲחוֹרַי

"I have never in my life said anything and looked behind my back" (Shabbath 118b).

This is one of R. Yose's statements concerning himself. Rashi offers two interpretations to this ambiguous declaration. (1) He would not say anything about a person while "looking behind his back" to see whether that person was nearby, i.e., he would say it to his face, for he held that this does not constitute "slander." (2) He would "not retract" [going back] his unfavorable opinion about others, because he did not state them in the first place without being perfectly sure of their truth" (Rashi, Arakhin 15b).

Rabbi Yosef Zundel of Salant interprets the above declaration in the following manner: "One who always tells the truth does not need an excellent memory. Since he is always truthful, he is never concerned that he may eventually contradict himself. On the other hand, an inveterate liar must have a phenomenal memory so as not to contradict himself and be caught in the web of his many lies.

This is what R. Yose is proclaiming. 'Since I have always embraced the [unadulterated] truth, I was never compelled to "look back" to search my memory regarding what I once may have said about a particular matter'" (Menachem Baker, *Parperaot LaTorah*, vol. 3, p. 137).

"Volumes have been written about what is proper speech . . . . But even if one does not have time to master all of the scholarly works on the subject, a reliable rule of thumb is to ask, 'Do I need to look behind me before I say it?' If the answer is yes, do not say it" (Rabbi Abraham J. Twersky, *Growing Each Day*, p. 150).

⦙ 864 ⦙   מָל וְלֹא פָּרַע אֶת הַמִּילָה כְּאִילוּ לֹא מָל

"If one circumcised but did not peel back the exposed membrane [*periah*], it is as if he did not circumcise" (*Shabbath* 137b).

If he removed the foreskin but did not sever the membrane underneath it, it is as if he did not perform the circumcision.

Rabbi Dov Ber (Schneuri) interprets this *mishnaic* dictum in terms of man's metaphysical relationship with the Almighty. "He who performs upon himself the commandment of circumcision, i.e., he circumcises the foreskin [obstruction] of his heart [Deut. 10:16], and he begins to serve the Almighty in love and awe, but he has not completely severed his ties with the past . . . such a person is not deemed 'circumcised' at all" (Rabbi Joseph I. Schneersohn, *Kuntres Toras HaChassidus*).

In this regard, it is significant to note Rabbi Aharon Soloveitchik's analysis of this precept. He writes: "The *mitzvah* of *bris milah* consists of two unique aspects, or *kiyumim*. First there is the aspect of *krisas ha'orlah*, of removing the foreskin. Then there is an additional *kiyum* of *hatafas dam bris*, letting of blood during the process of removing the foreskin."

Rav Soloveitchik believes that *hatafas dam bris* typifies the concept of sacrifice and suffering coupled with commitment.

"A Jew . . . is dedicated to the improvement of both the physical and the moral imperfections in the world, as symbolized by the removal of the foreskin, and in his readiness to suffer commitedly, as symbolized by *hatafas dam bris"* (*The Warmth and the Light*, pp. 25-30).

Cf. *Shir HaShirim Rabbah* 7:7, "How beautiful you are with milah and how pleasant you are with *periah."* See #847.

▯ 865 ▯

מְלַמְּדִין אוֹתוֹ כָּל הַתּוֹרָה כּוּלָה . . . . וְכֵיוָן
שֶׁבָּא לַאֲוִיר הָעוֹלָם בָּא מַלְאָךְ וְסְטָרוֹ עַל פִּיו
וּמְשַׁכְחוֹ כָּל הַתּוֹרָה כּוּלָה

"It [the embryo] is taught the entire Torah . . . . As soon as it is about to be born an angel approaches, slaps it on its mouth and causes it to forget the entire Torah" (*Niddah* 30b).

"This is why one sometimes has the vague feeling of having already known a fact one is just learning" (Rabbi Elie Munk, *The Call of the Torah,* vol. 1, p. 114).

Why was it necessary to teach the unborn child the Torah, only to cause him to forget it upon birth? It is suggested that it is easier for one to master a subject he once knew but forgot, than to master material which he never learnt before. Had the embryo not studied the entire Torah "in utero," it would have been extremely difficult for him to understand the Torah afterwards (Rabbi Samuel Alter, *L'kutei Bosar L'kutei* [*Aggadoth*] vol. 5, p. 283).

It is significant to note that one of the reasons for having a *Shalom Zachor* [welcoming the male] on the Friday night after a boy is born, is to console him [as a mourner] for the Torah which he has forgotten [*Taz, Yoreh De'ah* 265:13]. Since the infant is in mourning, chick peas or lentils [mourner's food] are customarily served at this occasion (*Zachor HaBris* 3:6).

Other authorities maintain that the proper name for this "festive gathering" is *Shalom Z'chor* [peace-*remembering*] or *Ben Zochor* [son of *remembrance*], signifying the prayerful hope that the child will study Torah and "remember" what he has forgotten (Rabbi Yaakov Emden, *Migdal Oz*, intro. 15).

〚 866 〛 מִן שִׁטַיָּא לֵית הֲנָיָא אֶלָּא מִן קְצִיָּא

"There is no benefit to be derived from acacia-wood except when it is cut down" (*Shemoth Rabbah* 6:5).

The acacia plant serves no substantial purpose while "alive," but when cut down, several species furnish timber of good quality. Hence, there is no benefit to be derived from acacia-wood except when it is cut down.

Similarly, there is no substantial purpose — no benefit is derived from the wicked until they are cut down and punished, thereby manifesting Divine Providence and the retributive principle in the universe.

See midrashic commentary *Yafeh Toar* [*Beraishith Rabbah* 2:5], who suggests that one may arrive at an "awareness of G-d" through punishment meted out to the wicked.

Cf. *Va'yikrah Rabbah* 24:1, "When is the name of the Holy One, blessed be He, magnified in the world? When He executes justice on the wicked."

〚 867 〛 מַנִּיחִין חַיֵּי עוֹלָם וְעוֹסְקִים בְּחַיֵּי שָׁעָה

"They forsake eternal life and occupy themselves with temporal life" (*Shabbath* 10a).

This was Rava's criticism of Rav Hamnuna when he saw him prolonging his prayers at the expense of Torah study.

Rabbi Chaim of Volozhin comments: "Torah study lies at the core of the existence of the universe. The preservation of the world depends on it . . . . If, G-d forbid, there would arrive an instant at which no one in the entire world would be studying Torah, the entire universe would instantly revert to nothingness. This is not so with the fulfillment of *mitzvoth*, not even the *mitzvah* of prayer. If, for a moment, all Israel would fail to pray to G-d, this would not cause the world to end. The Torah is therefore described as 'eternal life,' whereas prayer is characterized as 'temporal life' . . . . In *halacha*, 'a synagogue may be converted into a house of study' [Megillah 27a]" (*Nefesh HaChaim* 4:26).

Rabbi Joseph Ber Soloveitchik put it succinctly: "It was not the synagogue but the *beis midrash* — the house of study — which occupied the central place in Jewish life" (*The Lonely Man of Faith*).

⎱ 868 ⎰

מִנְעוּ בְּנֵיכֶם מִן הַהִגָּיוֹן

"Restrain your children from *higayon*" (*Berakoth* 28b).

Rashi interprets the ambiguous term *higayon* as excessive reading of Scripture or, alternatively, as childish chatter.

"Rabbeinu Saadiah Gaon translated the term [*higayon*] as *almanask*, which the Christians call "logic" — [it is disparaged] because it distracts people [from more important studies]. Rabbeinu Hai agrees and explains that it is intriguing and may cause someone to become so involved, that he abandons the Torah and forgets what he has learned" (*Nimukey Yosef, Megillah* 25b).

Similarly, Rabbi Yaakov Emden writes: "My son, who permitted you to attend their schools, learn their manners, pursue vanities and errors, and waste time on logic which is entirely theoretical and which our sages never used? That is what our sages meant when they said, 'Restrain your children from *higayon*'" (*Sheilath Ya'avetz* I 41).

The *Chasam Sofer* comments: "One who admixes *higayon* and Torah is guilty of 'plowing with an ox and a donkey'" (*Responsa, Orach Chaim* 51).

⎱ 869 ⎰

מְנַשֵּׁק לְכֵיפָתָא דְעַכּוֹ . . . עַד כֹּה הִיא
אַרְעָא דְיִשְׂרָאֵל

"[Rabbi Yosi ben Chanina] would kiss the stones of Acre [and say], 'Until here is [the boundary of] the Land of Israel'"
(*Yerushalmi, Shevi'ith* 4:7).

Acre was the [northern] boundary of *Eretz Yisrael,* and Rabbi Yosi ben Chanina would show his love for even the boundaries of the Holy Land (*Pnei Moshe*).

Rabbi Yekusiel Yehudah Halberstam [the Klausenberger Rebbe] asks:

"Why did he kiss the stones of Acre in particular? The reason is because the traditional borders of the Holy Land run through that city, half of which lies inside of Israel, and half on the outside. Where Rabbi Yosi stood in Acre, he could appreciate the difference between the sanctity of Israel and the secular nature of other countries. As a mark of this appreciation, he would kiss the stones which lay in the portion of Acre within Israel" (Rabbi H. Rabinowicz, "Tzanz Reborn," *Jewish Life* 41, no. 1 [Winter 1974]: 35).

Cf. *Kethuboth* 112a, "R. Abba used to kiss the cliffs of Acre." See Tosaf. s.v. *Menashek*.

⁑ 870 ⁑

מְסָאנָא דְּרַב מִכַּרְעַאי לָא בָּעֵינָא

"A shoe too large for my foot I do not want" (*Kiddushin* 49a).

If a man deceives a woman to her "advantage of birth" [*shevach yuchsin*], i.e., he betroths her on condition that he is a Levite and he is found to be a *Kohain*, all sages agree that she is not betrothed, for she can say, "I do not want a shoe too large for my foot."

This applies to an advantage in birth [he is found to be in a higher caste]. However, if she is deceived through a monetary advantage [*shevach mamon*], then there is a controversy [in the Mishnah] and Rabbi Shimon holds that she is betrothed.

Being deceived into marrying above one's "station" in life may present certain psychological problems. Metaphorically, "it is a shoe too large for her foot."

Cf. *Yebamoth* 63a, "Come down a step and take a wife." See #891.

⁑ 871 ⁑

מַעֲלִין בַּקֹּדֶשׁ וְאֵין מוֹרִידִין

"We promote [raise] in matters of sanctity but we do not reduce [lower] it" (*Shabbath* 21b).

This is illustrated by the kindling of the Chanukah lights according to the opinion of Beth Hillel. "On the first day one [light] is lit, and thereafter they are progressively increased [up to eight] . . . for 'We promote in sanctity but we do not reduce.'"

See scriptural derivation of this talmudic principle in *Menahoth* 99a.

Rabbi Moshe Avigdor Amiel offers a homiletical interpretation to this well-known principle. "In life there is no standing still, there is no middle ground — there is either ascension or descension. Life is constantly in a state of flux and development, and if one does not go up, most assuredly he will go down" (*Derashoth El-Ami*, vol. 3, p. 4).

Similarly, the Vilna Gaon writes: "If a person doesn't constantly strive to ascend higher and higher, he inevitably descends lower and lower" (*Even Sheleimah*, ch. 4:9).

"In spiritual matters there is no lukewarm, only hot and cold" (Rabbi Yosef Yozel Hurwitz, *Madreigoth Ha'odom*).

In commenting on the verse "A land which devours those who dwell in it" [Num. 13:32], Rabbi Yitzchok of Vorki said that this verse can be understood to mean that *Eretz Yisrael* is a land which devours those who sit in one place. It is therefore especially important to keep rising higher and higher in spiritual levels in Israel (*Baith Yitzchak: Shlach*).

〚 872 〛

מַעֲשֶׂה מוֹצִיא מִיַּד מַחֲשָׁבָה

"A deed can erase a thought" (*Kiddushin* 59b).

See talmudic discussion on the efficacy of deeds and thoughts with regard to the "unclean" and "clean" nature of utensils (ibid.).

Rabbi Yisrael Salanter applied the above maxim in a moralistic fashion. "He was once treated contemptuously by an obnoxious young Torah scholar. Rabbi Yisrael not only forgave the man when he apologized, but he did everything to help him find a good job. When Reb Yisrael was asked why he had troubled himself to do such favors for him, he answered: 'When you first came and apologized, I said that I forgave you completely and had no resentment at all against you. But a person cannot completely control his emotions, and I was concerned that maybe I did have a trace of bad feeling in me. And it is an important principle that "Deed erases thought." So I decided to do you a favor, to remove any possible trace of resentment in my heart, and that I would truly be your friend. For it is human nature that when you do a kindness for someone, you come to love him and feel yourself his friend" (*Midos Dor*, vol. 1, #782).

Cf. *Derech Eretz Zuta*, ch. 2, "If you wish to be joined together in a loving relationship with your friend, do business (provide) for his good."

See *Insights*, vol. 1, #71.

⫿ 873 ⫿   מַעֲשֶׂיךָ יְקָרְבוּךָ וּמַעֲשֶׂיךָ יְרַחֲקוּךָ

"Your own [good] deeds will bring you near [to them] and your own [evil] deeds will remove you [from them]" (*Eduyoth* 5:7).

When Akavya ben Mahalalail was about to die, his son said to him, "Father, commend me to your colleagues [instruct them to accept me as being worthy to be amongst the sages]." Akavya replied, "I do not commend you." His son inquired, "Have you found something wrong with me?" He replied to his son, "No — your own deeds will bring you near . . . ."

Rabbi Chaim Halberstam, the Sanzer Rav, applied the above maxim in a responsum concerning the right to inherit the position of *Admur* [chassidic Rebbe] from one's father. The Sanzer Rav maintained that the concept of *chazakah*, or established right of ownership, does not apply to the position of *Admur* and hence, the laws of inheritance also do not apply.

He distinguishes between the "public office" of a Rabbi, when it is accepted that the son has first claim on his father's position, and that of a chassidic Rebbe. "It is clear," he writes, "that the concept of inheritance does not pertain to the choice of a Rebbe's successor, but rather, 'it is his deeds which will draw a man near or push him away'" (*Divrei Chaim*).

Cf. *Sifra, Va'yikrah* 16:32, "A son is prior to any other man . . . ." See *Insights*, vol. 1, #107.

⏸ 874 ⏸

מִפְּנֵי מָה אֵין מְצוּיִין תַּלְמִידֵי חֲכָמִים לָצֵאת
תַּלְמִידֵי חֲכָמִים מִבְּנֵיהֶם . . . . שֶׁאֵין מְבָרְכִין
בַּתּוֹרָה תְּחִלָּה

"Why is it not usual for scholars to have sons who are scholars?
. . . . Because they did not first utter a blessing over the Torah
[before studying it]" (*Nedarim* 81a).

They did not study the Torah *lishmah* [for its own sake]. It was not
precious enough in their eyes to cause them to recite a benediction before
studying (*Ran*).

"In the blessing for the Torah we say, 'Who . . . gave us His Torah,' and
we conclude, 'Who *gives* the Torah' — 'gives,' in the present tense. He who
recites this blessing is conscious that even now he receives the Torah from
G-d. Not to 'pronounce a blessing over the Torah first' means to forget,
Heaven forbid, about the Giver of the Torah even while actually studying
Torah" (Rabbi Menachem M. Schneerson, the Lubavitcher Rebbe, *L'kutei
Sichot*, vol. 1, *Beraishith*, p. 17).

Cf. *Baba Mezia* 85b, "Why is the land in ruins? . . . because they did not
utter a benediction over the Torah first." See *Insights*, vol. 1, #437.

⏸ 875 ⏸

מִפְּנֵי מַה זָכוּ בֵּית הִלֵּל לִקְבּוֹעַ הֲלָכָה
כְּמוֹתָן? מִפְּנֵי שֶׁנּוֹחִין וַעֲלָבִין הָיוּ, וְשׁוֹנִין
דִּבְרֵיהֶם וְדִבְרֵי בֵּית שַׁמַּאי

"What was it that entitled Beth Hillel to have the *halachah* fixed in
agreement with their rulings? Because they were kindly and modest. They studied their own rulings as well as those of Beth
Shammai" (*Erubin* 13b).

Rabbi Yehudah Loew b. Bezalel commented: "Modesty should not be the
decisive factor in any halachic determination. But arrogant self-assertion
blinds a person to truth, whereas patient humility allows one to see the

opponent's logic or force of argument. The former is motivated by ill-will, and often hatred of the other side, whilst the latter knows no good except attaining truth and justice. Truth resides in the mansion of the humble searcher after its meaning" (Maharal miPrague, *Be'er Hagolah*, 5).

Cf. "These [statements] and these [statements] are the words of the Living G-d" (*Erubin* 13b). See #548.

⟦ 876 ⟧

מִצְוָה בּוֹ יוֹתֵר מִבִּשְׁלוּחוֹ

"It is more meritorious [to act] through oneself than through one's agent" (*Kiddushin* 41a).

"When one is occupied with the performance of *mitzvoth* [and does not delegate others to do them for him], he receives a greater reward" (Rashi).

"Even if one is a person of very high rank and does not, as a rule, attend to marketing or other household chores, he himself should nevertheless perform one of these tasks in preparation for the Sabbath, for that is the way of honoring it . . . . Indeed, the more one does in the way of preparation, the more praiseworthy he is" (*Mishneh Torah, Hil. Shabbath* 30:6).

Rabbi Chaim Soloveitchik of Brisk points to the *Akedah* [the binding of Isaac] as a scriptural illustration of the principle *"mitzvah bo yosair me'bashlucho"* [It is more meritorious . . .]. Abraham could have charged others to "bind" Isaac for him — but he did it himself, for it is "more meritorious through himself than through his agent" (*Mesorah* vol. 5 [Adar, 5751]: 16-17).

⟦ 877 ⟧

מִצְוָה לְקַיֵּים דִּבְרֵי הַמֵּת

"It is a *mitzvah* to fulfill the words of a dying man" (*Ta'anith* 21a).

"It is a *mitzvah* to fulfill wishes expressed by a person since deceased, even if a healthy person leaves instructions and then dies" (*Shulchan Aruch, Choshen Mishpat* 252:2).

Rabbi Moshe Avigdor Amiel cites the above "*mitzvah* to fulfill the words of a dying man" in conjunction with the *mitzvah* to fulfill the words of the sages [*Yebamoth* 20a], and bemoans the fact that not many pay attention to the second "*mitzvah*," while even the most irreligious Jews are concerned with the *mitzvah* of fulfilling [and honoring] the words of the dead through the observance of *Shiva, Yizkor* and *Yartzeit*.

He writes: "It is a fact that the major part of the work of a Rabbi today is confined to the 'Laws of Mourning' — the remaining part of the *Shulchan Aruch* is hardly referred to. Let me illustrate this. A man comes to me and asks whether he may open his shop on Sabbath. It seems that he is asking about a law pertaining to the Sabbath. But when he is questioned, 'Do you not know that "buying and selling" are forbidden on Sabbath?' he explains his meaning more fully. He is sitting *Shiva* and naturally his business is closed during the week, but having been informed that the laws of mourning are somewhat relaxed on the Sabbath, he has come to inquire whether, in these circumstances, he may open his shop!" (*Derashoth El-Ami*, p. 13)

﹝ 878 ﹞   מִצְווֹת בְּטֵלוֹת לֶעָתִיד לָבֹא

"The commandments will be abolished in the Hereafter"
(*Niddah* 61b).

Rabbi Moshe Chaim Ephraim of Sudylkov related that he heard from his grandfather, the Baal Shem Tov, that the reason [for the above dictum] is that "in the Hereafter" the world will understand the nature of a *mitzvah* and its source of life — through which it can cling to the blessed Divine Source of all life . . . .

What the Talmud means is that *mitzvoth* — the name *mitzvah* will be abolished because it is derived from the verb *tzivah*, "to order, command." Divine directives will no longer be called by a name which implies "orders" that we are bidden to follow. Instead, people will eagerly and of their own accord observe them. All will know the root reason and inner, mystic meanings of a *mitzvah* — how it brings Divine illumination to man and to the world (*Degel Machneh Ephraim*).

879

מִקְדָּשׁ שֵׁנִי מִפְּנֵי מָה חָרַב, מִפְּנֵי שֶׁהָיְתָה בּוֹ
שִׂנְאַת חִנָּם

"Why was the Second Sanctuary destroyed . . . ? Because therein
prevailed hatred without cause" (*Yoma* 9b).

Rabbi Joseph Grunblatt suggests that *"sinas chinom"* does not mean hatred
without cause, but *without a purpose* — wasted hatred. "It is hatred that does
not stem from love, that does not want to redeem the 'image of G-d' beset
by the evil in the person . . . . In short, *sinas chinom* is the root of all forms
of *ad hominem* hatred [stemming from one's prejudices], no matter what the
apparent 'cause' seems to be.

The mark of religious perfection is to treat the other, to love the other, as
'yourself,' with a standing equal to your own. The other end of the spectrum is *sinas chinom*, back to primitive man and distant from religious man.

Sinas chinom means that, in spite of all the external manifestations of
Torah experience ['being occupied with Torah, *mitzvoth* and acts of kindness'], we have failed; we have not internalized Torah values; we have not
become Torah — civilized. This is the failure of the Second Commonwealth,
and is why *Churban* [Destruction] was inevitable" (*Exile and Redemption*, pp.
103-106).

Cf. *Baba Mezia* 30b, "Jerusalem was only destroyed because they based
their judgments upon the law of the Torah." See *Insights*, vol. 1, #343.

See #692 for Rabbi Eliyahu E. Dessler's definition of *sinas chinom*.

880

מָקוֹם יֵשׁ לוֹ לְהַקָּדוֹשׁ בָּרוּךְ הוּא וּמִסְתָּרִים
שְׁמוֹ

"The Holy One, blessed be He, has a place and its name is '*Secret
Places*'" (*Hagigah* 5b).

A poignant homiletical interpretation was suggested by Rabbi Moshe
Avigdor Amiel. "If you feel that you have sought G-d in all places, and have
not found Him; in city and village, in field and in forest, in public and in

private, in house and in Synagogue — but all are devoid of His Presence . . .
then you must seek in the depths of your soul — 'in the *Secret Places*' within
you, your inner sanctuary, your holy of holies. Then you will see the truth
of the rabbinical saying, 'G-d does possess a place whose name is *mistarim.*'
Although you have driven Him, so to speak, from you and you have
shunned him — He still remains in the *secret places* of your heart and cannot
be dislodged" (*Derashoth El-Ami*, p. 43).

⟦ 881 ⟧   מַקִּישׁ הֲוָיָה לִיצִיאָה

"'Becoming' [betrothal] is assimilated to 'departure' [divorce]"
(*Kiddushin* 5a).

Betrothal and divorce are scripturally stated in proximity to each other,
showing that they have similar halachic regulations. "And when she is
departed [divorced] and be [another man's wife]" (Deut. 24:2).

Rabbi Moshe A. Amiel comments: "*Hava'ya* [betrothal] literally means
'being' and *yetzia* [divorce] literally means departure or 'non-being.' We
assimilate or compare 'being' to 'non-being.'

"It is human nature to experience *hava'ya* only after *yetzia*. One appreciates his marital state only after experiencing 'It is not good for man to be
alone' [Gen. 2:18]. Consequently, we assimilate the marital state to the state
of separation, for through *yetzia* we arrive at *hava'ya.*

"This is a universal axiom, when the Torah records: 'The earth was
without form and empty, with darkness on the face of the depths . . . . And
G-d said: "Let there be light"' [Gen. 1:2,3], this encompassed all that was
made under the sun. In all things, we see the *hava'ya* [the being] coming
from the *yetzia* [non-being]; the positive from the negative force. In the
language of the Torah, at creation we see light emerging from darkness"
(*Hegyonoth El-Ami*, pp. 228-231).

Cf. *Niddah* 16b, "The angel appointed over conception is called '*Lailah*'
[night]." See *Insights*, vol. 1, #406.

⎾ 882 ⏋   מַרְבֶּה עֵצָה מַרְבֶּה תְּבוּנָה

"The more counsel, the more understanding" (*Aboth* 2:8).

When one seeks advice from others, he gains more understanding.

"There is a popular saying, 'Ask others for advice — then do what your own mind tells you.' The question arises: If you will ultimately do what you believe is correct, why consult with others?

"The answer is that each person has a better knowledge of himself than anyone else can possibly have. However, every individual has some knowledge and understanding which you do not possess. Therefore, before making any major decisions, it is wise to consult with as many people as you can, to absorb ideas and information that you might not have known or thought of" (Rabbi Chaim of Volozhin, *Ruach Chaim* 2:7).

⎾ 883 ⏋   "מֹשֶׁה מִן הַתּוֹרָה מְנַיִן, „בְּשַׁגַּם הוּא בָשָׂר"

"Where is Moshe alluded to in the Torah? [In the verse] 'For that he also [*be'shagam*] is flesh' [Gen. 6:3]" (*Hullin* 139b).

The word *be'shagam* has the same numerical value as Moshe (345). Moreover, Scripture continues: "Therefore shall his days be a hundred and twenty years," which corresponds with the years of the life of Moshe (Rashi).

"This verse indicates that man could no longer live for centuries, as did the first ten generation recorded in the Torah. Because of Adam's sin, death had to be decreed upon his descendants, and a hundred and twenty years would become an ideal lifespan with the passage of time" (Rabbi David Feinstein, *Kol Dodi on the Torah*, p. 291).

Rabbi Aaron of Zhitomir suggests the following novel interpretation. "'*Moshe min haTorah mena'yin*' is a question pertaining to the possibility of ever achieving spiritual greatness comparable to Moshe Rabbeinu. Is there some allusion in the Torah pointing to that possibility? Yes, there is — *be'shagom* 'for he also is flesh' — Moshe, like everyone else, was composed of flesh and blood. Nevertheless, his 'flesh' did not in any way distance him from his Creator and he was able to achieve unparalleled spiritual heights. One can indeed learn from him" (*Toldoth Aaron, Succoth*).

◖ 884 ◗   מְשָׁלָן בֶּעָפָר, מְשָׁלָן בַּכּוֹכָבִים

"They [Israel] were compared to dust and they were compared to the stars" (*Bamidbar Rabbah* 2:13).

In this world, they were compared to dust. As the dust of the earth is trodden by all, so is Israel trampled by the nations of the world . . . . In the Hereafter, however, they are compared to stars. As the stars sparkle throughout the firmament, so will Israel sparkle in the Hereafter" (ibid.).

On the verse, "He counts the number of stars, to all of them He assigns names" [Psalms 147:4], Rabbi Mordechai Shulman comments: "Every star has a unique role to play, a distinctive job that makes it indispensable for the continued existence of the universe.

Man is compared to a star in that he, too, has his unique function . . . . The farther away man is from his true self [like the stars whose light is often invisible], the more irrelevant and unimportant he appears. The closer he comes to discovering inner being, the more he searches to discover his unique 'name' in Creation, the more he will find that his soul does not shine like a tiny star, but possesses a great light, and that he has been given a crucial spiritual function that cannot be fulfilled by anyone else" (Rav Reuven Grossman, *The Legacy of Slabodka*, p. 120).

◖ 885 ◗   מְשֶׁרַבּוּ מְקַבְּלֵי מַתָּנוֹת, נִתְמַעֲטוּ הַיָּמִים וְנִתְקַצְּרוּ הַשָּׁנִים

"When receivers of gifts multiplied, the days became fewer and the years shorter" (*Sotah* 47b).

"As it is written, 'He who spurns gifts will live long'" [Prov. 15:27]. What is the rationale of the above dictum? The more man "gives," the more he manifests the "image of G-d" within him, for only G-d truly gives [He never takes]. The more man "takes" [receiving unearned gifts], the further he removes himself from the Almighty, the source of all life. Hence, his days and years are automatically shortened (Rabbi M. Miller).

Similarly, Rabbi Yitzchak Hutner explains the verse, "He who spurns gifts will live long," thusly: "The attribute that most closely identifies us as G-d's children is the attribute of self-sufficiency . . . . Being a 'hater of gifts' puts us in sync with G-d, as miniature self-sufficient 'living wellsprings' [for G-d is the Living Wellspring of all] (*Pachad Yitzchak, Shavuos* 7).

⎰ 886 ⎱   מָתַי יַגִּיעוּ מַעֲשַׂי לְמַעֲשֵׂי אֲבוֹתַי

"When will my deeds equal those of my fathers?"
(*Tana D'vei Eliyahu* 28).

"We are obligated to say, 'When will my deeds reach the deeds of Abraham, Issac and Jacob?'" How can we reach the elevated heights of the patriarchs?

The Chafetz Chaim writes: "The Torah described Abraham's hospitality at length, so as to teach us by example how to treat guests . . . . Even though we are not accustomed to act in this [Abraham's] way we can, at least, learn from him that one should go after guests and receive them most cordially" (*Ahavath Chesed*, part 3, ch. 2).

Rabbi Menachem Mendel of Kotzk commented upon the above dictum: "We must at least touch the deeds of our forefathers. Even though we might not actually reach their level, we must follow in their footsteps" (*Emeth Mi'Kotzk Titzmach*, p. 115).

❏ 887 ❏ מַתָּנָה טוֹבָה יֵשׁ לִי בְּבֵית גְּנָזַי וְשַׁבָּת שְׁמָהּ

"I have a precious gift in My treasure house called the
Sabbath . . ." (*Shabbath* 10b).

The Sabbath is the Almighty's gift to Israel.

The Chafetz Chaim compares the non-observance of the Sabbath to a
bride who returns the gifts she received from her groom — indicating her
unwillingness to get married. Similarly, a Jew's desecration of the Sabbath
is tantamount to returning G-d's precious gift to Him. It is, in effect, a
proclamation that he no longer desires that special bond that has existed for
so many generations between Israel and the Almighty (*Parperaot LaTorah*, vol.
2, p. 179).

Sf. *Bezah* 16a, "On the eve of the Sabbath, the Holy One, blessed be He,
gives to man a *neshamah yetherah* (an additional soul) . . . ." See #897.

נ

⌐ 888 ⌐

נַהֲרָא נַהֲרָא וּפַשְׁטֵיה

"Every river has its own course" (*Hullin* 18b).

Every place has its own customs and usages (Rashi).

In his introduction to his *Siddur*, Rabbi Yaakov Emden writes: ". . . and in matters that depend upon local custom . . . I left both [traditions] and invoked the talmudic phrase '*nahara nahara u-pashtei*,'" which Rashi, in his commentary, interpreted as 'each place follows its customs.'"

"The principle is: whenever you are uncertain as to the law, go and observe how the community acts, as long as it does not contradict the talmudic view. Each [opinion in a] controversy for the sake of Heaven found in the Talmud has validity, for each has its root in Heaven above. This as well as that are the words of the living G-d" (*Siddur* I: 117a, cited by Rabbi Jacob Joseph Schacter [unpublished doctoral thesis] *Rabbi Jacob Emden: Life and Major Works*, part 1, p. 278).

Cf. *Beraishith Rabbah* 48:14, "When you enter a town, follow its customs." See *Insights*, vol. 1, #440.

Cf. *Pesahim* 50a, "We lay upon him the stringencies of the place which he has left and the stringencies of the place to which he has gone."

▯ 889 ▯

נוֹחַ לוֹ לְאָדָם שֶׁיַּעֲבוֹר עֲבֵירָה בְּסֵתֶר וְאַל
יְחַלֵּל שֵׁם שָׁמַיִם בְּפַרְהֶסְיָא

"It is better that a man should commit a transgression secretly, so
that he should not profane the Name of G-d publicly"
(*Kiddushin* 40a).

R. Ilai the Elder said: "If a man sees that his *yetzer* [Evil Inclination] is
strengthening itself over him, let him go to a place where he is unknown,
don black and cover himself with black, and do as his heart desires, but let
him not publicly profane G-d's Name" (ibid.).

Rabbeinu Chananel comments: "G-d forbid that a man is permitted to
commit a sin! But the sages stood firmly against the Evil Inclination and
believed that one lusts only for that which is forbidden, and that if a man
were to go a long distance and put on dark garments, then his heart would
be broken [it would subdue his lust] and he would refrain from sin. But as
far as doing something which is forbidden, absolutely not. It is just that his
type of conduct [wearing somber garments, etc. . . . .] breaks the grip of the
Evil Inclination and restrains one from sinning."

Cf. *Hagigah* 16a, "When anyone commits a transgression in secret, it is as
though he thrust aside the feet of the Divine Presence."

▯ 890 ▯

נוֹשֵׂא בָּעוֹל עִם חֲבֵרוֹ

"He shares the burdens of his fellow man" (*Aboth* 6:6).

This is one of the forty-eight qualifications by which the Torah is acquired.

"Reb Chaim Shmulevitz once passed by a shoemaker's store where rows
of children's shoes were drying in the sun. Reb Chaim was deeply moved
by this scene and later, in one of his *mussar* talks, he related the following
to his students. 'I imagined a poor young boy who notices these shoes and
wishes he could have a pair. His mother, knowing how expensive they are,
realizes that she cannot purchase them immediately, but promises her child

that soon, soon, they will be his. The exciting day finally arrives. The sweet little boy tries on the shoes, his face radiant with the wonder of the moment. I can feel,' said Reb Chaim, 'what the father felt at that moment; what emotions surge through a mother at such a time I cannot even imagine.'

"Reb Chaim went on to utilize this poignant scene to instill in his students the great principle of sharing in another person's joys and sorrows. 'Although I cannot imagine the depth of that mother's joy,' Reb Chaim declared, 'I can at least be a partner to her *simcha*'" (*Sefer Hazikaron*, p. 112, cited by Rabbi Yaakov Feitman, "Vessels of Holiness," *The Jewish Observer* 22, no. 7 [Oct. 1989]: 19).

⎗ 891 ⎗

נְחֵית דַּרְגָּא נְסֵיב אִיתְּתָא

"Come down a step and take a wife" (*Yebamoth* 63a).

One should not marry a wife of superior rank for she may behave arrogantly and be disgruntled at her husband's "social inferiority."

"True harmony can only exist amongst people with comparable intelligence and backgrounds. Each person, however, has a tendency to exalt and magnify his own true worth. Our sages, therefore, advise a man who is about to get married, 'Come down a step' from what you imagine you really are, and then 'take a wife.' This will lead to equality and marital compatibility" (*Chumdei Daniel*).

Cf. *Kiddushin* 49a, "A shoe too large for my foot I do not want." See #870.

⎗ 892 ⎗

נְטִירוּתָא דְּכַסְפָּא קַבִּילִי עֲלַי, נְטִירוּתָא
דְּזַהֲבָא לָא קַבִּילִי עֲלַי

"It was silver that I undertook to take care of, but
I never undertook to take care of gold" (*Baba Kamma* 62a).

"One who gives a *golden dinar* to a woman saying: 'Be careful with it, for it is a *silver dinar*' . . . if she was neglectful, she must repay [only] a silver dinar because she can say: 'I accepted responsibility for silver, but not for gold'" (ibid.).

The *Bais HaLevi*, Rabbi Yosef Ber Soloveitchik, applied this talmudic reasoning to a vital Jewish communal policy that was about to be implemented in Russia during the last century. The Russian government was about to close down the "Jewish schools" throughout the country.

The Torah authorities decided to appoint a permanent representative in Petersburg who would be on guard to defend Jewish education. As candidate for this responsible task a certain name was put forward, but Reb Yosef Ber opposed the appointment. When asked to explain his opposition, he replied: "The candidate certainly is a G-d-fearing man, nonetheless my opposition to him is based on a Gemara [cited above]. For me, the *Cheder* — the old educational system — is a golden dinar . . . . It is the basis of our existence. The *Cheder* is also precious to my dear friend, but in his eyes it is, as it were, a silver dinar. He does not think that without the *Cheder* Judaism is in danger of extinction . . . . Of course, he will guard the dinar [Cheder] faithfully, but he will not give his life for it, as we will . . . . I want a guardian who values the dinar exactly as I do, as a golden dinar, and not one who, like him, thinks of it as silver" (*The Rav Speaks*, pp. 180-182).

▯ 893 ▯ נָטַע אֹהֶל שָׂרָה תְּחִלָּה וְאַחַר כָּךְ נָטַע אָהֳלוֹ

"He [Abraham] pitched Sarah's tent first and afterwards he pitched his own tent" (*Beraishith Rabbah* 39:16).

"He did this because of modesty, as it is written, 'All glorious is the king's daughter within'" (Moshe Aryeh Mirkin). See *Insights*, vol. 1, #305.

Rabbi Zalman Sorotzkin comments: "This Midrash teaches us a timeless lesson. In a wayward, skeptical age, Sarah's tent takes precedence over Abraham's: that is, it is more important to bring women close to G-d than men. That is because women are more predisposed to faith to begin with. So by starting with women, one goes from the easy to the difficult, the accepted method in education. The women will then influence the men.

"Thus, before the Jews became G-d's people at Sinai, G-d first commanded Moshe [Ex. 19:3], 'So shall you say to the house of Jacob' — the women — 'and tell the sons of Israel — the men' [Rashi]" (*Oznayim LaTorah*).

⟦ 894 ⟧   . . . . נִיסִיתִיךָ בְּכַמָּה נִסְיוֹנוֹת וְעָמַדְתָּ בְּכוּלָן

"I have tested you on numerous occasions and you have success-
fully passed them all. Now, be firm for My sake in this test as
well, so that it not be said: There was no reality in the earlier
ones" (*Sanhedrin* 89b).

The Almighty tested Abraham ten times [*Aboth* 5:3]. The final test was the
Akedah, the binding of Isaac upon the altar. Our sages explain why G-d
pleaded with Abraham to sacrifice his son. "I have tested you on numerous
occasions."

Rabbi Menachem M. Schneerson raises an obvious question on the above
dictum. "Even if Abraham's self-sacrifice would not have been strong
enough to withstand the final test, in no way would this have negated his
ability in withstanding the previous ones, since the last test was by far the
most difficult of all. Why, then, would it be said that 'there was no reality
in the earlier ones'?"

Says the Lubavitcher Rebbe, "Had Abraham not withstood the final test
of the *Akedah*, it could well be said that his previous successes were a result
of the fact that they made spiritual sense to him. We would still not know
how he would respond to a test that required absolute and total *mesirus
nefesh* [self-sacrifice].

"By rising to the challenge of the *Akedah*, Abraham not only proved that
he was now capable of absolute *mesirus nefesh*, but also proved that this spirit
of total self-abnegation had permeated him when he withstood the earlier
tests as well" (*The Chassidic Dimension*, pp. 19, 20).

895 נַעֲשׂוּ מַלְאֲכֵי הַשָּׁרֵת כִּתִּים כִּתִּים . . . מֵהֶם אוֹמְרִים יִבָּרֵא וּמֵהֶם אוֹמְרִים אַל יִבָּרֵא

"The ministering angels formed themselves into groups, some of them saying, 'Let him be created,' and others saying, 'Let him not be created'" (*Beraishith Rabbah* 8:5).

"*Chesed* said: 'Let him be created' . . . *Emeth* said: 'He should not be created'; *Tzedek* said: 'Let him be created' . . . *Shalom* said: 'Let him not be created' . . . . What did G-d do? He took *Emeth* [Truth] and cast it to the ground . . . . While the angels were arguing with each other, the Holy One, blessed be He, created him . . ." (ibid.).

When the Almighty threw Truth to the ground, there remained a majority [*Chesed* and *Tzedek*] in favor of man's creation.

Rabbi Shlomo Kluger of Brody asks: "Since *Shalom* was also in opposition to the creation of man, why was Truth selected to be thrown to the ground? The reason is that were Truth left in opposition, a majority in favor of man's creation would not have availed, for truth is higher than any majority against it" (*Imrei Shefer*).

Rabbi Irving Filler offers the following homiletical interpretation: "A truth, be it ever so honest and accurate but whose logical conclusion is *al yebarei* — don't create, don't do — must be rejected . . . . Years ago Jews said 'In America you will never be able to build Torah and create an environment favorable to Jewish learning and *Yiddishkeit* . . . .' There was a great deal of truth in this assertion. But there were men of vision and courage who challengingly asked whether the policy should be *al yebarei,* to sit idly by and watch our children die a spiritual death. Such a 'Truth' was rejected and today, with the help of the Almighty, we have 'created' a chain of Yeshivoth and Day Schools from coast to coast!"

⫿ 896 ⫿

נָשָׂאתָ וְנָתַתָּ בֶּאֱמוּנָה

"Did you conduct your business affairs with faith?" (*Shabbath* 31a).

"When a man is led in for judgment he is asked, 'Did you conduct . . . .'"

Rabbi Avraham Pam notes that the Gemara uses the term *b'emuna* [with faith] instead of *b'tzedaka* [with righteousness] or *b'mishpat* [with justice]. He points out that *emuna* has a two-fold meaning — "integrity" and "faith in G-d," suggesting that this faith would prompt one to act with the utmost integrity and would imbue him with a higher sense of ethics ("Did You Conduct Your Business Affairs With Faith," *The Jewish Observer* 13, no. 3 [May, 1987]: 3).

Rabbi Shimon Schwab, speaking before the "Association of Jewish CPAs," said: "A person who is dishonest in business is a *Kofer B'Ikor* (he doesn't really have faith in G-d)."

It is significant to note that Rabbi Avraham Danzig, the author of *Chayei Adam* and *Chochmas Adam,* instructed his family [in his will] that no eulogies be delivered for him. The only exception he made was that it may be said of him that "he conducted his affairs with absolute faith and integrity."

Rav Pam commented that any Torah Jew entering business must learn the *halachoth* of *Choshen Mishpat* 227-238, else he would be like a *shochet* slaughtering animals with no knowledge of ritual slaughtering.

Rabbi Joseph Ber Soloveitchik maintains, "It is the *Choshen Mishpat* (dealing with civil and criminal law) which reflects the essence of Judaism's greatness . . . . It is primarily in the area of *bein adam lechavero*, interhuman relations, that Judaism is unique.

"There are some who, though stringent in ritual observance, are less than meticulous in human relations. This, though inexcusable, may not be due to hypocrisy, but to the formidable standards of the *Choshen Mishpat* with its demands that we discipline our greed in recognition of the rights and feelings of others" (Abraham R. Besdin, *Man of Faith in the Modern World,* p. 153).

See *Insights*, vol. 1, #115.

897

נְשָׁמָה יְתֵירָה נוֹתֵן הַקָּדוֹשׁ בָּרוּךְ הוּא בָּאָדָם
עֶרֶב שַׁבָּת וּלְמוֹצָאֵי שַׁבָּת נוֹטְלִין אוֹתָהּ

"On the eve of the Sabbath, the Holy One, blessed be He, gives
to man a *neshamah yetherah* [an additional soul] and at the close of
the Sabbath He withdraws it from him" (*Bezah* 16a).

"*Neshamah yetherah*" denotes an expanded heart for *menuchah* and *simcha*
[physical and spiritual rest and delight] (Rashi).

In commenting on the verse, "The heavens and the earth and their entire
host were completed" [Gen. 2:1], Rabbi Chaim ben Attar explains that
"when G-d finished Creation, He had to save His creatures from the inertia
threatening every living being which lacks some higher aspiration, some
higher goal . . . . [This was] the gift of the Sabbath . . . . The Sabbath gave
a new soul to the works of Creation. This day continues as the day *par
excellence* devoted to the soul's aspirations for G-d. The Sabbath snatches the
soul from the grip of worldly cares and liberates it by providing a release
from the metaphysical longings of the soul; thus it offers the soul the means
of fulfilling its supreme purpose on earth. In this way the Sabbath has
become the day of *neshamah yetherah* — the new soul" (*Ohr HaChaim*, cited
by Rabbi Elie Munk, *The Call of the Torah*, vol. 1, p. 41).

See #887.

ס

‖ 898 ‖　　　סוֹפוֹ דִּבְרֵי תוֹרָה דִּכְתִיב,
　　　　　סוֹף דָּבָר הַכֹּל נִשְׁמָע . . .

"The end thereof [the book of *Koheleth*] are words of Torah, as it is written, 'The sum of the matter, when all has been considered: Fear G-d and keep His commandments for that is the whole of man'" (*Sabbath* 30b).

"What is meant by 'for that is the whole of man?' Said R. Eliezer, 'The entire world was created only for such a man'" (ibid.).

"This is the essence of man" (Ibn Ezra).

Rabbi Elchonon Wasserman elaborated: "One might think that the fear of G-d is merely one among several human virtues — that one may be a man even though he does not fear G-d. *Koheleth* teaches that this is not so. Fear of Heaven is the totality of man. Without it, one is not a man at all — he is merely one more animal."

"The human in man," he continued, "can be measured only by his fear of Heaven, whether more or less. Whoever possesses abundant fear of Heaven is a great man; one who possesses little is small. If someone lacks every vestige of the fear of Heaven, then he is not truly a human being, but an animal in human guise" (*Reb Elchonon, The Life and Ideals of R. Elchonon Bunim Wasserman*, p. 145).

300

⟦ 899 ⟧

סִיגְנוֹן אֶחָד עוֹלֶה לְכַמָּה נְבִיאִים וְאֵין שְׁנֵי
נְבִיאִים מִתְנַבְּאִין בְּסִיגְנוֹן אֶחָד

"The same 'communication' is revealed to many prophets, yet no
two prophets prophecy in the identical phraseology"
(*Sanhedrin* 89a).

Rabbi Aryeh Kaplan explains: "Ancient sources agree that every prophet
expresses his prophecy in a way that reflects his own unique style of speech
or writing. In the majority of cases, translating the spiritual experience is
done, to some degree, by the prophet himself, according to what he is
familiar with . . .

The prophet, therefore, has to be so totally involved in Torah that his
means of expression parallels those of the Torah. The amazing thing about
the Bible is that despite the fact that each prophet expresses himself in
almost every conceivable image and metaphor available, the basic unity of
the spiritual experience comes through with extreme clarity and precision"
(*Inner Space*, pp. 135, 136).

Cf. *Yebamoth* 49b, "All other prophets saw through a dull lens while
Moshe our Teacher saw through a clear lens." See #756.

Cf. *Shabbath* 104a, "A prophet may henceforth make no innovations." See
Insights, vol. 1, #37.

⟦ 900 ⟧

סַנְהֶדְרִין הַהֹרֶגֶת אֶחָד בְּשָׁבוּעַ נִקְרֵאת
חוֹבְלָנִית

"A Sanhedrin which executes one person in seven years is called
destructive" (*Makkoth* 7a).

"Rabbi Eliezer ben Azariah said: 'Once in seventy years.' Rabbi Tarfon
and Rabbi Akiva said: 'Were we in the Sanhedrin, no person would ever be
put to death'" (ibid.).

Although the Torah imposes the death penalty for a variety of crimes, in practice there were many limitations. The would-be criminal had to be given prior warning and witnesses were thoroughly examined, so that only on the rarest of occasions was the death sentence actually carried out.

"Still, by proclaiming the death penalty with such conviction for so many crimes, the Torah intends to sensitize the moral conscience of the people. It brands sinners and criminals as abject beings who deserve death, even if the actual execution is commuted through legal technicalities" (Rabbi Elie Munk, *The Call of the Torah, Shemos,* p. 303).

On the above dictum, the Maharal of Prague comments that this policy was followed only "when Israel was righteous . . . . When it became necessary to adopt a policy of worrying about murderers, the sages ruled that 'The court has an extraordinary power to punish even when normal procedures do not warrant such, in order to protect the Torah'" (*Sanhedrin* 46a) — See *Chidushei Agadoth* of Maharal to *Makkoth* ad loc.).

Rabbi Aaron Lewin [author of *Hadrash VeHa'iyun*] spoke out in favor of the abolition of capital punishment before the Polish Parliament [The Sejm] and at the conclusion of his address he quoted the *Mishnah* in *Makkoth* [cited above].

In a biographical essay on his father, Rabbi Lewin's son writes: "The Polish legislators had never known of these talmudic thoughts. They were accustomed to anti-Semites heaping abuse on rabbinic literature. Now they heard a Jewish spiritual leader, in superb Polish, revealing its ethical level . . . The Polish Jew-haters sensed that here was a man over whom they could have no control. Whenever Rabbi Lewin rose to the rostrum, an atmosphere of respect pervaded the auditorium" (Isaac Lewin . . . *Unto the Mountains,* p. 42).

⸩ 901 ⸩ סַנְהֶדְרִי שֶׁרָאוּ כּוּלָּן לְחוֹבָה פּוֹטְרִין אוֹתוֹ

"If the Sanhedrin unanimously find [the accused] guilty, he is acquitted" (*Sanhedrin* 17a).

"If in trying a capital case all the members of the Sanhedrin vote for conviction, the accused is acquitted. Only when some cast about for arguments in his favor and are outvoted by those who are for conviction is the accused put to death" (*Mishneh Torah, Hil. Sanhedrin* 9:1).

Rabbi Zvi Hirsch Chajes explains: "There are always mitigating circumstances that might be cited in favor of the accused in an attempt to save him from the death penalty . . . Hence, if this court was immediately convinced of his guilt and could find nothing in his favor, even in the remotest way, then it is an indication that this court is either not competent and their judgment is not valid, or that they rendered judgment in haste without due deliberation and inquiry into the facts and the evidence" (*Annotations, Sanhedrin* 17a).

Rabbi Menachem Mendel of Kotzk offers an insightful explanation of the above paradoxical ruling. In a case where the accused is found guilty by a majority vote, since there are some judges who found points in his favor, the accused does not fully repent or atone for the sin which he committed. However, 'if the Sanhedrin unanimously find him guilty' then the accused acknowledges his sin with a broken heart for he believes that not even repentance can save him, therefore he is acquitted" (*Amud HaEmes*, p. 65).

It is significant to note that one of the Rishonim, Rabbi Meir HaLevi Abulafia [*Ramah*] interprets the above dictum in a diametrically opposite fashion. He translates *"pohtrim"* not as acquitted but as "finished" or "concluded," i.e., "If the Sanhedrin unanimously find him guilty, the matter is concluded — he is sentenced immediately, for there is no need to postpone the sentence till the morrow in the hope of finding new points in his favor since it cannot be anticipated in this case" (cited by Rabbi Baruch HaLevi Epstein, *Mekor Baruch*, vol. 3, pp. 1373-1379). See also *Torah Temimah*, Ex. 23:2, n. 17 for a detailed analysis of this interpretation.

This translation, however, is a *daas yachid* [the interpretation of one individual] and is *not* cited by later rabbinic decisors.

⫫ 902 ⫫   סְעוּדָּתְךָ שֶׁהֲנָאָתְךָ מִמֶּנָּה מְשׁוֹךְ יָדְךָ הֵימֶנָּה

"If you are enjoying your meal overmuch, withdraw your hand"
(*Gittin* 70a).

Do not indulge too freely in a meal which you enjoy. "While eating and still feeling hungry one should leave over some of what he desires in honor of the Creator" (Rabbeinu Yonah).

Rabbeinu Saadia Gaon, in a letter to an Egyptian community, wrote: "You eat to live, you do not live to eat" (*Treasury of Jewish Letters*, i, 89).

Overeating is like a deadly poison to the human body. Most illnesses which befall man arise either from bad food or from excessive eating of good food" (*Mishneh Torah, Hil. Daioth* 4:15).

"There are two advantages in this [dictum]. First, his eating will have no harmful effects. Secondly, this is an act of subduing the Evil Inclination and the breaking of lust . . . This should be the manner of treating all pleasures and delights of the world. One should never totally satisfy his desires" (*Orchoth Tzaddikim, Sha'ar HaTeshuvah*).

Rabbi Eliyahu Lopian writes: "Excessive enjoyment and the visible pleasure which arises from gluttonous eating . . . simply shows that the person is steeped in lust. The Talmud states [*Megillah* 12a] that the Jews of Shushan were deserving of destruction 'because they derived *pleasure* from the banquet of that wicked man' [Ahasueres]. Notice it says 'they derived pleasure' and not 'they ate.' It was the 'pleasure' and not the actual eating that precipitated the Divine wrath" (*Lev Eliyahu*, p. 166).

The commentary *Zikukin D'Nura* [a kabbalistic work by Shmuel Chida] explains that all sins result from overindulging in food and drink. We learn in the Torah that satiation leads to forgetting or even rejecting G-d. See Deut. 8:12-14.

Rabbeinu Bachya ben Asher writes: "For this reason we are commanded not to eat on *Yom Kippur*, since improper eating has the power to turn our souls to wrongdoing" (*Shulchan shel Arba'a*).

The *Chazon Ish* sent the following recommendation to a student who aspired to Torah greatness: "Scrupulously avoid indulgence in food . . . it is an exceedingly low mode of conduct and a hindrance to learning . . ." (Rabbi Shmuel Greineman, *Kovetz Igroth Chazon Ish*, I:20).

⟦ 903 ⟧

סַקְבָא דְּשַׁתָּא רִיגְלָא

"The sorest spot of the year is the Festival" (*Kiddushin* 81a).

The time of the greatest danger to chastity is the festive season when people of all sorts congregate.

"It is the duty of the court to appoint officers for festival days to patrol and inspect parks, orchards, and river banks, to make sure that men and women do not congregate there to eat and drink together and thus lead to immorality (*Mishneh Torah, Hil. Yom Tov* 6:21).

Rabbi Meir Simchah HaKohen of Dvinsk comments: "Since one does not labor on the Sabbaths and on Festivals, this [idleness] may lead to transgression. Moreover, in the Sanctuary the women who bring their personal offerings may come in contact with men who are required to sacrifice their festive offerings. This is a time when immorality is most to be feared" (*Meshech Chochmah*, p. 267).

Cf. *Keth.* 59b, "Idleness leads to unchastity." See *Insights*, vol. 1, #100.

ע

∐ 904 ∐

עֲבֵירָה מְטַמְטֶמֶת לִבּוֹ שֶׁל אָדָם

"Sin blocks [dulls] a person's heart" (*Yoma* 39a).

Rabbi Eliyahu E. Dessler writes: "In fact, the sin itself is the blockage. The will to sin will not *allow* the person to become interested in anything that might deflect his mind from the sin. This is called *"timtum ha-lev"* [blockage of the heart].

Rabbi Yitzchok Blaser maintained that a person can easily find out whether he has succeeded in obtaining Divine forgiveness on *Yom Kippur*. Since 'sin blocks a person's heart' — if the sin has been removed, the obstruction must also have been removed. It follows that if after *Yom Kippur* a person feels his heart is pure and obstruction-free, this is a sure sign that his sins have been forgiven. If, however, his heart is in the same state as before, as obstructed and obtuse as ever, it is clear that his sins have not been forgiven" (*Strive For Truth*, part 3, p. 134).

Cf. Saadiah Gaon, *Emunoth V'Daioth*, [Treatise 5]. "When merits predominate in the soul, it is thereby purified . . . when demerits are in the majority, the soul becomes turbid and darkened."

"Evil deeds bring about the materialization [in body and soul] of ugliness and deficiency" (R. Moshe Chaim Luzzato, *Derech HaShem*, part II, ch. 2).

306

⎮ 905 ⎮

עֲבֵירוֹת שֶׁבֵּין אָדָם לַמָּקוֹם יוֹם הַכִּפּוּרִים
מְכַפֵּר, עֲבֵירוֹת שֶׁבֵּין אָדָם לַחֲבֵרוֹ אֵין יוֹם
הַכִּפּוּרִים מְכַפֵּר עַד שֶׁיְרַצֶּה אֶת חֲבֵרוֹ

"For sins between man and G-d, *Yom Kippur* provides atonement,
but for sins between man and his fellow, *Yom Kippur* does not
provide atonement until he appeases his fellow" (*Yoma* 85b).

Even after he makes restitution to his fellow man and appeases him, he
must still repent. "One who has injured a person or damaged his property,
even though he pays what he owes him, is not pardoned unless he confess-
es and resolves never to commit such an offense again . . . (*Mishneh Torah,
Hil. Teshuvah* 1:1).

Rabbi Joseph B. Soloveitchik, in commenting on the above dictum points
out that a number of *baale mussar* [ethical preachers] maintained that *Yom
Kippur* does not provide atonement even for sins between man and G-d until
one appeases his fellow man. Atonement of *Yom Kippur* is not "achieved" for
isolated [single] transgressions, but only as a result of the individual's
purification. As Rabbi Akiva states: "Just as a *mikveh* purifies the contaminat-
ed, so does the Holy One, blessed be He, purify Israel." Just as it is impossible for one to immerse himself partially in a *mikveh*, to purify himself limb
by limb — but he must immerse his entire body in the *mikveh*, so too,
regarding the purification of *Yom Kippur*, there can be no atonement for some
transgressions unless the individual undergoes a total purification for all his
transgressions (*Mesorah*, 2 [*Tishrei* 5750], p. 23).

Rabbi Yisrael Salanter would quote the verse, "Let us fall into the Hand
of G-d . . . and let me not fall into the hand of man" (Samuel II 24:14), and
interpret it, "It is better to stumble over the *mitzvoth* between man and G-d
than to stumble over *mitzvoth* between man and man" (Rabbi Dov Katz,
Tenuath HaMussar).

⎰ 906 ⎱   עַד שֶׁלֹּא נִבְחֲרָה אֶרֶץ יִשְׂרָאֵל הָיוּ כָל הָאֲרָצוֹת כְּשֵׁרוֹת לְדִבְּרוֹת

"Before the Land of Israel had been especially chosen, all lands were suitable for [Divine] utterances" (*Mechilta*, Ex. 12:1).

"After the Land of Israel had been chosen, all other lands were eliminated" (ibid.).

Once the Land of Israel was chosen as the site for the people of Israel, this land alone became the seat of prophecy.

Rabbi Yehudah Halevi maintained that the centrality of the Land of Israel in Judaism was confirmed by the fact that all the prophets prophesied either in it or in its behalf. Moreover, he believed that only the Holy Land is suitable for the highest religious experiences (*Kuzari* 2:14).

Cf. *Baba Bathra* 158b, "The climate of the Land of Israel makes one wise." See *Insights*, vol. 1, #11.

Cf. *Va'yikra Rabbah* 13:5, "There is no Torah like the Torah of the Land of Israel and no wisdom like the wisdom of the Land of Israel" See #540.

⎰ 907 ⎱   עַד אַבְרָהָם לֹא הָיָה זִקְנָה

"Until Abraham there was no old age" (*Baba Mezia* 87a).

Until Abraham appeared on the scene, old age did not exist. "Abraham prayed and old age came into existence."

Rabbi Chaim Halberstam, the Sanzer Rav, comments: "We all know that in the 'Higher World,' days in which there is no spiritual growth do not count. They are non-existent. Before Abraham's time the world existed in a spiritual vacuum. Most people frittered away their lives in idle pursuits. Time had no meaning; their days did not count in the 'Higher World.' Abraham, by teaching mankind to believe in G-d, infused spirituality into the world. He made the days and years of temporal life count in the 'Higher World.' Thus, he introduced the concept of old age into the world" (*Divrei Chaim, Chayei Sarah*).

⟦ 908 ⟧

'עַד בְּלִי דָי' . . . עַד שֶׁיִּבְלוּ שִׂפְתוֹתֵיכֶם
מִלּוֹמַר דַי

"'There shall be more than enough' . . . Until your lips grow
weary of saying 'Enough'" (Ta'anith 9a).

This refers to the reward for setting aside *ma'aser* [a tithe]. It is based on
the following scriptural verse: "Bring the full tithe into the storehouse, and
let there be food in My house, and thus put me to the test, said the L-rd of
Hosts, I will surely open the floodgates of the sky for you and pour out for
you a blessing that there shall be more than enough" [Malachi 3:10]. What
does this mean? — Until your lips grow weary of saying, "It is enough."

Rabbi Avraham Mordechai Alter, the *Imrei Emeth*, distinguishes between
wealth which one receives as a reward for giving *ma'aser* and other kinds of
wealth. Regarding the latter, we know that "He who possesses one hundred,
desires two hundred," however, regarding the reward for tithing, one can
say, 'Enough' for it is a blessing that only brings contentment (Rabbi A. Y.
Bromberg, *Rebbes of Ger*, p. 294).

Cf. *Shabbath* 119a, "Give tithes so that you may become wealthy." See
Insights, vol. 1, #448.

Cf. *Koheleth Rabbah* 1:13, "He who possesses one hundred desires two
hundred." See *Insights*, vol. 1, #397.

⟦ 909 ⟧

עַד שֶׁבָּא ר' עֲקִיבָא וְדָרַשׁ 'אֶת ה' אֱלֹקֶיךָ
תִּירָא' לְרַבּוֹת תַּלְמִידֵי חֲכָמִים

"Until Rabbi Akiva came and taught: 'You shall fear *eth* the L-rd
your G-d 'is to include Torah scholars'" (Pesahim 22b).

"Shimon Ha'masoni interpreted every *eth* in the Torah [as an extending
particle]; but as soon as he came to 'You shall fear *Eth Hashem* your G-d'
[Deut. 6:13], he desisted [holding it impossible that this fear should extend
to another]. Said his disciples to him, 'Rebbe, what is to happen with all the
ethim which you have interpreted?' He replied, 'Just as I received reward for

interpreting them, so will I receive reward for separating myself from them [since the *eth* in one verse does not signify extension, it cannot do so elsewhere].' Until R. Akiva came and taught . . ." (ibid.).

Rabbi Mordechai Gifter asks: Wasn't Shimon Ha'masoni as great a scholar as Rabbi Akiva — couldn't he interpret this *eth* as Rabbi Akiva did — why was he forced to retract from all the *ethim* which he interpreted so well? Says Rabbi Gifter, do you know what prompted R. Akiva to interpret this "difficult" verse in the manner in which he did — *Shimon Ha'masoni himself!* He saw this great scholar who was ready to retract all the numerous midrashic interpretations he had compiled over the years, simply because he couldn't in all honesty fit this one *eth* into his midrashic structure. Such Torah scholars as Shimon Ha'masoni are indeed worthy of reverence as an extension of Divine reverence. Hence, "You shall fear *eth* the L-rd your G-d includes Torah scholars."

The Maharal of Prague writes: "Rabbi Akiva did not refrain from expounding 'You shall fear *es* the L-rd your G-d' — your G-d means to include scholars, — for there is no implication of *L-rdship* whatsoever. The [grouping of scholars with G-d] is only in relation to other men. However, He Himself, Who is blessed, is apart from everything, with no co-equality to or association with any being. Only in relationship to other men can a scholar be said to have an association and conjunction with *Hashem Yisborach* [G-d Who is blessed]" (*Nesivos Olam, Nesiv HaTorah*, trans. by Eliakim Wilner, p. 201).

⟦ 910 ⟧ עַד שֶׁלֹּא מַלְתִּי הָיוּ הָעוֹבְרִים וְהַשָּׁבִים בָּאִים
אֶצְלִי, תֹּאמַר: מִשֶּׁמַּלְתִּי אֵינָן בָּאִים אֶצְלִי?

"Before I became circumcised, travellers used to visit me; now that I am circumcised, perhaps they will no longer visit me?" (*Beraishith Rabbah* 47:10).

This was Abraham's fear concerning the mitzvah of *brith milah* (circumcision). He felt that this precept would cause a complete rift with society. People would accuse him of being subhuman and he would no longer be able to influence and convert others to his way of life.

Rabbi Joseph Ber Soloveitchik, in one of his *shiurim* [Torah lectures], points out that indeed, history confirms Abraham's pessimistic prediction. The break between Judaism and Christianity was partly due to the fact that the gentiles refused to circumcise themselves. Throughout history, many more women converted to Judaism than men, simply because they did not have to face that "repugnant" prerequisite of circumcision, which they considered a form of mutilation. Rav Soloveitchik believed that if not for circumcision perhaps most of Western Europe would be Jewish.

Rabbi Soloveitchik concludes his analysis with the following poignant remarks: When Abraham subjected himself to the *mitzvah* of *milah*, his popularity dropped. No one knocked on his door. But suddenly someone knocked — "And G-d appeared to him by the terebinths of Mamre" (Gen. 18:1). This biblical verse portrays the destiny of the Jew as part of the covenantal community — we pay the price of loneliness.

⦙ 911 ⦙ עוּבָּרִין שֶׁבִּמְעֵי אִמָּן אָמְרוּ שִׁירָה עַל הַיָּם

"Embryos in their mother's womb sang the song at the Red Sea" (*Berakoth* 50a).

In the Sabbath morning prayer, *Nishmath*, we declare, "All my bones shall say, 'Hashem, who is like You.'" Further on we declare, "Bless Hashem, O my soul and let all my innermost being bless His holy Name." Why does this prayer initially limit the blessing to "my bones" and then extend the blessing to include "my soul and my innermost being"?

The *Chasam Sofer* raises this question and suggests that the first passage relates to one's prayers in Exile while the second passage applies to prayers recited in the Land of Israel.

Apparently, there are different levels of *shira* [song]. A *shira* may be so pervasive that it passes through your bones. But there is an even greater *shira*, and that is one which reaches the depths of your soul.

This is what the Talmud means when it says that even "the embryo sang the song at the Red Sea." Feelings were so deep and strong that they penetrated into the very womb and inspired the unborn child (Rabbi Bernard Maza, *Insights into the Sidra of the Week* pp. 78, 79).

In this regard it is significant to note Rabbi Shraga Feivel Mendelowitz's

comment on the *tefillah* [prayer] following *Nishmath*:
"By the *mouth* of the upright shall You be lauded;
by the *words* of the righteous shall You be blessed;
by the *tongue* of the devout shall You be exalted;
and by the *inner being* of the holy shall You be sanctified."

The higher the level of the person, the more meaningful the manner in which he praises G-d. While the *upright* praises G-d with his *mouth*, the *righteous* uses articulated *words*. The *devout* uses his *tongue*, implying that the praise comes from within himself. The *holy person*, however, praises G-d with his very essence — his *inner being*" (*The Complete ArtScroll Siddur*).

⦗ 912 ⦘

עוֹלָם הָפוּךְ רָאִיתִי עֶלְיוֹנִים לְמַטָּה
וְתַחְתּוֹנִים לְמַעְלָה

"I saw an upside-down world — the high-placed ones were below and the inferior ones were on top" (*Pesahim* 50a).

Rav Yosef the son of Rav Yehoshua ben Levi became ill and fell into a trance. When he recovered, his father asked him, 'What did you see' [in the World to Come]?" He answered, that those who are honored in this world will be lightly esteemed in the next world and vice versa.

Rabbi Eliyahu Eliezer Dessler writes: "In the World to Come an intelligent, sharp-witted fellow who with faultless memory has amassed an encyclopedic amount of Torah knowledge will not be highly regarded. Conversely, a dull-witted person, with a weak memory and minimal intellectual achievement, who exerted himself, straining every nerve to learn Torah, will enjoy great prominence in the World to Come . . . The upshot is that in the next world a bright fellow who does not study intensely will be a dullard, while the ambitious, hardworking student will be the brilliant one, for this is the reward of his diligence" (*Michtav MeEliyahu*, vol. 3, "On Laboring for Torah").

〖 913 〗

עוֹלָמְךָ תִּרְאֶה בְּחַיֶּיךָ

"May you see your world in your lifetime" (*Berakoth* 17a).

As the Rabbis departed from the school of R. Ammi, they said to him: 'May you see your world . . . i.e., may you see your requirements provided in your lifetime (Rashi).

Rabbi Elimelech of Lizhensk interprets the above rabbinical blessing in a metaphysical vein. "May you experience the delights of the *World to Come* in your lifetime."

"The *tzaddik* attaches himself to eternal life, and even when he is in this world he experiences the delight of the *Upper World* and of eternal life. That is what the *Gemara* means when it says [as an expression of blessing] 'May you see your [eternal] world in your lifetime — that through all your deeds and movements being done with holiness and purity, with *d'vekuth* and joy, and with love and fear of G-d, you will experience the delight of the *Upper World* in this world (*Noam Elimelech, Terumah*).

〖 914 〗

עוֹמְדִים צְפוּפִים וּמִשְׁתַּחֲוִים רְוָחִים

"The people stood closely pressed together, yet they prostrated themselves amid ample room" (*Aboth* 5:7).

This is one of the "ten miracles that were wrought for our ancestors in the Sanctuary."

Cf. *Beraishith Rabbah* 5:7, "When they bowed down each person had four cubits, a cubit on each side, so that none should hear his neighbor's prayer."

"They could prostrate themselves amid ample room for within the Sanctuary space was 'supernatural.' Those who prostrated themselves in the Holy Temple had reached such a degree of purity that they did not occupy natural space" (Maharal miPrague, intro. to *Gevuroth HaShem*).

In a homiletical interpretation of the above miracle, Rabbi Menachem Mendel of Kotzk said: "If a person *stands* with false pride, haughty and arrogant, then *he will always feel cramped*. There is never enough room for him. Every bit of the surrounding space is filled with his contemptuous snobbery. When he is ready *to bend*, however — to bow his head in humility — a spirit of relief enters him and *he is enveloped in a feeling of spaciousness*. No longer crowded, he becomes a more satisfied individual" (Rabbi Ephraim Oratz, . . . *And Nothing But The Truth*, p. 122).

◊ 915 ◊   עַז פָּנִים לְגֵיהִנֹּם

"The bold-faced are [destined] for *Gehinnom*" (*Aboth* 5:23).

"What is bold-facedness? Transgressing in the sight of men and not being ashamed . . . walking erect and with a thrust-out forehead and not being ashamed" (Rabbeinu Yechiel b' R. Yekuthiel, *Ma'aloth Hamiddoth*).

See *Kallah Rabbathi* ch. 2 where the Talmud asks: "What if the bold-faced one repents [does he still go to *Gehinnom*?]. To which the answer is given: "There is no repentance for the bold-faced."

See, however, *Yerushalmi, Pe'ah* 1:1, Nothing stands in the way of those who wish to repent." How do we reconcile this statement with the dictum that "there is no repentance for the bold-faced"?

The Chafetz Chaim resolves the "contradiction" by raising another question. "Why does the Mishnah [above] say that only the bold-faced go to *Gehinnom* — are there not other people who commit various transgressions and are also destined to go there?"

"The answer is," says the Chafetz Chaim, "that the *Mishnah* is teaching us what we can expect of a sinner. An ordinary sinner will most likely repent. But those who are brazen, will, in all probability, never repent. Bold-facedness is a personality trait, it is not a specific sin; and this characteristic leads to sinning in general" (R' Paysach Krohn, *The Maggid Speaks*, p. 179).

916

עַיִן רָעָה וְרוּחַ גְּבוֹהָה וְנֶפֶשׁ רְחָבָה מִתַּלְמִידָיו שֶׁל בִּלְעָם הָרָשָׁע

"An evil eye, an arrogant spirit, and an insatiable soul are the traits of the disciples of the wicked Balaam" (*Aboth* 5:22).

Rabbi Menachem Mendel of Kotzk once asked: "Why didn't Balaam convert to Judaism considering his prophecy foretelling the greatness that the future holds for the Jewish people?"

His answer was based on the [above] dictum which points to Balaam's arrogant spirit. His haughtiness prevented him from accepting the truth, even when it was for his benefit (Rabbi Ephraim Oratz, . . . *And Nothing But The Truth*, p. 58).

See previous *mamor*, "The bold-faced are [destined] for *Gehinnom*."

917

עִיקַּר שִׁירָה בַּפֶּה

"The essential feature of the [Temple] music is the vocal singing" (*Sukkah* 50b).

There is a dispute amongst the sages concerning "the song" that accompanied the sacrifices [when the libation of wine was offered in connection with the continual morning and evening offerings]. R. Yose is of the opinion that "the essential feature of the music is the *instrument*" and the Rabbis maintain that "the essential feature of the music is the vocal singing" (ibid.).

Rambam codifies the halacha according to the Rabbis. " . . . There were never less than twelve Levites standing on the platform daily to chant during the sacrificial service . . . They sang by word of mouth alone, without instrument, because the essential feature of the singing is vocal music" (*Mishneh Torah*, Hil. Klei HaMikdash 3:3).

Rabbi Abraham Chill suggests a psychological rationale for the above dictum. "Under no circumstances can the mechanical robot-like manifestations of human expression be placed on the same plane as personal and intrinsic involvement. The mere mechanics can be cold, abstract, and withdrawn; personal involvement bespeaks warmth, closeness and passion" (*The Sidrot*, p. 65).

Cf. *Arakhin* 11a, "Whence do we know from the Torah the principle for the obligation of song? . . . from 'Because you would not serve G-d your L-rd with joy and gladness of the heart' (Deut. 28:47). Which is the service 'with joy and gladness of the heart'? You must say it is song."

It is significant to note that when Rabbi Shneur Zalman of Liadi was asked why he did not include *Shabbos zemiros* [songs] in his *Siddur*, he said, "Song must come from the heart, not from the *siddur*. If you sing only because it is written in the siddur, it is not true *zemiros*" (Rabbi Abraham J. Twersky).

〔 918 〕   עַל כָּל נְשִׁימָה וּנְשִׁימָה שֶׁאָדָם נוֹשֵׁם צָרִיךְ
לְקַלֵּס לַבּוֹרֵא

"For every single breath which a man breathes he should praise his Creator" (*Beraishith Rabbah* 14:9).

Rabbi Zechariah Fendel comments: "It is certainly difficult, if not entirely impossible, for an individual who is in robust health to appreciate the full significance of this remark. An individual, however, who has observed the suffering of a loved one who experienced a heart attack, empathizing with him as he lay gasping painfully for each and every breath, will begin to appreciate the deeper significance of the words of our sages."

"Similarly, Maimonides observes that the munificent kindness of the Almighty may be seen in the fact that those items which are indispensable to life, such as air, water, and food, are found cheaply and in abundance, while items which are less vital to life are often rare and expensive" (*Moreh Nevuchim* III, 12, *Anvil of Sinai*, p. 52).

◊ 919 ◊ עַל מָה קְטוֹרֶת מְכַפֶּרֶת עַל לְשׁוֹן הָרַע, יָבֹא דָבָר שֶׁבַּחֲשַׁאי וִיכַפֵּר עַל מַעֲשֶׂה חֲשַׁאי

"Why does incense obtain atonement for [the sin of] the evil tongue? Let that which is [performed] in secret [in the Holy of Holies] come and obtain atonement
for what is committed in secret" (*Yoma* 44a).

When the High Priest entered the Holy of Holies on *Yom Kippur*, he burnt incense before he performed any of the other services. This is meant to teach us a lesson. When we wish to mend our ways and repent, we must rectify our speech before anything else (R. Yisrael Meir Kagan, *Shmirath HaLashon* 2:5).

Cf. *Arakhin* 15b, "What is the remedy for slanderers? If he is a scholar, let him engage in the Torah, as it is said: 'The healing tongue is the tree of life' [Prov. 15:4] . . . and tree of life means only Torah . . . If he is an *am ha'aretz* [unlearned person] let him humble himself."

◊ 920 ◊ עַם הָאָרֶץ אָסוּר לֶאֱכוֹל בְּשַׂר בְּהֵמָה

"The *am ha'aretz* [unlearned person] may not partake of meat" (*Pesahim* 49b).

"For it is said, 'This is the law of the animal, and the fowl . . . ' " [Lev. 11:46]: whoever engages in [the study of] the Law is permitted to eat the flesh of animals and fowl, but whoever does not engage in [the study of] the Law may not eat the flesh of animals and fowl" (ibid.).

Rabbeinu Nissim, citing R. Sherira Gaon, explains that an *am ha'aretz* should refrain from eating meat because he has no knowledge of *shechita* [ritual slaughtering] and of examining the internal organs.

The *Maharsha* comments on the talmudic omission of any restriction upon the eating of fish, even though reference to "every living being that moves in the waters" is made in the very same scriptural verse that mentions animals and fowl. Says the *Maharsha*, that only the preparation of animal and fowl meat requires meticulous study of the complex dietary regulations. Consequently, the *am ha'aretz* who has no knowledge of these dietary laws is not permitted to eat the flesh of animals and fowl.

"This text has also been understood homiletically as underscoring the lesson that man was created to study Torah and that, should he fail to do so, he remains in a spiritual state analogous to that of lower animals. Since such a person has not developed his unique spiritual potential as a human being, he should not regard himself as endowed with superiority vis-à-vis members of the animal kingdom" (Rabbi J. David Bleich, *Contemporary Halachic Problems*, vol. III, p. 239).

〖 921 〗 עָמַד וְהִקְרִיב שׁוֹר שֶׁקַּרְנָיו קוֹדְמִין לִפְרָסוֹתָיו

"He arose and offered up a bullock whose horns were developed before its hoofs" (*Abodah Zarah* 8a).

"On the day that Adam was created, he saw the setting of the sun, and exclaimed, 'Woe is me, because I have offended, the world around me is becoming dark and is turning again to void and desolation — this is the death to which I have been sentenced from Heaven!' He sat up all night fasting and weeping and Eve opposite him. When dawn broke, he said: 'This is the usual course of the world.' He arose and offered . . ." (ibid.).

Rabbi Moshe A. Amiel comments: "The above [Midrash] contains a vivid commentary on the descendants of Adam and Eve who sit and weep and find no joy in this world . . . For the source of the continual dissatisfaction, envy and striving of man, is to be found in the Tree of Knowledge . . . 'And their eyes were opened and they knew that they were naked.' Until now they had been tranquil and contented with their lot, envying no creature . . . Then the poison entered their minds; their eyes were opened to seeking after vanity . . . They made themselves girdles of fig leaves . . . But the old tranquility had gone and a morbid spirit of unhealthy striving had taken its place.

"And so, 'the sun set upon him' . . . and when he sought the cause of his darkness he realized that it was because 'he had put the horn before the hoofs.' Every ox has hoofs to take up a firm stand on the ground, and horns to ward off attacks on his repose, but whereas the natural order is that first come the hoofs and then the horns, in Adam's case, since the animals were created fully grown, the horns came before the hoofs . . .

"The same principles animate man, the desire to go 'one better' on his neighbor, to have just that 'fig-leaf' which his neighbor does not possess . . . His position in the world ought to be 'the hoofs before the horns,' the establishing of *himself* before emulation of *others*" (*Derashoth El-Ami*, p. 3).

〔 922 〕

עָסַקְתָּ בִּפְרִיָּה וּרְבִיָּה

"Did you engage in procreation?" (*Shabbath* 31a).

"When man is led in for judgment he is asked . . . 'Did you engage in procreation?'" (ibid.).

"We are commanded to be fruitful and multiply for the perpetuation of the species" (Rambam, *Sefer HaMitzvoth*, #212).

"To fulfill this mitzvah, a man must beget at least one son and one daughter" (*Mishneh Torah*, Hil. Ishuth 15:4).

According to the *Minchath Chinnuch*, this *mitzvah* can only be fulfilled with the birth of two viable children. The act of cohabitation is only a *hechsher mitzvah* [preparatory to the commandment].

Reb Elya Pruzhaner, however, maintains that the essence of this *mitzvah* is the act of cohabitation itself, for not everyone is blessed with the ability of begetting children. The requirement of having a son and daughter merely serves as an exemption. With this interpretation of the *mitzvah* of procreation, the phraseology in the Heavenly question is proper and precise — "*did you engage* in procreation" i.e. "in trying" to have children, and not "did you fulfill the mitzvah of having children" (*Halichoth Eliezer*).

Cf. *Megillah* 13a, "Anyone who brings up an orphan boy or girl in his house, Scripture accounts it as if he had begotten him." see *Taz, Yoreh De'ah* 242, who maintains that raising an orphan in one's house is an actual fulfillment of the first commandment *pru ur'vu* ["be fruitful and multiply"].

See #736.

❲ 923 ❳   עֲרֵבִים עָלַי דִּבְרֵי דוֹדֶיךָ יוֹתֵר מִיֵּינָהּ שֶׁל
תּוֹרָה

"The words of Your beloved [the sages] are sweeter to me than
the wine of Torah" (*Abodah Zarah* 35a).

This is a midrashic interpretation of "For Your love is better than wine"
[Song of Songs 1:2]. Such is the proclamation of Israel before the Almighty.

Rabbi Zechariah Fendel asks: "How can this be? Is it possible that the
fence which protects the garden is more precious than the garden itself? . . .
No, indeed not! However, the Rabbis are making us aware of the deeper
significance of rabbinic law. By taking such painstaking measures to safeguard the Law, the Rabbis have not only manifested profound awe and
reverence for the Law, but they have also imparted a deep-rooted yearning
within the Jewish soul for compliance with the Will of the Creator, as
manifested in His Torah law.

"Therefore, while scrupulous compliance with the wine of Torah will
certainly manifest the individual's fear of the Almighty, compliance with
rabbinic law — with full awareness of its role as a precautionary safeguard
surrounding the law itself — will manifest the even nobler emotion of *ahavas
HaShem* — the love of the Creator. It is in this sense that the ordinances of
the Rabbis are sweeter than the wine of the Torah" (*Anvil of Sinai*, p. 262).

Cf. *Aboth* 1:1, "Make a hedge around the Torah." See *Insights*, vol. 1,
#447.

Cf. *Beraishith Rabbah* 19:3, "You shall not make the fence more than the
principle thing, lest it fall and destroy the plants."

‖ 924 ‖ עָשָׂה אַבְרָהָם אָבִינוּ אֶת כָּל הַתּוֹרָה כּוּלָהּ עַד שֶׁלֹא נִיתְּנָה

"Abraham our patriarch observed the whole Torah before it was given" (*Kiddushin* 82a).

The Maharal miPrague maintained that the patriarchs Isaac and Jacob observed only the positive commandments but not the prohibitions. Abraham was the only patriarch to observe the Divine laws, both positive and negative in their entirety (*Gur Aryeh* 46:6).

Rabbi Yechiel Michel, the Zlotchover Maggid writes: "Abraham was always conscious of G-d, and any action that would disrupt his attachment to G-d, he refrained from doing, any action that he saw which would increase his attachment to G-d, he performed as a *mitzvah*" (*Yeshuoth Malko*, p. 100).

Rabbi Chaim of Volozhin explains that the patriarchs observed the Torah before it was given not as binding commandments but as guides to achieve the proper *tikkun* [perfection]. Occasionally, they sought to achieve their desired goal through non-halachic means. After the Revelation at Mount Sinai, however, the Torah became legally binding and no exemptions were permitted on the basis of mystical insights (*Nefesh HaChaim* 1:22).

Rabbi Nachman of Breslov feared that the Gentiles would take him to a place where there were no other Jews, and he was concerned about fulfilling the commandments in such a place. After a while, the solution came to him. He would still be able to serve G-d even if he could not observe the *mitzvoth*, for he had grasped the manner of the Divine service of the patriarchs. Prior to the Revelation, they fulfilled all the commandments even though they could not observe them literally. In the course of time, he was able to perceive all the mitzvoth in this manner (*Shivchei HaRan*, no. 23).

⎮ 925 ⎮ עֲשֵׂה דְבָרִים לְשֵׁם פעלם וְדַבֵּר בָּהֶם לִשְׁמָם

"Do [good] deeds for the sake of their Maker, and speak of them
for their own sake" (*Nedarim* 62a).

"Do deeds for the sake of פָּעֳלָם, the Holy One, blessed be He, who
decreed them" (*Ran*).

"Do deeds for פָּעֳלָם, the *performance of them*," i.e., for the sake of doing
good" (Bachya ben Yosef ibn Pakuda, *Chovoth Halvavoth*, intro.).

"And speak of them for their own sake" — All your words and study in
Torah should be for the sake of Torah — in order to increase your knowl-
edge and deepen your understanding of the profundities of the Torah
(Rosh).

Rabbi Chaim of Volozhin cites the above Rosh to substantiate his thesis
that "*Torah Lishmah*" [Torah for its own sake] means exactly what the words
imply, in contrast to the Baal Shem Tov who maintained that *Torah Lishmah*
signifies studying with *d'vekuth*, i.e., an emotional awakening of the attachment of the student's soul to the Creator (*Nefesh HaChaim*, part IV).

Cf. *Aboth* 6:1, "He who occupies himself with the Torah for its own sake,
acquires many things." See *Insights*, vol. 1, #244.

⎮ 926 ⎮ עֲשֵׂה דּוֹחֶה לֹא תַעֲשֶׂה

"A positive commandment overrides a negative commandment"
(*Shabbath* 132b).

"A positive commandment issues forth from the attribute of love to that
of mercy, for he who does his master's command is beloved of him and his
master shows him mercy . . . A negative commandment goes to the attribute
of justice and issues forth from that of fear, for he who guards himself from
doing anything which does not please his master does so out of fear for him.

"It is for this reason that a positive commandment is greater than a
negative commandment, just as love is greater than fear, for he who fulfills
and observes the will of his master with his body and his possessions is

greater than he who guards himself from doing that which is not pleasing to him. This is why the Rabbis have said that a positive commandment overrides a negative commandment" (Ramban, *Commentary on the Torah*, Ex. 20:8).

The Vilna Gaon writes: "Failing to fulfill a positive commandment is worse than transgressing a negative commandment. As our sages have written, 'When a man sits idle and fails to fulfill a positive commandment, he transgresses a sin every second,' whereas transgressing a negative commandment is a sin only during the transgression" (*Even Sheleimah*, ch. 5:9).

See *Biur HaGra, Mishlei* 5:22.

According to the Kotzker Rebbe, "Every positive mitzvah dictates *'be wise'* and every negative mitzvah shouts, *'do not be a fool.'* Perhaps, we may homiletically assert that "the wisdom" of a positive commandment *overshadows* "the foolishness" arising from the violation of a negative commandment (S. W.).

927 עֲשֵׂה עַד שֶׁאַתָּה מוֹצֵא וּמָצוּי לְךָ וְעוֹדְךָ בְּיָדְךָ

"Perform [charity] while you can find, while you have the opportunity and while it is still in your hand" (*Shabbath* 151b).

"Give charity while you can still find someone to give it to; while you still have the money; and while it is still in your possession — before you die" (Rashi).

The Chafetz Chaim writes that this also applies to the mitzvah of supporting Torah scholars. Inasmuch as "Torah is destined to be forgotten in Israel" [*Shabbath* 138b], one should therefore give *tzedakah* and support Torah scholars while they are still to be found.

"While it is still in your hand," i.e., do not rely on the "will" you hope to make directing your children to give to *yeshivoth* for it often happens that the desire for money leads man to violate the trust of his Creator and the trust of his father (*Chomas Hadas*).

Cf. *Kethuboth* 66b, "The preservation of wealth is in its distribution." See *Insights*, vol. 1, #408.

Cf. *Shabbath* 119a, "Give tithes so that you may become wealthy." See
Insights, vol. 1, #448.

〗 928 〖 עֵשָׂו מִדַּעַת עַצְמוֹ הוּא הוֹרֵג אֲבָל זֶה מִדַּעַת סַנְהֶדְרִין הוּא הוֹרֵג

"Esau slew by his own volition, whereas he [David] would slay
only on the volition of the Sanhedrin" (*Beraishith Rabbah* 63:8).

When the prophet Samuel went to anoint David king of Israel, he saw
that David had a ruddy complexion. He was smitten with fear thinking that
he too [like Esau who was ruddy] might be a murderer. The Almighty,
however, reassured him that David would only slay on the sentence of the
Sanhedrin.

The Vilna Gaon makes the following observation: "A person should not
go completely against his nature even if it is bad, for he will not succeed. He
should merely train himself to follow the straight path in accordance with
his nature. For example, someone who has an inclination to spill blood
should train himself to be a *shochet* or a *mohel* (*Even Sheleimah*).

Cf. *Shabbath* 156a, "He who is born under [the planetary influence of]
Mars, will be a shedder of blood. R. Ashi observed: Either a surgeon, a
thief, a [ritual] slaughterer, or a circumciser."

〗 929 〖 'עָשִׂיתִי כְּכֹל אֲשֶׁר צִוִּיתָנִי' — שָׂמַחְתִּי וְשִׂמַּחְתִּי בּוֹ

"'I have done entirely as You have commanded me' — I have
rejoiced and I have given joy to others therewith"
(*Ma'aser Sheni* 5:12).

This is the final statement in the 'avowal' to be recited when giving the
tithe at the end of each three-year cycle. The Torah states: "When you have
finished tithing all the tithes of your produce in the third year, the year of

tithing, and you give it to the Levite, the stranger, the orphan, and the widow, . . . Then shall you say before the presence of G-d your G-d: 'I have cleared away that which is holy from the house . . .'" [Deut. 26:12-14].

Rabbi Samson R. Hirsch writes: "Concern for the welfare of one's needy neighbor was seen as a direct result of the landowner's enjoyment of his own harvest before G-d, and the Jew was taught not to rejoice in his personal happiness before G-d without first having done everything in his own power to give practical aid to his less fortunate brother, 'I have rejoiced and I have given joy also to others'" (*The Pentateuch*, Deut. 15:1).

Homiletically speaking, we may transpose the above two aspects of rejoicing to read: *simachti v'samachti* — "I have given joy to others, consequently, I have also rejoiced." One experiences personal *simchah* only after he dispenses it to others.

Moreover, it may be suggested that true *simchah* can only be achieved for oneself as well as for others if one can truthfully say, "I have done entirely as You have commanded me" (S.W.).

⎰ 930 ⎱

עָתִיד הַקָּדוֹשׁ בָּרוּךְ הוּא לַעֲשׂוֹת מָחוֹל
לַצַּדִּיקִים וְהוּא יוֹשֵׁב בֵּינֵיהֶם בְּגַן עֵדֶן

"In the days to come the Holy One, blessed be He, will hold a *machol* for the righteous, and He will sit in their midst in the Garden of Eden" (*Ta'anith* 31a).

"*Machol*" means "encircled" (Rashi). The righteous will revolve in a circle around the Almighty.

Rabbi Akiva Eiger explains that in this world every *tzaddik* worships the Almighty in his own manner, and the way of one righteous person is unlike that of another. In the days to come however, it will be revealed that all these ways are in reality one — all revolve about one central point, as does a circle. This is the *machol* that the Almighty will make for the righteous — that they will revolve in a circle about one point — the Holy One, blessed be He — which is the Truth" (Rabbi Y. L. Eger, *Toras Emes*, vol. 2, 101a).

❘ 931 ❘ עָתִיד הַקָּדוֹשׁ בָּרוּךְ הוּא לַעֲשׂוֹת צֵל לְבַעֲלֵי מִצְווֹת בְּצִלָּהּ שֶׁל בַּעֲלֵי תּוֹרָה

"The Holy One, blessed be He, will prepare a 'protection' for
those who carry out *mitzvoth* [of supporting Torah study] through
the 'protection' afforded to the masters of Torah"
(*Yerushalmi, Sotah* 7:4).

"The reward for those who support the Torah is equal to those who are
occupied in the study of the Torah. For the Torah 'is a tree of life for those
who support it' [Prov. 3:18]. The verse does not say 'for those that study it'
but 'for those who support it'" (*Pnei Moshe*, ad loc.).

Cf. *Va'yikra Rabbah* 25:1, "If a man has not learned Torah, and has neither
performed, observed, nor taught to others, but, though he had not the
means to maintain scholars, yet did maintain them, and though not strong
enough to protest yet protested, he is on this account included in the term
'blessed.'"

Cf. *Midrash Tanchuma, Va'yechi* II, "Zevulun is [always] placed before
Yissachar because they formed a partnership. Zevulun would occupy himself
in trade and Yissachar in Torah study [and they would share in the benefits
of each]. In this manner did Moshe bless them,' Rejoice Zevulun in your
going out [for trade in ships] and Yissachar in your tents [of Torah].' If not
for Zevulun, Yissachar would be unable to occupy himself in Torah."

Cf. *Hullin* 92a, "Were it not for the leaves the clusters could not exist."
See #519.

פ

⟦ 932 ⟧

פּוּק חֲזִי מַאי עַמָּא דְּבַר

"Go out and see how people conduct themselves" (*Berakoth* 45a).

Cf. *Yerushalmi, Pe'ah 7:3; Yebamoth 7:3*, "If the application of a law is uncertain in the Court and you do not know what its nature is, go and see how the community acts, and do likewise."

This talmudic principle, "Go out and see how the people conduct themselves," is cited by the Sephardic Chief Rabbi of Tel Aviv, Rav Chaim David HaLevi, in support of his and Rabbi Eliezer Waldenberg's "lenient" ruling regarding the prohibition of *Yichud* [a man and a woman being alone] in the situation of adoptive parents and their children.

As a matter of common practice, pious Jews adopt children and raise them as their own without adhering to the restrictions of *yichud* (Rabbi Azarya Berzon, *Journal of Halacha and Contemporary Society*, no. 13 [Spring 1987]: 107-112).

See Rabbi Eliezer Waldenberg, *Tzitz Eliezer*, vol. VI, pp. 226-228 and Rabbi Chaim David HaLevi, *Aseh Lecha Rav*, pp. 194-201. See also *Iggereth Moshe, Even HaEzer*, vol. IV, 64:2.

There are, however, many halachic authorities who are not as "lenient" regarding adopted children.

Cf. *Pesahim 66a*, "Leave it to Israel, if they are not prophets, yet they are children of prophets."

〚 933 〛

פְּלְגָּא בִּרְקִיעָא לָא יָהֲבִי

"Heavenly gifts are not given us on a half-way basis" (*Yoma* 69b).

See the talmudic discussion regarding the impropriety of requesting that the Evil Inclination function only for legitimate purposes. [Cf. *Beraishith Rabbah* 4:7, "'And behold, it was very good' — this refers to the Evil Inclination . . . But for the Evil Inclination no man would build a house, take a wife and beget children"]. The Talmud proclaims that "heavenly gifts are not given on a half-way basis." To ask that the Evil Inclination should live, but not tempt man to sin is to ask a thing which Heaven will not grant.

In expounding upon the above dictum, Rabbi Abraham Isaac Kook writes: "Every attribute of greatness is tied up with defects which correspond to it . . . All forces are created to have universal sway, and this is man's vocation: to exercise care in choosing his path so that the general force shall serve the good and not the evil. The great among the ancient masters already observed this, that the remarkable power of memory will recall to a person all the wisdom and the good he has observed, but also all the folly and the evil. This is true of all forces acting in the self. Thus the defect cleaves to them by their very nature. Inevitably, therefore, the greatest thoughts and the most precious dispositions are tied in with defects of corresponding dimensions" (*Iggrot* I, Letter 93).

〚 934 〛

פְּלְפֵּלְתָּ בְּחָכְמָה

"Did you engage in the dialectics of wisdom?" (*Shabbath* 31a).

This is one of the questions asked of man when he is led in for judgment.

"When man is led in for judgment he is asked, 'Did you conduct your business with faith; did you establish set times for studying Torah; did you engage in procreation; did you hope for salvation; did you engage in the dialectics of wisdom; did you understand one thing from another?'" (ibid.).

Why was it necessary to inquire of man if he was engaged in the "pilpul" [dialectics] of Torah wisdom after having asked him if he had established set times for Torah study? Why does *pilpul* loom so significantly on the Day of Judgment?

Rabbi Eliyahu E. Dessler suggests that the answer to this question may lie in the following rabbinic maxim: "The Holy One, blessed be He, rejoices *b'pilpulah d'ohraisah* [in the dialectics of the Torah]." "Simchah," Rabbi Dessler explains, "comes about when that which we lack and strongly desire, is acquired. The Almighty [so to speak] rejoices when His creation [which is lacking] is made 'complete' through the engagement of His creatures in *chiddushim* [Torah novelle]. The 'novel thought' [*chiddush*] which we 'discover' in our deep penetration of the Torah, awakens within us a love for Torah which otherwise would be lacking. Without this 'novel analysis' the Torah would appear 'old' and archaic, but now the Torah remains ever 'new' and vital. Hence, novelle and dialectics not only help us understand the Torah, but they instill within us a fundamental principle [of Judaism] — the enhancement of love of Torah and *mitzvoth* and the fear of Heaven" (*Michtav MeEliyahu*, vol. 4, p. 340).

See Insights, vol. 1, #115.

Cf. *Tosefta Ohaloth* 16:4, "One who studies [Torah] and does not toil in it, is like one who sows but does not reap." See #660.

⌡ 935 ⌠   פְּנֵיהֶם אִישׁ אֶל אָחִיו . . . פְּנֵיהֶם לַבָּיִת

"They faced each other . . . their faces were turned toward the house" (*Baba Bathra* 99a).

The Talmud cites a discrepancy between the scriptural verses regarding the structural position of the *Cherubim* in the Sanctuary. In Exodus 25:20, the Torah states that the *Cherubim* should be made "facing each other," while in Chronicles II 3:13, Scripture records "their faces were turned toward the house." The Talmud reconciles the two verses in the following manner. "Facing each other" alludes to when Israel obeys the Will of G-d and "their faces were turned to the house" alludes to when Israel did not obey G-d's Will.

Rabbi Yitzchok Elchanan Spector suggests that the direction of the Cherubim's faces, towards one another or towards the house reflects the attitude of one Jew towards his fellow Jew, i.e., "facing each other" implies taking an interest in one another, while "faces were turned to the house" implies being concerned only with the needs of one's house — turning a deaf ear to the suffering of others (*Torah Treasures*, p. 198).

Cf. *Baba Bathra* 99a, "The Cherubim stood by a miracle." See *Insights*, vol. 1, #327.

See next *mamor*.

⬩ 936 ⬩

פָּנָיו לְמַעְלָה סִימָן יָפֶה לוֹ . . . פָּנָיו כְּלַפֵּי
הָעָם סִימָן יָפֶה לוֹ

[If a man dies with] "his face upwards, it is a good omen [his face downwards it is a bad omen]; his face towards the public, it is a good omen, [towards the wall it is a bad omen]" (*Kethuboth* 103b).

"If one's entire life points upwards, in that he continually strives to elevate himself to reach higher and higher levels of spirituality, that indeed is a good omen for him. If one, however, faces downward — continually giving vent to his earthly passions and appetites, that is a bad omen for him.

"If one lives his life facing the public, i.e., striving for their welfare and spiritual elevation, that is a good omen for him. However, if he 'faces the wall' of his house [and is only concerned with his own welfare], that is a bad omen for him" (Rabbi Reuven Margolies, *Devarim B'ittam*, p. 96).

See preceding *mamor*.

⬩ 937 ⬩

פְּסִיעָה גַסָּה נוֹטֶלֶת אֶחָד מֵחֲמֵשׁ מֵאוֹת
מִמְּאוֹר עֵינָיו שֶׁל אָדָם

"A long stride takes away a five hundredth part of the light of a man's eyes" (*Shabbath* 113b).

"It is restored to him by the evening *Kiddush*" (ibid.). A hasty step reduces the light of a person's eyes and it is regained at *Kiddush*.

Rabbi Avraham Chaim Feuer writes: "The man who is engrossed in the frantic pursuit of all that he sees around him is doomed to lose sight of the candle that burns within him ['The candle of the L-rd is the soul of man . . .' (Prov. 20:27)]. Only the serene sanctity of the Sabbath, its tranquil cessation of activity and hot pursuit, can restore to man his awareness of the precious inner light of his vision and his soul" ("The Age of Illumination," *The Jewish Observer* 7, no. 2 [Dec. 1970]: 8).

938 〗 פְּעָמִים שֶׁבְּטוּלָהּ שֶׁל תּוֹרָה זֶהוּ יְסוּדָהּ

"There are times when setting aside Torah, preserves it"
(*Menachoth* 99a).

"This rabbinical teaching has numerous applications. Although one is aware that Torah is the lifeline of the Jew, he realizes that there are times when one must absent himself from Torah study and devotion for a while. He does this so that he will later be able to return to his study and devotion with renewed commitment and vigor" (Rabbi Chaim Kramer).

"When the Chafetz Chaim was studying in Minsk [in his early twenties] he fell ill and was compelled to return home. There the doctors ordered him to give up his studies for a while. For over a year he did not open a single holy volume, because concentration and serious thought were difficult for him. Even in prayer he was unable to contain and focus his mind, to reflect on the words" (Rabbi Moses M. Yoshor, *The Chafetz Chaim*, vol. 1, p. 85).

I have been told that, nevertheless, the Chafetz Chaim was able to master *Tanach* during that "difficult" year!

939 〗 פִּרְקוֹ נָאֶה: זֶה שֶׁלֹּא יָצָא לוֹ שֵׁם רַע בְּיַלְדָתוֹ

"His youth was unblemished: This is one against whom no evil reputation has gone forth in his youth" (*Ta'anith* 16b).

One of the qualifications of a "Reader" on a fast day is that he be one "whose youth was unblemished."

Before the *Musaf* service on *Rosh Hashanah* and *Yom Kippur* the "Reader" recites a personal prayer in which he beseeches the Almighty to accept his prayers "like the prayers of an experienced elder, and one whose youth was unblemished . . . "

In the twelfth century, one of the questions addressed to R. Yosef Ibn Migash was regarding a "Reader" who was about to be elected by a congregation but was objected to by some members on the grounds of a rumor that he had been a sinner in his youth.

In his responsum, Ibn Migash asserts that if there is a rumor that he is a sinner now, he should not be appointed. However, if it concerned transgressions which he committed in his youth, he is not to be disqualified, for even if the rumor were true, you can be certain that he has now repented. The talmudic dictum which disqualifies even such a person refers only to a "Reader" on a public fast day, for which function a special piety is required. *Teshuvah* [repentance] is accepted by the Almighty and a "Reader" must not be rejected for sins of which he has now repented" (Responsum no. 95).

⦗ 940 ⦘

פְּשׁוֹט נְבֵילְתָּא בְּשׁוּקָא וּשְׁקִיל אַגְרָא וְלָא
תֵּימָא כָּהֲנָא אֲנָא וְגַבְרָא רַבָּא
וְסָנְיָא בִּי מִלְּתָא

"Skin a carcass in the marketplace and earn wages and do not say,
'I am a *Kohen* and a great man and it is beneath my dignity'"
(*Pesahim* 113a).

Although it is embarrassing when one flays carcasses of dead animals in public, it is better than being dependent on others for support, for that is a defect in the very being of a person. An individual's excellence is in being self-sufficient, and not in a state of want. When one is dependent on other people he is an incomplete person. For this reason our sages said: "Skin a carcass in the marketplace . . ." (Rabbi Judah Loew of Prague, *Nesivoth Olam*).

"Our sages taught that one should never refuse to earn an honest living by engaging in manual labor with the attitude that such work is degrading for so important and noble a person as himself . . . 'Skin a carcass . . . .'

"Today, many have turned this teaching upside-down. They 'skin a carcass' in a marketplace with relish, not to earn the bare necessities of life, but to have extravagant luxuries; and they certainly do say 'I am a great man.' In fact, they declare, 'I am a great person and I simply must have every luxury, commensurate with my position!'" (Rabbi Menachem M. Schneerson, A Thought For The Week, vol. 8, p. 6).

⌂ 941 ⌂

פְּתַח פִּיךָ לְאִלֵּם

"Open your mouth for the dumb"
(Baba Bathra 41a, based on Prov. 31:8).

There are times when a litigant does not know how to argue his case, i.e., he is "dumb" in a figurative sense. In such cases the Judge should suggest an "argument" for him on the principle of "Open your mouth for the dumb."

On the scriptural admonition, "You shall not pervert the justice due to a stranger or to an orphan . . . " [Deut. 24:18] the Sforno comments: "At the time of argument, be careful [in dealing with] these [litigants] that their claim not be 'closed off' due to their humble standing. [Indeed,] under proper circumstances [you should fulfill the precept of] 'Open your mouth for the dumb.'"

In his explanatory notes on the Sforno, Rabbi Raphael Pelcovitz writes: "This concept is found in the Talmud in a number of cases such as a woman's claim for payment of her kesubah [Kethuboth 36a], and suggesting to one in possession of property that he should claim he had a shtar [deed], but had lost it [Baba Bathra 41a] and also in suggesting to a creditor that he write a pruzbul which would permit him to collect a debt after the Sabbatical year [Gittin 37b]. The responsibility of the court to suggest these claims to one of the parties, if they are otherwise unaware of those suggestions, is based on the [principle] 'Open your mouth for the dumb'" (Sforno, trans. vol. 2, p. 830).

צ

[942]

צַדִּיקִים בְּעוֹבְדֵי כּוֹכָבִים יֵשׁ לָהֶם חֵלֶק
לָעוֹלָם הַבָּא

"The righteous of the idolaters have a share in the World to
Come" (*Tosefta, Sanhedrin*, ch. 13).

Nonetheless, "It is a well known tradition that Esau hates Jacob" (*Sifri
Bamidbar*, 9:10; *Beraishith Rabbah* 33:4). See *Insights*, vol. 1, #178.

Rabbi Aharon Soloveitchik comments: "Whoever is a descendant of Esau,
be he the saintliest among the *chasidei umoth ha'olom*, has an innate prejudice
against the Jews . . . "

To illustrate his thesis, Rav Soloveitchik cites from a book by a certain
French journalist who tells of an interview he had with Thomas Masaryk
who was known as a great liberal, a man who fought against racial discrimi-
nation, a great friend of the Jewish people, certainly one of "the righteous
of the peoples of the world."

"Asked by the French correspondent whether in his heart he entertained
any prejudice against the Jews, Masaryk gave him the very honest answer.
'In my mind I do not have any prejudice against the Jews. Whenever I feel
that I am under the impact of pure logic, then I realize the Jew should not
be disliked. The Jew is as human as anyone else. But sometimes when the
control of the logic of the mind loosens, I fall prey to my feeling, then I take
notice of the fact that deep in my heart there is a prejudice raging against
the Jews. Why, I don't know'" ("Jew and Jew, Jew and non-Jew," *Jewish Life*
33, no. 5 [May-June 1966]: 12).

334

𐫂 943 𐫂 צַדִּיקִים יָרַד הַמָּן עַל פֶּתַח בָּתֵּיהֶם, בֵּינוֹנִים
יָצְאוּ וְלָקְטוּ, רְשָׁעִים שָׁטוּ וְלָקְטוּ

"Unto the righteous [the *manna*] fell in front of their homes; the
average folk went out and gathered, while the wicked had to
wander farther out to gather it" (*Yoma* 75a).

Rabbi Menachem M. Schneerson comments: "Thus, even the righteous
had to exert some measure of effort in gathering the *manna*, since it descended in front of their tents rather than appearing within their tents or upon the
table, in which instance no work at all would be necessary."

"Why indeed," asks the Lubavitcher Rebbe, "was labor involved in
obtaining this miraculous heavenly bread; why not have the *manna* appear
in a manner that completely obviated the need for human toil; since its
appearance was miraculous, why not have a totally miraculous event?"

He explains that the difference between earthly and heavenly bread is the
following. "Man-made bread is inextricably dependent upon human toil. A
man must labor to provide a natural vessel, a vehicle for G-d's bountiful
blessings. Heavenly bread, however, requires no man-made vehicle, toil is
thus not a prerequisite . . . .

"Were heavenly bread to be provided in a manner wherein the individual's labor was entirely irrelevant, it would then have no connection whatsoever with earthly bread. This might then lead to the erroneous conclusion
that complete faith and trust in G-d as Provider is necessary only when He
is entirely responsible for seeing to the person's needs; in the instance of
earthly bread, however, this faith and trust is not a prerequisite.

"Providing the *manna* in a manner whereby the Jew's labor was also necessary demonstrated that even then, complete trust in G-d is vital, for even
earthly bread is heavenly bread: man's labors are wholly secondary to G-d's
in providing him with his daily bread" (*The Chassidic Dimension*, pp. 78-80).

〔 944 〕

צְדָקָה עָשָׂה הַקָּדוֹשׁ בָּרוּךְ הוּא בְּיִשְׂרָאֵל
שֶׁפִּזְּרָן לְבֵין הָאוּמוֹת

"The Holy One, blessed be He, showed righteousness [dealt gen-
erously] to Israel by dispersing them among the nations"
(*Pesahim* 87b).

"So that their enemies would be unable to annihilate them [for they are
scattered all over the globe]" (Rashi).

During the First World War, a committee was established in St. Petersburg to deal with the refugee problem. "The committee decided that all the
Torah Scrolls in the war zone should be brought to the capital for safekeep-
ing, with only one left in each community. Rav Meir Simchah of Dvinsk
strongly objected to the committee's decision, arguing that one should never
'concentrate one's forces' in one area.

"Some thought that Rav Meir Simchah's suggestion was based on sound
military thinking. The Brisker Rav (R. Yitzchak Zev Soloveitchik), however,
revealed the true source of his advice, the *Gemara* [cited above] stating that
G-d dealt generously with the Jews by dispersing them among the nations'"
(Yaakov Mordechai Rapport, *The Light from Dvinsk*, p. 60).

Cf. *Beraishith Rabbah* 76:3, "A man should not put all his money in one
corner" See *Insights*, vol. 1, #348.

〔 945 〕

צוּרְבָא מֵרַבָּנָן דְּאִיכָּא בְּמָתָא כָּל מִילֵי דְמָתָא
עֲלֵיהּ רַמְיָא

"When a scholar resides in a city, all local matters devolve upon
him" (*Moed Katan* 6a).

Cf. Intro. to *Eichah Rabbathi*, "The true guardians of the city are her
scribes and Torah scholars [in contrast to the constables who are the destroy-
ers of the city]."

Rabbi Bachya Ibn Paquda explains that one who relies on his own efforts
[the constables], will be abandoned to circumstance, while one who trusts

solely in G-d will elicit Divine aid (*Chovos HaLevavos, Sha'ar HaBitachon*).

Rabbeinu Yonah writes: "It is known that Divine service endures by virtue of those who learn Torah and engage in its study day and night, for they teach knowledge and understand the times. They preserve Torah in Israel so that it is not forgotten by their children. In a place where there are none who occupy themselves with Torah, stumbling blocks abound and there is no righteousness" (*Shaarei Teshuvah*, Gate 3, Letter 148, cited by Rabbi Yoel Schwartz, *The Ben Torah and His World*, p. 148).

⟦ 946 ⟧   צְלוֹתָא דְּאַבְהָן קַיְּימוּ עָלְמָא

"It was the prayers offered up by the patriarchs that sustained the world" (*Zohar* I, 168).

Abraham instituted *Shacharis* [the morning prayer], Isaac instituted *Minchah* [the afternoon prayer], and Jacob, *Ma'ariv* [the evening prayer]. Cf. *Berakoth* 26b. See *Insights*, vol. 1, #500.

Rabbi Zalman Sorotzkin offers the following homiletical explanation: "Of the three patriarchs, Abraham knew the greatest contentment, wealth and honor . . . . Because his life was like the shining of the morning, it was both fitting and proper that he should establish *Shacharis*. By doing so, he taught that a man blessed with wealth and honor must offer thankful prayer to G-d for all the kindness shown him.

"Although Isaac, too, enjoyed wealth and honor, he was the first Jew to taste the bitterness of exile, to hear Abimelech say, 'Go away from us!' [Gen. 26:16]. The decree that 'your children shall be strangers' [Gen. 15:13], began with him. Thus Isaac's whole life was like *Minchah* time, as the sun is setting . . . . He established *Minchah*, his prayer for mercy to make the approaching 'night' endurable for his seed.

"Jacob's whole life was hard, as he himself told Pharaoh: 'Few and bad have been the years of my life' [Gen. 47:9]. He underwent one exile after another . . . . Jacob ordained *Ma'ariv* in expression of his steadfast service to G-d. 'He encountered The Place [i.e., he prayed] *because the sun had set*' [Gen. 28:11]. Thus he taught his children that even someone whose world has gone dark must pray" (*Oznayim LaTorah, Beraishith*).

▌ 947 ▐ צָלַלְתָּ בְּמַיִם אַדִּירִים וְהֶעֱלֵיתָ חֶרֶס בְּיָדֶךְ

"You have dived unto the depths of water and have brought up a
potsherd in your hand" (*Baba Kamma* 91a).

You went to a lot of trouble to no avail. [Eng. prov., "The mountain
labored and brought forth a mouse."]

Regarding the fundamental principle that the Holy One, blessed be He,
will justly reward the good and punish the bad, Maimonides writes: "Man
cannot grasp [the depths of] this justice, just as man's intellect cannot [begin
to] comprehend the knowledge of the Holy One, blessed be He. . . . 'For as
the heavens are higher than the earth, so are My ways higher than your
ways and My thoughts than your thoughts' [Isaiah 55:9]. For this reason
accept this fundamental principle, and do not lead yourself astray in this
subject, because whosoever of your Torah scholars or others who delved into
it, attained nothing, as our sages of blessed memory state, 'He dived into
depths of water and brought up a potsherd in his hand'" (*Commentary on the
Mishnah, Berakoth* 5:3).

▌ 948 ▐ צָפִיתָ לִישׁוּעָה

"Did you hope for salvation?" (*Shabbath* 31a).

This is one of the questions asked of man when he is led in for judgment.
See *Insights*, vol. 1, #115.

"Only through repentance will Israel be redeemed, and the Torah already
offered the assurance that Israel will, in the closing period of exile, finally
repent, and thereupon be immediately redeemed" (*Mishnah Torah, Hil.
Teshuvah* 7:5).

Rabbi Yitzchok b. Yosef of Corbeil writes: "The obligation to believe in
Moshiach is a consequence of the obligation to believe in the Almighty, His
providence and omnipotence. 'I am the L-rd your G-d who brought you out

of the land of Egypt.' As it is My will that you believe in Me, so it is My will that you believe that I took you out of Egypt. Likewise you should have faith that He will assemble you all together and help you" (*Sefer Mitzvoth Katan, Amude Hagolah*).

Rabbi Yechezkel Levenstein maintained that these three concepts are interdependent: Belief in the existence of G-d; Providence and the Exodus from Egypt; and trust that the Diaspora will culminate in the ingathering of all Jews and the arrival of Moshiach (Rabbi Elchanan Hertzman, *The Mashgiach*, p.54).

⟦ 949 ⟧ צְפַרְדֵּעַ אַחַת הָיְתָה שָׁרְקָה לָהֶם וְהֵם בָּאוּ

"There was one frog which croaked for the others, and they came"
(*Sanhedrin* 67b).

"And the frog came up and covered the land of Egypt" [Ex. 8:2]. [This was the second of the "Ten Plagues" in Egypt.] The Talmud cites the following, tannaitic dispute: "R. Akiba said, 'There was one frog which filled the whole of Egypt [by breeding].' R. Eleazar b. Azariah said, 'One frog croaked for the others, and they came'" (ibid.).

Rabbi Abraham R. Besdin, homiletically relates the dispute concerning "the plague of frogs" to the perennial plague of anti-Semitism. The two sages wondered, "how does anti-Semitic persecution break out in a land which was previously committed to freedom? Egypt was a land which had been liberal, tolerant, an open society which had enthroned a Semitic foreigner, Joseph, as second to the king, and had invited Jacob and his family to live in Goshen despite their abhorrence of sheep-herders . . . How can such a land become a vicious tyranny overnight?

"Rabbi Akiba felt that one charismatic and simple-minded tyrant can poison a society. All the hatred and vileness emanating from him can transform an entire people. Rabbi Eleazar disagreed. No evil man can do it. Anti-Semitism was embedded in their culture; it remained submerged because bigotry was unfashionable; but any evil king can call it forth . . . Hitler found the entire German culture and indeed, Western culture, readily responsive to his venom" (RCA *Sermon Anthology*, vol. 44 [1986] p. 408).

ק

𝄐 950 𝄐

קָבַעְתָּ עִתִּים לַתּוֹרָה

"Did you establish set times for studying Torah?" (*Shabbath* 31a).

This is one of the questions asked of man when he is led in for judgment. See *Insights*, vol. 1, #115.

The Vilna Gaon remarked that a person is asked in Heaven, "*Kavata* [did you establish] time for the Torah?" *Kavata* can also be translated as "did you steal?" A person is asked whether he stole away time, even when he was very busy, in order to learn Torah [*Divrei Eliyahu*].

Similarly, in commenting on this "heavenly" question, R. Yaakov Berlin [the Netziv's father] said: "This question, as well as the one which precedes it — 'Did you conduct your affairs with integrity,' seems to be directed towards the layman. The expression *kavata* can be interpreted to mean *overpower* or *subjugate*. Thus, the layman is asked, 'Did you forcibly subjugate your schedule to give yourself time for Torah study in the midst of all your everyday activities?'" (R. Baruch HaLevi Epstein, *Mekor Baruch*, cited in *Recollections*, p. 50).

Unlike the layman cited by R. Yaakov Berlin, the typical talmudic student need not concern himself about "fixing a time for Torah study" [at least while he is studying in the Yeshiva].

Rabbi Chaim of Volozhin once remarked facetiously, that at his Yeshiva the students do not "establish set times for studying Torah." They set aside a fixed time for *bitul Torah* [suspension of study] for at Volozhin they study day and night. They are required, however, to interrupt some portion of their studies to take care of their bodily needs — food, sleep, etc . . .

Cf. *Aboth* 1:15, "Make of your study [of Torah] a fixed practice." See

340

Insights, vol. 1, #446.

Cf. *Berakoth* 35b, "The earlier generations make their Torah fixed and their work temporary." See #610.

⦑ 951 ⦒ קְדֵרָא דְּבֵי שׁוּתָפֵי לָא חֲמִימָא וְלָא קְרִירָא

"A pot in the charge of two cooks [lit. 'of partners'] is neither hot nor cold" (*Erubin* 3a).

Each one of the cooks relies on the other, hence the 'pot' is not properly prepared.

[Eng. proverb: "Too many cooks spoil the broth."]

Rabbi Moshe Chafetz writes: "Woe to the house where everyone is [considered] "the head" [of the house]. For where there are many captains — the ship sinks" (*Mareh Hamussar*).

Cf. *Beraishith Rabbah* 60:3, "Between the midwife and the woman in travail the ill-fated child is lost." This maxim is illustrative of two individuals who adamantly refuse to relinquish their imagined rights.

⦑ 952 ⦒ קָדָשִׁים מְחַלְּלִין קָדָשִׁים וְאֵין חוּלִּין מְחַלְּלִין קָדָשִׁים

"Consecrated animals profane consecrated animals, but unconsecrated animals do not profane consecrated animals" (*Zebahim* 3b).

If one slaughters a consecrated animal, e.g, a *sin-offering* under the wrong designation of another consecrated animal — a *burnt offering*, then the *sin offering* becomes "profane" [unfit or invalid]. However, if one slaughtered a consecrated animal under the wrong designation of an unconsecrated animal [which is no sacrifice at all] it does not become "profane" — it is valid.

The Sanzer Rav, Rabbi Chaim Halberstam, homiletically interprets the above dictum as a poignant reminder of the greater sense of awe and responsibility inherent in being a spiritual leader.

'The unconsecrated do not profane the consecrated' — simple, unlearned and unsophisticated people who defame and disgrace that which is consecrated or holy — that is basically irrelevant. But when "consecrated things profane other consecrated things" — when those who are viewed as holy leaders and spiritual spokesmen, when they defame and desecrate — that is considered 'profane,' an absolute desecration of the holy" (*Divrei Chaim*).

953

קוֹדֶם שֶׁיֹּאכַל אָדָם וְיִשְׁתֶּה, יֵשׁ לוֹ שְׁתֵּי
לְבָבוֹת; לְאַחַר שֶׁאוֹכֵל וְשׁוֹתֶה, אֵין לוֹ אֶלָּא
לֵב אֶחָד

"Before a man eats and drinks he has two hearts, but after he eats and drinks he has only one heart" (*Baba Bathra* 12b).

There is a Yiddish proverb, "*Der zatteh kleibt nisht dem hungeren*" [the sated believes not the hungry]. However, if a man who generally is "sated" finds himself in a situation where he too has nothing to eat and drink, then 'he has two hearts' i.e., he experiences the faintness of his own heart and that of his neighbor who is always in this condition. But once he eats and drinks, he reverts to his general outlook on life and 'he has only one heart' [his own]. He no longer empathizes with the hungry.

"This is the meaning of '*Va'yishman Yeshurun va'yivat*' (*Yeshurun* [a poetic name for Israel] became fat and rebelled [Deut. 32:15]). Literally, it means 'became fat and kicked.' When a person's heart is satiated, he tends to push other people away; their misery leaves him cold" (Rabbi Mordechai Banet).

Our sages have therefore declared: "The merit of fasting is charity" (*Berakoth* 6b). The purpose and goal of the fast is not to afflict your soul but to experience hunger for a day, so that you will understand the necessity of providing for the hungry (*Knesseth Yisroel*, cited by Rabbi Reuven Margolies, *Devarim B'ittam*, p. 161).

See *Insights*, vol. 1, #3.

⦋ 954 ⦌

קוּשְׁטָא קָאֵי שִׁיקְרָא לָא קָאֵי

"Truth can stand, falsehood cannot stand" (*Shabbath* 104a).

Each of the letters of *sheker* [falsehood] is insecurely poised on one leg, whereas those of *emeth* [truth] are firmly set, each resting on two legs.

"What is the origin of the saying, 'Falsehood has no feet'? It was in the story of the serpent. He was the first to tell a falsehood and was cursed to go upon his belly" (*Tikkune Zohar*).

"Rabbi Samson Raphael Hirsch frequently climaxed his polemical writings on behalf of our Divine Judaism with the dictum 'Truth can stand . . . [truth prevails — falsehood fails']" (Rabbi Joseph Breuer, *A Time To Build*, vol. 3, p. 53).

⦋ 955 ⦌

קָטָן הַיּוֹדֵעַ . . . לְדַבֵּר אָבִיו לוֹמְדוֹ תּוֹרָה

"A minor who is able to speak, his father must teach him Torah"
(*Sukkah* 42a).

"What is meant by Torah? R. Hamnuna replied, [the scriptural verse] 'Moshe commanded us a Law, an inheritance of the congregation of Jacob'" [Deut. 33:4] (ibid.).

"Later on, according to the child's capacity, the father should teach him a few verses at a time, till he attains the age of six or seven years, when he should take him to a teacher of young children" (*Mishneh Torah, Hil. Talmud Torah* 1:6).

The *Shelah HaKadosh*, Rabbi Isaiah Horowitz, stresses repeatedly that children should be taught according to their ability, years, and intelligence. He also stressed the need of acquiring knowledge of all the three parts of the Torah [Pentateuch, Prophets and Sacred Writings] before proceeding to further study. He maintained that one should study systematically each verse and chapter of the whole Torah [and not jump from one *Parashah* to the other] so that he should know the translation of the words and meaning of the verse (*Shney Luchoth HaBrith* 1, p. 181a).

∬ 956 ∬

קִיְּמוּ וְקִבְּלוּ הַיְּהוּדִים,
קִיְּמוּ מַה שֶׁקִּיבְּלוּ כְּבָר

"'The Jews undertook and obligated themselves' . . . they undertook what they had [forcibly] obligated themselves to long before"
(*Shabbath* 88a).

After witnessing the miracles of Purim, the Jews willingly accepted the
Torah which was forcibly imposed upon them at Mt. Sinai.

"How is it possible," asks the Chafetz Chaim, "that the generation of the
desert, known as the 'generation of wisdom' had to be forced into receiving
the Torah while the generation of Mordechai would receive it willingly?"

"The truth is that the 'generation of the desert' were willing to receive the
Torah, for they said *na'aseh ve'nishma* [we will observe and listen]. However,
they were gnawed with doubts concerning the future. Observance of the
Torah meant that they would have to separate themselves from others by
not eating with them, not intermarrying with them etc. . . . . All this would
undoubtedly lead to hatred towards the Jews. They therefore, only reluctant-
ly accepted the Torah for they were fearful of not being able to withstand
the animosity of the nations.

"The generation of Mordechai, however, witnessed the wonderful miracle
which took place during Purim. They saw how the deputy of the king
[Haman] who demanded that Mordechai bow before him, suddenly, in a
mere instant, was sentenced to be hanged . . . . It then became evident that,
with the Torah to preserve them, it would indeed be possible to live in exile
among the nations of the world.

"This is why the sages declared that this generation received the Torah
willingly" (Rabbi Isaiah Dvorkas, *The Chafetz Chaim on the Sabbath and Festival
Days*, p. 206).

957 קִימְחָא טְחִינָא טְחִינַת

"You have ground flour which has already been ground" (*Sanhedrin* 96b).

See *Shir HaShirim Rabbah* 3:4, "Jerusalem spoke in this fashion to the daughters of Babylon: 'Had they not fought against me from Heaven, could you have prevailed against me? Had the Almighty not sent a fire in my bones, could you have prevailed against me? In truth you have ground flour which has already been ground, you slew a dead lion, you burnt a house already burnt.'"

Rabbi Chaim of Volozhin comments: "It was only because the strength of the Supernal Power was already weakened and diminished by our sins, and the Supernal Temple [which is a prototype of the earthly Temple] was made 'unclean,' as it were — that Nebuchadnezzar and Titus had power to destroy the Lower Temple . . . . You have ground flour which has already been ground — the sages said of the deeds of these men. Our own sins destroyed the Temple which is the Celestial Temple above, and they merely destroyed the lower dwelling" (*Nefesh HaChaim*, ch. 4).

958 קְרִיָּיתָא זוֹ הַלֵּילָא

"The reading [of the *Megillah*] itself is the *Hallel*" (*Megillah* 14a).

R. Nachman maintains that *Hallel* is not recited on *Purim* because the *Megillah* reading itself is a form of *Hallel*.

The *Meiri* comments that if one does not possess a *Megillah* he is obligated to recite *Hallel* on *Purim* (*Megillah*, end of first *perek*).

Rabbi Yitzchak Hutner explains: "Hallel commemorates the occurrence of a miracle. If it is a 'revealed miracle' [*nes nigleh*] then *Hallel* would be a halachic requirement. If, however, it is a 'concealed miracle' [*nes nistar*] as it was on *Purim*, then our sages required the recitation of *Hallel* in a 'concealed' manner. Consequently, on *Purim*, Hallel, so to speak, is chanted via the *Megillah* and is concealed much like the miracle. The *Megillah* does not take the place of *Hallel*, it is rather another form of it. Hence, in the absence of a *Megillah* one is required to recite *Hallel*."

See *Shaarei Teshuvah* [*Orach Chaim* 693]. In the absence of a *Megillah*, Hallel may be recited without a *bracha*.

See, however, *Responsa of Chasam Sofer, Orach Chaim* 192, who maintains that the halacha does not follow the *Meiri*.

◊ 959 ◊   קַרְנָא קַרְיָא בְּרוֹמִי בַּר מְזַבֵּין תְּאֵנִי תְּאֵנִי דַאֲבוּךְ זַבֵּין

"When the horn is sounded in [the market of] Rome — O son of the fig-seller, sell your father's figs" (*Berakoth* 62b).

When the horn is heard in the marketplace it is a signal that there are people interested in purchasing figs. The son of the fig-seller is told that if his father is not home [not to wait for him, but] to sell the figs while the buyers are still there (Rashi). This is an admonition against procrastination.

"The Vilna Gaon explains that this is an admonition to scholars to teach their wisdom to the public. Even one who is still in the learning stage himself [a 'son'] and is dependent upon his teacher [his 'father'] should teach whatever wisdom he knows [the supply of 'figs'] to anyone who desires to learn from him ['when the market opens up']; he should not relegate this obligation to his teacher" (*Beiur HaGra La-Aggados*, cited by Rabbi Aharon Feldman, *The Juggler and the King*, p. XXV).

◊ 960 ◊   קָשֶׁה גֵּזֶל הַהֶדְיוֹט יוֹתֵר מִגֵּזֶל גָּבוֹהַ

"Robbery of a private individual is worse than robbery of the [Most] High" (*Baba Bathra* 88b).

In an ordinary case of theft as soon as one removes an object from another's possession, he is deemed a sinner, whereas with regard to "holy objects" he is not deemed a sinner until he derives some pleasure from the object (Rashi).

In robbing "holy objects" there is no transference from one domain to another [for everything is in the Almighty's domain]. Hence there is no sin until there is actual use of the object (*Perushei Maharal MiPrague*).

The Almighty seems more concerned with human rights than with "Heavenly rights." In effect, since man is created in the image of G-d, by robbing from man, one is committing a dual transgression — against man as well as against his Creator.

Cf. *Sanhedrin* 108a, "Come and see how great is the power of robbery, for although the generation of the flood transgressed all laws, their decree of punishment was sealed only because they stretched out their hands to rob."

See #569.

⎰ 961 ⎱   קָשֶׁה עוֹנְשָׁן שֶׁל מִדּוֹת יוֹתֵר מֵעוֹנְשָׁן שֶׁל עֲרָיוֹת

"The punishment for unjust measures is more severe than the punishment for immorality" (*Baba Bathra* 88b).

"For the latter is a sin against G-d [only], and the former is a sin against one's fellowman. If one denies the binding character of the commandment relating to measures, he denies [in effect] the Exodus from Egypt, which was the basis of the commandments; but if one acknowledges the commandment relating to measures, he thereby acknowledges the Exodus from Egypt, which rendered all the commandments possible" (*Mishneh Torah, Hil. Geneivah* 7:12).

Rabbi Naftali Zvi Yehudah Berlin, the *Netziv*, raises two questions on the above dictum. (1) Why is the transgression of using unjust measures more culpable than other forms of theft? (2) What is the basis for the comparison between unjust measures and the prohibition of forbidden relations for the Talmud to conclude that one is more severe than the other?

The *Netziv* explains: "Of the three cardinal sins of Judaism — immorality, idolatry and murder — the sin of idolatry [total lack of faith in G-d] is the most despicable. Hence, the sin of unjust measures which one commits through his "lack of faith" in the Almighty who provides and sustains us all — a ramification of the sin of idolatry — is more severe than the sin of

INSIGHTS: A TALMUDIC TREASURY

immorality which one commits as a result of his inordinate desire and lust. Moreover, it is more difficult to do *teshuvah* — to repent from a sin committed as a result of a deficiency of faith than a sin committed as a result of unbridled passion" (*Ha'amek Davar*, Deut. 25:17).

∬ 962 ∬

קָשָׁה עָלַי פְּרִידַתְכֶם

"Your parting is difficult for me"
(Rashi's language based on *Sukkah* 55b).

The Almighty declares [so to speak] to His children on the festival of *Sh'mini Atzeres*, "I have detained you with Me like a king who invited his children to feast for a certain number of days [and], when their time came to depart, he said, 'My children, I request of you, tarry with me one more day, your parting is difficult for me'" (Rashi, Lev. 23:36).

This phrase, "your parting is difficult for me," expressing the longing of the Almighty for the children of Israel, was applied homiletically by Rabbi Moshe A. Amiel to the "longing" that many observant Jews experience on *Sh'mini Atzeres* towards their less observant brothers.

"During the month of *Tishrei* "most" congregants attend services on *Rosh Hashanah* and *Yom Kippur*, for the sounding of the *Shofar*, *Kol Nidre*, *Yizkor*, and *Neilah*. The month of *Tishrei* is blessed with religious events [culminating with *Succoth* and *Hakofos*] which attract many Jews to the Synagogue. Unfortunately, on *Sh'mini Atzeres*, a *siyum* [a conclusion] is made for the Torah without a new beginning. We must wait for a long and cold winter to pass before the entire congregation reconvenes for the festival of *Pesach*. Indeed, 'Your parting is difficult for me'" (*Hegyonoth El-Ami*, p. 207).

Rabbi Shmuel Zvi of Alexander interprets the above phrase as "the separation of Jews from each other." The separation of Jews, each traveling to his own home after being so close to each other during the festival [in Jerusalem] — this separation [says the Almighty] is difficult for Me (*Tifereth Shmuel*, cited in *P'ninei Hachassiduth*, vol. 4, p. 304).

ר

〔 963 〕 רָאִיתִי בְּנֵי עֲלִיָּיה וְהֵן מוּעָטִין

"I have seen the 'men of elevation' and they are but few" (*Sukkah* 45b).

"Bnei Aliyah" — those who will receive the Presence of the *Shechinah* [in the Hereafter] (Rashi).

Rabbi Yaakov Yosef of Polonoye comments: "There are seventy nations and the people of Israel; few are those who are close to the oneness of G-d. Among the people of Israel there are many who do the *mitzvoth* for show and fame, and study Torah in a like manner, few are those who are really devout. The closer one comes to the oneness of G-d, the fewer there are . . ."

"It seems to me that this is the explanation of the passage, 'I have seen the men of elevation and they are but few.' This [remarkable declaration made in the name of R. Shimon b. Yochai] refers to one who is able to raise himself along with his entire generation, causing them, through prayer or *mussar* to cleave to Him Who is blessed: men such as this are few" (*Ben Porath Yosef*, 14a, 66a).

349

964

רָאִיתִי לֹא נֶאֱמַר אֶלָא רָאֹה רָאִיתִי — אָמַר
לוֹ הקב״ה: מֹשֶׁה אַתָּה רוֹאֶה רְאִיָה אַחַת
וַאֲנִי רוֹאֶה שְׁתֵּי רְאִיוֹת

"It does not say, 'I have seen,' but 'seen I have seen.' The Holy
One, blessed be He, said to him, 'Moshe, you can only see one
vision, but I see two visions'" (Shemoth Rabbah 3:2).

This is the midrashic comment on the scriptural words, "G-d said: ra'oh
ra'ithi [seen, I have seen] the suffering of My people . . . [Ex. 3:7]. G-d said
to Moshe: "You see them coming to Sinai and receiving the Torah, and I
[can also] see them worshipping the Golden Calf" (ibid.).

Rabbi Levi Yitzchak of Berditchev raises the question: "Why, indeed, did
Moshe the greatest of all prophets, see only one vision, that of Israel
receiving the Torah? Why did he fail to see their downfall at the Golden
Calf? Were his prophetic powers impaired? Most emphatically not! However,
a prophet who sees Israel's shortcoming is no tzaddik and no prophet.
Moshe, the faithful shepherd, saw only the good in Israel, the receiving of
the Torah. He did not see the making of the Golden Calf" (Kedushath Levi,
Ex. 3:7).

Avraham Yaakov Finkel, in citing the above interpretation of Reb Levi
Yitzchak, notes: "This commentary mirrors the Berditchever's philosophy.
He was the great defender of the Jewish people seeing the sublime qualities
in the simplest of Jews, engaging in disputes with the Almighty Himself,
pleading the cause of his people" (The Great Torah Commentators, p. 244).

∬ 965 ∬

רִבּוֹנוֹ שֶׁל עוֹלָם הוֹאִיל וְלֹא זָכִינוּ לִהְיוֹת
גִּזְבָּרִין נֶאֱמָנִים, יִהְיוּ מַפְתְּחוֹת מְסוּרוֹת לְךָ

"Master of the Universe, as we did not merit to be faithful treasurers [of the Temple] let the keys be returned to you" (*Ta'anith* 29a).

"When the first Temple was about to be destroyed, bands upon bands of young priests with the keys of the Temple in their hands assembled and mounted the roof of the Temple and exclaimed, 'Master of the Universe . . . They then threw the keys up towards heaven and a hand reached out and received them . . . '

"When Rabbi Naftali Tzvi Yehuda Berlin, the *Netziv* died, he was eulogized by his oldest son, Rabbi Chaim Berlin, who cited the above passage, and then concluded: "The *mikdash* [Temple] of the Torah, the yeshiva of Volozhin was destroyed; and the key to the Yeshiva — my father — had no further reason to live. A fiery hand therefore descended from heaven to take him from us" (Rabbi Aharon Surasky, *Giants of Jewry*, vol. 1, p. 74).

∬ 966 ∬

רַבִּי טַרְפוֹן אוֹמֵר אֵין מַדְלִיקִין אֶלָּא בְּשֶׁמֶן
זַיִת בִּלְבַד

"Rabbi Tarfon said: 'Only olive oil may be lit [in the Sabbath lamp]'" (*Shabbath* 24b).

Rabbi Avraham Yitzchak Kook explains the inner meaning of this opinion: "The light of the Sabbath lamp alludes to the light of the intellect that emanates upon the soul that is sanctified by the holiness of the day of rest. Many types of oil produce light. The study of certain branches of wisdom elevates the soul with morals and positive character traits, and it is prepared to bring good to the world. But the purest light is the light of Torah; it is especially associated with the Sabbath day. It is the purest of all oils and is unclouded by error or darkness of man's Evil Inclination that is mixed in the light that comes from human wisdom. Therefore, Torah is compared to olive oil, the finest of oils, to teach us that the Sabbath day should be totally dedicated to exploring the wisdom of the Torah" (*Olath Reiyah*, p. 24).

The sages who disagree with Rabbi Tarfon and allow other oils, do agree, however, that olive oil is preferable because it produces a better flame than any of the other oils. See Tosaf. s.v. *Meireish, Shabbath* 23a.

⟐ 967 ⟐ רַבִּי עָשָׂה סְעוּדָה לְתַלְמִידָיו הֵבִיא הֵבִיא לִפְנֵיהֶם
לְשׁוֹנוֹת רַכִּים וּלְשׁוֹנוֹת קָשִׁים

"Rabbi [Rabbi Yehudah HaNasi] made a feast for his disciples and placed before them tender tongues and hard tongues"
(*Va'yikrah Rabbah* 33:1).

"They began selecting the tender ones, leaving the hard ones alone. Said he to them: 'Note what you are doing! As you select the tender and leave the hard, so let your tongues be tender to one another'" (ibid.).

The Rosh Ha'yeshiva of Brisk in Jerusalem, Rabbi Yosef Dov Soloveitchik explained: "Rabbi Yehudah Ha'nasi meant this as a lesson to his students to teach them just how careful we must be not to cause anyone pain with words . . . When he served tongue at his table, all the pieces were certainly edible. Nonetheless, as long as there is a slight variation in tenderness, one favors the piece that is even slightly softer.

"Not only are outright derogatory words and insults prohibited, but as long as there is a noticeable difference between two expressions, we are obligated to always select the more pleasant one. People are sensitive, and comments that are meant as light banter can cause untold anguish. A person should have the foresight to be aware of the consequences of every statement, concluded Rav Soloveitchik, and be continuously on guard to choose the softest possible approach" (R' Zelig Pliskin, *The Power of Words*, p. 24).

〚 968 〛 רַגְזָן לֹא עָלְתָה בְּיָדוֹ אֶלָּא רַגְזָנוּתָא

"A hot-tempered man [when he loses his temper] nothing ascends to his hand [nothing is achieved] but his anger" (*Kiddushin* 41a).

An irritable, quarrelsome person achieves nothing but the injurious effect of his irritability. "*Irate*" is generally an expression of "I rate" (Shraga Silverstein, *A Candle by Day*, p. 20).

Rabbi Nachman of Kossov interprets the above dictum literally, and explains why the term "to his hand" is used. It is known that every night, when the souls ascend to Heaven, each person records in his own hand every sin he has committed that day. Should he have lost his temper that day, however, then the *hand* only writes down the sin of anger. To write more would be superfluous, for anger leads to all other sins — it embraces them all. This is the meaning of the phrase "nothing ascends to his hand" [no angry soul ascends on high to write with his hand] anything other than the sin of anger (Rabbi Pinchas of Dinovitz, *Sifsei Tzaddikim*, *Mattos*).

Rabbi Avraham Grodzensky explains that there are generally no benefits in becoming angry. One's anger does not help him at all, and the subject of his anger usually pays less attention to what he is saying than if he would have spoken tactfully and patiently. Anger causes nothing but harm to one's health (*Toras Avraham*, p. 440).

"If one cannot control his anger and desires, he should isolate himself from humanity" (Vilna Gaon, *Even Sheleimah*, ch. 2).

Rabbi Avraham Pam, the Rosh HaYeshiva of Mesivta Torah Vodaath, highly recommends the *sefer Orech Apa'yim* by Avraham Yellin — a book containing practical suggestions on how to control one's anger (*Erev Shabbos Shiurim*).

Cf. *Nedarim* 22a, "Whoever is angry is exposed to all torments of *gehinnom*." See *Insights*, vol. 1, #266.

Cf. *Berakoth* 29b, "Be not wrathful and you will not sin."

∐ 969 ∐ רוֹאִין אֶת הַנִּשְׁמָע וְשׁוֹמְעִין אֶת הַנִּרְאֶה

"They saw what was audible and heard what was visible"
(*Mechilta* 20:15).

This is Rabbi Akiva's interpretation of the verse describing the Revelation at Mount Sinai — "All the people saw the sounds and the flames... [Ex. 20:15].

Rabbi Menachem M. Schneerson, the Lubavitcher Rebbe, points out that the above mentioned miracle was central to this supernatural event. "As a physical being, man is naturally closer to the material than to the spiritual. It follows that he will grasp a material object with his power of sight more intimately and thoroughly than something spiritual, which he will only grasp from 'afar' with his power of hearing.

"This then, is what is meant by 'seeing that which is heard, and hearing that which is seen.' Spirituality is generally only 'heard' [from afar]. When G-d gave the Torah to the Jewish people, however, He uplifted them to a level at which they became capable of 'seeing' and grasping spirituality through direct perception.

"Conversely, the physical world, which had always been clearly seen by them, now became distant from them. Their heightened spiritual state caused them to be unable to 'see' and fully grasp the corporeal; they were now only able to discern it with their weaker sense of 'hearing.'

"We thus understand that this miraculous occurrence was an integral element of receiving the Torah. Since at that time the Jews were granted a revelation of G-d's Essence, they then grasped spirituality with the more intense power of 'vision,' while they lost sight of their own corporeal being: they were only aware of it through the less direct sense of 'hearing'" (*The Chassidic Dimension*, pp. 86-88).

◊ 970 ◊

רוֹב בְּגֶזֶל וּמִיעוּט בַּעֲרָיוֹת

"Most [people are guilty] of robbery, a minority of illicit sexual relations" (*Baba Bathra* 165a).

Rabbi Yisrael Salanter once visited a wealthy merchant regarding a matter of communal importance. On the living room table there happened to be a large sum of money. Suddenly the merchant was called out of the room, but when he returned Reb Yisrael was gone, nowhere to be found. When the merchant looked outside, he saw the Rabbi standing in front of the door and he asked him why he ran out of the room. Reb Yisrael calmly explained that in the Torah there is a prohibition of *yichud* [forbidding a man and a woman to be secluded] for it may lead to *arayoth* [illicit relations]. Our sages have taught us that a minority of people violate these prohibitions. If that is the case regarding *arayoth*, said Reb Yisrael, then it stands to reason that in the case of *gezel* [robbery], where most people are guilty of this prohibition, there is an *issur yichud* [being alone] with unguarded money. He was therefore compelled to leave the house (Rav Avraham Pam, *Erev Shabbos Shiurim*).

◊ 971 ◊

רִבּוֹן הָעוֹלָמִים גָּלוּי וְיָדוּעַ לְפָנֶיךָ שֶׁרְצוֹנֵנוּ
לַעֲשׂוֹת רְצוֹנְךָ וּמִי מְעַכֵּב שְׂאוֹר שֶׁבָּעִיסָה
וְשִׁעְבּוּד מַלְכִיּוֹת

"Master of the Universe, it is clearly known to You that our wish is to do Your Will. What, then, prevents us? The yeast in the dough and our enslavement by the nations" (*Berakoth* 17a).

"The yeast in the dough" — The Evil Inclination which causes a ferment in the heart (Rashi).

"Controlled, the fermentation caused by the yeast creates bread which supports life; uncontrolled, the dough turns sour and inedible. Similarly, if man's drives for pleasure and the control of his surroundings are properly harnessed, they give him the impetus to conquer nature and provide the means for human life to survive and prosper. If left unharnessed, then the result is that 'jealousy, pleasure-seeking, and the lust for glory drive a man out of this world' [*Aboth* 4:21]: human personality decays and disintegrates along with the entire social structure."

"'Enslavement by the nations' — Foreign influences from the surrounding society can exert a tremendous pull on the Jews, drawing them away from spiritual endeavors" (Vilna Gaon, *Perush Al Kamma Agaddoth*, cited by Rabbi Aharon Feldman, *The Juggler and the King*, p. 24).

〚 972 〛 רַשָׁאִין בְּנֵי הָעִיר לְהַתְנוֹת עַל הַמִּדּוֹת וְעַל הַשְּׁעָרִים וְעַל שְׂכַר פּוֹעֲלִים וּלְהַסִּיעַ עַל קִיצָתָן

"It is permissible for the inhabitants of a city to regulate measurements, prices and laborer's wages, and to penalize [lit. to remove] those who violate their regulations" (*Baba Bathra* 8b).

"The residents of a city may agree among themselves to fix a price on any article they desire, even on meat and bread, and to stipulate that they will inflict such-and-such a penalty upon him who violates the agreement" (*Mishneh Torah, Hil. Mechirah* 14:9).

Rabbi Zechariah Fendel notes that "the prices of *shemurah matzah* for *Pesach, esrogim* for *Succoth*, and even kosher meat during the entire year (and particularly when a *Yom Tov* approaches) have skyrocketed and soared far out of proportion to their true value, making it extremely difficult for the non-wealthy Jew to observe these *mitzvoth* properly . . . ."

He suggests that "the leading Rabbinic and communal leaders can establish price guidelines in each of the areas specified above, thereby making it incumbent upon all Jewish merchants to abide by these communal guidelines" (*The Halacha and Beyond*, p. 76).

❡ 973 ❡

רְשָׁעִים שֶׁבְּחַיֵּיהֶן קְרוּיִין מֵתִים

"The wicked in their lifetime are called dead" (*Berakoth* 18b).

"Although the body of the wicked man appears to be alive and well, his soul is actually mortally wounded. The wicked corrupt their spiritual element and transform it into mundane, earthly matter. Thus their soul is dead even while their body lives. But in the Eternal Afterlife, the wicked will truly be dead, for all that exists in the Afterlife is the soul, and the wicked 'murdered' their souls in this life" (Rabbi Chaim ben Attar, *Ohr HaChaim*, Num. 25:14; Gen. 1:1; Gen. 6:3).

Cf. *Berakoth* 18a, "The righteous in their death are called living." See *Insights*, vol. 1, #460.

ש

〖 974 〗   שִׁבְעָה דְּבָרִים מְכוּסִּים מִבְּנֵי אָדָם

"Seven things lie hidden from man . . ." (*Pesahim* 54b).

One of them is *Omek HaDin* [the depths of judgment].
"What is hidden includes not only the type of punishment and its magnitude, but also what constitutes a sin and how a man is responsible for his actions. All this lies hidden. Slight sins and faults which we fail to take note of, or even consider to be *mitzvoth*, are included in the indictment above.

"The *Yalkut Shimoni* [II: 758] cites the following statement uttered by King David: 'You have given us 613 *mitzvoth* — both great and small. I have no fear on account of the major *mitzvoth*. But the minor ones, to which men pay scant attention and squash with their heel, those do I fear . . . .

"It is precisely those sins trodden upon by 'the heels,' which surround and harm a man . . ." (Rabbi Chaim Aryeh Bernstein, *Halichoth Chaim*, cited by Rabbi Shalom Meir Wallach, *Depth of Judgment*, p. 136).

〖 975 〗   שִׁגְגַת תַּלְמוּד עוֹלָה זָדוֹן

"An inadvertent error in [Torah] study is tantamount to an
intentional sin" (*Midrash Tanchuma, Va'yikrah* 6).

Cf. *Aboth* 4:16, "Be careful about study, for an error in study is accounted as intentional."
Cf. *Baba Mezia* 33b, "What is the meaning of 'Declare to My people their

transgression . . .' [Isaiah 58:1]? This refers to scholars whose inadvertent errors are accounted as intentional faults . . . ."

In commenting on the above dictum, Rabbi Yosef Shaul Nathanson suggests that a scholar's "inadvertent error is accounted as an intentional sin," for the people who witness the "wrongful act" are unaware that it was committed in error. Consequently, they will learn from his actions to do likewise, intentionally (*Divrei Shaul*).

▯ 976 ▯

שׁוֹחַד דְּבָרִים נַמִּי אָסוּר

"A bribe of words [or 'acts'] is also forbidden" (*Kethuboth* 105b).

Rabbi Yisrael Salanter cited numerous talmudic and midrashic dicta showing how far the slightest bias can pervert the mind of man. "Several case histories are recounted in the Talmud concerning Rabbi Yishmael ben R. Yose, Rabbi Yishmael ben R. Elisha and R. Anan, each of whom regarded themselves as 'bribed' and therefore incapable of judging fairly, merely because of some trivial benefit received from one of the litigants. Moreover, with their penetrating vision, they sensed how their views had become colored and were tending to the side of the particular party. They proved to themselves how much every man, even the greatest, is liable to err because of the slightest personal involvement, even where one is fully aware and conscious of everything going on" (*Ohr Yisrael*, p. 48, cited by Rabbi Dov Katz, *Tenuath HaMussar*).

Cf. *Kethuboth* 105b, "No man sees anything to his disadvantage." See *Insights*, vol. 1, #24.

Cf, *Kethuboth*, ibid., "What is [the meaning of] *shochad*? *Sh'hu Chad* that he [the recipient] is one [with the donor]" See #840.

"However, an exception (to the prohibition of *shochad*) was made during the Middle Ages when it was customary among Jews to offer large gifts to those magistrates or lords who judged their lawsuits with gentiles. *Chavos Yair* explains that in those days, Jews were in an inferior position, and so the judges were prejudiced *a priori* in favor of the gentiles and would accept their testimony and distorted facts unconditionally. Consequently, the bribes offered by the Jews were meant only to counterbalance the influence of these prejudices and to facilitate an equitable judgment" (Rabbi Elie Munk, *The Call of the Torah, Shemos*, p. 334).

〚 977 〛

שׁוֹחֵט מִשּׁוּם מַאי חַיָּיב, רַב אָמַר מִשּׁוּם
צוֹבֵעַ וּשְׁמוּאֵל אָמַר מִשּׁוּם נְטִילַת נְשָׁמָה

"One who slaughters [an animal on the Sabbath], on what account is he culpable? Rav said: 'On account of dyeing' [the blood that gushes from its throat dyes the flesh], while Shmuel said: 'On account of taking life'" (*Shabbath* 75a).

Rabbi Yaakov Yosef of Polonoye masterfully applies the above talmudic dispute to an eschatological doctrine in Judaism. The Talmud states: "In the time to come [the Messianic age], the Holy One, blessed be He, will bring the Evil Inclination and will slaughter it . . . (*Sukkah* 52a). The question arises, why should the Evil Inclination be punished for what it was created to do?

"This is the *Gemara's* question [above]. The Evil Inclination, who is a slaughterer — for he slaughters man by diverting him from the 'path of life' to the 'path of death' — on what score is he culpable, wasn't he created for that purpose?

"Rav and Shmuel, in answering this question, are not in disagreement. Rav said: 'On account of dyeing,' i.e., the Evil Inclination is culpable because he 'colors' the sin and makes it appear as a *mitzvah*, thereby deceiving man as to 'the true colors' of the deed which he is urged to perform. Shmuel simply adds, 'On account of taking life,' i.e., the Evil Inclination is therefore culpable for deceitfully causing man to sin and to lose his life in punishment for his transgression" (*Ben Porath Yosef*, 127).

❙ 978 ❙ שׁוּתָא דְּינוּקָא בְּשׁוּקָא אוֹ דַאֲבוּה אוֹ דְּאִימֵיה

"The talk of a child in the marketplace is either that of his father
or of his mother" (*Sukkah* 56b).

Parents are held responsible for the character and upbringing of their children.

On the scriptural verse, "Sarah saw the son of Hagar the Egyptian . . . mocking" [Gen. 21:9], the *Sforno* comments: "Sarah assumed that this scoffing was instigated by [Hagar] his mother, from whom he first heard it, as our sages say, 'The talk of a child in the marketplace . . . .'"

Rabbi Raphael Pelcovitz writes in his explanatory notes: "Since we are not told that Ishmael mocked, but 'the son of Hagar,' the implication must be that his behavior was influenced by his mother. She, of course, had an ulterior motive in questioning Abraham's paternity of Isaac, for then her son would be the sole heir of Abraham's considerable wealth" (*Sforno, Commentary on the Torah* [trans. and notes], vol. 1, p. 98).

Rabbi Yaakov Kamenetsky would often cite the above dictum when explaining that "education is, above all, by example." Someone once asked Reb Yaakov how he and his Rebbetzin had taught their children to say *berachos*. "We never taught them," he replied. "They saw us making *berachos* before and after eating, and because children naturally imitate their parents, they started making *berachos* too."

❙ 979 ❙ שִׁתֵּף הַקָּדוֹשׁ בָּרוּךְ הוּא שְׁמוֹ הַגָּדוֹל בְּיִשְׂרָאֵל

"The Holy One, blessed be He, joined His Name with Israel"
(*Yerushalmi, Ta'anith* 2:6).

Rabbi Yosef Ber Soloveitchik writes: "G-d does not proclaim His glorious Name through supernatural wonders unless they are performed to save the Jewish people. The salvation of Israel is the means of publicizing His glorious Name throughout the world. Thus, whenever Israel is in a lowly state, His glory, too, is concealed.

"This was G-d's message to Jacob when He said, 'I will go down with you to Egypt' [Gen. 46:3-4]. 'Going down' here figuratively alludes to the concealment of G-d's Name when Israel is in exile.

"This is what the sages meant when they said: 'The Holy One, blessed be He, joined His Name with Israel' . . . . The sages were saying that G-d brings glory to His Name only through the salvation of Israel. This is the greatest assurance that they will never be destroyed, Heaven forbid" (*Beis HaLevi, Va'yigash*).

〔 980 〕

שָׂח בֵּין תְּפִלָּה לִתְפִלָּה, עֲבֵירָה הִיא בְּיָדוֹ
וְחוֹזֵר עָלֶיהָ מֵעוֹרְכֵי הַמִּלְחָמָה

"He who talks between the placing of the *tefillin* on the hand and the *tefillin* on the head has committed a transgression, and returns home under the regulations pertaining to war" (*Sotah* 44b).

"The thoughts of a man going forth to battle must be in complete harmony with his actions. Nothing may intervene to disrupt this harmony. His intentions and motivations must be entirely pure and honest, and his actions must be in keeping with his ideals.

"An interruption between the act of donning the hand *tefillin* and the head *tefillin* symbolizes a disharmony between thought and action, and if this symbolic defect were to be carried out into the plans and activities of the warrior, the battle which he wages would no longer be a war fought for the sake of fulfilling a Divine commandment, but only a battle for selfish gain" (Rabbi Alexander Zusia Friedman, *Avnei Ezel*, cited in *Wellsprings of Torah*, p. 343).

In a similar vein, Rabbi Shmuel Zanvil Kahana writes: "The *tefillin* on the hand suggests action, while the *tefillin* on the head represents thought or belief. There must be no interruption, no dichotomy, no division between our belief and our actions" (*Heaven on Your Head*, p. 198).

981

„שְׁחוֹרָה אֲנִי וְנָאוָה . . . "שְׁחוֹרָה אֲנִי וְנָאוָה" כָּל
יְמוֹת הַשָּׁבוּעַ וְנָאוָה אֲנִי בְּשַׁבָּת . . . בְּיוֹם
הַכִּפּוּרִים . . . לְעוֹלָם הַבָּא

"'I am black, but beautiful' . . . . I am black all the days of the week and beautiful on the Sabbath; I am black all the days of the year and beautiful on Yom Kippur . . . . I am black in this world and beautiful in the World to Come" (Shir HaShirim Rabbah 1:5).

Rabbi Moshe Avigdor Amiel comments: "If permanent joy exists in this world, it is derived from that portion of the World to Come which exists here, i.e., the Sabbath; Yom Kippur, which is a 'Sabbath of Sabbaths'; and from the World to Come [itself], which is 'one long Sabbath day.'

"If we experience a neshamah yeseirah — contentment of soul on the Sabbath, something which eludes us on the other days of the week, if on Yom Kippur we are filled with a unique joy, the 'joy of trembling' which is not felt on any other day of the year, it is because the nearer we approach in spirit to the 'day which is one long Sabbath,' the more our joy in the world intensifies" (Derashos El-Ami, vol. 1, pp. 176-180).

"Every confession expresses itself in the call: 'I am black but beautiful.' If we do not see the 'beautiful,' we cannot discern the 'black' . . . . The sinner must see himself from two antithetical viewpoints — the nullity of self, and the greatness of self" (Rabbi Joseph B. Soloveitchik, The Rav Speaks, p. 133).

〔 982 〕

שַׁלִּיט בְּעוֹלָמוֹ יוֹדֵעַ שֶׁאֵין לְךָ דָּבָר שֶׁמַּפְרִיס
פַּרְסָה וְטָמֵא אֶלָּא חֲזִיר, לְפִיכָךְ פָּרַט בּוֹ
הַכָּתוּב

"The Ruler of the Universe knows that there is no other animal
that parts the hoof and is unclean except the pig, therefore the
verse particularly stated it" (*Hullin* 59a).

In *Va'yikrah*, ch. 11, the Torah lists the two signs of *Kashruth* for animals
— those that have "true hooves that are cloven, and that bring up its cud."
Scripture proceeds to name three animals that bring up their cud but do not
have split hooves — the camel, the hyrax, and the hare — and one animal
that does have split hooves but does not bring up its cud — the pig. The
Talmud thereupon comments that the Almighty knows that there are no
animals but those, that possess only one of the two signs of *kashruth*.

Reb Archik, Rabbi Aaron Yosef Baksht, would often cite the above dictum
to prove to skeptics and nonbelievers that the Torah is of Divine origin. Reb
Archik would exclaim: "Now in all these years, no one ever found an animal
to disprove those sentences in the Torah! Isn't that proof that the Torah was
written by G-d!" (Chaim Shapiro, *The Jewish Observer* 8, no. 8 [October 1972]:
16).

In reality, the Talmud itself cites the above dictum as proof of "*Torah min
Ha'shamayim*" (the Divine origin of the Torah) when it asks: "Was Moshe a
hunter or an archer?" How could he possibly know the biological characteristics of all animals? "This refutes those who maintain that the Torah was not
Divinely revealed" (*Hullin* 60b).

983

שֶׁלְךָ אִי אַתָּה רוֹאֶה אֲבָל אַתָּה רוֹאֶה שֶׁל
אֲחֵרִים וְשֶׁל גָּבוֹהַ

"Your own [chametz] you must not see; but you may see that of others and of the Most High" (Pesahim 5b).

"You may see," i.e., have in your possession leaven which is not your own — which belongs to others or is consecrated for use in the Holy Temple.

Rabbi Nachman of Kossov homiletically interprets the above dictum as an exclamation: "Your own chametz [sins] you do not see [for 'a person sees all faults save his own'], but you do see [the sins] of others! Indeed, you pursue an investigation into the sins of others . . . and even of the Most High, i.e., when something 'bad' happens to you, you do not attribute it to your own shortcomings, but see a defect in Divine Providence" (Rabbi Uziel Meisels, Tifereth Uziel, p. 64).

Cf. Nega'im 2:5, "A man may inspect all the leprosy symptoms save his own." See #757.

984

שְׁלֹשָׁה דְּבָרִים עָתִיד אֵלִיָּהוּ לְהַעֲמִיד לָהֶן
לְיִשְׂרָאֵל: צִנְצֶנֶת הַמָּן, וּצְלוֹחִית שֶׁמֶן
הַמִּשְׁחָה, וּצְלוֹחִית הַמַּיִם, וְיֵשׁ אוֹמְרִים אַף
מַקְלוֹ שֶׁל אַהֲרֹן

"Elijah [the prophet] is destined to deliver three things to Israel: the container of manna, the dish of anointing oil, and the dish of [purifying] water; and some say the staff of Aaron"
(Midrash Tanchuma, Beshalach 21).

Rabbi Aaron Lewin homiletically related the above four items to four aspects of a Rabbi's responsibility in the community. "The container of manna symbolizes his charitable activities for the poor to whom he provides 'manna.' The 'anointing oil' is symbolic of his educational activity as the teacher of his people, anointed with the oil of Torah. The 'purifying water' symbolizes his purifying the community by showing them the proper way of life. Aaron's staff is the symbol of peace, to which every Rabbi must aspire as a firm foundation for his position in the community" (*Isaac Lewin*, . . . *Unto the Mountains*, p. 34).

⟦ 985 ⟧ שְׁלֹשֶׁת אֲלָפִים הֲלָכוֹת נִשְׁתַּכְּחוּ בִּימֵי אֶבְלוֹ שֶׁל מ'שֶׁה

"Three thousand *halachoth* were forgotten during the period of mourning for Moshe" (*Terumah* 16a).

"They [the Israelites] said to Joshua: 'Ask' [through the Holy Spirit that the forgotten laws should be revealed to you]. He replied: 'It is not in Heaven' [Deut. 30:12]. They said to Samuel: 'Ask.' He replied: 'These are the commandments' [Lev. 27:34]. A prophet does not now have the right to introduce anything new" (ibid).

Rabbi Yitzchak Zev Soloveitchik, the Brisker Rav, points to an apparent redundancy in the above text. "The request addressed to Samuel is identical to the request earlier dismissed by Joshua. Yet, although Joshua applied the dictum 'It is not in Heaven,' Samuel invoked the doctrine 'No prophet has now the right to introduce anything new.'"

Rav Soloveitchik suggests [*Chiddushei haGriz*] that the request addressed to Samuel was significantly different from that which was addressed to Joshua. A void was created through failure to remember the laws in question. Samuel was asked to remedy the situation by means of his own prophetic prowess — to request Divine re-enactment of the forgotten laws. To this demand Samuel's reply was that prophets subsequent to Moshe do not function as lawgivers . . . . The demand earlier addressed to Joshua was not a demand for new legislation, but simply that Joshua use his prowess of prophecy in order to discover the law which had already been revealed to Moshe . . . . His function would have been that of a reporter, not a lawgiver. To this demand Joshua answered, "It is not in Heaven" (Rabbi J. David Bleich, *Tradition and Transition*, p. 72).

Cf. *Baba Mezia* 59b, "It is not in Heaven . . . ." See *Insights*, vol. 1, #333.

Cf. *Shabbath* 104a, "A prophet may henceforth make no innovations." See *Insights*, vol. 1, #37.

⟦ 986 ⟧ שְׁנֵי מַלְאֲכֵי הַשָּׁרֵת מְלַוִּין לוֹ לָאָדָם בְּעֶרֶב
שַׁבָּת מִבֵּית הַכְּנֶסֶת לְבֵיתוֹ
אֶחָד טוֹב וְאֶחָד רַע

"Two ministering angels accompany man on the eve of the Sabbath from the Synagogue to his house: one good [angel] and one evil one" (*Shabbath* 119b).

"And when he arrives home and finds the lamp burning, the table set and the couch [bed] covered with a spread, the good angel exclaims, 'May it be even thus on another Sabbath' and the evil angel unwillingly responds 'Amen'" (ibid.).

Rabbi Yehudah Aryeh Alter, the *Sfath Emeth*, comments: "This appears to be a scribal error, for no evil angel could be counted among the ministering angels."

The emendation of the *Sfath Emeth* is supported by manuscript texts that are quoted in *Dikdukei-Sofrim*. In further support of this view the *Sfath Emeth* refers to a manuscript edition of the *Rif* and *Menoras HaMaor*, Section 157 (Rabbi A.Y. Bromberg, *Rebbes of Ger*, p. 80).

⟦ 987 ⟧ שְׁנַיִם שֶׁיּוֹשְׁבִים וְאֵין בֵּינֵיהֶם דִּבְרֵי תוֹרָה הֲרֵי
זֶה מוֹשַׁב לֵצִים

"When two sit together and do not discuss Torah, it becomes a seat of scorners" (*Aboth* 3:3).

Rabbi Yechezkel Landau explains [in his *Tzelach*] the above dictum to mean that the actual seat on which the two sit becomes saturated with scorn, causing anyone who occupies it to be adversely influenced. He bases his interpretation on the fact that our sages use the expression "*moshav leitzim*" [it becomes a seat of scorners], rather than the more seemingly appropriate one, "they are likened to scorners."

Rabbi Yoel Schwartz cites the above *Tzelach* and comments: "Our sages explain that physical objects have the capacity to both absorb and impart spiritual states, an idea which finds expression in many sources" (*The Ben Torah and His World*, p. 26).

⟦ 988 ⟧   שָׁפִיל וְאָזִיל בַּר אַוְזָא וְעֵינֵיהּ מְטַיְּיפֵי

"Though a duck keeps its head down while walking, its eyes look afar" (*Baba Kamma* 92b).

Its eyes look above and beyond for its sustenance. Though a man be humble, he should never be embarrassed to ask for his needs, whether it be in Torah or sustenance (Rashi).

This popular saying is derived from Abigail who humbled herself before King David, and yet she was not embarrassed to mention [albeit in an indirect manner] that she yearned to be his wife in the future: ". . . and when the L-rd has prospered my lord, *remember your maid*" (I Samuel 25:31).

The Vilna Gaon translates and interprets the above maxim in a novel fashion: "*Humbly walks the duck, but its eyes are turned to Heaven*. Do not malign the words of a sage even if they seem trivial, for they contain the loftiest wisdom" (*Commentary by the Vilna Gaon*, ad loc., cited by Rabbi Aharon Feldman, *The Juggler and the King*, p. 2).

⟦ 989 ⟧   שְׁרֵי שַׂקָּיךְ וְעַיֵּיל לַחְמָךְ

"Open your mouth [lit. 'your sack'] and let your food enter" (*Shabbath* 152a).

"Shmuel said to Rav Yehudah: 'O keen scholar — open your mouth and let your food enter.' Until the age of forty, food is more beneficial; thenceforth, drink is more beneficial" (ibid.).

Rabbi Chaim Kramer of the Breslov Research Institute in Jerusalem writes:

"Fasting and leading a life of asceticism does not necessarily guarantee freedom from physical desires. Indeed, Rabbi Nachman of Breslov taught, 'A person who abstains from worldly pleasures and then retracts from his asceticism, falls into even greater physical desire than beforehand'" (*Aleph-Bet Book, Prishuth* 1).

"It is noteworthy that Rabbi Nachman himself, after having fasted a great deal in his youth, later remarked, 'Had I then known the power of prayer, I never would have destroyed my body with fasting'" *Likutei Moharan*, vol. 1B, #10).

Cf. *Ta'anith* 11a, "Whosoever fasts [for the sake of self-affliction] is termed a sinner." See *Insights*, vol. 1, #265.

⦉ 990 ⦊   שְׂרֵיפַת נְשָׁמָה וְגוּף קַיָּים
"The soul was consumed while the body remained intact"
(*Sanhedrin* 52a).

Such is the talmudic description of the tragic death of Nadav and Avihu, the two sons of Aaron.

In a sermon entitled "Living Bodies With Dead Souls," Rabbi Simon Dolgin homiletically applies the above metaphysical occurrence to the disturbing manner in which many view certain fundamentals of Judaism.

To reduce *Kashrus* to a health measure and divest it of its spiritual purity and nobility, is the consuming of the soul though the body is intact.

For anyone to view the rite of circumcision as an operation and see in it only the medical advantages . . . but fail to behold the Covenant of Abraham with G-d . . . is to destroy the soul and G-dly message while keeping only the physical benefits of the commandment.

To behold the Sabbath as a day of rest and relaxation which each can enjoy as he chooses — and not to feel the holiness of this day and the sanctity of prayer and Torah study, of scrupulous observance and abstinence from work . . . is to have developed a dead soul in a relaxed body.

To speak of Israel as a country in the Middle East where Jewish refugees can settle, but with which we have no [spiritual] kinship, is to set up a state in body, but without a soul. We're reminded of the refrain, "The Land of

Israel without Torah is as a body without a soul."

The same relates to our charity-giving. To give charity only because of pressure, or for glory, without feeling its importance, its need, is to give the body of money without the soul of man (RCA Manual, 1961, pp. 129-133).

Some of our sages suggest just the opposite opinion concerning the death of Nadav and Avihu, i.e., "the body was consumed while the soul remained intact." See *Tosaf.* s.v. *Ha'he sereifa* (ad loc.). "As the *Zohar* puts it, only physical death is meant here — their souls were not lost. According to this view, it is inconceivable that *Hashem's* infinite mercy would not take into consideration the merits of these two righteous people, the merit of their forefathers, and the merits of Moshe, their teacher" (Rabbi Elie Munk, *The Call of the Torah*, *Va'yikra*, p. 88).

ת

⟦ 991 ⟧ תֶּבֶן אַתָּה מַכְנִיס לְעָפָרַיִם

"You bring straw to Ofarayim" (*Menachoth* 85a).

When Moshe performed miraculous signs before Pharaoh, the chief sorcerers of Egypt assumed that they were performed through witchcraft. Consequently, they exclaimed to Moshe, "You are bringing straw to Ofarayim" [i.e., a city abundant with straw]. Seeing that Egypt is the place of sorcery, why are you bringing your sorcery here? Isn't there enough magic here, thus making your power unnecessary!"

Cf. Eng. Proverb, "Bringing coals to Newcastle."

Rabbi Nachman of Breslov suggests the following homiletical interpretation of the above maxim. *Teven* [straw] alludes to *Tevunah* [Torah understanding]. *Tevunah* preserves an individual spiritually, much as *Teven* [straw] preserves an individual physically.

The Egyptian chief sorcerers could not comprehend Moshe's bringing "Torah understanding" to the Jews when they had not as yet received the Torah. How could they be expected to rise to great spiritual heights — for without the Torah, they are likened to *offar* [dust]? Thus we interpret the phrase as "you are bringing *teven* [understanding] to *Ofarayim* [a low spiritual level]" (*Likutei Moharan*, vol. 1B, #11).

371

992

תּוֹרָה בְּעִידְנָא דַּעֲסִיק בָּהּ מַגְנָא וּמַצְּלָא

"Regarding the [study of] Torah, while one is engaged in it, it
protects and rescues . . ." (Sotah 21a).

The Gemara explains that this protective power of the Torah results not
only from Torah study *per se*, but also from acts that further Torah study —
for example, a woman merits this protection by virtue of her abetting the
Torah studied by her husband and sons [she encourages them and urges
them to study].

Rabbi Yitzchak Hutner asserts that Torah is the one *mitzvah* that has the
power to enclose within its embrace other activities, if they are used to
further the ends of Torah study. See *Pachad Yitzchak, Shavuos* 13 (Eliakim
Willner, *Maharal of Prague, Nesivoth Olam, Nesiv HaTorah*, p. 54).

"A man should direct his mind and thoughts to the words of the Torah
and enlarge his understanding with wisdom, for unchaste thoughts prevail
only in the heart devoid of wisdom" (*Mishneh Torah, Hil. Isurei Biah* 22:21).

Rabbi Eliyahu E. Dessler writes: "If this is true of any wisdom, any
intellectual pursuit that captures one's interest, how much more is it true if
the wisdom which engages his interest is that of the Divine Torah. Then
there is a very powerful force in operation. The sanctity of the Torah will
pervade his being and its spirituality will preserve him from defilement"
(*Michtav Me-Eliyahu*, vol. 1, p. 213).

In commenting on the above dictum, Rabbi Yisrael Salanter writes: "The
Torah protects and rescues a person from sin no matter which part of the
Torah he is occupied with. He may study the case of 'the ox which gores the
cow' [*Baba Kamma* ch. 5] or similar matters, and it will protect him from
loshon hara [evil speech] . . . for the spirituality of the Torah preserves him"
(*Iggereth Ha-mussar; Or Yisrael*, p. 106).

The Vilna Gaon, in commenting on the verse, "The tongue's medicine is
the tree of life . . ." (Prov. 15:4), declared: "If a person has spoken gossip or
slander, his remedy is to speak always of Torah" (Rabbi Yissachar Dov
Rubin, *Oros Hagra*).

∦ 993 ∦

תִּינוֹק שֶׁנִּשְׁבָּה לְבֵין הַנָּכְרִים

"A child who was taken captive among Gentiles" (*Shabbath* 68a).

"Concerning the Sabbath, the sages have laid down a fundamental rule: If a man forgot the principle of the Sabbath and forgot that commandments concerning the Sabbath were imposed upon Israelites, or if he was held captive among Gentiles while yet a child . . . even if he performed many acts of work on many Sabbaths, he is liable to but one sin offering, since they all count as a single transgression committed through error . . ." (*Mishneh Torah, Hil. Sh'gagoth* 7:2).

Rabbi David Zvi Hoffman regarded the vast majority of American Jews as "victims of two generations of the wilderness, whose transgressions of Sabbath law is due to their being 'children, captives of ignorance of Judaism' in a pioneering environment, and hence not to be treated as deliberate violators of the Sabbath laws" (*Melamed L'Hoil, Orach Chaim* no. 28).

Similarly, the *Chazon Ish* [*Yoreh De'ah*, Sec. 2, pars. 16 & 23] decided as a matter of *halachah*, that "since we do not know the wise art of 'reproof,' we should treat with infinite patience and love even *mamrim lehach'iss* [deliberate, provocative transgressors]. They are *tinokoth shenishbu* [children who were taken captive] who were deprived of a chance to learn Torah, live Torah, and to therein become wholesome types of Jewish men and women" (Rabbi Leo Jung, *Between Man and Man*, p. 210).

Rabbi Yitzchak Hutner asserts that "only one whose heresy is the result of rebellion or 'wickedness' is excluded from the Jewish people. One, however, who is not vindictive or rebellious is not totally excluded from *Klal Yisrael*. He is likened to a *tinok shenishba* [a child taken captive] or a child of the Karaites" (*Pachad Yitzchak, Pesach, Maamar* 111 [2]).

❘ 994 ❘

תֵּיקוּ [נוֹטָרִיקוֹן]: תִּשְׁבִּי יְתָרֵץ קוּשְׁיוֹת
וְאִבָּעְיוֹת]

"Teyku" [an acrostic for "The Tishbite (Eliyahu) will resolve all the difficulties and questions"] (Berakoth 8a).

The word "Teyku" (found throughout the Talmud) literally means, "It stands over" and is derived from "Taykum" (let it stand), indicating that the question still stands and the matter remains in doubt. Hence, unresolved problems in the Talmud are often characterized by "Teyku."

The acrostic (above) is recorded in Tosafoth Yom Tov on Edyoth 8:7 in his commentary on the mishnaic statement, "The sages say [Eliyahu will come] . . . to make peace in the world, as it is said, 'Behold, I will send you Eliyahu the prophet . . . . And he will turn the heart of the fathers to the children, and the heart of the children to their fathers.'" Says the Tosafoth Yom Tov, "Eliyahu will turn the hearts of the fathers to the children by resolving conflicts that exist in the area of statutes and laws of the Torah."

"It is frequently stated that Eliyahu clarifies halachic doubts. This clarification will take two forms, law and fact . . . . In law, he clarifies through his status as a great scholar whose decision we follow, but not through his status as a prophet, as no law may be determined on the strength of prophecy, for 'It is not in Heaven' [Deut. 30:12], and 'A prophet may not innovate in law' [Shabbath 104a]; but we will rely on him to clarify matters of fact by means of prophetic powers" [Encyclopedia Talmudith, s.v. Eliyahu].

See Torah Temimah (Lev. 27:34 [216]).

❘ 995 ❘

תַּלְמִידֵי חֲכָמִים אֵין לָהֶם מְנוּחָה לֹא בָּעוֹלָם
הַזֶּה וְלֹא בָּעוֹלָם הַבָּא

"The disciples of the wise [Torah scholars] have no rest either in this world or in the World to Come" (Berakoth 64a).

Cf. Tamid 33b, "A psalm, a song, for the Sabbath Day — for the day which will be all Sabbath [the World to Come] and rest for everlasting life."

The *Maharsha* reconciles the apparent contradiction between the dictum in *Berakoth* and that in *Tamid* in light of the midrashic interpretation of the verse, "And G-d finished on the seventh day His work . . ." [Gen. 2:2]. What was the world missing [in the six days of Creation]? Rest. When the Sabbath came, rest came and the work [of Creation] was finished. In *Berakoth* the *Gemara* tells us that Torah scholars who do intellectual work and toil in this world will have no rest and completion from this intellectual activity in the World to Come. That, indeed, is the intellectual *menuchah* or rest of the righteous who "sit" and enjoy the radiance of the *Shechinah* [Divine Presence].

The *Gemara* in *Tamid*, however, depicting the World to Come as "the day which will be all Sabbath and rest for everlasting life" — that refers to actual physical work which will indeed be totally abolished.

The Maharal of Prague writes: "Lest it be asked, 'How can a thing which causes a lack of repose for Torah scholars be a sign of their advantage?' — This is not a valid question, for to say that Torah scholars have no repose is not to say that they must bring exertion to bear . . . . [To say that there is no repose is simply to say that] there is no completion or culmination to the intellect . . . .

"Certainly, completion itself is a worthy trait, but its absence with regard to Torah scholars bespeaks the greatness of their status — a status superior [to that of a thing that achieves completion]" (*Nesivoth Olam, Nesiv HaTorah*, trans. by Eliakim Willner, p. 208).

〗 996 〖   תַּלְמִידֵי חֲכָמִים כָּל זְמַן שֶׁמַּזְקִינִין חָכְמָה
נִתּוֹסֶפֶת בָּהֶם . . . וְעַמֵּי הָאָרֶץ כָּל זְמַן
שֶׁמַּזְקִינִין טִפְּשׁוּת נִתּוֹסֶפֶת בָּהֶן

"As for Torah scholars, the older they grow the more wisdom they acquire; but the unlearned in Torah, as they wax older they become more foolish" (*Shabbath* 152a).

"If you do not suffer the toil of study, you will suffer the toil of ignorance" (R. Moshe Ibn Ezra, *Shiras Yisrael*).

In alluding to the above dictum, Ramban writes: "If he takes pride in wisdom — let him understand that G-d 'may remove the speech of the most competent and take away the wisdom of the aged' [Job 12:20]" (*Iggeres HaRamban*).

In his translation and commentary on the *Iggeres HaRamban*, Rabbi Avraham Chaim Feuer writes: "Ramban implies that the haughty person who prides himself as a Torah scholar entertains a distorted perception of Torah. Genuine Torah scholarship makes one humble, not proud. When one studies properly, the more he learns the more he is overwhelmed by how little he knows. Thus, the one who grows haughty from his studies attests to the superficiality of his knowledge" (*A Letter for the Ages*, p. 73).

Perhaps, the above dictum can be better understood in light of Rabbi Mordechai Gifter's observation that *our* sages are not called *chachamim* (wise) but *talmidei chachamim* (students of the wise). They do not merely possess wisdom but are guided by it; they are its students.

Cf. *Kinnim* 3:6, "As the elders of the untutored increase in years, so do they lose their intelligence . . . ."

〔 997 〕

תַּלְמִידִים קְרוּיִים בָּנִים

"Disciples are called children" (*Sifri, V'ethchanan* 6:7).

"And you shall teach them diligently to your children" [Deut. 6:7] — this refers to your disciples. ". . . Just as disciples are called children, so is the teacher called a father" (ibid.).

Rabbi Meir Shapiro, founder of Yeshivath Chachmei Lublin, proclaimed at an Agudath convention, "In my yeshiva, no student . . . will be called a 'yeshiva bachur' (yeshiva boy), but a 'ben yeshiva' (son of the yeshiva), and by us he will feel as if he was in his own home" (1929).

Rabbi Yitzchak Hutner points out that when Reb Chaim of Volozhin founded his famous yeshiva, he discouraged the use of the term "*talmidei yeshiva*" (yeshiva students) and replaced it with the term "*bnai yeshiva*" (yeshiva sons). The difference between a secular teacher and a Torah Rebbe, he said, is analogous to the distinction between receiving sustenance from a cook and sustenance from a nurse. The nurse feeds the infant with her body, while the cook supplies something from outside herself. The Rebbe likewise gives of himself to his disciple [*Pachad Yitzchak*, #74].

Rabbi Samuel Belkin writes: "This biblical and rabbinic doctrine, that the teacher is in *loco parentis*, is a concept which was unknown to the ancient non-Jewish world. There was hardly a more loyal and dedicated disciple than Plato was to Socrates, his intellectual master, but the former never looked upon himself as his master's son, nor did the latter consider himself the father of his disciple.

"This rabbinic doctrine . . . is reflected in the legal responsibilities which a student has to his teacher and which takes precedence even over the obligations which a son has to his parents" [*Essays in Traditional Jewish Thought*, pp. 25-26].

⫞ 998 ⫞

„תָּמִים תִּהְיֶה עִם ה' אֱלֹקֶיךָ", כְּשֶׁאַתָּה תָּם, חֶלְקְךָ עִם ה' אֱלֹקֶיךָ

"'Be wholehearted with the L-rd your G-d' — when you are wholehearted, your portion will be with the L-rd your G-d" (*Sifri, Devarim* 18:13).

"We are to direct our hearts to Him only, and believe that He alone does everything. It is He Who knows the truth about all future events . . . . We are not to inquire of the astrologers or from anyone else, or by any means to trust that their words will be fulfilled" (Ramban, Deut. 18:13).

Ramban includes this *mitzvah* among the 613 commandments of the Torah. He writes that "Maimonides presumably considered this *mitzvah* to be a general exhortation to walk in the path of the Torah . . . and therefore he did not include it in his enumeration of the commandments."

The Malbim suggests that Maimonides relies on the Sifri's comment [above] that "your portion will be with the L-rd your G-d" if you will be "wholehearted with the L-rd your G-d," i.e., it is a conditional declaration, not an imperative one. The Malbim, however, concludes: "The *Gemara* [*Pesahim* 113b] implies that it is a commandment, for it says: 'How do we know that you must not consult astrologers [lit. Chaldeans]? Because it is said in the Torah, "Be wholehearted with the L-rd your G-d"'" (*HaTorah*

VeHaMitzvah, Deut. 18:13).

Maimonides echoes the Sifri's commentary when he writes: "The greater the human perfection a person has attained, the greater the benefit he derives from Divine Providence. This benefit is very great in the case of prophets, and varies according to the degree of their prophetic faculty; as it varies in the case of pious and good men according to their piety and uprightness" (*Moreh Nevuchim* III, chap. 18).

"Rabbi Chaim of Volozhin (*Nefesh HaChaim* III:12-13) cites the Talmud (*Hullin* 7b), which teaches that if a person internalizes the verse: 'HASHEM, He is G-d, there is nothing else beside Him' (Deut. 4:35), he will be protected from harmful forces."

Rabbi Yitzchak Zev Soloveitchik testified that he never stopped reviewing this *statement of faith* which literally protected him throughout his life (*Rabboseinu*, p. 170).

999

„תַּעֲשֶׂה" וְלֹא מִן הֶעָשׂוּי

"'You shall make' (Deut. 16:13) [the *sukkah*] and not [simply use] that which is already made" (*Sukkah* 11b).

This is illustrated by the following *mishnaic* ruling: "If one hollows out a haystack [rakes in the heap] to make for himself a *sukkah*, this is not a *sukkah*" (ibid. 15a). "If one removes [from the haystack] some of the sheaves down below next to the ground, and goes in and makes a space according to the required dimensions of a *sukkah*, so that the *s'chach* is thus already made from beforehand on its own, this is not a *sukkah*" (Rashi, ibid. 12a).

"You shall make, and not that which is already made" is a general principle whenever the Torah requires that a thing be made (*Pnei Yehoshua*, ibid. 12b). See *Rashei Besamim*, responsa sec. 4 in this regard.

The Gaon of Vilna's favorite saying about *Eretz Yisrael* was that only two *mitzvoth* totally envelop the Jew performing them: dwelling in a *sukkah* and living in Israel. Both have something else in common as well — just as a *sukkah* is not kosher unless you build it anew ["You shall make, and not that which is already made"], *Eretz Yisrael* must be built up by each one of us.

1000   תֵּשְׁבוּ כְּעֵין תָּדוּרוּ

"Your sitting [in a *sukkah*] should be as your dwelling [at home]
(*Sukkah* 26a).

"All the seven days [of *Succoth*], one should make the *sukkah* his permanent abode and his house his temporary abode .... Whence do we know
this? From what our Rabbis have taught: 'You shall dwell' implies in the
same manner as you ordinarily live" (ibid. 28b).

"The *halacha* that one who is *mitzta'air* [in discomfort] is free from the
obligation of dwelling in a *sukkah* is derived from 'your sitting should be as
your dwelling,' for one does not dwell in a place where he is in discomfort"
(Tosaf. s.v. *Holchai* ibid. 26a).

Rabbi Abraham Shapiro (Chief Rabbi of Israel) writes: "Similar standards
to those used in determining whether one is required to dwell in a *sukkah* at
a particular time, can also be applied to the duty of living in Israel at a time
when conditions there are unfavorable."

The Gemara points out that Rav Kahana was released from the duty of
settling in Israel, for had he done so he would have forfeited the great
opportunity of studying Torah with his teacher, Rav [the greatest scholar of
his time] (*Pesahim* 49a).

One must not, however, equate "discomfort" with inconvenience. Now
that the Land of Israel has become the State of Israel where economic
conditions are greatly improved, the category of "*mitzta'air*" exists only
minimally [especially for those not yet married, who have no family responsibilities. They are certainly to be considered as duty-bound to perform this
commandment]" (*Torah From Zion*, pp. 13-19).

Just as we should adhere to the principle of *teishvu k'ein taduru* — "Your
sitting [in a *sukkah*] should be as your dwelling [at home]" — so conversely
[in a homiletical vein] we should adhere to the principle of *taduru k'ein
teishvu* — "Your dwelling at home should be as your sitting in a *sukkah*."

Rabbi Samson Raphael Hirsch noted that *Rosh Hashanah* is only one day
for the *teruah* mood, and *Yom Kippur* is only one day for the *kaparah* —
fasting — while *Succoth* is seven days, a whole cycle of days, for the joyful
building of our huts, and for enjoying our possessions before G-d. This is

what is most characteristic of the Jewish Law of Truth which teaches the normal mood of one's life to be, not the bowed down broken feeling, but the erect joy of life which runs equally through the year of a life faithfully devoted to duty (*The Pentateuch*, Lev. 23:33).

Hence, *taduru k'ein teishvu* — one should endeavor to live throughout the year in the spirit of true *simcha* as generated during the joyous festival of *Succoth* (S. W.).